unlocking

human resource management

Adrian Murton London Metropolitan University
Margaret Inman Swansea Metropolitan University
Nuala OSullivan U

First published in Great Britain in 2010 by
Hodder Education, An Hachette UK Company,
338 Euston Road, London NW1 3BH

Hachette UK's policy is to use papers that are natural, renewable and recyclable products and
made from wood grown in sustainable forests. The logging and manufacturing processes are
expected to conform to the environmental regulations of the country of origin.

The advice and information in this book are believed to be true and accurate at the date of going
to press, but neither the author[s] nor the publisher can accept any legal responsibility or liability
for any errors or omissions.

British Library Cataloguing in Publication Data
A catalogue record for this book is available from the British Library

Library of Congress Cataloging-in-Publication Data
A catalog record for this book is available from the Library of Congress

ISBN: 978 1 444 11186 6

1 2 3 4 5 6 7 8 9 10

Typeset in 10/13pt ITC Stone Sans by Servis Filmsetting Ltd, Stockport, Cheshire
Printed in Great Britain for Hodder Education, an Hachette UK Company,
338 Euston Road, London, NW1 3BH by The MPG Books Group, Bodmin and King's Lynn

What do you think about this book? Or any other Hodder Education title?
Please send your comments to educationenquiries@hodder.com

www.hoddereducation.com

Figure 1.1 MBI /Alamy; Figure 1.2 keith morris/Alamy; Figure 1.4 © TOBY MELVILLE/Reuters/
Corbis; Figure 4.2 © Thor Jorgen Udvang – Fotolia.com; Figure 4.4 © innocent drinks; Figure 5.2
PETER SKINGLEY/AFP/Getty Images; Figure 5.4 © Misha – Fotolia.com; Figure 6.5 Jupiterimages/
Getty Images; Figure 7.3 © Jetta Productions/Getty Images; Figure 7.4 © Sean Gladwell – Fotolia.
com; Figure 7.5 flashfilm/Getty Images; Figure 8.1 © Dragan Trifunovic – Fotolia.com; Figure 8.4
© Don Klumpp/Getty Images; Figure 9.1 Bob Aylott/Keystone/Getty Images; Figure 9.2 © Image
Source/Getty Images; Figure 9.3 © Kelly Young – Fotolia.com; Figure 9.4 © David Young-Wolff/
Getty Images; Figure 9.5 © Marcel Weber/cultura/Getty Images; Figure 9.6 Kent Fire & Rescue;
Figure 14.3 © TOBY MELVILLE/Reuters/Corbis.

Artwork for Figures 6.1, 6.4, 11.1, 11.2, 11.3, 11.4 and 11.5 by Peter Lubach. All other artwork
by Servis Filmsetting Ltd.

Every effort has been made to trace and acknowledge the ownership of copyright. The publishers
will be glad to make suitable arrangements with any copyright holders whom it has not been
possible to contact.

Contents

Features Guide

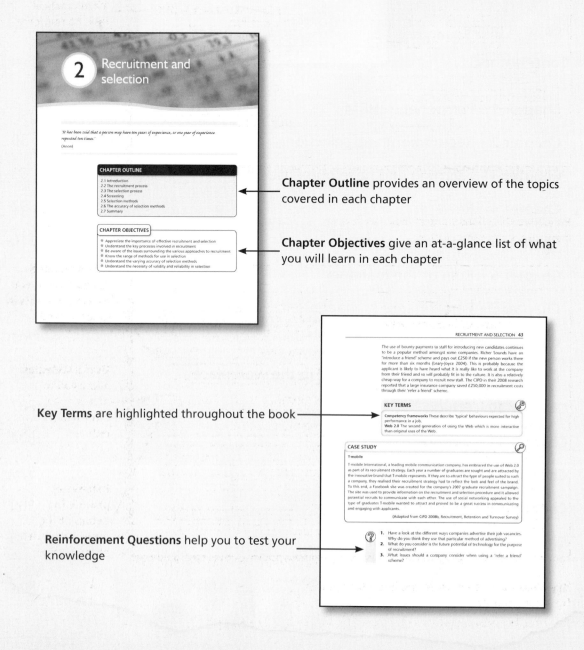

Chapter Outline provides an overview of the topics covered in each chapter

Chapter Objectives give an at-a-glance list of what you will learn in each chapter

Key Terms are highlighted throughout the book

Reinforcement Questions help you to test your knowledge

Case Study boxes include real-life examples to put your learning in context

Artworks and photographs illustrate each chapter and help to explain key ideas and concepts

Activities provide more practical tasks to reinforce your learning

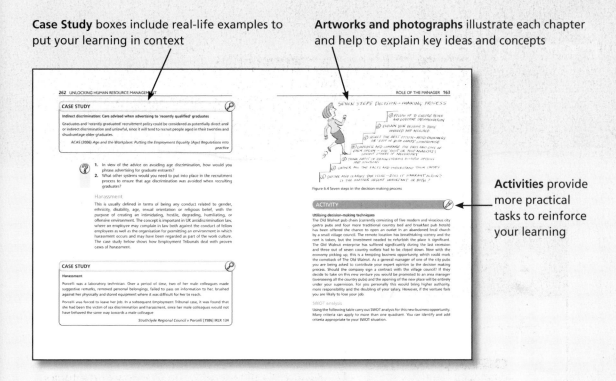

Reflective Questions suggest ideas for further discussion and consideration

Recommended Reading helps you to explore topics in greater detail

Useful Websites allow you to access more information online

References provide full details of the sources used in each chapter

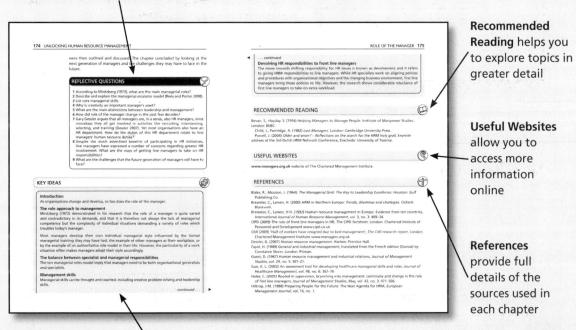

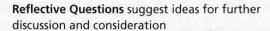

Key Ideas tables summarise the important points from each chapter

Contributors

Natasa Marinkovic

Susan Hutchinson
University of the West of England

John Neugebauer
University of the West of England

Fiona O'Conner
University of Westminster

Paul Smith
University of Hertfordshire

1 Personnel to HRM

'Personnel was perceived, to use Drucker's famous term, as a 'trash can' into which all unwanted tasks could be dumped rather than a key element in the search for competitive advantage'

(Guest 1990: 383)

'HRM represents the discovery of personnel management by Chief Executives'

(Fowler 1987)

CHAPTER OUTLINE

1.1 Managing people is straightforward isn't it?
1.2 Background
1.3 What is personnel for? (What is special about personnel?)
1.4 The growth of personnel management
1.5 The emergence of HRM
1.6 So what is different about HRM?
1.7 Looking ahead: human resource management in the twenty-first century
1.8 Summary

> **CHAPTER OBJECTIVES**
>
> - Understand the historical origins of personnel management and the ways these have shaped the nature and status of the profession in modern organisations
> - Appreciate the ambiguities and contradictions that operate in the personnel/HR role
> - Understand the contexts within which HRM emerged and how this is viewed as different from mainstream personnel management
> - Appreciate the links between large-scale organisation and the rise of the personnel function
> - Understand the various forms of human resource management and their implications for the effective management of people

1.1 Managing people is straightforward isn't it?

It is often assumed that because most people work because they need to – to earn money if nothing else – that they will come in, do their jobs to the best of their ability from the time they enter in the morning to when they leave at night and collect their pay cheques at the end of the week or month. The idea that managing people should present any difficulties or challenges, let alone require a separate department of professionally qualified staff to develop policies to manage them, strikes some people as strange and unnecessary.

Yet, those of you who work and indeed all of us who have experience of work organisations as customers know that things do not always go so smoothly. There are times when people are late for work, 'throw a sicky', are asked to do things they don't want to do or don't feel is part of their job, argue, get frustrated, bored and angry, and sometimes they leave. Although most of us need to work, what we need and what we want to do as human beings are not always one and the same thing. Also as we will try and show in this and other chapters, what people want from work as workers and what employers want from workers are often different and this can produce tensions which need to be managed carefully, particularly in a world of considerable change.

The aims of this chapter are to explain why the management of people is such a critical issue for organisations, and often more complicated than is realised. It also aims to explain why and how a profession dedicated to managing people came into being and why that profession has changed somewhat from what we used to call 'personnel management' to what is now 'human resource management'. Finally it aims at an assessment of whether this change represents something more fundamental about managing people in the twenty-first century.

1.2 Background

People are generally an essential element in any work organisation. From your other studies many of you will be aware that economists often talk about people as a 'factor of production' along with land (raw materials and land) and capital (finance, buildings, technology), which are combined together in order to produce an output. This may be physical products such as cars, computers, breakfast cereals, or services like banking, insurance, or sporting events. The essential differences between people and these other factors is that people can think, be creative, have feelings and demonstrate emotion, and may have concerns about how they are treated; fairly, reasonably and with respect at their place of work. This means we need to think particularly carefully about how we manage people and the techniques and policies we may wish to put in place in order to get the best from people at the workplace.

This is especially true in Britain today when most of us work in the service sector, and where people skills are particularly important in dealing with customers and fellow workers. Those of you who have part- or full-time jobs in organisations such as McDonalds, Pizza Hut, PC World or another high street outlet constantly deal with customers. In doing so you are developing a set of skills seen as highly desirable by potential employers in the long term. It is also the case that in an increasingly competitive world, employers are looking more for continuous improvement and knowledge work which means they are looking not only to recruit but also retain high quality staff required to deliver these elements. It follows that staff, and the people skills that they possess are seen as key elements for organisations in maintaining a competitive edge in the twenty-first century.

Figure 1.1 People skills are particularly important in the service sector

However, it was not always this way. Indeed there is a very influential view that despite personnel and HR managers, far from being 'our most important asset' people have often been seen as a cost, under-valued and treated as dispensable by those running organisations. It is not our intention to explore this view in detail except to point out that as well as being an asset, people do represent a significant cost for many organisations and if an organisation does experience difficulties in competing in markets, it is likely that they may look to people as a source of savings. What is important here is the balance – and the emphasis placed on each by senior managers.

Of course one person's wages are another person's costs and here lies one of the difficulties for managers trying to grapple with people issues in an organisation. The interests of those who own and run organisations and those who work in them clearly overlap. Owners need staff, and individuals generally need to work and both have an interest in an organisation being successful, but there may be differences between them in how this success should be achieved and conflicts over the details of the relationship between them. For example, how much they should be paid, how many hours and how hard they should work, where they should work and for whom? For those with responsibility for managing people these tensions present particular challenges.

1.3 What is personnel for? (What is special about personnel?)

Is the role of the personnel or HR manager to support employees, or at least to act as an advocate or 'champion' of the employee or is it first and foremost to meet the needs of the business?

In the early days of what came to be called personnel management, it was 'employee support' and welfare, often described as the 'tea and sympathy' role, which dominated and which helped shape a view of personnel as a necessary but low-key and marginal management function. The origins of what is now the Chartered Institute of Personnel and Development (CIPD), the main professional body for personnel and HR managers in the UK, came with the Welfare Workers Association in 1913, and more formally the Industrial Welfare Workers in 1924. Such origins created their own problems.

The Welfare Workers Association was mainly made up of women whose concerns were primarily to protect women and girls in employment. Although this was important it served to place such work at the margins of organisations. Also for many people, 'tea and sympathy' was something that could be done by almost anyone. In a world of heavy industry where manual skills dominated, welfare was seen as 'patching up', dealing with the 'casualties' of work and organisations and not part of the real business of producing goods and services. Crucially such people skills were seen as secondary to the real tasks of business, and because almost anyone had them, those who had largely failed to perform in other areas of management as in Drucker's (1961) 'trash can' vision, could 'do personnel'. More controversially, these were skills most closely associated (rightly or wrongly) with women, who at the time were often 'bit players' in the world of the industrial economy, a world largely dominated by men.

Although personnel work opened up considerable opportunities for women in management, these were often restricted to clerical positions and the sense that personnel was something that 'anyone could do' didn't help in raising its status within management. Even today, Keith Sisson's famous description of personnel as the 'Cinderella function' continues to cast a long shadow over the way the people management area is viewed by many in organisations (Sisson 1993). The obvious reference to gender is important here but also the question as to whether Cinderella would ever make it to the ball, in organisational terms, whether personnel would ever make it to positions of influence? As Anthony and Crichton have argued 'The history of the personnel specialists as a group is the history of a struggle for status to become full members of the management team' (Anthony and Crichton 1969).

Indeed, despite important work by the CIPD, there remains a sense that personnel/HR is still seen by those running organisations as the poor relation to finance, marketing or sales. Forty years on from Anthony and Crichton's observation there remains the feeling that the personnel and HR profession is one still struggling for identity and influence, a struggle that is partly based on a lack of clarity and conviction about what the basis of its claim to expertise is. Something that has not been helped by the fact that today, most managers are expected to manage people to varying degrees and to demonstrate 'people skills'.

We will return to this issue later in the chapter, but here we should note that one of the claims made for human resource management is that it is different in important respects from personnel management and this difference marks it out and requires senior managers as well as ourselves, to take it more seriously.

1.4 The growth of personnel management

With its origins in the late nineteenth century, welfare workers grew slowly, with around 1300 identified by the end of the First World War. The period between the two world wars in Britain saw the emergence of some very large organisations – ICI, Pilkingtons, Lever Brothers, Marks and Spencer – many of which had grown through merger, and the complexity of these new organisations helped to stimulate growth among what were now seen as labour managers, with an estimated 5300 employed in this area by 1943 (www.cipd.co.uk). Following the end of the Second World War, the number of personnel managers (the Institute of Personnel Management was formed in 1946) continued to grow steadily. This growth accelerated from the mid-1960s as a result of a growing number of large, complex organisations often formed by merger, and by the increasing power and influence of trade unions. Since then, numbers have been further stimulated by the growth of employment legislation since the mid-1970s (see chapter on employment law) and the need for staff to interpret and implement this. These developments have helped swell the numbers currently working in personnel to 150,000 (CIPD 2009). The significance of large-scale organisation for the growth of personnel is described in the insert below.

By the mid-1960s there was also concern to raise the professional standards of those working in personnel. Although a professional body had existed for some time, it was only in the early 1970s that a programme of accredited professional training was begun for those working in personnel. This was seen as an important basis for establishing a subject area of expertise (people management) and for helping to cement the idea of personnel as a profession and a career. Further, it was hoped that this would help to enhance the status of personnel and give greater credibility to the function and those working within it.

At this stage it should be remembered that the personnel profession is quite fragmented, containing within it a number of specialisms – recruitment and selection, manpower (now human resource) planning, training and development, reward, and industrial (employee) relations. These are reflected in a number of roles identified by the then IPM in the late 1970s (www.cipd. co.uk).

- Collective bargaining role
- Implementer of legislation role
- Bureaucratic role
- Social conscience of the organisation
- Performance improvement

(www.cipd.co.uk)

The importance of these varied from organisation to organisation. In some highly unionised industries, such as car manufacturing and other parts of engineering the collective bargaining role (what Tyson and Fell, page 8, referred to as the 'contract negotiator' role) was a central element in the work of the function and involved a large proportion of those employed in personnel. In others, such as high street retailers, bureaucratic and legislative concerns were more significant in determining the focus of personnel work.

Other companies revealed a range of different pressures on the development of personnel. Companies such as Cadburys, Clarks, Lever brothers and Marks and Spencer showed the importance of company founders and philosophy in shaping the development of personnel. Marks and Spencer in particular had acknowledged the importance of effective people management from an early stage. A wish to develop a reputation as a 'good employer' and 'employer of choice' as well as a concern to promote a strong paternalistic culture meant the company made a substantial investment in personnel-related activities which reaped benefits well into the 1990s.

Figure 1.2 Marks and Spencer acknowledges the importance of effective people management

Similar developments were also taking place in the United States and in the inter-war period a number of large organisations began to develop sophisticated people management policies around internal labour markets, careful recruitment and selection and developed career paths. Companies such as Kodak, IBM, Sears Roebuck and Maceys devoted considerable resources to this area partly to secure good quality staff and keep them but also to keep trade unions out, a concern shared by a number of British employers (Jacoby 1998). The view that strong personnel policies could be an important element in this emerged at this time and can be seen today in companies like Pret a Manger, DHL, McDonalds and Amazon.

Significantly, these large high-profile companies have tended to attract attention precisely because they are unusual, not because they are typical. We should not forget that the vast majority of organisations in Britain are small (employing fewer than 20 people) and where a personnel or HR presence continues to be rare or non-existent. Even in larger organisations the degree of sophistication in people management policies and presence varies considerably.

Tyson and Fell (1986): Personnel and the building site

In this famous description of personnel practitioners, Tyson and Fell use parallels with roles commonly found on a building site to identify three types of personnel practitioner found within organisations. These roles were:

- The *'clerk of the works'* – essentially an administrative and clerical role with much of the authority for dealing with the day-to-day management of staff lying with line managers.
- The *'contracts manager'* – here policies are well established and the role is essentially to maintain these and work within them. While there may be limited involvement in shaping or designing the policies the main focus of the role is in interpreting these. It follows that a significant emphasis is placed on industrial relations concerns.
- The *'architect'* role – here the organisation has well-developed policies and systems with the 'architect' normally responsible for developing and shaping these. Often with a seat on the most significant decision-making bodies within an organisation the 'architect' contributes to the direction and strategy of the organisation.

Frames of reference: unitarism and pluralism

People are assumed to see the world and frame their understanding of this through 'frames of reference'. These ways of seeing and making sense of the world are normally divided up between unitarist, pluralist and radical. Following the work of Fox (1966) we concentrate on the first two as these have been seen as most relevant for personnel practitioners. In his pioneering work on the profession, Fox made the distinction between those who adopted a unitarist frame and those a pluralist. For Fox, those who held to a unitarist view tended to see organisations as having clear objectives, shared by all, with managers having the accepted authority to make decisions on behalf of the majority. The view of the organisation as a team working together to achieve shared objectives is often used to describe a unitarist perspective. The difficulty that a unitarist view has is in coping with conflict in an organisation. For unitarists conflict is an aberration, the result of misguided individuals or poor communication within the organisation.

Fox's concern with this position was that he saw it as unrealistic in the world that most personnel practitioners operated in the 1960s. His view was that a more appropriate perspective was that of pluralism; one that emphasises the diversity of views and interests within organisations. For pluralists, a number of interests are represented in organisations and as a result conflict is a normal part of organisational life that has to be acknowledged and managed. Pluralism suggests that power, politics and influence play a critical part in organisations, as do the ways these play out through negotiation and consultation. A key concern for Fox was how personnel managers dealt with trade unions, a group representing the interests of employees. In his view personnel managers that held on to a unitarist view while in regular discussions with trade unions were in effect dealing with people they felt had no right to exist. If you believe organisations are teams with shared interests and objectives, a group representing a separate interest will inevitably present you with a problem. Furthermore, your interactions with these groups are unlikely to be constructive or positive and moreover are likely to give off the clear impression that their contribution is not valued. This in turn is likely to provoke a negative set of responses and set in train a downward spiral, and the negative feelings you had about these groups is likely to take on the features of a self-fulfilling prophecy.

1. One of the criticisms of personnel managers that is frequently heard by line managers is that personnel 'gets in the way', and stops them from doing what they want to do whereas personnel often feel they are saving 'the necks' of line managers. Personnel then get put in the same bracket as trade unions and governments who are also seen as limiting their freedom of action. Do you feel this is a fair criticism of personnel? In what ways could personnel/HR address these concerns in a way that achieves a positive outcome for them and line managers?

2. Why do you feel was Fox so insistent that, in his view, personnel practitioners needed to embrace a pluralist view of organisations and organisational life? Do you feel that Fox's argument remains relevant today? Give reasons for your answer.

3. In the light of the CIPD's identification of five distinct roles within personnel in the 1970s, what does this tell us about the nature of personnel work at that time and the skills and competencies that personnel practitioners may have needed to perform these roles adequately? Do you feel that today personnel/HR is required to perform different roles? If so is this reflected in a requirement for different skills and knowledge, and if so, in what ways?

Bureaucracy and the personnel function

As organisations increase in size their management becomes more difficult. The rise in complex large-scale organisations has created problems of coordination and control and with these, concerns about the need for consistent treatment of staff. Traditionally, large-scale **bureaucratic** organisations have provided a model for dealing with these issues, developing a range of employment rules to guide and shape behaviour. The basic employment rules have surrounded the jobs that people have performed and such organisations have tended to provide a large number of specialist jobs arranged in a hierarchy. The classic pyramid-type structure is normally used to describe this.

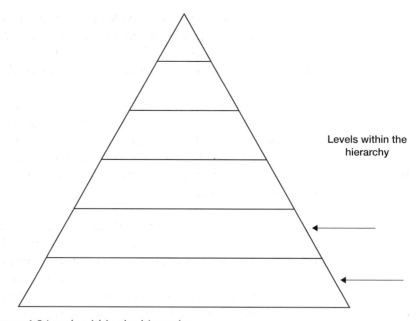

Figure 1.3 Levels within the hierarchy

Figure 1.3 illustrates this pyramid structure – jobs are arranged in a hierarchy with senior jobs at the top and with jobs becoming less senior, and generally less skilled, as we move down the hierarchy. Often organisations like this operate what economists call an internal labour market. That is people join the organisation at specific 'entry points' indicated by the arrows above, and then progress up through the organisation moving from job to job. In the past, many companies, including banks as well as parts of the public sector (Post Office, Armed forces, Police, Civil Service, and local authorities), operated such arrangements for their staff.

If we examine this model in detail we can see that the job is the basic unit, and for personnel managers, if we define a job carefully and precisely it allows us to provide a basis for managing people effectively. The job provides a set of rules (see the job description below) that defines clearly what people are expected to do when in work and from this a range of other employment rules can be defined and developed.

KEY TERMS

Bureaucracy An organisational form with a number of characteristics; bureaucracies are often large, hierarchical, centralised in decision-making, formal and rule-bound.

The job is arrived at through a **job analysis** and this provides the basis for something called a **job description** (simply that, a description of key tasks, responsibilities and reporting relationships) and a **person specification** (a description of what is required of the person to be able to perform the job). The job description and person specification are the basic documents used in recruiting and selecting staff. But a job description also enables us to do other things – we can use it to train and develop staff (as a basis for promotion for new jobs), to appraise them (to see if they are performing to the required standard), to reward them (through something called **job evaluation** that measures the worth of a job) and to discipline them if they are not performing to the required standard.

It follows that a large number of rules (around recruitment and selection, discipline, absenteeism, equal opportunities, pay and criteria for training) come into being as a result of organising on the basis of specific jobs, something that was seen as necessary in large-scale organisations. Furthermore, much of what we understand as personnel management is constructed on the basis of this idea of a job. Most of the tools personnel managers use derive from this and because of the precise nature of jobs in a bureaucratic organisation it is no surprise that this is where these techniques became established and personnel management with it.

KEY TERMS

Job analysis The various methods available to analyse the requirements of a job.
Job description Provides the job title together with a basic outline of the tasks, activities and broad functions of a particular job. In some organisations the focus has shifted towards role descriptions, reflecting the broader role rather than jobs individuals are expected to perform.
Job evaluation The CIPD defines this as 'a method of determining on a systematic basis the relative importance of a number of different jobs' (CIPD 2008b).

continued . . . ▶

◀ *. . . continued*

It could be argued that the real point of job evaluation is to provide some 'internal equity' to justify the different pay for often very different jobs.

Person specification Derived from the job analysis and matches the requirements the organisation wants to see in the ideal candidate in terms of skills and competencies to the job as defined by the job description.

Internal labour markets

The concept of an internal labour market was developed to better understand how people were recruited, developed and promoted within large-scale and bureaucratic organisations. Most commonly associated with the public sector; the civil service, the police, the army, local government, the NHS and the Post Office and with large-scale private sector organisations such as banks, and oil and chemicals companies. In these organisations staff were recruited at selected 'ports of entry' normally from school or university and were then given exposure to a number of areas of work before promotion opportunities arose. In addition, staff were often given considerable incentives to stay, through good pay and conditions, subsidised benefits (discounted mortgages in the case of banks) and opportunities for progression. The internal labour market helped organisations to cut down on recruitment costs by concentrating it at certain points (the graduate 'milk round) and by minimising turnover. It also helped to increase stability and loyalty to the organisation and develop staff who had an intimate knowledge of the various parts of the business. The downside of such arrangements is that staff have limited experience of and exposure to other organisations, and by having potentially a 'job for life' could become complacent and 'inward looking'. This may not be a significant problem in stable economic conditions but when change is required such people may have problems 'thinking out of the box' and embracing any changes that may be required.

CASE STUDY

In the 1990s Ford worked with an organisational model based on functional 'chimneys'. Its HR department was no different with a grading structure (for graduates at least) that extended from Grade 7 up to 19 or 20 although in practice 9 or 10 was the limit for most staff. Graduates joined on Grade 7 and spent about 18 months to three years in a number of roles, one of which had to be a plant/factory role normally involving employee relations at Dagenham or Halewood. Assuming that a person was performing well they could expect to progress to Grade 8 when they might take on one or two more specialist roles and within three to five years could then progress to a Grade 9 role. This was a goal for many Ford employees because the role normally came not just with more money but also a car. Many 'Fordies' never progressed beyond this role although some did get to Grade 10 or 11 and in some very exceptional cases to 13 or 14.

continued . . . ▶

◀ | *. . . continued*

What Ford provided was a classic internal labour market with possible progression to a number of HR roles in various locations. In the early 1990s Ford broke with its tradition of training its own staff and decided it needed to 'professionalise' its HR staff. It did so by using an external provider to deliver an accredited CIPD programme, something that also acted as a useful recruitment tool in a competitive market. The scheme was very successful, perhaps too successful as many staff left before getting to Grade 9. In the external labour market Ford was seen as providing good management training and experience, and people who had gone through the programme were highly marketable. It followed that Ford found itself with a limited number of staff to promote to Grades 9 and above and by 2001 had begun to seek external recruits to these posts. It also relaxed its entry into the HR grades by making it easier for non-graduates so pursue an HR career within the company.

Summary

The period from the mid-1960s until the present day has seen a rapid expansion in the numbers engaged in personnel work and we have identified a number of factors that have stimulated this expansion.

- The growing size and complexity of modern organisations, often as a result of mergers and takeovers.
- The growth and influence on trade unions in the 1960s and 1970s which stimulated the 'contracts manager' role identified by Tyson and Fell (1986).
- The growth of employment legislation since the mid-1970s which has required organisations to become legally compliant, procedures to be introduced or refined and in some cases, outcomes to be monitored.
- The growing importance of personnel as a profession; the rise of what is now the CIPD, as a professional body for those working in the field and a qualifications framework for those working in personnel.

However, we have also seen that despite this growth, personnel has often struggled to attain positions of power and influence within organisations. A number of reasons have been suggested for this: the belief that personnel lacks a clear claim to specific expertise, that it is not sufficiently business aware or business focused, and that it is marginal in a number of ways to the 'core business' of organisations. By the early 1980s, as the political and economic context shifted, these showed no signs of going away, but across the Atlantic something was stirring which was potentially to offer the profession the opportunity to 'get a leg up' to positions of influence, the emergence of what came to be known as human resource management, and it is to this that we now turn.

1.5 The emergence of HRM

As we have already noted, despite the growth in numbers working in personnel departments there were many who questioned the contribution and effectiveness of such departments for organisations. Robert Townsend's famous argument in *Up the Organisation* that personnel departments should be abolished (along with marketing!) hit a nerve and confirmed a need for personnel to be more assertive and positive about their contribution. But it was the work of an academic – Karen Legge – that was to provide the most searching and ultimately influential assessment of personnel in the UK and this work is discussed in the case study below.

Legge's contribution is important for a number of reasons but not least because it inspired some soul-searching within the profession as to how it could develop a position of power and influence within organisations – the elusive 'seat on the board'. However, its lasting legacy was probably to influence very significantly the knowledge base and skills set that those aspiring to careers in personnel should possess. The professional qualification for personnel and HR staff today is still partly influenced by Legge's work.

CASE STUDY

Karen Legge and the problems of personnel management

Karen Legge had spent time in the 1970s reflecting on the contribution of personnel and its continuing problems in gaining influence within organisations. The result, a book called *Power, Innovation and Problem Solving in Personnel Management,* offered an assessment of why personnel continued to be a low-status management function and why it failed to gain influence at senior levels within organisations, and provided clear options for the profession in terms of moving forward. The book remains one of the most influential and important studies of personnel ever written and although many of its analyses reflected concerns raised by others, its suggestions for change were genuinely innovative and had a major influence on the profession.

One issue that has remained central to concerns about personnel was the view that personnel managers did not really understand the business, and as such were not taken seriously. Worse still, was the view that they were often seen as not really part of the management team, 'of management' rather than 'with management', and therefore not really to be trusted. Legge acknowledged these problems and suggested two radical ways forward for the profession, either to become in her terms 'conformist innovators' or 'deviant innovators'. The former would seek to influence decisions by acknowledging where power lies in organisations and seek to work with the dominant power relationships within organisations. This meant speaking the language of accountants or at least to have a much greater understanding and appreciation of finance and to acknowledge that to have influence personnel needed to include costings in plans, to consider the financial implications of any proposed projects and in general to become more business aware. It is significant that today, many companies expect prospective HR staff to work or have worked in other business functions before

continued . . . ▶

. . . continued

moving into personnel – gaining a broader understanding of the workings of the business before specialising.

Deviant innovators in contrast would seek to influence by challenging the dominant thinking and management cultures found in organisations. This is clearly more radical, and risky, and in a profession that is already struggling for credibility, requires exceptional skills to carry off. It is no surprise that evidence for deviant innovation is still hard to find in personnel departments in Britain.

Although a development that began separately from Legge's work, human resource management or HRM came to prominence in the early 1980s following the publication of an American textbook (Beer et al. 1984) that used the term and identified what it saw as important differences between this and personnel management. The fact that HRM originated in the United States is important, as Guest (1989, 1995) has pointed out, and reflects many aspects of the individualistic culture of that country. Behind this was a largely unitarist philosophy, one which emphasised the overwhelming importance of shareholder and senior management interests in setting goals and driving behaviour within organisations and one which challenged the pluralism of personnel management, a pluralism that gave legitimacy to other (not just business) interests within organisations (see above). The significance of this lay in the challenge it posed for established ways of working, and arrangements for the shared development of objectives with bodies like trade unions, something that had become well-established in many areas of British organisational life by the 1960s and 70s.

Lying behind this interest in 'new approaches' to managing people in the 1980s was a view that countries like America had fallen behind economies such as Japan in terms of economic success. This led some to argue that there had been a failure of management (Hayes and Abernathy 1982) and a belief that in a more competitive international economy 'new times required new solutions'. At the risk of over-simplifying and in the language of the time, a 'Fordist' industrial model where volume and price were emphasised was seen to be giving way to a post-Fordist model where niche, quality and flexibility became priorities. Many influential writers explored the implications of this for organisations, suggesting that old style bureaucracy was no longer appropriate to the needs of a modern economy (Peters and Waterman 1982) and that what was needed in a dynamic, globalising and competitive economy was more agile, flexible and dynamic organisational forms. If bureaucratic organisation had provided the 'seed-bed' for the emergence of personnel, a move to a different form of organisation, a more networked form was likely to pose a challenge to this. Moreover, traditional methods for managing people might also be less appropriate than in the past. A further impetus to such change has come from more recent concerns to develop a knowledge economy and to emphasise work-life balance issues. Clearly if organisations are more concerned to retain the services of valuable knowledge workers then HR policies need to be geared more to interventions that seek to secure commitment and engagement from staff, something that received little attention from personnel management.

Before proceeding further it is worth reflecting on this a little more. If the world of organisations was facing unprecedented change and the traditional 'industrial Fordist model' no longer appropriate then what would this mean for the traditional job and the profession that had been built up around it? Could we still talk about people doing a job, rather than a number of jobs? Could we now talk as O'Doherty (2001) has done, about the demise or end of the job? If they were doing a number of jobs, having to be more flexible and essentially 'multi-tasking' what did this mean for traditional job descriptions? If traditional job descriptions were no longer appropriate then what was, in this brave new world of work (Beck 2001). Furthermore, if we could no longer talk about job descriptions, then what would happen to the other elements of personnel work – reward, resourcing, succession planning – that in our discussion of bureaucratic organisation were seen as being derived from the idea of a clear, distinctive job? This could have heralded a major crisis for personnel; the fulcrum around which a profession had been based appeared to be eroding away and unless personnel could modernise, become relevant to the challenges of a changed world it would become further marginalised within organisations. What was needed was a personnel for the late twentieth and early twenty-first centuries, at the very least a 'rebranding' but arguably something more fundamental which addressed many of the key issues organisations appeared to be facing.

 ## 1.6 So what is different about HRM?

If these were some of the external pressures that were forcing a rethink of the profession, the work by Beer and his colleagues provided a template for what might be different under the title of human resource management. This work then spawned a raft of studies that attempted to define, develop and critique the concept of HRM both in America and in the UK (see for example Schuler and Jackson 1982, Storey 1991, Blyton and Turnbull 1992). The important point for us is how this study and others at the time attempted to identify elements that they argued made HRM distinctive and distinguished it from personnel management. The main factors identified were as follows.

- That HRM is seen as offering a more strategic perspective on people management with personnel seen as mainly operational.
- That HRM is more clearly integrated, both with the business (business strategy – vertical integration) and with other policies. HR policies are integrated with each other and HR initiatives are integrated with those in other areas – marketing, sales, procurement, etc. – to provide a form of

horizontal integration. Furthermore, that HRM is seen as a more integrated line management activity.

- That 'people are our most important asset' and that people management is the responsibility of everyone and far too important to be left to personnel managers. It follows that HRM needs to be owned by line managers and by senior managers and by implication is 'too important to be left to personnel managers' (Guest 1991).
- HRM is 'business driven' people management and adds value to the business through (1) to (3) above.

These points are expanded upon further in Chapter 14 but it should be noted that they not only mark a break with the more 'nuts and bolts' world of personnel but they also carry with them some important tensions. A key element of this view of HRM is that it is 'business aware and business driven' – the *'resource'* view of HRM – so that HRM and HR departments should follow a business-driven agenda and serve the business. If the company decides that it will compete on the basis of particular strengths or a particular market position (providing high quality or low cost) then HR should support this by recruiting, rewarding, and developing staff who will best deliver to that strategy.

To put this another way, this is saying that HRM is *contingent* upon business considerations – there is no one best way of managing people. One of the best illustrations of this can be seen in the work of two American writers Schuler and Jackson (1987) who argued that the key responsibility for HR is to 'fit' HR strategy and initiatives to the business strategy, an approach developed further in Chapter 14. In their terms, an organisation pursuing a 'quality enhancement strategy' will need very different 'employee role behaviours' (their term) and HR policies from one following a 'low cost' or an 'innovation' route. The BA and Ryanair insert below provides a good illustration of how HR initiatives may differ depending on the business strategy being pursued.

Similarly it follows that how HRM operates in organisations like McDonald's is likely to be very different from other organisations in its sector because they are pursuing different business strategies. In the high street restaurant business, companies like Pizza Express and Café Rouge are trying to target a particular group of customers, and provide them with a different dining experience from that at McDonalds or Pizza Hut. Whether they actually receive such an experience will depend critically on the way they are treated by staff, and the necessary staff treatment will be encouraged and facilitated by appropriate HR policies. As a result we would expect Pizza Express and Café Rouge to operate with different criteria and priorities from McDonald's with respect to HRM in areas such as recruitment and selection, rewards, training and development, and the management of staff (employee) relations. (See Chapter 14 Strategic HRM for further details on this.)

CASE STUDY

British Airways and Ryanair

Since privatisation BA has arguably pursued a 'quality enhancement strategy' based on high levels of distinctive customer service. Over time this has been increasingly focused on 'high end' first and business class customers on long-haul and transatlantic routes. Although the strategy has not always been consistent it has emphasised the importance of staff in delivering the high quality service that this requires, and the training that is necessary to deliver the service. Historically BA has emphasised recruitment of the right people, and HR policies such as competitive pay, promotion opportunities, generous pension arrangements and on-going training and development aim at retention of those staff once they are recruited. In contrast Ryanair has followed a policy of 'cost leadership', taking out costs from every stage of the business in order to give customers low price fares. Recruitment is frequently outsourced and many staff recruited on fixed-term contracts through agencies so that Ryanair is often not the direct employer. It is usual for Ryanair cabin crew to 'multi-task', so they may check-in passengers and then reappear at the departure gates and then again on the flight itself. Once on the flight, cabin crew function as sales staff with part of salary in the form of a commission on in-flight sales. The Ryanair business model is one based on volume, high passenger volumes and high capacity utilisation on planes. Unlike the BA model where quality is seen to be critical, for cabin crew at Ryanair productivity and flexibility are key, managing the large volumes of passengers in what Ryanair's Chief Executive once described as 'buses in the sky'.

CASE STUDY

Tesco and Aldi

As with BA and Ryanair, supermarkets provide an interesting example of companies seeking to cater for specific target markets or niches. Traditionally, Tesco had established itself as a 'no frills' 'pile it high sell it cheap' supermarket but in the 1980s invested heavily in repositioning itself, taking itself more 'up market' to target groups of consumers with rising disposable income. Companies like Aldi, Netto, and Asda sought to explore the market that Tesco had left, focusing on low cost. Schuler and Jackson would anticipate that these differences in market strategies would be reflected in differences in approaches to managing staff. However both parts of the sector rely heavily on part-time staff for flexibility (in Tesco and Sainsbury 60 per cent of staff are on part-time contracts) and although pay and conditions differ, any differences are probably more visible in terms of management and management development.

This business-driven agenda has greatly helped to focus HR departments on 'the bottom line' and to emphasise business needs in HR considerations but there is a danger, as Tom Keenoy (1991) has argued that rather than being distinctive, HRM becomes whatever the business decides it should be rather than having any value of its own. It also sits uncomfortably the point made above – that 'people are our most important asset'. In a company like

McDonalds, people are clearly important to the business but many of the job roles are low skilled and the people who perform them easily replaceable. Indeed, in order to maintain a fresh and enthusiastic attitude to customer service in a world of deskilled jobs, McDonalds may be happy to have a high level of staff turnover among certain groups of staff, precisely because it does not want many of these staff to stay with it indefinitely. Its targeting of certain groups (e.g. students) who are less likely to stay for a limited period is one way in which this is achieved.

A number of points follow from this:

1 Ethical considerations in HR (for example relating to equal opportunities, 'whistle blowing', handling grievances) may be downgraded in importance if business considerations dominate (see the parallel debates in the airline industry over the possible safety issues with the low-cost operators).
2 That people issues may also be relegated in importance and individual needs neglected (see below). As Bolton and Houlihan (2007) have argued, 'The unitarist frame of reference underpinning mainstream HRM is directed towards the desired outcomes of the organisation, apparently to the exclusion of the individual needs and values of the employee' (Bolton and Houlihan 2007: 3).

   This is a theme that also appears in the writings of Paauwe (2004). That issues of fairness and justice might be relegated in importance where business needs get prioritised to the exclusion of other considerations.
3 If it is the case that business needs do dominate HR policy concerns, then it is difficult to talk of a 'best practice' HRM which is applicable to all organisations, because any 'best practice' HRM is decided by the business. It follows that what is best practice for one organisation, may not be for another.
4 If HR strategy is simply 'read-off' from business strategy it raises a question of what is distinctive about HRM and its contribution to the business. It also assumes that HR 'follows' rather than initiates ideas to shape the direction of the business – something that carries with it a rather negative message for HR.
5 It ignores an increasingly influential body of opinion that suggests that people may be a key source of core competence or capability for organisations and that how they are nurtured and developed and how HR policies are 'clustered together' (Huselid 1995) may be critical in explaining why some organisations are more successful than others (this is explored further in Chapter 14 Strategic HRM). That is, that far from being largely passive, in the 'business-driven' model, HR may through its role in recruiting and developing the human resource be a key influence in what is described as *competitive advantage*. The text on resource-based strategy below explains this point further.

Resource-based strategy (RBS)

Derived from the work of an economist Edith Penrose in the 1950s, RBS starts from the proposition that organisations are composed of resources and it is these, together with how they are combined that provides *distinctiveness* in what an organisation does and ultimately its competitive advantage (a sustainable advantage as perceived by customers that means they deal with you rather than others). This idea was revived in the 1990s following work by Hamel and Prahalad (1990) which viewed organisations as having *core competencies* or *distinctive capabilities*. The key element of which is that competitive success comes from within organisations, rather than scanning the market and attempting to find a niche or a new opportunity. In the RBS, it is the core competencies developed within organisations that can then be exploited in a range of markets that are the key to competitive success. The example is often given of Honda with core competencies around engine technologies that have then been exploited in a number of distinct markets – cars, motorbikes, powerboats and lawnmowers.

Figure 1.4 Honda and resource-based strategy

The significance of this for HR is that a key resource in organisations is people, so that people are often integral to the development and sustainability of core competences. This is clearly true in knowledge-based organisations, examples of which would include Apple, Nokia and most famously, Microsoft where much of the asset value of the company comes from its people but it is arguably true more widely. The resource-based view also carries another positive message for HR. As well as reinforcing the 'people are our most important asset' view, it also suggests that instead of merely following business strategy as in the 'hard' matching model, HR may take more of a lead in initiating developments in strategy because of their claimed expertise in people management.

In truth what is being described here is not as 'clear-cut' as it appears. We are discussing a tension first identified by John Storey (1992) in his path-breaking study of the take-up of HRM practices in Britain, between 'hard' or business-driven HRM and 'soft' HRM, with the 'soft' version stressing the 'human' in HRM and representing what we have called 'best practice' HRM, itself linked to 'resource-based' views of the firm.

In practice this tension can be exaggerated. Even where organisations follow a 'hard' version of HRM they will be advised to take account of aspects of 'best practice', so that many often opt for an 'adopt and adapt' approach, taking aspects of 'best practice' and adapting them to their particular requirements. Furthermore, much of the work that links HRM with business performance suggests that in attempting to be distinctive and to prevent others from easily mimicking initiatives, it is the ways in which HR initiatives are combined, how they are 'clustered' that may be critical for success (HR clusters) and how they are embedded into wider organisational networks. The example of Honda is often used to illustrate a company that works hard on what John Kay (1993) has called 'strategic architecture', part of which concerns the ways in which policies are integrated and blended to suit the particular needs of an organisation at any point in time.

1. On the basis of what you have learned in this chapter, how different do you feel HRM is from personnel management? To what extent do you agree with Michael Armstrong that HRM is merely a case of 'old wine in new bottles'?
2. There has been much debate between 'business-driven' and so-called 'best practice' HRM. What is the basis of the difference between these and what difference do you feel it is likely to make to how HRM operates in practice? In light of your reflections, how useful do you feel the concept of human resource management is as a basis for effective people management?

1.7 Looking ahead: human resource management in the twenty-first century

In moving forward, it is possible to identify two themes that have dominated discussion of human resource management in the past fifteen years. Both connect with the long-standing concerns we have discussed throughout this chapter, namely how personnel/HRM can 'raise its game' and be seen as a credible and legitimate player in organisations.

Theme one, which we can call 'the business contribution', is in two parts. First, does HRM improve business performance and second, if it does, what are the mechanisms by which it does this? That is, identifying the links between HRM and business outcomes and then establishing the specific HR policies and initiatives that HR practitioners can identify that 'make a difference' to business metrics (various measures of business performance). This is more difficult than it sounds. Identifying a clear link between HRM and business performance is hard because so many factors affect performance and it is extremely difficult to isolate the impact of one factor. A further problem is that even if you find an association between the two, it is very difficult to establish that HRM actually *causes* changes in business performance.

Clearly, establishing a link has been particularly important for professional bodies like the CIPD in Britain, which has funded some of the research in this area but the overall evidence has been inconclusive. Indeed recent work (Guest and Bryson 2009) has painted a fairly 'downbeat' picture of the links between the two.

A further criticism of such work has been that even if an association is found, it tells us little about *how* HRM makes a difference. In terms of our earlier discussion, the theory tells us that HRM could make a difference by being 'business driven', 'matching' with the business strategy, or it could foster the growth and development of core competencies and capabilities (Ulrich 1997). Furthermore, this could then lead to consideration of the specific policies or clusters of policies (Huselid 1995) that might lead to changes in behaviour and performance, but even this tells us little about what actually takes place within organisations. That is, how are these theories and the policies associated with them translated into practice within organisations 'on the ground'.

We should note that the problem of translating strategy into effective operations has been a feature of organisational life for many years and only recently have these begun to be effectively addressed through for example, Kaplan and Norton's (1996) work on 'the balanced scorecard'. The technique provides a mechanism whereby strategic goals are translated into a series of measures, targets and initiatives at a departmental or other local level. HR clearly forms an important part of this in terms of meeting key performance targets and it allows key areas of HR to be identified and monitored for priority and/or improvement.

This takes us some way into the area of how we translate strategy into practice but other factors are also important. In the late 1990s a group from Bath University (Purcell et al. 2003) set out to try and explore a further aspect of the 'how' in terms of how these were operationalised at the 'grass roots' of organisations. That is, how the lofty ideas of strategy were actually translated into action 'on the ground' (see Chapter 14 for a development of this). Their 'people and performance' model derived from research on organisational case studies examined what went on in the 'black box' of organisations, that is how HRM practices do impact on organisational performance. Such an approach has the potential to examine what HR practitioners actually do to make a difference and takes us in to the worlds of organisational climate and cultures, of organisational power, politics and influence. As a result it emphasises the importance of HR professionals being able to draw on networks, interpersonal relations and their own resources as well as the policies that might be in place within their organisations. These factors are frequently played down in our often 'rational' treatment of management and decision-making within organisations and it is important to remind ourselves that organisations are often very political spaces. To influence, we often need to use the resources available to us sparingly and strategically, and often in liaison with others and these require refined organisational skills which frequently get ignored in many 'textbook' treatments of management. Indeed, Legge's seminal contribution was probably to make this explicit for personnel/HR practitioners. To gain influence you might need to 'play the game', to curry favour with those who have power and influence in organisations. This might mean some strange 'bedfellows' at times but it might also get results.

The second and related theme has focused on the HR function itself. Gaining credibility, legitimacy and influence has been seen not only to be about 'professionalising' the function but also emphasising the business relevance and contribution through 'business partnering'. This has faint echoes of Legge's concept of 'conformist innovation', rebranded for the twenty-first century but still about working with a dominant business model. In answer to the question 'how can the HR function gain influence, be taken seriously and contribute to the business', voices today emphasise **'business partnering'** and 'centres of expertise'. These ideas have been associated with the work of an American academic Dave Ulrich.

The Ulrich model and classification of HR roles

It is useful to contrast the aspirational and prescriptive focus of Ulrich's work with Tyson and Fell's description of personnel roles as they saw them in the 1970s:

- Strategic or business partner
- Administrative expert
- Change agent
- Employee champion

Whereas the business partner model attracted considerable interest and attention when the classification first appeared, significantly the change agent and **employee champion** have since become more important with current concerns about effective change management and employee engagement.

The model is now most commonly described as the three-legged stool model – business partnering, shared services, centres of expertise are now the most common HR function structure (CIPD 2007) and in recent years Ulrich has focused on human capital and organisational capabilities.

KEY TERMS

Business partner The business partner role (previously entitled the 'strategic partner') is seen as working closely with senior business leaders in executing strategy and in designing HR systems and processes that ensure that strategic business issues are addressed (CIPD 2008).

There is considerable evidence that in the UK the Ulrich model has been extremely influential in reshaping and organising the work of HR departments with the recent CIPD survey indicating that around 30 per cent of HR departments had implemented it in full and a further 30 per cent in part. The same survey (CIPD 2007) has shown evidence for the 'three legs' of the model; centralised provision of shared administrative services (the 'administrative expert' providing payroll, resourcing, administrative advice), strategic business partners (working with senior strategists in the business) and centres of expertise (links to change agents with experts providing 'leading edge' HR advice and solutions to the business). However, at present, the extent to which the Ulrich model has led to a significant raising of the profile and influence of the HR role, and moreover a contribution to business performance, is less clear. As a recent assessment of change over the past twenty-five years has put it: 'While we have seen a growth in the presence of personnel specialists, and while they have become more qualified, this does not seem to have been reflected in any pioneering of new human resource practices . . . if anything, personnel specialists have been bringing up the rear' (Guest and Bryson 2009: 149).

KEY TERMS

Employee champion The 'employee champion' is seen as supporting the rights and needs of the employee. The recent interest in trying to secure employee engagement has focused particular attention on raising the profile of the employee champion role.

1. If HR departments in large organisations are taking on strategic business partner roles as Ulrich's model and CIPD evidence suggests, how might we expect that to be translated in terms of what HR actually contributes to the business? That is, what might we expect to see them doing that they are not currently?
2. To what extent does the Ulrich model offer a potential way of addressing the tensions and ambiguities that we have described as lying within the personnel/HR role? In what ways is the model different from that offered by Tyson and Fell?
3. How far do you feel Legge's commentary on the function continues to be relevant today?

(1.8) Summary

We began this chapter presenting something of a dilemma for those engaged in managing people: that it is assumed that managing people is rather straightforward, common sense, something that all of us can do, and indeed are increasingly expected to do as part of our everyday jobs. We suggested that this could create problems for those whose main function at work is to provide advice, support and leadership in the area of people management, and much of the evidence we have presented suggests that the personnel function has continued to strive often unsuccessfully for status, influence and credibility. Part of this problem has lain with the contradictions and ambiguities in the role itself. In Ulrich's terms, is it a strategic business partner first and foremost, or an employee champion, and can it be both things at the same time?

The position here, and in the remainder of this book, is that managing people is far from straightforward. It is an essential element in effective management and business performance but it does require considerable skill, expertise and is underpinned by a body of knowledge that is continually evolving. Moreover, there is something vital and unique that personnel/HR has to offer. Yes, it needs to be taken seriously by the management team, and following Legge that does mean learning the language of those in positions of power and influence so that personnel/HR can present proposals and influence in ways that 'tick the right boxes' and get their proposals noticed. But, it is also about the fact that personnel operates on a number of important boundaries; between the organisation and its employees, and the organisation and the wider society. That is, that sometimes it does need to 'champion employees' and a good recent example of this has been the concern to embrace employee engagement.

It can also be seen as the 'conscience of the organisation'. We have noted at various points the importance of ethical considerations in personnel work and the potential tensions between these and a more overt 'business-driven HRM'. The interface between personnel/HR and the wider society is also one we should not ignore and increasingly the influence of the European Union, particularly through legislation is one that is having a profound effect on the function and the skills requirements of those who work in it.

Finally we would encourage you to reflect on one point as you embark on the remainder of this book. The recent debates on engagement suggest that the dangers of a narrowly focused 'business-driven' HRM are as much of a problem as one that is focused overly on people. If HRM becomes whatever the business wants it to be, it potentially loses any claims to distinctiveness, and certainly ethical considerations could be downplayed significantly. Furthermore, there is a danger that it reinforces the idea that anyone could do it because there is no unique knowledge base. In practice, as we try and show in the remainder of the book, it is often the complexities of personnel/HR work that not only make it challenging but also extremely interesting and when done well there is little doubt can make a major contribution to organisations and those who work in them.

REFLECTIVE QUESTIONS

1 In view of the historical importance of internal labour markets for aspects of personnel management:
   a) What do you see as the advantages of having such arrangements for employers and employees?
   b) Under what conditions might such arrangements become a problem for employers and why?
2 Throughout the chapter reference has been made to the tensions, contradictions and ambiguities that lie at the heart of the personnel/HR role that serves to make it particularly challenging:
   a) What is the nature of these tensions and ambiguities?
   b) Are they just an inherent part of managing people, which we have to accept?
   c) Does the Ulrich model offer a potential way of addressing these tensions and ambiguities and if so, how?

KEY IDEAS

Background
- The importance of retaining skilled staff.
- The conflict between human resources and other demands on the organisation.

What is personnel for? (What is special about personnel?)
- The role of personnel management.
- The development of personnel management through workers' associations.

The growth of personnel management
- The growth of personnel management due to the increasing number of large, complex organisations.
- The emergence of professional standards and training for those working in personnel.
- The fragmented nature of personnel and the specialisms it encompasses, for example, recruitment and selection, human resource, planning, training and development, reward and industrial relations.
- The developing influence and status of personnel management and policies.
- Tyson and Fell's (1986) three types of personnel: the clerk of the works, the contracts manager and the architect.
- Unitarist and pluralist perspectives.
- Bureaucracy and the problems it can create for the personnel function.
- The internal labour market and its effect on the organisation.

The emergence of HRM
- Karen Legge's influence.
- New approaches to managing people in a dynamic, globalising and competitive economy.
- The new focus for human resources managements as a result of the demise of the traditional job description and expectations demanded of employees in the twenty-first century.

So what is different about HRM?
- The new strategic perspective.
- The clear integration of HRM with the business and other policies.
- The emphasis on the importance of people to the business.
- HRM is 'business driven' – emphasis on staff as a resource.

Looking ahead: human resource management in the twenty-first century Conclusions and reflections
- The business contribution – identifying the links between HRM and business performance.
- 'Professionalising' HRM and business partnering as ways to legitimise the HR function.
- The classification of HR roles: Tyson and Fell's description of personnel roles and Ulrich's three-legged stool model.

RECOMMENDED READING

For a useful background to the development of personnel management in Britain, a valuable book is Hall and Torrington's (1998) *The Human Resources Function: The Dynamics of Change and Development*.

The same authors, with the addition of Stephen Taylor and Carol Atkinson, have also written *Fundamentals of Human Resource Management: Managing People at Work* (2009), a more accessible text for undergraduate students than the CIPD text Torrington, Taylor and Hall (2007) *Human Resource Management* but for those who want more on the essential features of human resource management either text is valuable.

In general any standard HR text will provide some basic coverage of 'what is HRM' but the early chapters of Storey's (1992) book *Developments in the Management of Human Resources* and his chapter in his (1995) text *Human Resource Management a Critical Text* still provide a valuable introduction into the complexities of the term. Arguably the debate has moved on considerably since this time but his work still highlights some of the conceptual problems with a term that has become part of the fabric of modern organisations.

If you are not sure that Storey will give you what you want, another valuable text that provides additional information on human resource management is Marchington and Wilkinson's (2008) *Human Resource Management at Work: People Management and Development*. Again this is a CIPD set text so is pitched very much towards postgraduate students although is written in a fairly accessible way.

Finally the 2007 CIPD report, *The Changing HR Function*, is a useful way in to appreciating both how the function has been changing and the influence of Ulrich's work on the direction of change.

REFERENCES

Beer, M., Spector, B., Lawrence, P., Qui Mills, D., Walton, R. (1984) *Managing Human Assets*. New York: Free Press.

Blyton, P., Turnbull, P. (eds) (1992) *Reassessing Human Resource Management*. London: Sage.

Bolton, S., Houlihan, M. (2007) 'Searching for the H in HRM', in Bolton, S., and Houlihan, M. (eds) *Searching for the Human in Human Resource Management*. Basingstoke: Palgrave Macmillan.

CIPD (2007) *The Changing HR Function*. London: CIPD.

CIPD (2009) *Panel on Fair Access to the Professions: Report to the Cabinet Office* (March 2009). London: CIPD.

Drucker, P. (1961) *The Practice of Management*. London: Mercury.

Fox, A. (1966) *Industrial Society and Industrial Relations*. Royal Commission research paper No. 3.

Guest, D. (1990) 'Human Resource Management and the American Dream', *Journal of Management Studies*, vol. 27, no 4, 149–75.

Guest, D. (1995) 'Human Resource Management, Industrial Relations and Trade Unions', in Storey, J. (ed.) *Human Resource Management: A Critical Text*. London: Routledge.

Guest, D., Bryson, A. (2009) 'From industrial relations to human resource management: the changing role of the personnel function', in Brown, W., Bryson, A., Forth, J., Whitfield, K (eds), *The Evolution of the Modern Workplace*. Cambridge: Cambridge University Press.

Hall, L., Torrington, D. (1998), *The Human Resources Function: The Dynamics of Change and Development*. London: FT/Prentice Hall.

Hamel, G., Prahalad, C. (1990) 'The Core Competence of the Corporation', *Harvard Business Review*.

Hayes, R., Abern... 67–7.

Holbeche, L. (20... Butterworth-F

Huselid, M. (199... financial perf

Jacoby, S. (1998... University Pre

Kaplan, R., Nor... Harvard Busi

Kay, J. (1993) F...

Keenoy, T. (199... *Journal of H*

Legge, K. (197... Hill.

Marchington, ... *and Develop*

O'Doherty, D. ... *Human Res*...

Paauwe, J. (20...

Pfeffer, J. (199... Boston MA

Pfeffer, J. (199...

Schuler, R., Ja... practices', ...

Sisson, K. (19...

Sisson, K. (19... *Text*. Lond

Storey, J. (19...

Storey, J. (19...

Torrington, ... *Managing*

Torrington,

Tyson, S., Fe

Ulrich, D. (1

...ne', *Harvard Business Review,*

...London:

...er, productivity and corporate ...no. 3.

...)eal. Princeton: Princeton

...tegy into Action. Boston MA:

...nd Contradiction, *International*

...el Management. London: McGraw-

...nt at Work: People Management

..., in Beardwell, I., Holden, L. (eds), ...on: Prentice-Hall.

...bility. Oxford: OUP.

...nding the Power of the Workforce.

...ss School Press.

...uman resource management

...lations, vol. 31, no 2.

...) Resource Management: A Critical

...ources. Oxford: Blackwell.

...don: Routledge.

...s of Human Resource Management:

...ment. Harlow: FT/Prentice Hall.

...n: Hutchinson.

...d Business School Press.

2 Recruitment and selection

'It has been said that a person may have ten years of experience, or one year of experience repeated ten times.'

(Anon)

CHAPTER OUTLINE

2.1 Introduction
2.2 The recruitment process
2.3 The selection process
2.4 Screening
2.5 Selection methods
2.6 The accuracy of selection methods
2.7 Summary

CHAPTER OBJECTIVES

- Appreciate the importance of effective recruitment and selection
- Understand the key processes involved in recruitment
- Be aware of the issues surrounding the various approaches to recruitment
- Know the range of methods for use in selection
- Understand the varying accuracy of selection methods
- Understand the necessity of validity and reliability in selection

2.1 Introduction

Recruitment and selection is a core element of HR activity in developing sustained competitive advantage for the organisation. In fact Taylor and Collins (2000) believe recruitment and selection is the **most** important part of HR work. This is because recruitment and selection determines who works in the organisation and shapes candidates' perceptions about other HR practices and the company in general. The knock-on effects of poor recruitment and selection may have long-term consequences for an organisation. For example, an employee who doesn't perform as expected results in significant time spent on performance management issues, time spent on training that person to enable them to work more effectively and can result in loss of motivation for the individual and for those they work with. One of the most extensive pieces of research to date on the impact of recruiting and selecting poor performers has been carried out by Schmidt and Hunter (1998). They calculated that the difference between a high performing worker and a low performing worker is on average 40 per cent of salary. If we put that in monetary terms it means that if a manager is earning £40,000, then the difference in effectiveness is £16,000 of their salary. This is obviously a lot of money for any organisation to waste should they have made the wrong selection decision.

In today's dynamic business environment, it is no longer acceptable for organisations to use recruitment and selection as a means of replacing departed employees. It is expected to be a means of acquiring people with the right skills, knowledge, experience and attitude to enhance the future of the organisation. In order for it to meet this tall order, recruitment and selection needs to be seen within the context of the overall environment that the organisation operates within. For example, a small high-tech company wishing to set up business in a new area would need to consider the skill level of the local labour market, the age profile of the work force, the availability of suitable premises in the area, the extent of customer demand for their product, employment regulations and so on.

Recruitment and selection should also be a two-way process. It is just as important for the candidate to get to know the company and see if they really want the job as it is for the company to discover if the prospective employee suits the business needs. Sadly some companies don't realise this and I'm sure you may have experienced both good and bad recruitment and selection procedures. However, the best companies do realise the importance of this two-way process.

An example of good recruitment and selection is Microsoft, who have so many applications for each role they give plenty of information early on so that people can see if the job will suit them. The British Army do the same. If you go on their website www.armyjobs.mod.uk you can take an assessment and participate in 'virtual training' to see if the army would be the right career for you before you even look at the application procedure.

So far the terms 'recruitment' and 'selection' have been used together, but they are in fact distinct in that they involve different activities. **Recruitment** is the part of the process concerned with finding applicants. It requires positive action by employers to sell themselves in the relevant labour market to generate interest and applications of suitably qualified candidates. **Selection** is that part of the process that involves choosing between applicants and identifying who would be the most suitable for the job on offer and rejecting the rest.

KEY TERMS

Recruitment The process used to attract candidates.
Selection Choosing between applicants and identifying who would be most suitable for the job.

The time, cost and importance of each stage depends on the state of the labour market. When the economy is buoyant and the labour market is tight, recruitment activities become very important, companies have to work harder in finding potential suitable employees. Conversely when the economy takes a downturn and jobs are in short supply, there is usually little shortage in suitable applicants. This means that more attention is given to the selection stage as organisations focus on ways to correctly differentiate between suitable candidates. Many companies who were struggling to find suitable applicants in 2007 were overwhelmed by the increase in number and quality of applicants for posts advertised in 2009 when the world economy was in recession. For instance, John Lewis had 250 people chasing each of its graduate jobs in 2009 which is an increase of 87 per cent from 2008. Microsoft had 5,000 applications for 25 vacancies and Tesco applications were up 50 per cent in 2009.

1. What do you think are the reasons that these companies are so popular with graduates?
2. How can companies ensure the most suitable people apply for the job vacancies?

As we have already seen, getting recruitment and selection right is not easy. It is a complex and critical process for companies and as a result it has become an essential feature of HRM in all organisations irrespective of their size, sector or design. Making the right choices must result from a thorough and systematic process. This chapter aims to introduce you to some of the issues involved in recruitment and selection and give you an understanding of the processes necessary for them to be effective.

2.2 The recruitment process

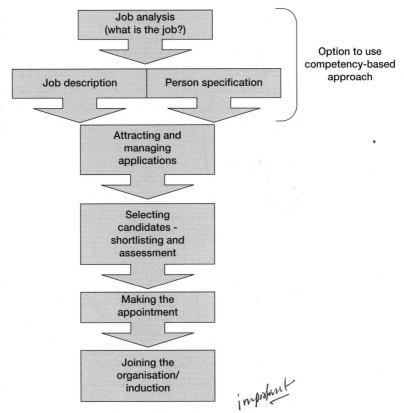

Figure 2.1 Flow diagram to illustrate the recruitment and selection process (CIPD 2009, with the permission of the publisher, the Chartered Institute of Personnel and Development, London (www.cipd.co.uk))

There are two main stages involved here; analysing the job that is available and then advertising it in the most appropriate way. When a vacancy occurs, it is necessary first to establish the need to fill it. The job may have changed or may not be required anymore. This is often a good chance for the company to review their requirements and make changes to vacant jobs in the light of the external and internal environment relevant to the organisation.

Job analysis

Assuming that the need to fill the vacancy has been established, the first stage in the process is to acquire knowledge about the job and the skills and qualities required of an employee to fulfil the role. To do this, we need to carry out a job analysis. This involves some type of research to find out exactly what the job entails. There are various techniques of doing this which are summarised in Table 2.1.

Technique	Method	Advantages	Disadvantages
Observation	Observing and recording the information of a post holder over a period of time	Simple Comprehensive information could be collected Most suitable for straightforward, physical jobs	Some activities cannot be observed Time-consuming Employee may not behave in usual way due to being observed
Interviews	Trained analyst asks job-holders, supervisors and colleagues to describe the job concerned	Skilled interviewers can identify the detail of the job and probe for clarification	Interviewees may focus on more interesting parts and downplay the routine aspects
Group discussions	Conduct a group interview with several job holders at the same time	More balanced information as 'talking up' the job will be discouraged	May result in 'group think' Time-consuming and logistically difficult to arrange
Critical incidents	Focus attention on outcomes of the job Interviewee is asked to describe actual events or incidents to identify what aspects of the job make the difference between success and failure	More specific and detailed information is gathered Most significant tasks are identified	Complex Time-consuming Requires highly trained interviewers
Questionnaire	Employers can develop their own or use a questionnaire from a licensed provider which has been developed using data gathered from a cross section of jobs from a number of industries	Less opportunity for bias, higher level of objectivity Efficient and straightforward	Time in preparing a suitable questionnaire If it is not correctly designed, information gathered may be inappropriate or difficult to analyse Buying from a provider may be too generic and not specific enough
Work diaries	Employees are asked to detail the tasks they complete each day for later analysis	Systematic and avoids missing detail Most suitable for higher level, more complex jobs	Time-consuming for the individual Difficult to analyse depending on the way the information is recorded

Table 2.1 Job analysis techniques

Ultimately a job analysis is trying to find answers to the following questions:

1 What are the initial requirements of the employee?
   (Qualifications, experience, personality, attitude)
2 What are the duties and responsibilities of the job?
   (Responsibilities for other staff, routine work or use of own initiative, equipment)
3 What is the environment and conditions of the job?
   (Potential hazards, physical surroundings, level of pay, benefits in terms of holidays, career prospects, etc.)
4 What is the physical and social context of the job?
   (Size of the department, teamwork or individual work, type of people expected to deal with – members of the public, managers, etc.)

ACTIVITY

John is an assistant manager of a small supermarket based in the Midlands. On average he works a 40-hour week but this can vary as the shop is open from 6 a.m. to 10 p.m. Monday to Saturday. He is often left in charge of the shop and is expected to ensure the smooth running of all its operations. This involves a wide range of tasks from ordering stock and dealing with deliveries to organising the staff rota and dealing with customer complaints. No day is the same. As business is good, the owner has decided to branch out and open another store ten miles away. He has already appointed a manager and now needs to appoint an assistant manager to perform a similar role to that of John's.

1. Which method, or combination of methods, would you recommend to gain a thorough job analysis of John's role?
2. What problems would you anticipate in carrying out a job analysis of this role?

Job description/accountability profiles

The research involved in the job analysis should provide enough information that can be then used to write a job description. Although organisations will have their own format for how they describe their jobs, most include the following elements:

- Job title, department, pay and grade
- Job summary
- List of the main tasks involved in the job
- Reference to other documents that may clarify or expand on areas (e.g. collective agreements over breaks, holiday allowance, legal aspects, health and safety and so on).

A problem with job descriptions is that they describe a job at the time of the analysis. Due to the rapid pace within which many organisations now operate job descriptions can quickly become outdated. Employers are also increasingly expecting employees to be flexible in what they do. As a result some organisations consider job descriptions to be too rigid and may even encourage post holders to only do what is outlined in their job description, focusing on inputs rather than outputs. I'm sure you have come across the 'job's worth' person who refuses to help 'because it is not their job'! As a response to this, many organisations are now using **job groupings** rather than job descriptions for each job type and some are adopting **'accountability profiles'** that focus on performance measures for each job (Taylor 2008). This means that the focus moves from 'what workers are expected to do' to 'what gets done'. So rather than state that the job involves 'dealing with the public' (what the employee is expected to do), the job profile uses phrases such as 'assisting with queries to solve common problems' (to stipulate more clearly what gets done).

KEY TERMS

Accountability profiles Details of performance measures for each job type.
Job groupings Putting similar types of jobs together and providing a generic description to include all of these jobs.

An example of a job description and an accountability profile for John's job is given in Table 2.2.

Person specifications

This is the other piece of information derived from the job analysis. Here the focus is on the ideal person to do the job as described in the job description or accountability profile. Although the format may vary between organisations, their purpose is the same: to detail the 'essential' requirements that an applicant must possess before they can be considered for the job vacancy. Most person specifications also list 'desirable' requirements which are particularly useful for screening purposes when large numbers of candidates are likely to meet the 'essential' criteria. An example of a person specification for John's job is given in Table 2.3. You will see that the method of assessment is also included. In the 'selection' section of this chapter, we will discuss these methods further, but it is good practice to detail them in the person specification so that applicants know how they will be expected to provide evidence of meeting the criteria listed.

Job description	Accountability profile
Job title: Assistant Manager **Salary**: 17–20 K **Reports to**: Manager **Main purpose of the job** To work closely with the manager to ensure the smooth and profitable running of the store. **Main duties:** • Opening and closing of the store • Ordering stock • Organising the staff rota • Handling and distributing deliveries • Dealing with customer complaints • Coordinating and delivering staff training	**Job title**: Assistant Manager **Salary**: 17–20 K **Reports to**: Manager **Main purpose of the job** To work closely with the manager to ensure profitability targets are met and customer and staff complaints are minimised. **Key responsibilities:** • Ensures timely opening of the store and security at the end of business • Ensure stock is kept at optimum levels • Communicates with staff to ensure sufficient cover in line with business needs • Organises the distribution of deliveries and ensures the relevant paperwork is completed and recorded accurately • Provides solutions to customer complaints promptly and courteously • Analyses staff training needs and implements appropriate training to fulfil staff training requirements. Gives advice, guidance and feedback in a constructive manner.

Table 2.2 Job description and accountability profile

Discrimination and person specifications

Particular care needs to be taken when constructing person specifications that items included are not discriminatory in any way. In the UK and under European law, there are various discrimination laws which prevent direct or indirect discrimination on the grounds of race, sex, age and disability as summarised in Table 2.4. If the person specification details requirements that

Category	Essential job requirements	Desirable job requirements	Method of assessment
Qualifications	Educated to a minimum of A level standard or equivalent GCSE (or equivalent) maths and English	Business-related degree	Certificates Application form
Experience	Working in a retail environment Managing staff Organising and distributing stock Dealing with members of the public Analysing training needs Delivering training	Working in food retail	Application form Interview Practical assessment
Knowledge, skills and abilities	Able to demonstrate effective interpersonal skills to deal with customers and staff Good communication skills (verbal and written) Excellent organisational skills Good IT skills Able to manage and prioritise work loads	Report writing skills Excel and database knowledge	Application form Interview Practical assessment/ test
Other	Understanding of and a commitment to equality of opportunity both for customers and staff		Interview

Table 2.3 Person specification

could be considered discriminatory then an applicant can bring their case to an Employment Tribunal. It is therefore necessary for HR to check all information on a person specification to ensure it is relevant to the requirements of the job.

As an example of discriminatory wording, a person specification accompanying a job recently advertised in a national newspaper asked for 'five years continuous experience'. This could be deemed as indirect discrimination as a significant proportion of the population could not comply with the requirement. This is because younger people may not have been in employment for the required length of time due to their age and women may not be able to comply because

Type of discrimination	Legislation to prevent discrimination	What it prevents
Age discrimination	Equality Act 2006	Discrimination on the grounds of age
Disability discrimination	Disability Discrimination Act 1995 (Amendment) 2003	Discrimination for a: 'physical or mental impairment that has a substantial and long-term adverse effect on a person's ability to carry out normal day-to-day activities'
Equal pay	Equal Pay Act 1970 (Amendment) Regulations 2003	Unequal pay for men and women for the same work
Race discrimination	The Race Relations Act 1976 (Amendment) Regulations 2003	Discrimination on the grounds of 'race or ethnic or national origins'
Religious discrimination	The Employment Equality (Religion or Belief) Regulations 2003/2007	Discrimination on the grounds of 'any religion or religious or philosophical belief'
Sex discrimination	The Sex Discrimination Act 1975 (Amendment) Regulations 2003/2008	Discrimination on the grounds of gender or marital status
Sexual orientation discrimination	The Employment Equality (Sexual Orientation) Regulations 2003 The Equality Act (Sexual Orientation) Regulations 2007	Discrimination or harassment of a person on the grounds of sexual orientation

Table 2.4 A summary of key legislation to prevent discrimination relevant to recruitment and selection

they may have taken time off on maternity leave. A better way would be to ask for the type of experience required, as the number of years is not very meaningful anyway.

Research by Robertson and Smith (2001) has found that years of job experience gives virtually no indication of high performance. You may have worked with somebody or experienced a teacher who has been doing the job for a long time who you consider is not very effective. They probably weren't very effective in their first week and after 20 years they are still not very effective!

1. Why is it necessary to have both a job description and person specification?
2. Make a list of the various purposes that a job description and person specification could be useful for.
3. Try and think of other requirements that may be listed on a person specification which could be deemed as discriminatory.

ACTIVITY

Have a go at interviewing a colleague about their job using the questions listed on page 35 as guidelines. From the information you have gained, try and construct a job description and person specification for that job. Show these documents to your colleague. Ask them to assess if they are an accurate portrayal of their job and its requirements.

Competency frameworks

As we have seen, there are some drawbacks associated with the job analysis/ job description/person specification approach to identifying the right person for a job. Not least because it is very difficult to identify what we mean by some of the criteria typically written on a person specification. Indeed if you look at the example in Table 2.3 what is really meant by 'good communication skills' and 'effective interpersonal skills'? The main alternative to this approach is the use of **competency frameworks**.

Competencies are used to describe 'typical' behaviours and have been defined as 'the behaviours that employees must have, or must acquire, to input into a situation in order to achieve high levels of performance' CIPD (2008a). They are therefore person-centred rather than job based. So instead of a job analysis being carried out, an analysis of people is carried out to try and identify what behaviours are associated with a superior performance of a job. This involves identifying employees in an organisation whose work is consistently better than 'average' performers and then finding out, through questionnaires or interviews, what attributes differentiate these high performers from others in the organisation. A profile of competencies can then be drawn up for use in recruitment and selection. According to the CIPD (2007) Learning and Development Survey, the most popular competencies asked for by employers are: communication skills, people management, team skills, customer service skills, results-orientation and problem solving.

A good example of a competency framework is used by the Football Association, the governing body for football in England. Tom Harlow, the Learning and Development Manager, introduced a competency framework for all its 290 staff in 2006. Although staff shared a common 'love for the game', Tom felt there was a need to recognise the similarity of tasks across the various roles and to identify the behaviours necessary to achieve high performance. The new framework was based on six behaviours: team working, communication, leadership, customer service, delivery and fairness and inclusion. It is now a useful tool for recruiting the right staff in to the organisation as well as rewarding existing staff who demonstrate these behaviours (CIPD 2007).

However some are particularly critical of the competency approach. Taylor (2008) suggests the most persuasive arguments are those that suggest it leads to 'cloning' of employees as all new employees are expected to exhibit similar behaviours. As you can imagine this may ultimately reduce the diversity of the people within the organisation and can lead to 'group think' with employees behaving and approaching work in similar ways. This is obviously a disadvantage for those organisations which require creativity!

1. Can you think of other drawbacks of the competency approach?
2. If you are in work, what are the key competencies required to do your job effectively?

Advertising

The ultimate aim of any recruitment process is to attract good quality candidates by the most objective, cost effective and swift means possible. This means that careful consideration needs to be given to how the vacancy should be advertised, where is the most suitable place for the advertisement and when is the appropriate time for it to be advertised.

Recruitment activities can vary significantly from company to company. The results from the annual CIPD Recruitment, Retention and Labour Turnover Survey (2009) in Table 2.5 show the methods of advertising which are most common in organisations in the UK.

While it can be seen that traditional methods of advertising are still common (newspapers, trade press and agencies), e-recruitment is increasing in popularity as organisations embrace technology and use online methods to address their recruitment needs. Using their own website is now the most popular method of advertising a vacancy particularly for those companies who operate in a global market and potentially could attract employees internationally.

Methods used to attract applicants	Total %
Own corporate website	78
Recruitment agencies	76
Local newspaper advertisement	70
Specialist journals/trade press	55
Employee referral scheme	46
Job Centre Plus	43
Links with schools/colleges/universities	34
National newspaper	31

Table 2.5 The most common recruitment advertising methods (CIPD 2009, with the permission of the publisher, the Chartered Institute of Personnel and Development, London (www.cipd.co.uk))

The use of **Web 2.0** is the latest technology advancement which some companies are beginning to embrace for recruitment purposes. The CIPD (2008b) propose this as the second generation of using the Web. Instead of companies using the internet to provide information, new web developments allow applicants to interact with the information, through services such as blogs, twittering or social networking sites, such as Facebook. Web 2.0 allows potential candidates to 'experience' what it is like to work for the organisation and reach a global audience.

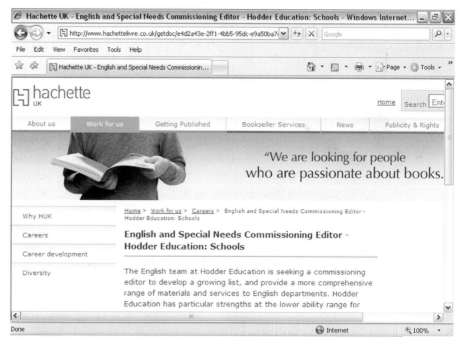

Figure 2.2 A website recruitment advertisement

The use of bounty payments to staff for introducing new candidates continues to be a popular method amongst some companies. Richer Sounds have an 'introduce a friend' scheme and pays out £250 if the new person works there for more than six months (Leary-Joyce 2004). This is probably because the applicant is likely to have heard what it is really like to work at the company from their friend and so will probably fit in to the culture. It is also a relatively cheap way for a company to recruit new staff. The CIPD in their 2008 research reported that a large insurance company saved £250,000 in recruitment costs through their 'refer a friend' scheme.

KEY TERMS

Competency frameworks These describe 'typical' behaviours expected for high performance in a job.
Web 2.0 The second generation of using the Web which is more interactive than original uses of the Web.

CASE STUDY

T-mobile

T-mobile International, a leading mobile communication company, has embraced the use of Web 2.0 as part of its recruitment strategy. Each year a number of graduates are sought and are attracted by the innovative brand that T-mobile represents. If they are to attract the type of people suited to such a company, they realised their recruitment strategy had to reflect the look and feel of the brand. To this end, a Facebook site was created for the company's 2007 graduate recruitment campaign. The site was used to provide information on the recruitment and selection procedure and it allowed potential recruits to communicate with each other. The use of social networking appealed to the type of graduates T-mobile wanted to attract and proved to be a great success in communicating and engaging with applicants.

(Adapted from CIPD 2008b, Recruitment, Retention and Turnover Survey)

1. Have a look at the different ways companies advertise their job vacancies. Why do you think they use that particular method of advertising?
2. What do you consider is the future potential of technology for the purpose of recruitment?
3. What issues should a company consider when using a 'refer a friend' scheme?

2.3 The selection process

In an ideal world, an effective recruitment process should ensure only suitable applicants want to apply for the job vacancy. Although it may go some way in dissuading totally unsuitable candidates, organisations may find that they have a large number of people interested in the job, particularly in times of recession. To avoid a costly and time-consuming selection process, organisations need to have in place effective methods of screening applicants. This should be the first stage of the selection process. Traditionally application forms and curriculum vitaes (CVs) have been the most popular methods of doing this. In 2003, 80 per cent of respondents used some format of application form/CV. Although according to the CIPD 2009 recruitment survey their use has declined to 68 per cent, they are still the most common method of screening applicants. More recently organisations have embraced the use of technology to enhance the screening process both in terms of time and accuracy in screening out (or in) applicants.

2.4 Screening

Application forms

An effective application form will be tailored to the job vacancy. It will not only ask questions for reference purposes such as name, address, employment history and so on, but also provide the organisation with information about the candidates' abilities and potential match for the job vacancy. Using a standard application form irrespective of the job vacancy is not going to give all the information required. Unfortunately you may have noticed that some organisations still carry out this practice. A competency-based application form is one way in which organisations can ensure applicants tailor the information they provide more closely to the job vacancy. Many organisations now use competency-based application forms such as the prison service, the police and British Airways.

ACTIVITY

Go on to the prison service website at www.hmprisonservice.gov.uk and have a look at their application process and form. This will give you an insight in to a competency-based application form.

Curriculum vitae (CV)

The alternative to an application form is to allow applicants to design their own CV. This allows candidates to tailor their application to fit the job vacancy and sell themselves, rather than trying to fit information into predetermined sections on an application form. The issue for organisations screening CVs is that there will be no consistent format or content which makes it not only difficult to differentiate between candidates, but also time-consuming. A well-presented CV may falsely favour a weaker candidate, particularly if it has been professionally produced, and conversely, a poorly produced CV may detract from an applicant who is better qualified for the job.

Online screening

In order to deal with huge number of applications, employers need to screen applicants in the fastest and most efficient way. The majority of larger employers require candidates to apply online. Online applications not only save money, time and paper but also allow employers to monitor applicants. Technology has been designed to screen candidate applications by scanning for key words and phrases used by the applicant to check for job match. It also allows acknowledgement letters, acceptance and rejection letters to be produced in a timely manner. While this improves the efficiency of the screening process it can impact on the candidate perception of the organisation. You may have heard stories of applicants who have spent hours completing an online application form only to receive a rejection email within five minutes of submitting the application! Organisations need to assess the public relations aspect of such a procedure, particularly when these applicants are also likely to be potential customers.

ACTIVITY

Have a go at an online application simulation. www.selectsimulator.com enables you to complete a typical online application form and gives advice on how to answer the questions.

 A Mori poll in 2002 found that one third of respondents admitted to lying on their CV. A survey by the CIPD in 2004 found a similar result. What do you think organisations can do about this?

Other organisations have embraced technology for screening by rejecting the traditional application/CV process and instead have opted for 'person-fit' as the first stage in screening. This is particularly popular for those jobs which require significant customer contact. Asda and B&Q, for example, ask applicants to complete a personality questionnaire online before they can progress to further stages in the selection process. This is because they believe that personal attributes such as personality, sociability and warmth are more important than specific experience and abilities (Clapperton 2008).

Vodafone, the mobile solutions company, use a 'dependability' psychometric measure to assess those applying for contact centre roles. It is used at the pre-screen stage to assess how an individual may work in a customer-centric environment. Early indicators have shown high scoring participants were three times more likely to be client focused, over ten times more likely to comply with company policies and procedures and four times more likely to cope with pressure and be reliable (SHL newsline 2009).

CASE STUDY

Lego

Lego sells 20 billion bricks a year and is the third largest toy brand. Although they are now two separate companies, its theme parks in Denmark, Germany, Britain and California were originally set up to showcase the product and to allow people to sample the Lego brand. If the company was to sustain and build its reputation, it realised it must have employees who had the skills and motivation to deliver the brand. One of Lego's values is 'creativity'. To bring 'creativity' to life Lego needs 750 people each season with the skills to bring the best out of others and who have a natural motivation and skills to interact successfully with customers. The recruitment process Lego developed involved two critical stages. The first was a web-based application form and a motivation questionnaire. The questionnaire quickly identified and screened out people who did not have the 'fit' for the job and the Lego brand. The second stage was an interview to identify those who had a natural empathy with customers. Two thirds of managers said the process was better at selecting people who engage with guests and letters of complaint were soon replaced by letters of praise.

(Eglin 2004)

Telephone screening

Telephone screening has become another popular choice of screening amongst those organisations where large volumes of applicants are likely or for roles which involve telephone contact. Applicants are asked to ring a number which is answered by a trained operator who asks a series of questions related to the job vacancy. The operator usually uses a computer-based scoring system to log the responses and to calculate if the respondent should be put through to the next stage of the selection process (Roberts 2005). Amazon, the online retailer, when seeking staff for a new distribution centre in Swansea, required applicants to answer a series of questions on the telephone as the first stage in screening. Marks and Spencer make similar use of the telephone to screen out applicants for new store openings. The advantages of cost savings in terms of time and resources are obvious but a hidden advantage is that it allows more flexibility of where and when the applicant can apply and it removes potential issues of discrimination, particularly of race and disability.

(2.5) Selection methods

Below is a summary of the various methods used by organisations to select candidates.

Interviews

As you can see some form of interview is still the most popular form of selection. Although there is no data from the 2009 survey, the 2008 CIPD survey suggested that the 'classic trio' (Cook 2004) of application form, interview and references is still what most applicants expect when applying for a job. This is rather curious because research (Schmidt and Hunter 1998; Robertson and Smith 2001) has shown that interviews are a notoriously poor indicator of applicant potential and suitability for a job. Unstructured interviews where the candidate is encouraged to talk freely in response to an open question and where the questions may be different for each candidate, are particularly poor in accurately assessing the ability of the candidate. Structured interviews where the same set of questions are asked of each candidate and based around the requirements of the job are better indicators of suitability (Cooper et al 2003).

Method used	Percentage of organisations using the method
Competency based interviews	69
Interviews following contents of a CV/application form	68
Structured interviews (panel)	59
Tests for specific skills	50
General ability tests	44
Literacy/numeracy tests	39
Personality/aptitude questionnaires	38
Assessment centres	35
Group exercises	26

Table 2.6 Selection methods (CIPD (2009) Recruitment, Retention and Turnover Survey)

The continued popularity of the interview is probably because not only do candidates expect an interview and so it gives the process credibility but it also allows them to get a feel for the organisation. On the organisations behalf they are seen as relatively versatile, quick and cheap to arrange and allows representatives of the organisation to meet a potential employee (Taylor 2008). Of course an effective interview is neither quick nor cheap in terms of the human resources tied up in the interviewing process nor does it measure mental ability, conscientiousness or emotional stability (Robertson and Smith 2001), all of which are important aspects of most jobs in today's organisations. It could be argued that the problem with the effectiveness of interviews is not in the method but with the person doing the interviewing. If you look at Table 2.7 on page 49, which lists some of the problems of interviews, most could be rectified if the interviewer was effectively trained. Alternatively carrying out interviews as a panel of two or more interviewers could challenge any inherent prejudices of one interviewer. This does depend on the inclination of the panel members to challenge other panel members.

1.   How would you feel if you were not given an interview for a job but a series of assessments instead?
2.   In what ways could some of the problems of interviews as shown in Table 2.7 be overcome?

Employee references

This is the third element which completes the 'classic trio'. Despite references being almost a universal requirement, they are increasingly seen as a poor predictor of a candidate's suitability for a job. There is no legal requirement for an employer to provide a reference but it is generally considered acceptable practice to give one. Referees must ensure that what they do write is truthful and accurate and hold a legal liability to those who are the subject of the reference. The legal implications of withholding information or giving false information has meant that references today are rather bland and cover the most basic facts. The source of the references is usually chosen by the candidate and so they are not necessarily impartial or objective reviews of the candidate (Searle 2003). The motivation of the referee for writing a reference may also be questionable. While most will write a reference to assist the applicant in to a new role the reasons for doing this may be questionable. For example, writing a favourable reference may be a chance to get rid of a poor employee. It is for these reasons that many employers are becoming cynical about the actual value of references. The Recruitment Confidence Index (RCI) produced by Cranfield School of Management (2006) found that 86 per cent of HR managers did not find written references useful predictors of future success (Cockerton 2008). Robertson and Smith (2001) put references among the lowest measures of good selection decisions, only just above astrology.

Stereotyping	When the interviewer makes a prejudgement according to their own belief as to how someone should behave. This may be in relation to age, status, ethnic origin or gender.
Halo and Horns effect	Where the interviewer generalises about the candidate in either a favourable light (halo) or a less favourable light (horns). This could be for any number of rather superficial reasons such as the clothes the candidate is wearing, the way they speak, their body language or how they answer the first question asked.
Similarity	Where the interviewer is more favourable to candidates who are more similar to themselves or to others in the organisation.
Contrast effect	Where the interviewer may compare candidates and overemphasise differences. If a weaker candidate follows a particularly good candidate the contrast may make the interviewer score the weaker candidate more harshly than if all the candidates are of a similar ability.

Table 2.7 Some problems with interviews

Selection testing

In order to improve the validity of the selection interview, researchers have found that combining the interview with some sort of test significantly improves the accuracy of the selection procedure (Schmidt and Hunter 1998). Selection testing can be divided in to two broad categories:

1 Tests of proficiency and attainment which measure an individual's competence in a particular job related skill. Proficiency tests measure someone's current ability such as typing accuracy or the use of spreadsheets. Attainment measure the standard achieved at a particular skill eg. NVQs.
2 Psychometric tests measure psychological factors such as aptitude, intelligence and personality.

Tests of proficiency and attainment

There is a wide range of these tests available to test different aspects of a candidate's competence at a variety of skills. The UK driving test is a classic example of a test of proficiency.

An 'in tray' exercise is a common test to assess a candidate's ability to prioritise and organise their work. A sample of materials is given to a candidate which would represent a typical workload that someone doing the job would find in their 'in tray' first thing in the morning. It could be a collection of email and phone messages, letters, memos and reports. The candidate then has to prioritise each and decide on the action to be taken within a tight time constraint.

ACTIVITY

Try this example of an in tray exercise. For the purpose of this exercise, assume you are employed by a small mail order business called 'Toys for Kids' as a manager of the customer services team. Most of your work involves dealing with customer enquiries either by letter or telephone. You have just returned from a two-week holiday. You arrive at your desk and find an in tray piled with memos, letters, email print offs and telephone messages which have been received during your absence. The papers are arranged in date order. Write down what actions you would take in response to each of the items and in what order you would tackle them. Briefly justify your decision in each case.

1. A memo from the Chief Executive asking you to comment on the annual report. The deadline was over a week ago.
2. A doctor's note from a member of staff who is absent due to a fall at work.
3. A complaint letter from a regular customer (Mrs Jarvis) who has not received her order.
4. A letter from a children's hospital inviting you to bid to supply the hospital with toys on a regular basis.
5. A memo from the finance manager complaining about the attitude of one of your members of staff.
6. A confidential note from a member of your staff complaining about those who consistently left early in your absence.
7. A questionnaire from a student at the local college who is carrying out a project on e-business.
8. A further complaint letter from Mrs Jarvis saying she still has not received her order.
9. A resignation letter from a member of your staff who has one week's notice left.
10. The results of the recent customer satisfaction survey.

Written exercises such as case studies are another common method of assessing proficiency. For example a candidate applying for a HR position may be given a case study of an employee facing disciplinary action. The candidate would have to demonstrate their employment law knowledge and problem solving skills in answering the questions related to the case study.

Psychometric tests

Aptitude tests

These are designed to measure and predict candidates' potential to perform a job or learn new skills. There are a range of aptitude tests available from recognised providers such as SHL. Some of these are listed in Table 2.8.

 Can you think of jobs where each of these aptitude tests would be a good way of assessing suitability?

Type of aptitude test	Assessment	Example
Verbal reasoning	Ability to read and understand pieces of information	A candidate is given a paragraph of writing and asked questions on it.
Numerical reasoning	Arithmetic calculations to inferences that need to be drawn from business data	A motorist travelled for 1½ hours at a speed of 60km/h. What distance did he travel?
Diagrammatic	Tests of logical reasoning ability presented in the form of abstract shapes and diagrams	Choose the diagram which will complete the sequence
Mechanical	Mechanical problems usually presented in pictorial form which need to be solved by the candidate	Which shelf will support the heaviest load?
Spatial	Assesses the ability to imagine the rotation of shapes in space or how pieces of equipment fit together	Choose the 2 drawings which are identical
Dexterity	Measures hand speed and fine precision skills and coordination	A candidate is given a piece of equipment to put together in a tight time frame.

Table 2.8 Aptitude tests

ACTIVITY

Visit the SHL website (www.shldirect.com) and have a go at a range of psychometric tests.

Intelligence tests

The IQ test is a traditional measure of intelligence as are the eleven-plus tests used for school entrance in some grammar schools. The role in selection for jobs is limited as traditional measures of intelligence are not necessarily a good indicator at success in a job. However it does provide an indicator of how easily a candidate may be trained, which is something organisations have a vested interest in.

Personality assessments

Henry Ford's famous lament: 'Why is it I always get a whole person when what I really need is a pair of hands', goes some way to suggesting why personality assessments remain a popular selection method for some employers. Research across the world shows how personality impacts on issues such as learning, absenteeism, team performance and conscientiousness (Burke, 2004). In fact for some jobs, up to 70 per cent of attributes associated with success at work are due to aspects of a person's personality rather than ability.

ACTIVITY

Below is a list of typical characteristics need for a managerial position in a retail outlet. Put an 'A' by those attributes associated with ability and 'P' by those attributes associated with personality. How important is personality in this role?

Influence
Able to take charge and control a group towards an objective. Motivates subordinates effectively.

Communication skills
Able to understand and express ideas accurately and persuasively both orally and in writing.

Organising and planning
Able to think ahead, prioritise and organise work.

Motivation
Shows energy, drive and enthusiasm.

Creativity
Generates and is receptive to new ideas. Seeks to innovate.

Empathy
Able to understand the strengths, weaknesses, views and feelings of others.

Emotional maturity
Responds well to criticism. Is frank and open.

Decision making
Has the confidence to take own decisions and balance risk with outcome.

Commercial awareness
Able to analyse numerical problems and takes an interest and understanding in financial/profit implications of actions taken.

The main issue is that it is very difficult to change someone's personality. Changing habits, let alone personality is very hard. If you have ever tried to lose weight, give up smoking or chocolate, reduce drinking, you will know what I mean. A study in New Zealand looked at all the children born in the 1970s, tracking them for more than 30 years (Deary 2001). They found that personality characteristics at 3 years predicted a range of behaviours at the age of 26, including alcoholism and attempted suicide. Other studies (Bouchard 1998) on twins found that they got more alike over time despite being more exposed to different environmental influences. This means that for organisations, what you see at the selection stage is really what you are going to get. No amount of training and coaching will change the personality of that employee. As the service industries expand, increasingly jobs are becoming more personality dependent as positive interactions with fellow workers and customers are crucial to organisational success, then personality fit becomes more critical (Furnham 2003). As we saw from the case study of Legoland, selecting for certain aspects of personality was felt crucial to ensure delivery of the company brand.

Measuring personality

The measurement of personality is a relatively recent phenomenon. Personality assessment became particularly significant during the Second World War. As the army had suffered from large number of officers having mental breakdowns it was seen as a useful means of assessing the suitability of new recruits for extreme conditions.

Most personality assessments today are based on the 'big five'. These are five aspects of personality that numerous studies dating from the 1960s have shown to be good indicators of job performance. They are:

- Extraversion/introversion (traits such as assertiveness and expressiveness)
- Emotional stability (traits such as anger and worrying)
- Agreeableness (degree of social conformity, forgiveness, tolerance)
- Conscientiousness (how hard working, careful, organised a person is)
- Openness to experience (how broad-minded, imaginative and curious someone may be)

(Roberts 2005)

The well-researched assessments generally provide accurate measures of different facets of personality and made meaningful connections with how people are likely to perform at their jobs. Among the most well researched and common types of personality questionnaire are SHL Occupational Personality Questionnaire (OPQ), Catell's 16 Personality Factors (16F) and the Californian Psychological Inventory (CPI).

Below is a sample of typical statements in a personality assessment. Candidates are asked to respond on a scale, usually from one (strongly disagree) to five (strongly agree) to the statements.

1 I enjoy taking to new people
2 I like to keep things well organised
3 I like to help others
4 I worry about deadlines
5 I tend to be assertive at work

(SHL 2009)

Of course there is no 'right' personality, just one more suited to the type of job on offer. Kimberley-Clark, which produces household brands such as Kleenex, Andrex and Huggies believe psychometric assessments play a key role in effectively selecting the right people to work in their company. They estimate that the overall cost of recruitment is £26,000 per candidate so appointing the wrong person is potentially costly. The financial case for using psychometric tests (which cost around £10 per head to administer) to gain additional information on candidates is therefore easy to make.

CASE STUDY

Asda

During 2003/4, Asda developed several bespoke psychometric tests for use in its recruitment and selection processes for shop floor staff and managers. The items used in the tests were designed to reflect the tasks involved in these jobs and to give candidates a realistic idea of whether they would be suited to the role for which they were applying.

Asda is the third largest supermarket chain in the UK and has been part of the Wal-Mart family since 1999. It has over 250 stores offering a mix of food and non-food products, employing around 122,000 staff.

The personality questionnaire makes up the third step of the application process. It consists of 84 items based around Asda's company values. Each of the items takes the form of a statement, such as: 'I tend to take a polite but reserved approach with customers'. Applicants are required to rate themselves according to how much they agree or disagree with the statement. Their responses are compared to a norm group of high performing staff at Asda. The system will automatically respond with either a rejection letter or an invitation to an assessment centre.

This process ensures that there is virtually no administration required on the part of Asda's HR department and it saves time and effort for candidates as they do not have to attend an assessment centre unless there is a good chance of reaching the company's required standard. It also means those applicants who 'fit' the Asda brand are identified quickly.

(Income Data Services 2004)

Assessment centres

This is not a place but an approach. An assessment centre is made up of a range of exercises designed to simulate the job on offer. They can also include individual psychometric tests, assessments and interviews. Assessment centres are usually based around competencies identified for the job role. Exercises are designed to assess these competencies, with each competency assessed at least twice throughout the centre.

Typically a range of assessments are administered to between eight and twelve candidates over the course of a day and they are observed by trained assessors. In doing so they give selectors a longer opportunity to study candidates and reveal how candidates might perform in similar situations in the job role.

Below is an example of an assessment centre for the role of a sales executive.

	Interview	Group discussion	In tray exercise	Presen-tation	Numerical and verbal reasoning psychometric tests
Communication skills	X	X		X	X
Analytical skills			X		X
Problem solving		X	X		
Negotiating and influencing skills	X	X		X	
Time management		X	X	X	
Decision making		X	X		X

Table 2.10 Assessment centre example

As you can see the main competencies needed for a sales executive have been identified. Each candidate participates in five activities where each competency is assessed at least twice. This gives the assessor a good opportunity to observe the potential of the candidate and also gives the candidate a fair chance of demonstrating their abilities.

CASE STUDY

Mercer

Mercer is a global provider of consulting, outsourcing and investment services, with more than 25,000 clients worldwide. Every year Mercer uses a three-stage selection process to choose the 80 or so candidates who will join one of the company's graduate schemes. It includes a well established assessment centre comprising of a presentation, verbal and numerical reasoning tests, two competency-based interviews and a leaderless group discussion. The assessment centre is designed to evaluate a candidate's ability to demonstrate the following six key competencies:

- Team working
- Communication
- Commercial awareness
- Planning and organising
- Personal drive
- Creativity and innovation

The assessment centre is well respected in the business and they have found that those selected in this way have gone on to be excellent employees (Income Data Services 2008).

1. If an assessment centre was used to select call centre staff, what do you think would be the competencies that they would want to assess the candidates against?
2. Think of suitable methods they could use to assess these competencies.
3. Can you think of any drawbacks of using assessment centres?

The accuracy of selection methods

The purpose of recruitment and selection is to ensure the best candidate is selected to fulfil the job role. Described in the previous pages are various methods to do this. Research has shown that some methods are better than others in measuring and assessing the right candidate accurately.

Figure 2.3 below illustrates the varying degrees of accuracy of different selection methods. It is virtually impossible to get 100 per cent accuracy, but structured interviews, ability and work sample tests are generally considered to be the most effective. The more information an organisation can collect about a candidate, the more accurate the selection decisions are likely to be. That is why by combining assessments methods accuracy improves significantly.

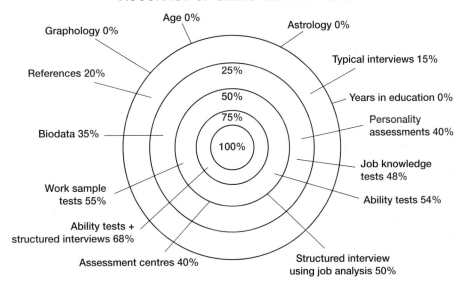

Figure 2.3 Accuracy of selection methods (adapted from Robertson and Smith 2001)

It is necessary to understand the two key concepts of validity and reliability to ensure accurate selection measurement and prediction.

Validity of selection methods

There are different types of validity but the two key aspects of validity for selection purposes are **concurrent validity** and **predictive validity**. Concurrent validity describes if the selection method is measuring what it is supposed to be measuring. For example a candidate might be asked to read a company report and make recommendations in order to assess communication skills. Although communication skills will be demonstrated, the focus of the assessment may really be on the ability of the candidate to work under pressure and analytical skills. For selection methods to be credible to both the candidate and the organisation, they must have high concurrent validity. Predictive validity measures to what extent the assessment measures some future outcome. In other words is the selection method likely to predict what the candidate will be like in the role? If you look at the validity ratings in Figure 2.3 you will see that tests of general mental ability (GMA) have a higher validity than an interview. If an interview is combined with a test of GMA the validity further increases. This means that if a company were to administer these methods in their selection procedure, then the chance of getting the right person for the job is significantly higher than by just doing an interview alone. In other words the predictive validity of using both should ensure they predict more accurately the right person for the job.

Reliability of selection methods

KEY TERMS

Concurrent validity measures what it is supposed to measure.
Predictive validity measures to what extent the assessment measures some future outcome.
Reliability Consistency of an assessment over time.
Validity means the assessment is credible and meaningful.

Reliability of the selection method is equally as important as validity. An assessment would be reliable if it gives the same result over and over again. Reliability is essential for any assessment method as selection cannot be valid and unreliable. There are many factors which can affect reliability such as human errors in administering or scoring selection methods, different conditions when candidates take assessments –particularly the case when candidates do online assessments – and if different people are carrying out the selection procedures. It is therefore important for organisations to control the environment and have trained assessors carrying out assessments to ensure the selection process is standardised as much as possible. A structured interview is more reliable than an unstructured interview as each candidate is treated in the same way. If the questions are relevant to the post and can elicit information about the skills and abilities of the candidate then the structured interview will also be more valid.

1. In what other ways can organisations ensure their selection methods are reliable and valid?
2. How do you think they can measure reliability and validity?
3. Which do you think is the more important – reliability or validity?

(2.7) Summary

Recruitment and selection is costly both in terms of time and resources. The cost of making a wrong decision is even greater. The average cost of recruiting and selecting a new employee is approximately £5,000 (Berry 2007). The cost is even greater for graduate and management jobs. As we saw at the beginning of this chapter, a poor employee is worth up to 40 per cent less than a high performing employee. Organisations therefore need to ensure they are using the most effective recruitment methods to firstly attract the right type of people to the job vacancy and then select the most suitable candidate for the position available. Making use of technology has the potential to speed up the recruitment and selection process and offers cost savings, flexibility and objectivity. By choosing valid and reliable methods, it is hoped that a job vacancy is filled by the right person who will not only be effective in the job but will continue to be a productive and motivated employee of the organisation for years to come.

KEY IDEAS

The recruitment process
- Recruitment is the part of the process involved in finding enough of the right candidates who want to apply for the vacancy on offer.
- This is a two-stage process. The first stage involves analysing the job that is available and producing either an accurate job description and person specification or an accountability profile for the job. Care needs to be taken so as not to include any requirements which may be considered discriminatory.
- The second stage is using an appropriate method to advertise the vacancy. The CIPD (2009) survey suggests the majority of organisations today use their own corporate website, recruitment agencies and local papers to advertise.

The selection process
- Selection is the part of the process which involves choosing between applicants.
- There are two stages to the selection process. The first is screening candidates to eliminate those who are totally unsuitable for the job vacancy; the second is applying a variety of selection methods to try and accurately predict who would be the best candidate for the job.
- Selection should be a two-way process. It should allow for the candidate to select themselves in or out of the process as well as for organisation selection purposes.

Screening
- Application forms and curriculum vitaes are still the most common method of screening applicants. However care needs to be taken to ensure the information requested and supplied is relevant to the job for effective screening to take place.
- Organisations are increasingly embracing technology to speed up the screening process, reduce the cost and to allow for more flexibility for the candidate and the organisation.
- Some organisations such as B&Q and Asda use personality assessments to screen candidates as well as an application form to ensure better 'person fit' with the organisation.

Selection methods
- The 'classic trio' of application, interview and references are still the most common methods of selecting candidates despite research such as that of Robertson and Smith (2001) showing that these methods are a very poor predictor of the right applicant for the job.
- The use of testing can improve the accuracy of selection decisions. There are two types of tests: tests of proficiency and attainment which measure a candidate's knowledge and skills and psychometric tests which measure psychological factors such as aptitude and personality.
- Assessment centres are a good way of combining a number of selection methods and by doing so improving the accuracy of selection decisions.

The accuracy of selection methods
- The validity of a selection method is critical as it means how accurate the selection method is in predicting and measuring a candidate against the requirements of the job. The higher the validity of a selection method, the better the chance of selecting the most suitable candidate for the job.
- Reliability is how consistent the selection method is over time in selecting candidates. Without reliability, the assessment method would be invalid.

REFLECTIVE QUESTIONS

1 Review a job description and person specification or accountabity profile of a job of your choice. What recommendations would you make to improve them?
2 Thinking of an organisation known to you, suggest in what ways they could use technology more effectively to enhance their recruitment and selection process.
3 Why is a systematic approach to recruitment and selection beneficial?
4 Why are some selection methods better at identifying the best candidate for a job than others?
5 How could you justify the continued use of some selection methods despite their low validity?

RECOMMENDED READING

If you would like to learn more about some of the issues in the five sections within this chapter you might like to consider the following books and articles:

The recruitment process
Malcolm Martin and Tricia Jackson's book *Personnel Practice* contains a detailed chapter on the recruitment process. It provides some good illustrations of job analysis techniques, job descriptions, person specifications, competency profiles and advertisements.

The selection process
Gareth Roberts book *Recruitment and Selection* provides an easy understandable account of the various elements of the selection process.

Screening
Stephen Taylor's book *People Resourcing* provides a detailed section on methods of screening applicants. The CIPD recruitment, retention and labour turnover surveys are also a good way of finding out and keeping up to date with what methods organisations are using.

Selection methods
Selection and Recruitment by Rosalind Searle gives a detailed coverage of the different selection methods. It can be quite complex but is useful if you want a more in-depth understanding. If you want to find out more on assessment centres, Charles Woodruffe has written a book just about these in *Development and Assessment Centres*. It is a good practical guide, particularly if you are thinking of setting up an assessment centre yourself.

The accuracy of selection methods
The article by Schmidt and Hunter, *The validity and utility of selection methods in personnel psychology: practical and theoretical implications of 85 years of research findings*, gives the most comprehensive review of the accuracy and validity of selection methods. Although the article is quite complex it is worth persevering if you want to be able to fully justify the cost savings made by using more valid selection methods.

USEFUL WEBSITES

www.acas.org.uk has lots of useful information and produces booklets and advisory fact sheets.
www.cipd.co.uk This is the Chartered Institute of Personnel and Management website. It contains a wealth of information including fact sheets, surveys and articles, many of which are available to non-members, but please note that some are only available to members.
www.equalityhumanrights.com. Independent statutory body. Good for up-to-date information on discrimination and advice.

REFERENCES

Berry, M. (2007) Hidden cost of recruitment, *Personnel Today*, 19 March 2007.

CIPD (2007) *Learning and Development Survey*. Accessible at www.cipd.co.uk/surveys

CIPD (2008a) *Competency Fact Sheet*. Accessible at www.cipd.co.uk/surveys

CIPD (2008b) *Recruitment, Retention and Turnover Survey*. Accessible at www.cipd.co.uk/surveys

CIPD (2009) *Recruitment, Retention and Turnover Survey*. Accessible at www.cipd.co.uk/surveys

Clapperton (ed.) (2008) *Britain's Top 100 Employers 2008*. London: Guardian Books.

Cockerton, T. (2008) Selection in Muller-Camen, M., Croucher, R., Leigh, S. (eds.) (2008) *Human Resource Management. A case study approach*. London: CIPD.

Cook, M. (2004) *Personnel Selection. Adding value through people*, 4th edition. Chichester: Wiley & Sons.

Cooper, D., Robertson, I., Tinline, G. (2003) *Recruitment and Selection: A framework for success*. London: Thomson.

Deary, I.J. (2001) *Intelligence. A very short introduction*. Oxford: Oxford University Press.

Eglin, R. (2004) 'Finding staff who fit your brand', *The Sunday Times* 17 October 2004.

Income Data Services (2004) Psychometric tests, No. 774, March 2004.

Income Data Services (2008) Assessment Centres, No. 876, August 2008.

Leary-Joyce, J. (2004) *Becoming an Employer of Choice*. London: CIPD.

Roberts, G. (2005) *Recruitment and Selection. A competency approach*. London: CIPD.

Robertson, I., Smith, M. (2001) 'Personnel Selection', *Journal of Occupational and Organisational Psychology*, vol. 74, no 4, 253–77.

Schmidt, F.L., Hunter, J.E. (1998) The validity and utility of selection methods in personnel psychology: practical and theoretical implications of 85 years of research findings, *Psychological Bulletin*, vol. 124: 262–74.

Searle, R.H. (2003) *Recruitment and Selection: A critical text*. Milton Keynes: Palgrave/Open University Press.

SHL (2009) Improving recruitment with SHL's Dependability and Safety Instrument. *SHL Newsline*, Spring 2009.

Taylor, M.S., Collins, C.J. (2000) 'Organizational recruitment: enhancing the intersection of theory and practice', in Cooper, C.L., Locke, E.A. (eds.), *Industrial and Organizational Psychology: Linking Theory and Practice*. Oxford: Basil Blackwell, 304–34.

Taylor, S. (2008) *People Resourcing*. London: CIPD.

3 Learning and development

'A Journey of a thousand miles begins with a single step'

(Chinese Philosopher, Laozi)

CHAPTER OUTLINE

3.1 Introduction
3.2 The importance of learning and development
3.3 Government initiatives to encourage learning and development
3.4 The 'learning organisation'
3.5 What do we mean by education, training, learning and development?
3.6 How do people learn?
3.7 The training process
3.8 Summary

CHAPTER OBJECTIVES

- Why learning and development is important for organisations and UK prosperity
- The initiatives introduced by the UK Government to try and 'upskill' the UK workforce
- The meaning and importance of the learning organisation
- Definitions used when discussing education, training, learning and development
- Ways in which people learn and an appreciation of why this is important to know
- The four stages of the training process including how to analyse training needs, devising a learning plan, how to meet the development need through a variety of formal and informal methods and how to evaluate training and development

3.1 Introduction

The competitiveness of the UK and any other country depends on the skills and capabilities of its people. New Labour's slogan of 'education, education, education' in its pre-election campaign in 1997 highlighted the importance of this. Over the past 20 years a number of government initiatives have been aimed at 'upskilling' the UK workforce. Similarly with the increase in technology and the growth of the 'knowledge economy' organisations are realising the importance of a skilled workforce to compete in the global market place. Despite worsening economic conditions of 2008/9, results from the CIPD (2009a) Learning and Development Survey suggest that investment in learning and development, has not, on the whole been decreased. In fact 79 per cent of respondents agreed that learning and development was an important part of business improvement. This chapter looks at some of the Government and organisational initiatives used to improve the skill set of the UK workforce and the main principles involved in managing learning and development initiatives.

3.2 The importance of learning and development

Globalisation, technological advancements and a free-market economy has meant that organisations have similar access to capital, customers and to employees. Consequently the key differentiator between organisations is the skills and knowledge of the people they employ. Within this context, learning and development have become critical success factors for organisations to be able to effectively compete within competitive markets. Skills are increasingly seen as the key lever not only for an organisation but for the economy as a whole to compete internationally (Leitch 2006).

You may have seen frequent reports in the media highlighting the low skills level of the UK compared to its European counterparts. In fact one third of adults in the UK do not hold the equivalent of a basic school leaving qualification and almost a half of adults have difficulties with numbers (LSC 2006). If we look at how this compares internationally, it can be seen that the UK is not keeping up with its competitors. The UK ranks 24th out of 29 developed countries for the number of young people staying in education and training after the age of 16. The UK ranks 17th out of 30 countries for the number of adults in work without level 2 skills, which is equivalent to 5 GCSEs at grades A*–C (QCA 2006). The situation doesn't seem better at graduate level. India and China are creating four million graduates a year compared with 250,000 produced in the UK. Of course the total population is much greater in these countries but nevertheless we cannot ignore employers who are still complaining that UK universities do not produce enough graduates with the skills that they need (Association of Graduate Recruiters 2007). Sixty-one per cent of respondents in the CIPD Learning and Development

Survey (2009a) said that new employees joining them from school, college or university were deficient in business skills and particularly lacked commercial awareness. Ninety-nine per cent believed communication to be very important, a skill in which sixty per cent said were lacking in school and college leavers. This obviously affects the UK's ability to compete.

1. What do you think are the reasons for this lack of business skills among school, college and university leavers?
2. What would you suggest could be done to improve these skills in this age group of people?

The Institute for Employment Research suggests that the majority of new jobs created will need degree-level qualifications and that by 2020 65 per cent of all jobs will require skills at level 3. The number of unskilled or low skilled jobs will significantly decrease as most are outsourced to countries which offer cheaper labour such as India, China and Eastern Europe. An important review of the level of skills in the UK workforce, 'Prosperity for all in the Global Economy – World Class Skills', often referred to as the Leitch review (2006) after the author of the study, Lord Sandy Leitch. This report further influenced the way the Government and organisations think and talk about skills and reiterated the importance of 'upskilling' the UK workforce.

3.3 Government initiatives

Following the UK recession of the 1980s and a number of influential reports (Handy 1987; Constable and McCormick 1987), the Government introduced a range of initiatives to encourage employers to invest in the training and development of their workforce. The three main initiatives were the introduction of National Vocational Qualifications (NVQs), the development of the Investors in People Award (IiP) and the implementation of Modern Apprenticeships. Since the Leitch report the Government has introduced a further range of initiatives such as the 'Train to Gain' initiative, which aims to directly engage with the needs of the employer and to provide courses and policies specifically aimed at nurturing business skills. In the latest CIPD Learning and Development Survey (2009a) 31 per cent of employers were using 'train to gain' services and 19 per cent had made a skills pledge to develop their employees to a minimum of NVQ level 2.

National Vocational Qualifications (NVQs)

NVQs were one of the first initiatives by the Government in the 1980s to address the shortfall in skills within the workforce and to address the weaknesses in the vocational qualifications available at that time. NVQs were introduced in 1986 and are a competence-based qualification. This means that they are designed to help people develop their skills and knowledge so that they can do their job more effectively. They are delivered in the workplace or other settings that replicate the working environment and are based on national standards for various occupations. NVQs range from level 1 (most basic) to level 5 (Masters level) and are available in most business areas. Assessment is through practical assignments and a portfolio of evidence. By 2001 3.2 million NVQ certificates had been awarded and it is estimated that 12 per cent of the national workforce have attained a NVQ (www.direct.gov.uk). According to the CIPD Learning and Development Survey (2009a) 53 per cent of respondents were using NVQs with a further 16 per cent considering their use. Unfortunately this is not across all sectors of business. Seventy five per cent of NVQs awarded were in engineering and the service sector and tend to be concentrated in the lower-skilled jobs (www.qcda.gov.uk). Research on the role of NVQs in the NHS by Cox (2007) found that they had been valuable in stimulating learning, particularly in the less skilled employees and had increased the knowledge, skills and confidence of those achieving a NVQ. However, those in more senior positions were more critical of NVQs, giving excessive paperwork as a reason, and suggested they were less relevant at more senior level.

CASE STUDY

Superdrug

Superdrug is national chemist retail outlet with 913 stores nationwide, employing 16,000 people. In November 2007 they launched a pilot scheme to offer employers an NVQ in retail skills. There are currently 400 employees enrolled on the NVQ and it is run in conjunction with a national college. Each learner is given an individual plan and guidance and all training and assessment takes place in the learner's place of work. Recent customer service satisfaction survey results and financial figures suggest the focus on employee skills have had a significant impact in benefiting the business in both these areas. Superdrug now intends to extend offering NVQs in warehousing and distribution, team leadership and business administration.

(Income Data Services, 2008)

Investors in People (IiP)

Investors in People is a flexible and easy-to-use business improvement framework, which helps organisations transform their business performance through their people.

The Investors in People framework is outcome focused, outlining what organisations need to achieve, but never prescribing how. This flexible approach allows thousands of different employers of every sector and size to use the same framework. Investors in People's flexibility is enhanced by focusing all their advice and assessment around meeting organisations' needs. This means the process starts with Investors in People finding out what organisations' performance targets or key priorities are. These targets and priorities then become central to all their work with the organisation, so they support the business plan and maximise the value customers can gain from working with Investors in People.

The Investors in People framework has three core principles:

- **Plan:** Develop strategies to improve performance.
- **Do:** Take action to improve performance.
- **Review:** Evaluate and improve performance.

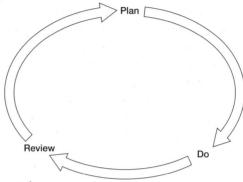

Figure 3.1 IiP framework

The three principles breakdown into ten indicators. 'Plan' has four strategies, starting with Business Strategy and followed by Learning & Development Strategy, People Management Strategy and Leadership & Management Strategy. There are then four action-focused indicators to help organisations 'Do' what is in their plan (these are Management Effectiveness, Recognition & Reward, Involvement & Empowerment and Learning & Development). Finally, 'Review' encourages organisations to evaluate results and feed them into continuous improvement for the future. The indicators that make up this principle are Performance Measurement and Continuous Improvement.

Much of Investors in People's success is down to the versatility of these three core principles. Essentially you can take any business issue and apply their plan, do, review approach to it.

Investors in People now have additional recognition for organisations that would like an extra stretch. The Standard is now complemented by Bronze, Silver and Gold recognition, which are designed to celebrate success as well as signpost areas for further improvement.

Figure 3.2 IiP logo (© Investors in People 2010)

Several pieces of research has confirmed the impact that achieving IiP has had on organisations. Cranfield School of Management (2008), for example, researched the impact of IiP on organisational financial performance and found there to be a positive link between achieving IiP status and increased financial performance. There are currently 35,000 organisations in over 50 countries who have the IiP award. Ninety per cent of organisations stay with the standard once accredited. However, 73 per cent of IiP awards are concentrated in organisations with 50 plus employees (Kitching 2007) with particular focus within the public sector. This does not mean that small organisations do not invest in training and development but it is not always recognised in a formal sense as it tends to be in the form of informal, 'on the job' training which is problematic when needed to provide evidence necessary for the IiP award certification process.

CASE STUDY

McDonald's

McDonald's is recognised world wide as a leading food retailer, with more than 30,000 restaurants in over 110 countries. In 2005 McDonald's successfully achieved accreditation against the revised IiP standards. The IiP recognition covered the company head office and company-owned McDonald's, of which there are 800, employing nearly 45,000 people. It encourages its 400 franchises to gain IiP status and currently about half of its franchises have recognition.

All branches of McDonald's have at least one PC that staff can access so the IiP survey was carried out on these. The surveys were completed anonymously and all responses were sent directly to the assessor. Employees were encouraged to complete the survey by being given 20 minutes during their shift to complete the questionnaire. The interview stage of the IiP assessment took place over a three-week period. Two hundred and fifty face-to-face interviews were carried out by the IiP assessor and two assistants at restaurants selected by the assessor.

McDonald's met all the requirements of the new IiP standard and exceeded the criteria in seven of the ten indicators. Particularly impressive areas were the company's open communication style, its learning and development activities and its approach to flexible working. McDonald's viewed the benefits of IiP as being an excellent way of gaining an objective report on its performance and it has enabled them to see how it compares to other British competitors. It also serves as a very public recognition of the value the company places on its staff.

(Income Data Services 2006)

Apprenticeships

Apprenticeships have always been a traditional way of learning a trade in sectors such as engineering and particular crafts. 'Modern Apprenticeships' were introduced in 1994 to extend training across a wider range of sectors in order to plug the growing skills gap and to provide an alternative to the academic route. They are now in over 80 sectors, many of which did not have a tradition of apprenticeships such as retailing, nursery care and health.

The basic apprenticeship leads to NVQ level 2 and consists of work-based training programmes designed around the needs of employers. Progression is available to the advanced apprenticeship at NVQ levels 3–4. The majority of training is provided 'on the job', the remainder by a local college. The National Apprenticeship Service will fund 100 per cent of training to 16–18 year olds and up to 50 per cent of the training for those over the age of 19 (www.apprenticeships.org.uk).

Apprenticeships are a key part of the Government plan to develop young people, although the 25-year age barrier has now been removed. The UK Government has committed that from 2013 all young people should either be studying for A levels, Diplomas, International Baccalaureate or an Apprenticeship. Outside the government-supported apprenticeships there is evidence that some companies are developing their own 'apprenticeship' schemes. Tesco, for example, developed its own training to meet its specific needs and this has now been accredited with an NVQ level 2. The CIPD Learning and Development Survey (2009a) suggested that 33 per cent of organisations use apprenticeship style development to train lower skilled entrants. As you may have experienced, the downturn in the economy in 2008 has been particularly hard on young people gaining employment. With this in mind the Government has promised an extra 35,000 apprenticeship places and is promoting and supporting 5,000 'internships' (Davies 2009). These are opportunities for people to gain work experience but are generally unpaid. Lloyds banking group have 52 internships and report community and business benefits. More than half of their first year intake now work part time at the bank whilst studying for degrees (Phillips 2009).

CASE STUDY

Sheffield Forgemasters International Limited (SFIL), a manufacturer of large-scale steel components came very close to closing in 2004. Following a management buyout, SFIL now has a turnover of £120 million which they attribute to a renewed investment in learning and development, and in apprenticeships in particular. Out of a total of 800 employees, 70 apprentices are currently training for specialist careers to ensure long-term company security. Apprentices are trained in the workplace and at college achieving a range of qualifications such as NVQs, BTECs, degrees and post-graduate certificates as well as following a work-based key skills learning programme. The scheme is proving popular with 250 applicants in 2008 applying for 30 apprenticeship places. 'There will always be a requirement for dynamic apprentices who are willing to learn and who can carry British Manufacturing forward,' said the head of apprenticeship and HR director, Steve Tagg (CIPD 2009b).

1. If you were a training manager in an organisation, how would you promote introducing NVQ's, IiP or Modern Apprenticeships in to the organisation?
2. How would you deal with any resistance to your ideas?

Qualification and credit framework (QCF)

In a bid to modernise the current qualification framework and to make it easier to understand the different types of qualifications that learners hold, the Government has decided to implement a new qualification and credit framework. This includes the replacement of NVQs. From 2010 the new qualification framework will consist of three sizes of qualification (award, certificate and diploma) at eight levels. Level 1 will be entry level, level 2 will be the same level as GCSEs A*–C, level 3 equivalent to GCE A levels right up level 8 which will be the same level as a PhD. If you want to find out more about these changes please visit the Government website at: www.qcda.gov.uk/19674.aspx.

3.4 The 'learning organisation'

All these initiatives were aimed at encouraging a culture of lifelong learning both within the UK and within organisations. Senge (1990) popularised the idea of learning in the organisation. Pedlar et al (1991) developed this further and with Senge were one of the first to write about the importance of continuous learning of employees within an organisation. They introduced the concept of a 'learning organisation'. By that they meant an organisation which 'facilitates the learning of all its members and continuously transforms itself' (Pedlar et al. 1991). Such an organisation creates the atmosphere at work where learning is encouraged throughout everyday tasks. Sharing of ideas, letting people try out these ideas without fear of mistakes and learning from each other is actively promoted as part of the company strategy.

Becoming a learning organisation can be a long process because it often means changing people's thoughts and the way they work. It is also about getting people to realise that every task should be a learning opportunity. Sharing such learning is a critical part of an organisation becoming a 'learning organisation'. This may be through feedback, teamworking and cross-teamworking so different parts of an organisation can benefit from each other's learning. In other words employees are not 'reinventing the wheel' all the time but moving on and learning from each other's mistakes and successes.

Results from the CIPD Learning and Development Survey (2009a) suggest organisations are moving in a positive direction towards a 'learning organisation'. Fifty per cent of organisations were trying to develop a learning and development culture across their organisations. In fact 76 per cent of respondents agreed that learning and development was seen as an important part of business improvement.

Continuing professional development (CPD)

Encouraging employees to regularly update their knowledge, skills and experiences is part of a learning culture. CPD is a term used to describe this continuous nature of learning. Members of professional bodies, such as the Chartered Association of Accountants (ACCA); Chartered Institute of Managers (CIM) and the Chartered Institute of Personnel and Development (CIPD) are required to demonstrate evidence of their own CPD. This encourages individuals to reflect on what they have learnt and apply this to future situations. Learning isn't restricted to work, CPD is about learning from all situations. In other words it is encouraging 'learners to learn'. That is probably why many of *The Times* Top 100 Companies to Work For actively encourage their employees to be involved in community projects and learning out of work. For example Vodafone UK, the communications company, encourages employees to take up to 24 hours paid volunteering time each year, whilst Atkins (an engineering consultancy) employees, mentor young people to help them plan for their future.

 3.5 ## What do we mean by education, training, learning and development?

So far we have used these terms almost interchangeably. Although distinctions between the terms are not clear-cut, there are important differences.

> **KEY TERMS**
>
> **Development** Longer-term changes which take place as a result of training and learning.
> **Education** Usually a formal way of learning knowledge and skills over a long period of time often resulting in a qualification of some kind.
> **Learning** Changes which occur in an individual's skill, knowledge or attitude over a period of time.
> **Training** Usually instructor-led, aimed at developing a particular skill or gaining specific knowledge.

Education tends to be more formal and 'aims to develop people's intellectual capability, conceptual and social understanding and work performance though the learning process' (Marchington and Wilkinson 2008). The outcome is usually seen in terms of some sort of qualification or formal recognition, for example Degree, MBA.

Training tends to be more specific. It is usually instructor led and aimed at developing a particular skill or changing behaviour, for example training in how to use a new software package.

Learning focuses on the changes which take place within the individual. This may be in terms of their skill, knowledge or attitude and may have been brought about consciously through training or unconsciously through experience.

Development is a term which really covers both training and learning but tends to cover the longer-term changes which take place as a result of training and learning.

 ## How do people learn?

This is an important question to consider if education, training or development are to be effective. There are many theories developed which try to explain how people learn, but among the most well known is the work of Kolb (1974) and Honey and Mumford (1982). Kolb argued that for learning to be effective, individuals needed to go through a cycle of learning.

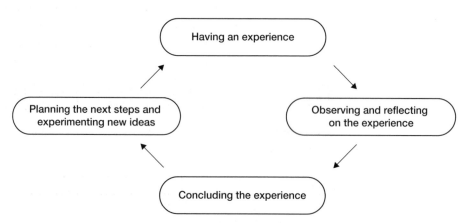

Figure 3.3 Kolb's learning cycle (Kolb 1974)

Honey and Mumford (1982) developed this concept further and suggested that individuals tended to be better at one stage than another. They acknowledged that individuals were different and consequently people learn in different ways. Have you ever put up flat packed furniture? Some people learn more effectively by just having the experience, learning from doing (stage 1 of Kolb's cycle). These are the type of people who will get out all the pieces of furniture and try and put it together without looking at the instructions, even though they may end up with the door on the wrong way. They learn by trial and error. They called these people 'Activists'. Others need time to observe and reflect upon information, preferring to sit back and listen before coming to a decision (stage 2 of Kolb's cycle). These types of people will get out the pieces of furniture, look what they have, look at the picture of the finished product and think about how they are going to put it together, perhaps with consultation of the instructions. They called these types of people 'Reflectors'. There are those who enjoy forming concepts, thinking problems through in a logical step-by-step approach (stage 3 of Kolb's cycle). These people would get out all the pieces of furniture, put them in to piles, count what they have, read the instructions and put it up in a systematic way piece by piece. Honey and Mumford called these people 'Theorists'. Finally some people have a preference for practical approaches to solving problems. They are keen to establish links between what they are learning and the 'real world' (stage 4 of Kolb's cycle). These people are probably quite happy about putting up the flat pack furniture as long as they can see the purpose of the furniture in the end. They are unlikely to volunteer to put up anyone's furniture just for the pleasure of doing it! These they called 'Pragmatists'.

Of course there is no right or wrong learning style and some people may have a preference for two or more learning styles. However, these theories have important implications for learning and development. Taking them in to account should determine the choice of methods used in development initiatives and make them more effective for the individual learner.

ACTIVITY

Look at the following methods used in training and development. Decide which learning style they would most suit.

Activity	Learning style
Putting together a piece of equipment to learn how it works	
Reading an instruction booklet	
Taking part in a discussion to decide on the best way of tackling a task	
Listening to a presentation	
Being coached by an expert	
Watching a training programme	
Using a computer 'game'	

3.7 The training process

The basis of most training and development still lies in the classic training cycle. Although it could be argued that it oversimplifies the training and development process and doesn't pay enough attention to the transfer of learning or the sometimes ad hoc nature of training needs within an organisation, it does provide a structured way of managing training and development. It is this cycle we will go through now to understand the process of training and development.

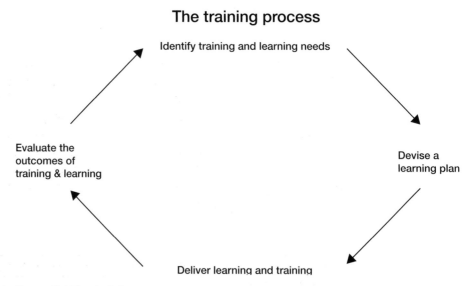

Figure 3.4 The training process

Identifying training needs

Training needs to occur for any number of reasons, external and internal, to the organisation. External needs could be because of economic, social, legal, environmental or technological changes affecting the organisation. These changes may lead to new products, services, standards and competitors which in turn demand new skills and abilities (Martin and Jackson 2005). Internal training needs may be due to promotion, returners to work, retirement or the introduction of new machines, technology or health and safety initiatives.

Training needs may be at different levels within the organisation: organisational, job or individual level. It is important to identify at which level the need is. A training needs analysis detects and specifies the training needs and provides solutions as to how these training needs can be met.

Organisational training needs

These could arise from a change in direction for the organisation, whether it is a change in culture, product or service which has implications for the whole organisation. Business plans, mission statements, succession plans, financial statements, data on productivity, discussions with managers, personnel statistics and exit interviews all provide information that may be useful in identifying the training needs for the whole organisation. Obviously this process is very time-consuming but may be necessary if training is seen as a means to improve, or change, the whole organisation.

Job training needs

A job analysis is the 'process of identifying the purpose of the job and its component parts, and specifying what must be learned in order for there to be effective work performance' Harrison (2003: 269). Various methods can be used including analysing job descriptions and job specifications, giving employees who perform the same job a questionnaire to find out specific details of the job, carrying out group discussions or observations. A popular technique is to ask job holders to keep a work diary, which is then analysed or interviewing the supervisor and job holder. Sometimes job holders are asked to note and analyse key tasks of the job.

A simple key task analysis

How to photocopy two sheets of paper on to one piece of paper		
Stage (breakdown of each stage of the process)	Instructions (how to perform each stage)	Key points (anything which needs to be particularly noted)
1. Preparing the photocopier	• Press the 'on' button • Wait for the copier to warm up • Open the drawer that contains paper • Check there is enough paper for the job you are doing	Make sure the paper in the tray is flat otherwise the photocopier is likely to jam Ensure you close the paper drawer properly

▶

◄

Stage (breakdown of each stage of the process)	Instructions (how to perform each stage)	Key points (anything which needs to be particularly noted)
2. Setting the photocopier	• Put both sheets of paper the same side up in the feeder tray on the lid of the photocopier • On the control panel, select 'one single side – double side' • Input how many copies you want • Press 'start'	Make sure both sheets of paper are pushed up against the 'feeder' part of the photocopier
3. Collecting the photocopies	• Wait for copies to come out of the side of the photocopier • Take the original two sheets of paper from the top of the photocopy	Don't pull the copies out of the machine – wait for the machine to stop

Table 3.1 Key task analysis

ACTIVITY

Now carry out a key task analysis of a function that you are familiar with. Draw three columns with the same headings as in the example.

The issues with all of these methods depend on the capability of the post holder to analyse their own job objectively and to avoid confusion with training needs associated with the individual rather than the job.

Individual training needs

Analysing individual training needs shares some of the methods as described above. More focus is likely to be on information from appraisals, performance data, interviews, work samples and observation to identify where a training gap arises. This does depend on honest communication between the individual and the person doing the analysis. Any link to reward is not likely to encourage individuals to admit to weaknesses or areas for possible improvement through additional training.

1. How would you analyse the training needs of a charity worker who has been transferred from a project working with disadvantaged people in rural communities to working with homeless people in London?
2. How would you establish the training needs of a small group of experienced call centre staff, externally recruited following their redundancy from a competitor's firm?

Devising a learning plan

Once training needs have been identified, a learning plan to meet these needs is devised. There are a number of factors which need to be considered before a suitable learning plan can be agreed.

1 What resources are available to be put into workplace learning? This includes money, time and physical resources such as equipment, a place for the learning to take place and who is available and skilled to deliver the learning.
2 What is the level of commitment of the organisation to workplace learning? Some organisations value learning and will try and ensure any training needs identified will be met while others may only be prepared to meet the need if it is seen as critical to the organisation.
3 What are the costs of the training or development? It is important to ensure the benefits of the development intervention outweighs the cost of its implementation.
4 Is training and development the solution to a training need? An employee may be underperforming due to lack of motivation, not because they need more skills.
5 What are the characteristics of the trainee? Consideration needs to be given to the level of their existing knowledge and skills, their level of motivation for new learning and their learning style.

Methods to meet the learning need

There are various ways in which learning needs can be met. You may have met the type of person who laments that they have had no training. What they really mean is that they have not been on a formal training course. They may have had a number of learning experiences which they have discounted as they were not 'formal' and planned. It is important to appreciate that there are many ways in meeting a learning need, most of which, can be more effective than attending a training course. If you look at the results below taken from the CIPD Annual Learning and Development Survey (2008), it can clearly be seen that in fact on-the-job training is deemed far more effective than formal training courses by the respondents with a 32 per cent increase in its use between 2007 and 2009 (CIPD 2009a).

On the job learning	Off the job learning
Apprenticeships	Attending talks or presentations
Placements or secondments	Seminars and workshops
Rotating the job to experience new types of work	Attending local meetings of professional bodies such as the CIPD branch events or the Chartered Management Institute (CMI) events
Enlarging the job by giving more tasks to the post holder	Reading appropriate texts or manuals
Enriching the job by giving higher level tasks or more responsibility	Educational videos/DVDs
Projects	Computer assisted learning (e.g. e-learning)
Job instruction	Simulations
Trial and error	Business games
Observation	Visits to other organisations or different sites of their own organisation
Coaching and mentoring	Outdoor training and development
NVQ programmes	Formal instructor led training courses
Keeping work diaries or log books	Discussion groups

Table 3.2 Learning methods

While there is still a place for formal training, other methods such as work experience, coaching and mentoring are also valuable learning opportunities for employees. A method used in the companies listed in *The Times* The Best 100 Companies to Work For is to provide 'real-time' challenge in the workplace by giving people new work that stretches them. By doing so it ensures that learning is tied to work, not to a classroom. Table 3.2 lists some of the learning methods available as part of the everyday job (on the job learning) and away from the workplace (off the job learning).

1. Try and think of the benefits and drawbacks of some of the methods mentioned in Table 3.2.
2. In what circumstances would each method be most suitable?
3. Referring to the definitions in section 3.5, can you classify the methods in to training, education and development?

Formal development initiatives

While Table 3.2 divides training and development into activiti͟
place while the trainee is working (on the job learning) or away from theɪɪ ͟ɷ͟
job (off the job learning), they also consist of a combination of formal, planned
development events and informal, more self-managed style learning and
development. We will first look at some of the more formal types of learning
and development.

Training courses

These are usually designed to last for a specific period, for example half a day,
a couple of hours or delivered over several days. Although they could consist of
a variety of activities, they are usually led by a trainer or expert, either internal
to the organisation or bought in and therefore external from the organisation.
The objectives of the course are known and the content planned to reflect the
business needs.

The culture of the organisation could have a significant effect on the style of the
training course. An organisation which is very hierarchical and autocratic might
favour a presentation-style approach where the trainer imparts knowledge to
the trainees who may make notes followed by a question and answer session.
A culture which is much more participative and team focused would probably
favour a more hands on approach where the training course would consist of
lots of group work and practical exercises.

Of course as we have seen, if training courses are to be effective and address all
learners needs they should be a combination of both. The problem with training
courses is sometimes they take a 'sheep dip' approach where employees are
told to attend, but don't really know why and everyone goes through the same
process irrespective of how appropriate it is for them. The focus becomes more
on attendance than learning (Favell 2008).

Induction programmes

The purpose of induction training is to: 'welcome new employees and provide
them with the information and skills that they will need to carry out their role
and to contribute to the organisation's objectives' (Robson 2009: 41).

The best induction programmes are planned over a number of weeks or
months so the new starter has time to digest the information and apply their
learning as they develop into their new job. Too much information given to a
new starter will make them feel overwhelmed and is unlikely to be effective.
Some companies carry out a pre-induction where they provide new employees
with information and support before they start the job. There is always quite a
lot of information a new employee needs to understand about the organisation

they have joined and the job that they will be doing. Initial information that a new starter will need surrounds what Herzberg (1968) called 'hygiene' factors. These are things that won't necessarily motivate an employee but without knowledge and access to them, they are likely to be demotivated and may result in the new starter not staying long with the organisation.

Information on pay, company policy, the organisation's vision and values, health and safety issues, holiday and sickness arrangements and who's who in the organisation will ensure new employees understand the organisation that they have joined. According to Leary-Joyce (2004) who studied the top 100 companies to work for, the best inductions left new employees inspired about work and understanding the behaviours expected in the company. People were brought in to tell 'stories' of life in the company to help people understand what was really important and why, which consequently helped to build a sense of belonging.

Further information on the job itself, their role and responsibilities should be addressed early on and by the appropriate people. In fact induction usually works best, according to Fiona Robson, author of the CIPD *Induction Tool Kit* (2010), when it is neither written nor delivered solely by the HR department. Managers and colleagues, including those who have recently joined the company, should be involved in delivering some elements of the programme. A buddy system in which experienced employees partner up with the new employee, introduce them to the appropriate people and answer questions is usually a successful way of making the individual feel welcome and secure. At Asda, new recruits are put on 100 days of induction and move around all the different departments in the company to understand the interconnections between departments, concluding with a lunch with senior leaders.

1. What else would you consider is important to include in an induction programme?
2. How could an organisation assess the success of an induction programme?

Placements and secondments

These are more typical in larger organisations which may have a number of departments or sites located across a wide geographical area. The individual is placed in a department or location different to their normal workplace in order for them to gain an insight in to a different aspect of the organisation. It is formal, in that it is planned for and can vary in length of time from a day a week to months or even a year. Apprenticeships and graduate programmes often use this type of development so that they gain a breadth of knowledge and experience before specialising in a particular type of work.

CASE STUDY

Carphone Warehouse

The Carphone Warehouse was founded in 1989 and has grown from a mobile phones business to a wider based telecommunications company with significance presence across Europe. It currently employs 13,000 people. Secondment opportunities are a form of development used within the company, particularly used in management development. Secondments include working in an overseas business, joining a project team to help establish a new market or working in a different function to broaden their skills, such as working in Finance or IT. The benefits of secondments have been in enabling idea sharing across the business as well as significant learning opportunities for the individual.

(Income Data Services 2005)

Job rotation, enlargement or enrichment

These are techniques which are often used in an organisation to give the individual more variety and experience in a range of jobs than their normal work would allow. They are particularly common in 'flatter' organisations where there is limited opportunity for promotion. Job rotation is similar to a secondment in that the learner tries out a new job but it is usually for a shorter period and within the same department. With job enlargement the learner would be given more tasks to do so that they can experience a wider range of work whereas in the case of job enrichment they may be given more responsibility. While all these are good learning opportunities some consider them to be a way for the company to get more out of the employees without actually paying them any more. For this reason you can appreciate that the way these initiatives are implemented needs to be carefully considered and planned with the full involvement of the employee.

Coaching

In a formal scheme an expert staff is allocated to an employee and a meeting schedule is arranged over a period of time. The trainer and learner develop a learning partnership and share control of the learning process. Although coaching is often considered as an individual partnership, it can be used for groups and teams. There are four key steps within the coaching process using the GROW model. Where a **G**oal or learning objective is identified, the **R**eality in relation to the goal is explored, **O**ptions are worked through and considered, then pinning down exactly what the learner **W**ill do by when and what help is needed for effective implementation (Hackett 2007). Coaching is not a short-term fix to a problem, it should be seen as a long-term development tool. Coaching is gaining in popularity, particularly at senior management level. The

CIPD (2009a) report that over two thirds (69 per cent) of respondents to their Learning and Development Survey use coaching within their organisations, with public sector (78 per cent) and large organisations with more than 5000 employees (83 per cent) are most likely to use coaching. Coaching is particularly common in management development programmes and is seen by most, according to the CIPD (2009a) survey, as a positive development opportunity.

E-learning

This is learning via electronically based technology (Harrison 2003) and with the increased sophistication of technology, its potential, as a learning tool is enormous. It can be an economic way of developing large groups of people which are not necessarily time or place dependent. Information can be delivered to all employees quickly and consistently with access to a wide choice of company specific information or 'off the shelf' training packages. It is likely that because of these advantages, 42 per cent of respondents in the 2009 CIPD Learning and Development Survey said that they have used e-learning more in the last two years. Xerox, the photocopier firm had been forced to move some classroom based training to the virtual world in an attempt to keep costs down but interestingly according to the company's head of learning and development, it has also boosted staff satisfaction (CIPD 2009c). Similarly B&Q, the DIY retailer, back in 2003 realised the potential of e-learning as a way for staff to improve their capabilities and achieve greater job satisfaction. They now have 90 e-learning modules available, some of which are compulsory, such as the module on Health and Safety. Of course if e-learning is to be really effective it must be carefully tailored to the organisation's and individual's needs. The e-learning material needs to be of a high quality with good resources available to support the learner both in the technology available but also with access to someone who can offer guidance when needed (Harrison 2003).

1. If you were a trainer in a company, how would you justify the use of each of the of the learning methods so far discussed?
2. In what situations do you think each would be really effective?
3. Write a list of situations when e-learning would not be appropriate.

Informal learning opportunities

This is when the learning is not planned and can happen by accident. A true 'learning organisation' will provide the culture where informal learning is an everyday process. Learning by just doing the job is the most obvious form of informal learning, but experiential learning and discussions encourage more reflection about the learning taking place.

Experiential learning

This is often called 'trial and error' learning. An employee might try a new way of doing something, find it doesn't work the first time, but after thinking about it may try to do it in a different way. This time it works. They learnt from their mistakes the first time round and applied this. Dyson for example, made 5,000 prototypes of his now famous bagless 'Dyson' vacuum cleaner until he had got the model that he was happy with. He didn't attend a training course, nor was he assisted by any type of formal development. His final success came from experimenting. Of course with experiential learning, the experience alone is not enough. It is necessary to think about what we have done and how we are going to do it differently the next time round for learning to take place.

Discussion groups

Staff rooms, common rooms, staff canteens encourage employees to meet and informally discuss issues about work. It is increasingly being recognised that this type of informal interchange is a valuable way of sounding out and developing new ideas. Some organisations have deliberately designed new buildings with areas set aside for informal discussion.

British Airways built a new head office at Waterside near Heathrow airport in 1998. On the ground floor is an 'office street' designed as a social space that brings the airline together with cafés, seating areas and shops to encourage discussion from people in all areas of the business. Everything about the new building is designed to encourage discussion and creativity – even the shape of the meeting tables and the installation of cordless telephones. This is in stark contrast to their old building which consisted of many offices in dark corridors with doors firmly shut, indicative of the hierarchical, traditional way of working which used to exist in the previously publicly owned organisation (Duffy 1998).

Blended learning

This describes the use of a variety of approaches which may be taken from informal and formal methods of development to enable learning. That can mean mixing all kinds of new technologies such as combining e-learning, an online lab exercise and a series of virtual classroom sessions, or it could mean using a traditional training session with the use of printed handouts, practical sessions and reflective discussion. If we refer back to how important it is to consider how individuals learn, it would make sense to select a mixture of approaches to suit the individual and by doing so, be more effective. Of course this also means it can be more time-consuming and difficult to plan but the advantages are that it should mean less 'blanket' training with more development which meets the business and individual needs as well as less time spent in the classroom away from the office. The benefits, if done carefully, should outweigh the costs. In fact in the UK, blended learning is rated as 'generally' or 'very' effective by 57 per cent of organisations, while in North America 79 per cent rate it as effective. By introducing blended learning, Barclays Bank was able to reduce its number of training units from 26 in 2000 to 1 in 2005 with a cost saving of £30 million over two years, while making learning more effective for its employees (Charles 2005).

CASE STUDY

Microsoft

Microsoft, the winner for the best training and development in *The Sunday Times* best companies to work for (2009) is dedicated to helping employees reach their full potential through a range of formal and informal development initiatives. These range from 'class room based learning, to taking on increased responsibilities, mentoring colleagues and learning by listening to pod casts' (Rodrigues and Clayton 2009: 10). They also recognise that learning and development shouldn't be restricted to the workplace. Microsoft supports staff on further education courses, allows sabbaticals and offers a range of resources at the in-house learning centre from cookery books to language courses. By 'blending' such a variety of learning methods, it ensures that all staff are developed in a way that suits their interests and learning needs.

Evaluating training and development

If training needs analysis was carried out and a learning plan devised, then the aims and objectives of the learning event should have been clear. The learning should also have been appropriate to the learner and the overall organisations strategy. In order to identify if this was the case and that the training and development was worthwhile, the training should be evaluated. At Asda they 'measure everything that moves, lives and breathes' Leary-Joyce (2004: 120). Successful companies are keen to track carefully what is done and how it contributes to the goals they are reaching for. Unfortunately this is often not done by organisations or only a half-hearted attempt is made at really seeing if the training had met its original objectives.

The reason for this lack of rigour in evaluation is often down to time and resources. It is also sometimes difficult to make a direct link between the learning and improved performance until some time after the training event. By this time other factors may have also contributed to improved performance. The more the learning event is concerned with 'soft' skills, by that we mean people skills which are non-technical such as listening, negotiating and communication skills, the less easy it is to measure.

The higher up the organisation the learning event, the less easy it is to measure the impact training has had, due to the complexity of the job.

The result is that often the only type of evaluation that is carried out is a questionnaire; often called a 'happy sheet' which is given immediately after the training. If you have ever been on a training course you may have been given one of these. It was probably given to you when the course finished, just as you were ready to rush for your train. You can see that these are not ideal in really assessing the usefulness of the training. What they really tell the organisation is if the employee felt the training was useful and how much they enjoyed it. In fact you will probably find most people want to comment on superficial aspects of the day such as the quality of the lunch and the availability of free drinks! More useful to the organisation would be how effective the training was and whether it has improved performance. Kirkpatrick (1967) devised a model which outlines four levels of evaluation which, if carried out, would assess if the training and development was meaningful and worthwhile.

The levels	Purpose	Methods of evaluation
Level 1 – Reaction level	To find out reaction of the trainees to the content, methods of training and the effectiveness of the trainer	Questionnaires Interviews Discussion
Level 2 – Immediate level	To measure what was learnt during the learning event	Quiz Test Examination Case study or structured exercise Observation
Level 3 – Intermediate level	To assess if trainees were able to transfer what was learnt during the training event to their jobs	Sampling Appraisal Supervisor evaluation Performance level Sampling Observation Work diary Customer and colleague feedback
Level 4 – Ultimate level	To assess if the learning has had an impact on the department and the organisation's performance	Quality indicators Sales Targets

Table 3.3 The four levels of evaluation for measuring the effectiveness of training

Levels 1 and 2 are usually done either during or immediately after the learning whereas level 3 and level 4 may be weeks, months or even a year afterwards, when the impact can really be assessed. However, the longer the delay in measuring the learning event, the less easy it is to do.

ACTIVITY

Evaluating training at Bizworks

Bizworks provides secretarial support to a number of small businesses. They have just introduced a new computer system to provide a more efficient and professional way of meeting their clients secretarial needs. It was decided that a training course was needed for all the secretaries so that they could use this new system as soon as possible.

Sally Periwinkle had recently been taken on by Bizworks as the new trainee in the learning and development department. She was asked to design, run and evaluate a training course for the secretaries on the new computer system. She was informed by the department manager, Grace Smith, that the training objectives of her course should be that the secretaries should have enough basic knowledge of the new system so that they could use it straight away in their day-to-day work.

Sally ran a day training course on the new system and, knowing the importance of evaluation, asked the secretaries to complete a questionnaire at the end of the day to see what they thought about the training. The questionnaire asked the secretaries to respond with a 'yes' or a 'no' to questions such as 'Did you enjoy the course?', 'Have you learnt a lot from the course?' and 'Do you think you can use what you have learnt back in the workplace?'. Sally was pleased that the responses were all very positive with all the secretaries saying that they had increased their knowledge of the new computer system, they had enjoyed the course and had learnt a lot.

Four weeks later, Sally received a phone call from Grace Smith complaining that the secretaries still didn't seem to know how to use the new computer system, with many resorting to going back to the old system. This meant that the improvements that the new computer system should have made were not happening and a backlog of work was piling up. She was afraid that this would mean losing business and cancelled orders. This apparent lack of knowledge puzzled Sally as her evaluation had shown that the course was effective.

1. What level of evaluation did Sally use for her training course?
2. What mistakes did she make in evaluating the course?
3. What other method(s) of evaluation might she have used to ensure the training was more effective?
4. What could she have done to ensure all levels of Kirkpatrick's model were evaluated?

Of course training may not be the only solution. Job redesign, better communication or more employee involvement may be more beneficial to the individual and the organisation. In all circumstances training needs to be seen as important to the future of the organisation. There should be some form of recognition or reward made by the organisation to ensure employees are also committed to learning and development and the whole culture of the organisation needs to be open to experimentation and applying training. Those organisations which operate in a 'blame' culture are not going to encourage individuals to try new methods or implement what they have learnt.

CASE STUDY

Bob Henry, the former CEO of CORGI, the national watchdog for gas safety in the UK, believed in risk taking for learning and development of the individual and the company. In an interview with Leary-Joyce who was researching the top 100 companies to work for he said the following: 'We want people to take risks, be adventurous, not foolhardy, and we don't want them to be afraid of losing their job. It's OK if the outcome is unexpected – OK but share it with others and look at what went on. If you repeat the behaviour and the outcome is the same, it is not unexpected any longer, and that's not acceptable – because you are not learning and we take a dim view of that. In that case we want to identify the development need that has to be addressed' (Leary-Joyce, 2004: 115).

(3.8) Summary

The chapter began by outlining the importance of learning and development and the various initiatives that the UK Government have implemented to improve the capabilities of the UK workforce. The idea of the 'learning organisation' was then introduced and how lifetime learning is becoming essential as the pace of change increases in the twenty-first century. The key terms of training, education and development were defined, followed by a discussion of how people learn. This is important to understand if any training and development initiative is to be really effective.

Progressing through the training cycle is an important way of identifying training and learning needs and deciding on the most appropriate methods to meet those needs. Recognition of the benefits of more on the job provision in learning and development has led to the rise of methods to facilitate learning 'on the job' rather than sending employees on generic training courses. The increased use of coaching, e-learning and blended learning have proven particularly popular with organisations trying to achieve more meaningful development. New technology is making a growing impact on learning and development. E-learning and blended learning give greater choice about training delivery and more choice about how and when learning takes place. Evaluation of training and development initiatives was seen as an important way of assessing the benefit of any development initiative.

KEY IDEAS

Some of the main points covered in this chapter are listed below. If you feel unsure about any of them revisit the appropriate section. If you would like some additional reading on the topic try out the books listed below in recommended reading.

The importance of learning and development
- Investment in learning and development is seen as the key way in which organisations can effectively compete.
- The skills levels of the UK are falling behind other advanced industrial nations.

Government initiatives to encourage learning and development
- Since the 1980s, the Government has introduced a range of initiatives to encourage employers to invest in the training and development of their workforce.
- National Vocational Qualifications (NVQs), Investors in People standard (IiP), Apprenticeships and 'train to gain' have been the main initiatives that the Government have introduced to try and 'upskill' the UK workforce.

The 'learning organisation'
- Pedlar et al (1991) were one of the first to write about the importance of continuous learning and introduced the idea of the learning organisation.
- Organisations which develop a learning and development culture have found significant business improvements.

What do we mean by education, training, learning and development?
- Education is about more formal type learning largely focusing on acquiring knowledge whereas training is seen to be more specific, often with a focus on improving skills.
- Learning and development are more continuous and focus on longer-term changes to an individual's knowledge, skills and abilities.

How do people learn?
- Kolb (1974) suggested that for learning to be effective individuals need to go through a four-stage process starting with having the experience and ending with making changes following reflection about the learning.
- Honey and Mumford (1984) suggest that people learn in different ways and that it is important to understand the best ways in which people learn in order to provide effective learning and development opportunities.

The training process
- In order for any training or development initiative to be effective, it is first necessary to identify what the training needs are. This can be done at three levels; organisation, job or individual.
- Once training needs have been established, a learning plan needs to be devised in order to meet the training needs. A range of factors need to be considered such as the resources available, the cost of training and the characteristics of the learner if the plan is to be effective.
- Meeting the learning needs can be through a variety of methods, both formal and informal, off the job and on the job. Usually a combination of methods, known as blended learning, is the most effective way to meet the learners' needs.
- Evaluating training and development is the final part of the training process and is an essential, although often forgotten, way of ensuring the development initiative is effective in both meeting the learning need and adding value to the organisation.

REFLECTIVE QUESTIONS

1 Despite the usefulness of informal methods of training and development, why do you think the Government has focused its initiatives such as NVQs, IiP and apprenticeships on formal types of learning?

2 When designing a learning plan, what considerations would you need to take in to account?

3 For what reasons would you justify the importance of using a variety of methods for training and development purposes?

4 Why is it important to evaluate any training and development initiative?

RECOMMENDED READING

If you would like to learn more about some of the issues in the five sections within this chapter you might like to consider the following books and articles:

The importance of learning and development
Rosemary Harrison's book *Learning and Development* provides an in-depth coverage of the importance of learning and development, backed with a number of enlightening studies to illustrate. A joint discussion paper published in June 2009, produced by ACAS and the CIPD *Meeting the UK People Management Skills Deficit*, sets out evidence and discusses the importance of learning and development for good people management.

Government initiatives to encourage learning and development
Mick Marchington and Adrian Wilkinson, in their book *Human Resource Management at Work*, discuss and assess the impact of government initiatives for improving the learning and development of the UK workforce.

The 'learning organisation'
The CIPD have produced a report entitled *Training to Learning*, published in April 2005, which outlines ways in which organisations can move from just delivering training to focusing on learning and the benefits that this brings.

What do we mean by education, training, learning and development?
Training in Practice by Steve Truelove provides definitions and a short discussion on the difference between these terms.

How do people learn?
Laurie Mullins' book *Essentials of Organisational Behaviour* provides a comprehensive chapter on the nature of learning and discusses a range of theories on the way people learn.

The training process
Penny Hackett's book called *Training Practice* provides a systematic review of the training process, which is easy to read and outlines the main steps in the training process. The CIPD have produced a number of fact sheets covering the varying aspects of the training process from training needs analysis,

to methods used in training and how to evaluate training and development. All are available from their website www.cipd.co.uk.

USEFUL WEBSITES

www.investorsinpeople.co.uk This is the official website responsible for promoting and developing the standard. It provides information on the standard, plus research materials and support services.
www.direct.gov.uk/en/EducationAndLearning This is a Government website designed to provide all the information that you may need about education providers and learning opportunities for young people and adults.
www.lsc.gov.uk The Learning and Skills Council website aims to inform readers of courses on offer to develop the skills needed for the future.
www.cipd.co.uk The Chartered Institute of Personnel and Development is the United Kingdom's leading professional body for those involved in the management and development of human resources. Their website contains a variety of information ranging from research and reports to details of qualifications that are available to develop people involved in human resource management.
www.qcda.gov.uk/19674.aspx The Qualifications and Curriculum Development Agency website.

REFERENCES

Association of Graduate Recruiters (2007) at www.agr.org.uk
Charles, B. (2005) Ingredients for Success in *Blended Learning*, Skills Report ITtraining, 2005, 6–7.
CIPD (2008) *Learning and Development Survey*, London: CIPD
CIPD (2009a) *Learning and Development Survey*, London: CIPD
CIPD (2009b) Sheffield Forgemasters International in *People Management,* 27 August 2009: 25.
CIPD (2009c) Xerox, *People Management*, 27 August 2009: 10.
Constable, J., McCormick, R. (1987) *The Making of British Managers.* London: BIM/CBI.
Cox, A. (2007) Re-visiting the NVQ Debate: 'Bad' Qualifications, Expansive Learning Environments and Prospects for Upskilling Workers. SKOPE Research Paper No. 71. Oxford/Cardiff: SKOPE.
Cranfield School of Management (2008) *Investors in People,* available at www.investorsinpeople.co.uk/MediaResearch/Research/Pages/Provingthebenefits.aspx
Davies, G. (2009) *Jobs Crisis Ahead for the Young*, Impact, Issue 28. CIPD.
Duffy, F. (1998) Working at Waterside, *Business Publications*, available at www.findarticles.com
Hackett, P. (2007) *Training Practice*, London: CIPD.
Handy, C. (1987) *The Making of Managers.* London: NEDO.
Harrison, R. (2003) *Learning and Development.* London: CIPD
Honey, P., Mumford, A. (1982) in Mumford, A. and Honey, P. (1992) 'Questions and answers on learning styles', *Industrial and Commercial Training,* vol. 24, no 7, 10–13.
Income Data Services (2005) Carphone Warehouse, No. 804, August 2005.
Income Data Services (2006) McDonald's, No. 816, February 2006.
Income Data Services (2008) Superdrug, No. 874, July 2008.
Kirkpatrick, D. (1967) 'Evaluation and Training', in Craig, R. and Bittell, L. (eds.) *Training and Evaluation Handbook.* New York: McGraw-Hill.
Kitching, J. (2007) 'Regulating employment relations through workplace learning: a study of small employers', *Human Resource Management Journal*, vol. 17, no 1, 42–57.

Kolb, D. (1974) in Zuber-Skerritt, O. (1992) *Professional Development in Higher Education.* London: Kogan Page Limited.

Leary-Joyce, J. (2004) *Becoming an Employer of Choice.* London: CIPD.

Leitch, S. (2006) *Prosperity for all in the global economy – world class skills.* HM Treasury.

Marchington, M., Wilkinson, A. (2008) *Human Resource Management at Work.* London: CIPD.

Martin, M., Jackson, T (2005) *Personnel Practice.* London: CIPD

Mulllins, L. (2008) *Essentials of Oganisational Behaviour.* Haslow: Prentice Hall.

Pedlar, M. Burgoyne, J., Boydell, T. (1991) *The Learning Company: A strategy for sustainable development.* Maidenhead: McGraw-Hill.

Phillips, L. (2009) Plan to end internship elitism in *People Management,* 30 July 2009. London: CIPD.

Robson, F. (2009) How to deliver effective inductions in *People Management* 18 June 2009. CIPD.

Robson, F. (2010) *The Induction Tool Kit* (forthcoming). London: CIPD.

Rodrigues, N., Clayton, M. (2009) A positive difference: Microsoft, *The Sunday Times 100 best companies to work for,* 8 March 2009.

Senge, P. (1990) *The Fifth Discipline: The art and practice of the learning organisation.* London: Century.

The story of NVQs available at www.qcda.gov.uk

Truelove, S. (2007) *Training in Practice.* London: CIPD.

4 Reward

'*In the arena of human life the honours and rewards fall to those who show their good qualities in action.*'

(Aristotle)

CHAPTER OUTLINE

4.1 Introduction
4.2 What motivates people at work?
4.3 Financial rewards
4.4 Employee benefits
4.5 Non-financial rewards
4.6 Total reward
4.7 Summary

CHAPTER OBJECTIVES

- Gaining an understanding of what motivates people and its link with reward
- Knowledge of the types of financial reward including base pay, variable pay and share ownership
- Awareness of the nature of employee benefits
- Understand the importance of non-financial rewards
- Understand the meaning and benefits of a total reward approach

Introduction

Why do people work? The obvious answer is for money. Attractive financial rewards are necessary to attract and retain the best employees. Would you still work if you won the lottery? Maybe not, but million-pound-scratch-card-winner Maria Murray did. She returned to her £5 an hour café job serving fry ups from 6 a.m. because 'all her friends were there'.

Many people work in jobs when they could earn more if they moved to another organisation. This is because people do not usually work purely for financial return. Obviously money does matter for the majority of people but the reasons people work in one company rather than another are sometimes more complex than just the wage they will get. Rewarding people for what they do needs to be seen in the context of what motivates people. Just giving financial reward is not usually enough to retain the best people. This chapter aims to introduce you to some of the ideas behind reward, recognition and motivation and to give you an insight in to how and why different companies reward their people.

 ## What motivates people at work?

If you have ever been in an office on a Friday afternoon you will probably have noticed how the noise volume has risen, clock watching increases, people start packing their bags and clearing their desks all in preparation for a swift exit as soon as 5 p.m. is reached. Motivation to stay a minute longer is not apparent among the majority of employees. To get the best from their employees, organisations need to create conditions where staff actively want to get in early and stay late because they enjoy what they do and associate the company's success with their own. Just getting paid for attending work is not going to do this. According to Scase (2007) what is required is an employment relationship (rather than just a wage contract) where the employee regards themselves as a stakeholder in the long-term success of the company. It is also important to understand what motivates people in the first place to work. If this is understood then organisations can tailor their reward systems to motivate people to want to be in such an 'employment relationship'.

In order to understand what an effective reward system looks like, it is first necessary to understand the link it has with motivation.

The study of motivation is concerned with why people behave in a certain way. Mitchell (1982:80) defines motivation as: 'the degree to which an individual wants and chooses to engage in certain specified behaviours'. Motivation is complex, personal to the individual and is influenced by many factors. The various needs and expectations at work can be categorised as extrinsic and intrinsic motivators (Mullins 2008). Extrinsic motivators are related to tangible rewards such as salary, benefits, promotion prospects, the conditions at work and training and development. Intrinsic motivators are related to 'psychological' rewards of being appreciated and recognised for good work, being valued and treated in a considerate manner, gaining a sense of achievement and being able to apply your abilities and skills to interesting and challenging work. If you have ever read *The Times* The Best 100 Companies to Work For, researched and printed each year, you will be able to identify those companies who consistently score in the top 100. They go a long way in meeting the extrinsic and intrinsic needs of their employees. Gathering pace are also the broader concerns of work/life balance opportunities, flexible working and the ethical policies of companies which are increasingly seen as important factors in motivation among its workers.

KEY TERMS

Extrinsic motivators Those aspects of work which are tangible and can easily be recognised such as salary, benefits, conditions of work.
Intrinsic motivators Those things which motivate people but are usually more personal to an individual such as being appreciated, being treated in a considerate manner, gaining a sense of achievement.

1. Think about a company that you might like to work for. What are your reasons?
2. What are the benefits to the organisation of meeting the extrinsic and intrinsic needs of its employees?

Theories of motivation

There are many competing theories, which attempt to explain motivation. The complexity of motivation means that there is no simple answer to what motivates people. Although it is not my intention to go through each theory, understanding the most common ones provides an insight into possible ways to motivate people at work.

Most theories of motivation can be divided into either content theories of motivation, which focus on human needs related to motivation, i.e. the 'contents' of the motives (for example money and safety needs) or process theories, which focus on the relationship between different variables which lead to motivation.

One of the earliest writers on motivation was F.W. Taylor (1856–1915) who believed in the power of money to motivate. He suggested that workers were only interested in earning as much money as possible. As this was the case he applied the principles of scientific management to work. This meant that each job was analysed through time and motion studies so the most efficient way of doing the job could be calculated and a 'best' method devised. Workers were instructed in the 'best' method and rewarded accordingly. Workers in effect became like robots where there was no place for innovation or creativity. Although today, it seems unrealistic to expect workers to perform in such a way, if you consider the fast food industry there is a striking resemblance to elements of scientific management. Even some call centres have applied a 'best' method to conduct a conversation. A conversation has been broken down into its constituent parts and operators are expected to open and close a call in a specific way, prompted by cues throughout the conversation. In this way the work is carried out as efficiently as possible and the employee earns money related to successfully carrying out the task in the specified manner.

1. Think of a time when you rang a call centre. Did the conversation appear to follow a set formula? If so, for which things do you think they were being rewarded?
2. Do you need to be a chef to work in a fast food restaurant? Explain your answer.

The human relations approach in the 1920s, primarily through the Hawthorne experiments, placed more emphasis on the broader context of work rather than the simple maximisation of earnings (see Chapter 6 for a more in-depth discussion). This led the way for other theorists to consider multiple aspects of motivation linked to reward. The first of these was Maslow in the 1940s who suggested that there was no single source of motivation but a 'hierarchy of needs'. He listed nine needs which workers ascend once the lower need is satisfied, although he did concede that the hierarchy isn't necessarily a fixed order. Maslow claimed that the hierarchy is relatively universal among different cultures (Mullins 2008), but Buchanan and Huczynski (2004: 247) provide evidence that this may not be so. For example Scandinavian cultures place a high value on quality of life and social needs whereas Anglo-American cultures place a high value on productivity and efficiency and individual self-actualisation. This is in contrast to Chinese culture which values collectivism and community rather than individualism.

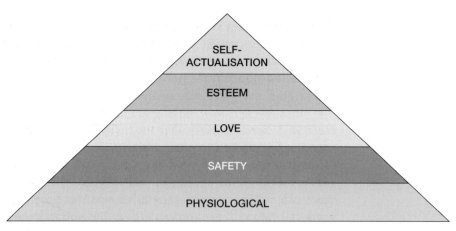

Figure 4.1 Maslow's hierarchy of needs

CASE STUDY

George Cadbury's chocolate factory at Bourneville in Birmingham was ahead of its time. This was because when the factory was first moved to Bourneville in the late nineteenth century, he built 24 houses for his key workers. Cadbury later added another 300 houses to form Bourneville village. The houses were superior to working-class houses of that time with larger rooms and big gardens. A school, hospital, reading room and washhouses were built for the people in the village. He also provided training and education, and in 1906 he paid £60,000 into a pension fund for his employees. He already had a good reputation as an employer but by introducing half-days on Saturdays and bank holiday closing, this was further enhanced. In the factory there was a kitchen for heating up food and later he added a canteen as well as providing medical and dental treatment.

1. Which of Maslow's hierarchy of needs did George Cadbury focus on?

Herzberg's (1966) two-factor theory of motivation and job satisfaction was influential in that following interviews with 203 accountants and engineers, he suggested that there were two different sets of factors affecting motivation and work. One set of factors related to the job environment which did not necessarily motivate but if they were not present would demotivate. He called these 'hygiene' factors. The other set of factors were related to the content of the work itself and, depending on the strength of these factors, would motivate. He called these 'motivators'. However, some have criticised these assumptions as people employed in mainly unskilled jobs may not be interested in the job content of their work and consequently the 'motivators'. Despite this the value of this theory is that some believe it has had a significant impact on rewards and remuneration packages today.

1. In what ways do you think Herzberg's theory has had an impact on the rewards and pay that organisations provide today?

If motivation comes from the job content then it is important for managers to consider the nature of the jobs they ask their employees to do. If you want people to do a good job, then you must give them a 'good' job. The question is, what is a 'good' job?

The 'motivators' has led some organisations to think more carefully about the non-financial rewards that they offer while paying closer attention to the 'hygiene factors' to ensure satisfied employees. Hackman and Oldman (1976) attempted to refine our understanding of what a 'good job' actually looks like: what are the characteristics of motivating jobs? They suggested that workers react differently to jobs (not as universal as Herzberg suggests) and found that workers who aspired to promotion and development within the organisation responded positively to jobs which had high motivating potential, but those who just wanted to do the job, did not. They found that there were five key motivating factors which made a 'good' job. These were:

1 Skill variety
2 Task identity
3 Task significance
4 Autonomy
5 Feedback

For a job to be intrinsically motivating all five characteristics must be simultaneously present.

Figure 4.2 The production line job

1. Is this what Hackman and Oldham believe is a 'good job'? Justify your answer.

While content theories of motivation do not recognise individual choice or social influence, process theories of motivation attempt to identify the relationships 'among the dynamic variables that make up motivation and the actions required to influence behaviour and actions' (Mullins 2008: 187).

Equity theory, developed by researchers such as Adams (1963, 1965), has particular implications for management practice and how effort and reward is linked. The theory is based on our perception of fairness. Inequity occurs when you get more or less reward than perceived as deserved. The more intense the perceived inequity, the greater the motivation to act. Adams proposed that employees compare rewards such as pay and recognition with the level of contribution such as time, effort and ideas. If there is a perceived imbalance particularly of 'under reward' it is not easily tolerated. Of course this depends on individuals 'threshold' of tolerance and perception of inequity. That is why it is important for reward systems to be transparent and as much as possible, to be related to effort.

The expectancy theory developed by Tolman in the 1930s argued that high levels of motivation can only be achieved if productive work is seen as a path to valued goals (Buchanen and Huczynski 2004). So if you value money and want to get more money and you believe working harder will get you more money, then that is the path to reach your goal. Of course this assumes that we are rational in our behaviour and we make a conscious effort to meet our desired goals. Unlike content theories of Taylor and Maslow which suggest all employees are alike and motivated by the same sort of thing, equity and expectancy theories suggests employees weigh up their inputs against their outputs and will be motivated accordingly. Motivation is much more personal to the individual and is an important point to note when creating effective reward strategies. While a high salary may motivate some, others would be more motivated if they could balance their work and personal lives more easily.

1. If motivation is personal to an individual, how can an organisation try and motivate all of its employees?
2. Try and think of examples of organisations which seem to motivate their employees based on one or more of the theories discussed.

Relevance of theories of motivation

As you can see, most motivation theories date back many years and so their relevance to today's work environment, could be questioned. Some believe that motivation in the twenty-first century should be based on a different set of criteria such as friendship, the benefits of work and respect (Reis and Pena 2001). In fact in Mercer's Global Total Reward Survey (2008) 'respect' was rated as the highest factor in employee motivation (80 per cent), followed closely by 'type of work' (73 per cent), the 'people who work with you' (71 per cent) and 'work-life balance' (69 per cent). Pay and benefits were amongst the lowest rated motivators. Despite this, there is a general support for some of the early theories, particularly those of Maslow and Herzberg, as they are seen to provide basic principles on which organisations can motivate and support their employees (Mullins 2008). Being aware of the different motivational theories coupled with more recent research will ensure that the complexity of motivation is not forgotten when deciding appropriate reward strategies.

Reward systems

Rewarding people for a good job done should be linked to the values or strategy of the organisation. So if an organisation wants to encourage good customer service then it would make sense to reward those who give good customer service. Similarly those organisations who value teamwork, should reward effective teamworking. The value individuals in the organisation put on different types of reward should also inform decisions of how much and in what form, to reward their employees. Reward is not just about the money paid in a salary. Reward can come in many forms. Financial rewards can be in the form of basic salary, but it can also be through share ownership and financial benefits such as pensions or private health care. People can also be rewarded in non-financial ways such as through recognition, career opportunities or a good quality of working life. Whatever form of reward a company operates, the fairness of how people are rewarded is essential. Any reward system which is perceived as unfair will not be effective and is likely to leave employees disillusioned and demotivated. We will first look at the types of financial reward which operate in organisations.

Financial rewards

Base pay

This is the amount of money which is paid for a particular job. It is often called 'payment by time' where an individual is paid for a specified amount of time at work. This can be based on an hourly rate or as a weekly or monthly salary. There are many different types of pay structures but they tend to fall into two categories, spot pay and graded pay.

Spot rates involve payment of a single rate of pay per period of time and type of job. There is usually little opportunity for pay progression other than via a general increase in all rates, often related to inflation. A spot rate pay system is simple to administer and is easy for everyone to understand. The minimum wage set by the government is a form of spot rate. So for example, as of October 2009 the minimum wage for a 16–17-year-old is £3.57 per hour, for an 18–21-year-old it is £4.83 per hour and for those over the age of 21 it is £5.80 per hour. This means that anyone within the age bracket who is going to be paid the minimum wage will know what the rate will be per hour. Spot rates can vary within an organisation depending on their geographical location. For example Laura Ashley, the clothing retailer, pay an extra 10 per cent per hour for staff working in inner London (Income Data Services 2008). Some organisations group spot rates in 'job families' where everyone doing a similar job will be paid the same and is determined not only by the market rate but also the knowledge, skills and experience needed to do the job.

The other main type of pay format is a graded structure. Jobs are assessed according to their worth and put on a 'scale'. Typically the scale will be divided into grades or bands into which groups of jobs that are similar are placed. There are a variety of types of graded structure but the most commonly used are broad bands, job families and narrow-graded pay structures (CIPD 2009). Broad-banded structures consist of about four or five grades within each band, whereas narrow-graded pay structures consist of a sequence of narrow grades of perhaps ten or more (Armstrong 2007). Job family structures are when groups of jobs with similar characteristics are each divided into levels. The levels between job families may differ depending on the going market rate of each job family. The salary received by the employee will depend on where their job is placed within the band or grade.

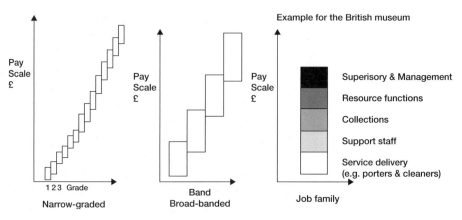

Figure 4.3 Grade, band and job family structures (adapted from Armstrong 2007)

Although this type of pay arrangement rewards experience and is relatively cheap to administer, it provides little incentive to do a job well as the payment will be the same however much effort is put in. Each year an employee stays

CASE STUDY

The British Museum

In 2005 the British Museum introduced a new pay system. It created a single grading structure with five job families: collections (museum assistants, conservators and curators), service delivery (security, cleaners, porters, ticketing and gallery staff), resource functions (finance, HR, marketing and designers), supervisory and management (all forms of management across the museum) and support (administrators, secretarial staff and personal assistants). Each family was subdivided into the knowledge, skills and competencies required in each of the roles. Jobs were then slotted into the structure by considering which job family they were in and then assessing each role against five criteria including: knowledge and skills, decision making, complexity, use of resources and communication. Employees progress up through the pay scales through annual increments within their job family 'band'.

Adapted from Income Data Services (2009a)

in the job, they move up one more point on the salary scale. This can result in 'grade drift' where organisations that have many long serving employees, all end up at the top of the scale. Once they have reached the top within their pay structure, unless they gain promotion, their salary will not rise.

1. What do you think may be some of the issues of grade drift?
2. If organisations pay for time, how can they encourage quality and effort?

Job evaluation

In order to decide where a job should be placed on a pay structure, job evaluation has become a widely used method of assessing the job's worth. It can be defined as 'a method of determining on a systematic basis the relative importance of a number of different jobs' (ACAS 2008). As soon as people realise that different people are being paid different amounts for a job, they start to assess the relative importance of that job. If an employee perceives what they are getting paid is not fair, it is sometimes hard for a manager to justify why one job has higher pay than another. A well-thought-out and executed job evaluation scheme provides an objective way of assessing the relative importance of some or all of the different jobs within an organisation. Job evaluation does not determine pay levels but it produces a hierarchy of jobs that can then be put on to a salary structure. The problem is that the importance allocated to a job may be influenced by societal stereotypes as well as individual perception and prejudice.

ACTIVITY

1. Place the following list of jobs in rank order according to what you think is their importance or worth.

Type of job	Importance of job	Pay of job
MP		
Train driver		
Nurse		
Checkout operator		
Foster parent		
HR manager		

2. Now place them in rank order according to what you think they get paid.
3. If your two columns are different, why is this?
4. Why are jobs sometimes not paid what they are worth?

Variable pay

Where pay varies according to performance, contribution, skill, experience or effort and is paid as cash bonuses it is described as 'variable pay' (Armstrong 2007). This links closely to what we have already seen about motivation and reward. This type of variable pay is based on the assumption that those who are motivated by money will work harder as they will get paid more. A bonus is usually a lump sum payment paid either to individuals or to groups. Wright (2004: 135) lists the different types of variable pay in the following way:

- Sales commission or sales incentives designed to increase the performance of the sales force
- Bonus payments related to output of a team or business unit
- Executive incentives that my be profit-related to the success of the business unit
- Piecework where individual output is measured and paid accordingly.

Payment by results

Performance-related pay (PRP) in the form of payment by results usually makes up a part of the employees pay. The actual percentage of salary which is related to performance varies between organisations and types of jobs, but usually those jobs which focus on output rather than input, have a large part of their salary based on PRP. For example an employee may be paid a set rate for completing a job. However if the job is completed in a reduced time or more is produced, a bonus payment is given. For sales staff, a bonus payment may be received for exceeding their sales target.

Sony UK Customer Information Centre have a team-based bonus scheme which is dependent on results from customer satisfaction surveys and the weekly average abandonment rate of telephone calls. Weekly targets are set for each call centre team and a maximum of £500 per half year is paid to members of the team if the targets are met. (Income Data Services 2007)

Merit-based pay

PRP in the form of merit-based pay is becoming a more common way of incentivising employees who do not necessarily have targets to meet or who produce quantities of work which can't be counted. Instead employees can receive a bonus payment above their standard salary based on their overall job performance. Of course for this to be effective, employees must know what they need to do in order to achieve such a bonus. Clear performance objectives need to be set out and a transparent method of evaluating performance needs to be agreed. Employee appraisal ratings are a common form of determining how much bonus an employee receives.

1. What do you think are the main advantages and disadvantages of PRP?
2. Can you think of any potential issues for an employee's variable pay being based on a managers ratings in an appraisal?

CASE STUDY

Ladbrokes, a betting and gaming company with 2000 shops in the UK, redesigned its salary and bonus scheme in 2008 to better reflect individual performance. Ladbrokes felt that the relationship between individual performance and overall company performance was so closely linked that more was needed to be done to incentivise employees to give of their best. As a result employees are assessed on a scale from one to five. One is given when an employee did not meet the performance criteria to a rating of five where an employee meets all the performance criteria 'all of the time and did more than was expected'. The score on the scale is combined with results from a mystery shopper to determine the value of the bonus payment that each employee receives at the end of the year. Jeremy Trevor, the Retail HR Director, believes that the business benefits from measuring individual performance includes being better able to serve their customers, having employees who are clearer as to what is expected of them and enabling the business to focus on the important issues so that they can make money in the right areas.

Income Data Services (2009b)

Share ownership

There are a variety of schemes in operation which encourage employees to have a financial 'stake' in their employing organisation. They became particularly popular in the 1990s when tax incentives were introduced by the government. Today about a third of companies have some form of share ownership scheme (CIPD 2009).

Tesco operate a 'Save As You Earn' scheme (SAYE). Employees can save up to £50 per month in the scheme over a three- or five-year period. In March 2009 those Tesco staff that had paid in to the scheme were able to have a share in the £126 million payout from SAYE. The staff who had paid the maximum of £3,000 over the five-year period, received £5,638 each (http://www.tescoplc. com/plc/corporate_responsibility_09/news/press_releases/pr2009/2009-02-09/ 2009).

Although such schemes can be a way to attract and retain people in the hope of a large payout, there are also a number of problems. The main one is how much control the individual employee has over the level of profits and hence the amount of payment received. As you are well aware, shares can go up as well and down. This is not necessarily linked to effort by individual employees, but factors beyond the control of the ordinary employee. While it can be motivating for employees to receive a good bonus when shares do well, in harder times many employees could become disillusioned by a payment system which doesn't pay!

4.4 Employee benefits

Employee benefits are those aspects of reward made by the employer to the employee in addition to their basic pay. Benefits make up the remuneration package of an employer and in some cases can be up to a third of the basic pay costs of each employee. Table 4.1 shows the most common benefits provided to employees within organisations in the UK.

You may be surprised to see some of the items listed as a 'benefit'. Having 25 days leave for example is considered a benefit. Before the Working Time directive in 1998 there was no statutory obligation to provide any paid holiday other than bank holidays. Currently employers have to pay a minimum of 28 days paid holiday per year, inclusive of bank holidays (www.direct.gov. uk). Any organisation who pays for more than the statutory minimum is considered a benefit to the employee as it costs the employer extra money. Due to the environment agenda and the decrease in space for parking, many organisations now charge employees to park their cars at work. Free parking is now seen as a benefit. For example hospital workers are expected to pay for

Type of benefit	Percentage using the benefit
Pension plan	95%
Training and development	71%
25 days or more paid leave	67%
Free tea/coffee/ cold drinks	62%
Christmas party/lunch	60%
On-site car parking	60%
Child care vouchers	56%
Life assurance	51%
Eye care vouchers	46%
Enhanced maternity and paternity leave	43%

Table 4.1 The most common benefits for employees (CIPD Reward Management Survey (2009), with the permission of the publisher, the Chartered Institute of Personnel and Development, London (www.cipd.co.uk))

their parking. Indeed a recent report which appeared in a Scottish newspaper claimed that nurses who parked for longer than four hours had to pay a £40 fine for exceeding the parking limit.

The type of benefits offered by organisations depends on the cost and the relative value to the employees. An attractive benefits package helps to attract employees to an organisation and retain them. Organisations can compete with each other on basic pay but it is often the benefits package which makes the organisation more or less attractive to their competitors. Those companies which need to compete for the best employees often have quite complex benefits packages offering rewards which are particularly valued by the type of employee they wish to attract. Some even go one step further by offering benefits which are unique and sometimes rather quirky which are difficult to replicate by other companies. For example, Tokyo-based Hime and Co offer 'heartache' leave to female employees. The older the employee, the more 'heartache' leave they are given as the company believes they need more time to cry and so come back to work refreshed after having their heart broken!

Flexible benefits

These are schemes which allow employees to choose their benefits package and sometimes vary their pay, to suit their personal requirements. In most schemes employees can keep their existing salary and are given a benefit

CASE STUDY

Innocent Drinks, the health drink maker based in London, puts sales target on the side of a large smoothie bottle called the Drinkometer (Armistead 2002). When each target is met, the managers organise fun days as a reward. The last one was a sports day in the park, the next one is a group yoga session. They give free breakfasts to all staff to encourage a bright start to each morning, with every member of staff having their own breakfast bowl, mug and plate. They also run a two-hour bar tab every Friday after work at a selected pub. Other benefits include extra holidays to newlyweds, an annual company weekend away, a £2,000 bonus to expecting couples and each quarter they run an Innocent scholarship where employees get the opportunity to win £1,000 to pay for something they have always wanted to do. For those who see career development as a benefit, they run 'mini Innocent MBAs' which consists of eight courses in Leadership and Management over a year to give staff a taster of a real MBA programme. Sales representatives get a company car but it is dubious if this is a real benefit. The reason being it is in the form of a van decorated to look like a cow, complete with eyelashes, udder, tail and horns that moo! (Chomka 2005).

Figure 4.4 An Innocent cow van

allowance from which they can buy their benefits. Some can adjust their salary up or down by either buying or selling benefits. Although this type of system is more costly and time consuming to set up and administer it does allow employees to tailor their benefits to their own needs. So for example a company providing childcare vouchers as part of a fixed benefits package is worthless to those without children. In a flexible benefits system they could choose an alternative benefit of the same value which would be more useful to them. The other main advantage of offering flexible benefits is that employees gain an idea of the true worth of the benefits package that they receive. Many take benefits for granted such as pension and holidays but when the real cost is identified, a value is placed on them. However due to the cost of administration and the feasibility of offering a range of benefits, generally it is only organisations with over 5000 employees who tend to offer flexible benefits (CIPD 2008).

CASE STUDY

London Stock Exchange (LSE)

In 2003, LSE moved to a flexible benefits system for its 500 staff. The old benefit system was administration heavy, paper based and a 'one size fits all' benefit scheme. The newer flexible benefit scheme has been computerised and employees can choose the benefits that best suit their lifestyle each year. Benefits include a discretionary bonus linked to individual and company performance, a non-contributory pension scheme, a season ticket to cover travel expenses to work, private healthcare, life insurance, gym membership, company cars and season ticket loans. Employees can now see the value of their package and can choose what to have in the privacy and comfort of their own PC. Within the first year of its introduction, 95 per cent of staff changed the make up of their previous package. This is a strong indictor that a flexible benefit scheme had been welcomed by staff.

(Personnel Today 2003).

Voluntary benefits

Unlike flexible benefits where the cost of the benefits is paid for by the employer, with voluntary benefits the cost of the benefits are paid for by the employee. The advantage of offering them is that due to the size of the organisation they are often able to negotiate discounted rates. Some benefits can be paid for directly out of an employee's salary and by doing so are tax-exempt, for example as childcare vouchers, pension contributions and bicycle loans. As a result the opportunity to offer voluntary benefits can contribute to the overall package of reward for an employee and by doing so can enhance their image as an employer of choice.

There are three main types of voluntary benefits:

1 Health benefits such as discounted dental care and private medical insurance.
2 Financial benefits such as voluntary contributions to pension schemes or discounted holiday insurance.
3 Leisure/lifestyle benefits such as offers on gym membership, holiday offers, discount vouchers for restaurants, childcare vouchers and discounted shopping (CIPD 2009).

The most commonly offered being private medical insurance, life assurance, additional pension contributions and gym membership (Employee benefits, 2007).

1. What do you think are the advantages and disadvantages for offering both flexible benefits and voluntary benefits to employees?
2. What do you anticipate are likely to be the most attractive benefits in the future?

4.5 Non-financial rewards

If we refer back to the earlier theories on motivation, we have seen that people are motivated by a range of factors, many of which are not financial. For example, the Hawthorne experiments showed that people can be motivated just by feeling valued. It has increasingly been recognised that rewards don't necessarily always have to be financial. Non-financial benefits can be seen as rewarding.

Recognition

This is a very powerful type of reward, yet relatively simple to do. It is surprising then, that many managers don't thank or praise an employee for a job well done. Feedback on performance is very rewarding and public recognition can raise an employee's self-esteem. Some organisations go a step further and have an 'employee of the month' whose picture is displayed on the department notice board. Others print their picture in the in-house magazine or have an award ceremony. However it doesn't have to be that grand. Immediate, constructive feedback from a manager to an employee can increase an employee's confidence, motivation and status within an organisation.

Opportunities to develop skills

Giving employees ways and means to improve and develop their skills ensures their work experience is satisfying and self-enhancing. This can be learning on

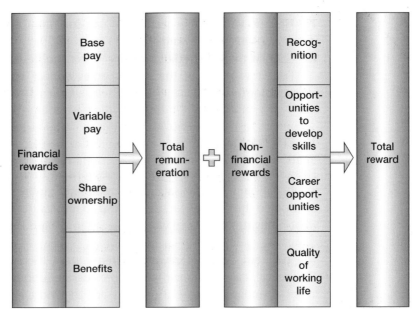

Figure 4.5 Total reward (Armstrong 2007, with the permission of the publisher, the Chartered Institute of Personnel and Development, London (www.cipd.co.uk))

W.L. Gore & Associates, a manufacturing firm producing waterproof clothing, has reaped the benefits of a total reward approach. Four times winner of *The Times* Best 100 Companies to Work For award, it offers its employees a combination of financial and non-financial rewards such as opportunities for personal growth, team spirit, flexible working, private healthcare, dental insurance and on-site massage.

Although many organisations offer a benefits package, not many are good at showing how the range of benefits are integrated in a total reward structure and then communicating this to their employees.

CASE STUDY

Nottingham City Council had recruitment and retention problems, when in 2005 it launched its 'works perks' benefits package. The benefits package was already in existence but by distributing a DVD and booklets listing all the benefits available, it served to communicate more clearly to employees what was on offer. The communication of the works perks package seemed to have paid off. Staff turnover dropped from 15 per cent to 9 per cent and there was an increase in the proportion of the local people employed by the Council (North 2008).

1. How do you think organisations can communicate to managers the value of non-financial rewards?
2. Look at the latest edition of *The Times* The Best 100 Companies to Work For. How many of these companies appear to operate a total reward package?

 ## 4.7 Summary

This chapter began with some suggestions as to why people work and why it is beneficial for organisations to create an employment relationship. It then considered the theoretical background to motivation and the need to consider what motivates people to work if we are to reward them appropriately.

The different types of reward systems were then outlined and discussed. Theoretical, case study and research evidence suggests that a combination of financial and non-financial rewards are the most effective means to ensure motivated employees. We saw how a total reward approach can be a very powerful tool in attracting, retaining and motivating the best employees.

KEY IDEAS

What motivates people at work?
- The study of motivation is concerned with why people behave in a certain way. Motivation is complex and many theories have been developed to try and explain what motivates people at work.
- Content theories of motivation focus on human needs related to motivation. These range from simple needs such as money, to more complex reasons such as the content of the job.
- Process theories of motivation try to identify the relationship between reward and motivation.

Financial rewards
- Basic pay can either be in the form of a spot rate or it is decided by where the job is placed on a scale. Job evaluation is the usual method of deciding where the job is placed.
- Variable pay is when employees can earn extra money on top of their basic pay. This may be due to results achieved because the employee met a target or merit pay where the individual or team are rewarded for good overall performance.
- Share ownership is a way in which employees can have a stake in the organisation and can be rewarded if it performs well.

Employee benefits
- Benefits are in addition to basic pay. An attractive benefits package can help to attract and retain the best employees. The most common benefit is a pension plan.

continued . . .

. . . continued

- Flexible benefits allow employees to choose their benefits so they can tailor them to their individual needs. Due to the complexity of administering flexible benefits these schemes tend to be found in larger organisations with over 5,000 employees.
- Voluntary benefits are paid for by the employee but employees can sometimes gain from discounted rates or tax exemptions.

Non-financial rewards

- Rewards don't always have to be financial in nature. Motivation theories suggests that people can also feel rewarded by non-financial rewards. Recognition, giving employees the opportunities to develop skills and enhance their careers, are all very powerful ways to motivate people.
- Increasingly, providing a good work-life balance is seen as rewarding as a high salary. Providing flexible ways of working both in place and time is highly valued by many employees.

Total reward

- Combining salary, financial and non-financial benefits in an integrated package for employees is termed as 'total reward'.
- Armstrong (2007) suggests a total reward approach creates a longer-lasting impact on motivation and commitment of employees while ensuring an effective way for an organisation to become an 'employer of choice'.

REFLECTIVE QUESTIONS

1 Why do you think so many theories have been written on motivation?
2 Explain why employers should concern themselves with producing an equitable reward structure.
3 Discuss why it is necessary for organisations to offer benefits in addition to a basic salary.
4 Imagine you had to justify the introduction of a total reward approach. What would you say?

RECOMMENDED READING

If you would like to learn more about some of the issues in the five sections within this chapter you might like to consider the following books and articles:

What motivates people at work?
David Buchanan and Andrzej Huczynski have written a detailed and easy to read chapter on motivation in their book *Organizational Behaviour*. Similarly Laurie Mullins' book, *Essentials of Organisational Behaviour*, also contains good illustrations and more detail of motivational theory.

Financial rewards

ACAS have produced some very readable guides on aspects of financial rewards including pay scales and job evaluation. Michael Armstrong's book *A Handbook of Employee Reward Management and Practice* is probably one of the most informative and authorative texts on this subject area.

Employee benefits

Angela Wright's book *Reward Management in Context* discusses employee benefits in detail and offers a number of different perspectives surrounding the debate about employee benefits. The CIPD have also produced fact sheets on employee benefits with supplementary fact sheets specifically on voluntary and flexible benefits. These can be accessed on their website www.cipd.co.uk

Non-financial rewards

Judith Leary-Joyce in her book *Becoming an Employer of Choice* discusses many examples of how non-financial rewards have assisted organisations to become one of the best companies to work for. It is an easy read, very insightful and based on extensive research from *The Times* The Best 100 Companies to Work For.

Total reward

The Income Data Service has produced comprehensive information sheets on understanding total reward. They cover many of the components which make up a total reward structure and give guidelines for designing a total reward package.

USEFUL WEBSITES

www.acas.org.uk ACAS is an organisation devoted to preventing and resolving employment disputes. This site provides information on how to contact ACAS as well as online advisory information and case studies.

www.cabinetoffice.gov.uk/workforcematters/pay_and_rewards.aspx This website provides information and practical guidance on current and emerging workforce issues regarding pay and rewards in the public services.

www.cipd.co.uk The Chartered Institute of Personnel and Development is the United Kingdom's leading professional body for those involved in the management and development of human resources. Their website contains a variety of information ranging from research and reports to details of qualifications that are available to develop people involved in human resource management.

www.e-reward.co.uk The latest thinking and research in reward management is given on this website through a variety of forms such as electronic newsletters, journals and case studies.

www.statistics.gov.uk Free access to data produced by the Office for National Statistics and some data from government departments and devolved administrations.

REFERENCES

ACAS (2008) Advisory booklet – *Job evaluation: considerations and risks*, available at www.acas.org.uk
Armistead, L. (2002) 'Happiness is a bigger motivator than money', *The Sunday Times*, 14 July 2002.
Armstrong, M. (2007) *Employee Reward Management and Practice*. London: CIPD.
Buchanen, D., Huczynski, A. (2004) *Organizational Behaviour*. Harlow: Pearson Education Limited.

CIPD (2009) *Voluntary Benefits*. London: CIPD.

Chomka, S. (2005) 'No concerns over staff treatment here – this company's Innocent' 7 February 2005, 58. Available at www.foodmanufacture.co.uk

Employee Benefits (2007). Voluntary benefits and salary sacrifice research 2007. Available at www.employeebenefits.co.uk

Hackman, J., Oldham, G. (1976) 'Motivation through the design of work: test of a theory', *Organizational Behavior and Human Performance*, vol. 16, 250–79.

Income Data Services (2006) Tower Hamlets Council. *IDS HR Studies 820*, April 2006.

Income Data Services (2007) Sony UK Customer Information Centre. *IDS HR Studies 843,* April 2007.

Income Data Services (2008) London Allowances. *IDS HR Studies* 882, November 2008. Available at www.idshrstudies.com if you subscribe.

Income Data Services (2009a) British Museum. *IDS HR Studies* 894, May 2009.

Income Data Services (2009b) Ladbrokes. *IDS HR Studies* 886, January 2009.

Mercer (2008) *Global Total Reward Survey*. Available at www.imercer.com/products/global-total-rewards.aspx

Mullins, L. (2008) *Essentials of Organisational Behaviour*. Harlow: Prentice Hall.

North, S. (2008) Nottingham City Council. *People Management*, April 2008.

Personnel Today (2003) 'Valuing staff benefits at just one click of a mouse', *Personnel Today* 18 February 2003.

Reis, D., Pena, L. (2001) 'Reengineering the Motivation to Work', *Management Decision*, vol. 39, no. 8, 666–75.

Roberts, Z. (2003) Learning leads the way, *People Management*, 6 November 2003, 34. (Subscription required for any articles over a month old.)

Scase, R. (2007) *Global Remix: the fight for competitive advantage*. London: Kogan Page.

Thomas, D. (2006) 'Asda to allow unpaid leave for football fanatics', *Personnel Today* 24 April 2006.

Wright, A. (2004) *Reward Management in Context*. London: CIPD.

5 Employee relations

'Those who cannot learn from history are doomed to repeat it'

(George Santayana)

CHAPTER OUTLINE

5.1 Introduction
5.2 What is or are employee relations?
5.3 The nature of employment rules
5.4 Employee relations as the study of the employment relationship
5.5 What next?
5.6 Employee involvement
5.7 Employee relations: change and possible futures
5.8 Summary

CHAPTER OBJECTIVES

- Appreciate the changing nature of employee relations in Britain and the reasons for these changes
- Appreciate the shifting concerns of employee relations and the renewed interest in the employment relationship as the appropriate focus of study in employee relations
- Understand the concept of an industrial or employee relations system and how this can help us analyse developments in the area
- Understand the significance of employee involvement for contemporary employee relations together with its potential to help secure change in organisations
- To appreciate different interests and positions in employee relations and develop awareness of the issues involved in managing effective change in modern organisations

5.1 Introduction

It is probably true to say that of all the elements that are part of human resource management none has experienced as much change over the past thirty years as the area of employee relations. Indeed, if you were to be transported back into the workplace of the 1970s you would immediately be confronted by a world that in important respects would be quite alien to the one you are familiar with. For a start you would be talking about something called 'industrial relations', reflecting the fact that many more of us worked in 'industry'. You would most probably be observing an organisation where many people were members of **trade unions** and where these played a key role in the management of people, exerting considerable influence on people's daily working lives. If you were in industry you would also have been working in a world that was populated mainly by men, working full-time for at least 40 hours a week – 'the male breadwinner'. This was also a world where the vast majority of us had our most important terms and conditions of employment (pay, hours, holidays) determined by something called 'collective bargaining'.

To illustrate the extent of change Table 5.1 draws on survey data to detail some of the main indicators of change in Britain from 1980 until 2004.

Trade unions and collective bargaining

For much of the period after 1945 until the late 1970s these were seen as the core elements in what was generally understood as industrial relations in Britain and many other industrialising countries. The focus was very much on collective relations between 'the two sides of industry'. Employers and their representatives on the one side, and trade unions; as 'collective, organised associations of working people formed for the protection and promotion of common interests' on the other. Underpinning these collective relations was a form of **industrial pluralism** (see Chapter 1) which treated the workplace as largely independent of the wider society, acknowledging different interests between the two sides and emphasising how such differences could be resolved. In practice, this model advocated the resolution of differences through the mechanism of **collective bargaining**; negotiation between employers representatives and trade unions; the fulcrum of the industrial relations system (see discussion of Dunlop below).

KEY TERMS

Collective bargaining The process of joint decision-making through negotiation between two or more parties, normally involving employers or their representatives and trade unions, and backed up by the potential to use economic sanctions.

Industrial pluralism The theory that acknowledges different interests coexisting within organisations and in particular between capital and labour, although such differences are not necessarily rooted in class.

Shop stewards Workplace union representatives – normally elected – who play a key role in the maintenance of union organisation and activity inside organisations.

Trade unions 'organised associations of work people formed for the protection and promotion of common interests' (Webbs 1891).

This collectivist model was supported by public policy (Government) initiatives that provided legal support to trade unions and collective bargaining. Despite coming under strain in Britain in the 1960s and 1970s, it was not until the changed economic and political contexts of the 1980s and 1990s that we see a significant dismantling of collective industrial relations in Britain.

The data in Table 5.1 provides a striking set of comparisons. Britain's continuing shift from a manufacturing to a post-industrial, service-based economy is evident from the table and associated with this is both a growing **flexibilisation** and **feminisation** of work and employment. Furthermore, the table shows clearly that this shift in the form, nature and location of work has been associated with a substantial erosion of the established pillars of collective industrial relations as measured by the conventional indicators of trade union strength, and of the importance of collective bargaining.

KEY TERMS

Feminisation In employment relations this refers to the growing employment of women, normally in specific sectors and occupations, so that it may be possible to talk about occupations having become feminised over time.

Flexibilisation To make more flexible, normally used in terms of work, working patterns and employment generally.

However, these headline changes mask important variations between groups and across sectors, and for some people at work trade unions and collective bargaining remain important, for example those who work in the public sector. It is also important to note that in a number of other

Dimension	1980	2004
Trade union membership	12.95 million	6.7 million
Trade union density (%)	53.6	28.8
% Workplaces recognising trade unions	64	38
Numbers shop stewards (WIRS/ WERS estimate)	328,000	128,000
Collective bargaining coverage (%)	75	39
% Workplaces with any collective bargaining	66	32
Numbers of strikes	1330	130
Numbers employed in manufacturing	6.7 million	3.28 million
Numbers employed in services	15.36 million	21.47 million
Women as % of all in employment	43.2	49.9
Numbers working part-time (and as % of all employed)	3.9 million	7.4 million
Sources: TUM, TUD, Burchill, F. (2007); % workplaces recognising trade unions, shop steward numbers and collective bargaining data from Brown et al (2009); manufacturing and service sector employment – ONS; women as % of all employment data relates to employee jobs – ONS; strike data – ONS; numbers working part-time – ONS (2004) and Hakim (2004) for 1980.		

Table 5.1 Change in employee relations

countries, particularly within Europe, some of what we have described as part of collective industrial relations continues to be both established and influential. It is certainly the case that in many mainland European countries, it remains normal for managers who wish to bring about change at the workplace to have to negotiate such changes with trade unions or worker representatives.

Before we proceed further it is worth pointing out that there is also an influential body of opinion that argues that the extent of change has been exaggerated. That some areas have experienced limited change and that the essential nature of the employment relationship between those who provide work and those who perform it, has changed little and certainly far less than figures on trade union membership and collective bargaining coverage would suggest (Ackers and Wilkinson 2004, Brown and Edwards 2009, Marsden

2004). As we will see, these writers have been particularly influential in recasting the subject matter of industrial or employee relations in terms of the employment relationship.

 ## 5.2 What is or are employee relations?

So far we have said something about the nature of collective industrial relations but as we have seen the props for this have gradually been removed and in its place it has become common to use the terms employee or employment relations. Perhaps confusingly, many writers use the terms employee relations and industrial relations interchangeably, whereas others suggest the change in terminology reflects a deeper change in the way in which the area has evolved. Certainly, Table 5.1 indicates the extent of change in aspects of industrial relations and it is certainly the case that 'bargaining power' over the period in question – the extent to which certain groups can secure their objectives through their ability to mobilise resources – has shifted in many workplaces in favour of employers. As we shall see, one result of this has been that managers have more scope to make changes at work and are more able to do so unilaterally – that is without having to negotiate with workers or their representatives. It follows that if there is an important difference between industrial and employee relations, for many this lies in the emphasis placed on the role of management in determining how employment is regulated. We return to this theme below.

To try and set the scene we will begin by discussing probably the most influential theoretical contribution to the study of industrial relations and use this as a basis for the remainder of the chapter. In 1958, John Dunlop, an American academic published his ideas on an 'industrial relations system', arguing that like other systems there were inputs which were transformed into outputs. In doing so he provided the 'nuts and bolts' of the subject which has largely framed the study of industrial relations for most of the subsequent period. A simple representation of Dunlop's 'systems' framework is provided below in Figure 5.1.

In Dunlop's framework the contexts operate on what he calls the 'actors' in the system. Dunlop's approach is pluralist (see Chapter 1), accepting that the 'actors' have different interests and that they make choices about how these different interests are resolved. For Dunlop, industrial relations is about employment regulation (see below), with regulation possible through a number of 'processes'. He also acknowledges that although the processes can produce rules, sometimes conflicts arise because there is a failure to agree rules. Like other systems approaches, Dunlop's model incorporates feedback – the outcomes can influence the attitudes and behaviours of the actors, and

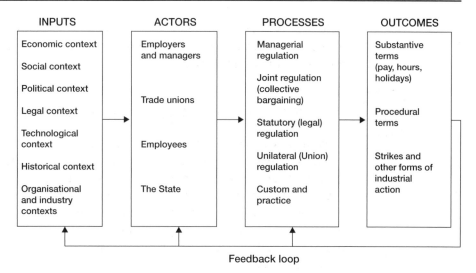

Figure 5.1 Dunlop's systems framework

through these, the processes and outcomes for the future. In extreme cases the outcomes may affect the inputs, as in the case study that follows.

CASE STUDY

The 1984/85 miners' strike

In February 1984 the National Coal Board (NCB) and the Government of the day made the decision to close a large number of what they termed 'uneconomic pits'. The decision precipitated the longest and most bitter strike in recent British history between the union (the NUM) and the NCB, the legacy of which still affects many mining communities today (Bradley 2008).

In terms of Dunlop's framework a number of key political changes are relevant. A Government under Margaret Thatcher was unsympathetic to the industry, to the unions generally and to the miners' leader Arthur Scargill in particular. The Government had already introduced laws to curb the power of unions and make certain forms of industrial action unlawful. It was also committed to a programme of privatisation, including the electricity generating industry, the NCB's major customer. There was also some history between the miners and previous Conservative governments, with a major set piece confrontation in 1974 leading to electoral defeat for the then Conservative government. In 1984 the miners leaders clearly believed they could win again, with the government equally determined to ensure that this would not happen.

The political and economic contexts had changed – coal was no longer the energy source of choice and alternatives meant that miners did not have the same bargaining power as they had in the past. Power stations had also stockpiled coal prior to the start of the strike and had secured significant supplies from other countries. In the end, the miners returned to work in the summer of 1985 having achieved none of their demands and it is generally accepted that the failure of the miners to secure concessions had a major impact on strike activity in the economy more generally – if the miners were

continued . . . ▶

◀ *. . . continued*

Figure 5.2 1984/85 miners' strike

unable to do it, how could we? When Ian McGregor, the then Chairman of the NCB, was asked after the strike had ended what had been achieved his response was telling: 'There was no way I was going to let their (NUM's) leadership stand in the way of establishing management's right to manage. From now on there didn't need to be any ritual genuflection to the NUM, every time we want to do anything' (McGregor 1986, 237, 358).

In terms of Dunlop's framework, the inputs had changed which affected the approach of the actors. For the NUM, the NCB had ignored established joint procedures to consider coal mine closures, preferring instead to make decisions without consultation or negotiation. The strike then had longer-term consequences for the future. Within the industry, the NUM was marginalised and with a massive closure programme introduced, lost huge numbers of members and changes took place to processes which affected future outcomes. The wider repercussions affected strike activity in the industry and elsewhere, but also influenced subsequent public policy, including legislation.

Ultimately the industry was privatised in 1995, at which point it employed around 10 000 miners (from over 200,000 in 1982), in 16 pits (170 in 1984). Today there are fewer than 6,000 working in the industry.

Following Dunlop's contribution, the 1960s and 1970s saw industrial relations emerge not only as a serious subject of academic study in Britain but also one of public policy interest and concern. In Britain, Dunlop's work had particular influence on the so-called 'Oxford School', who in turn helped to define the essential concerns of industrial relations: that it was about a system of employment rules, 'how these were made, how they were changed and how they were administered' (Flanders and Clegg 1954).

The 'Oxford School' and the Donovan Commission

So-called because of their work together at Oxford in the 1950s and 1960s, the key individuals, Allan Flanders, Hugh Clegg, Alan Fox and William McCarthy had a profound influence on the development of the academic study of industrial relations in Britain and on developments in public policy. At the time strongly wedded to the ideas of industrial pluralism the group's influence reached its peak in the mid 1960s when they were all in various ways involved with the Royal Commission on Trade Unions and **Employers' Associations** established by the then Labour Government (the so-called Donovan Commission). Clegg and Flanders were members of the Commission, McCarthy was its research director and Fox contributed to a number of research papers. The Donovan Report, as it has become known, remains a classic of pluralist industrial relations thinking, arguing strongly that any problems of industrial relations were amenable to reform by the parties themselves. Heavily influenced by the ideas of the 'Oxford School' the Commission was generally opposed to legal regulation of industrial relations, advocating that management and trade unions should be free to resolve their own issues, albeit with a strong 'steer' from the Commission. As for collective bargaining, this needed to be reformed but in the Commission's view it remained the proper method for conducting industrial relations.

KEY TERMS

Employers' Associations Employers that grouped themselves together to form associations originally to negotiate with trade unions.

1. Pluralists generally believe that the state should keep its involvement in employee relations to a minimum, leaving the parties (management and unions) to resolve their own differences, for example through collective bargaining. What do pluralists see as the dangers of too much involvement of the state in employee relations?
2. Because pluralists accept that there are different interests at work and that these need to be acknowledged and resolved, why do they see trade unions as such a necessary part of employee relations?

3. After the miner's strike Ian McGregor made a very revealing comment about managerial prerogative (see case study on the miner's strike). What do you understand by this term and why do you feel some managers are still willing to recognise the need for, and legitimacy of, joint decision-making in some areas of business?

4. Link the data in Table 5.1, with the Dunlop's framework in section 5.2. Using this data, and your knowledge of changes taking place in Britain at the time, identify the factors that you feel account for the shift away from collective bargaining and collective employee relations more generally over this period.

(5.3) The nature of employment rules

As we noted in the discussion of Dunlop's framework, the rules in question are of two types:

- **substantive** – How much were you to be paid? How many days holiday? How many hours would you work?
- **procedural** – the processes by which rules were to be made and administered, which could cover negotiating, disputes, discipline, grievance.

In principle these rules could be made and administered in a number of ways, these could be via

1 **Management regulation** – senior managers made, changed and administered rules themselves. This links to an important concept in employee relations of managerial prerogative – 'management's right to manage' (Purcell 1991). The quote from Ian McGregor earlier is a good illustration of this position. In any organisation at least some rules are made this way, but in some, other methods are important, most notably joint regulation.

2 **Joint regulation** – through collective bargaining. Management and trade unions negotiate together to reach an agreement on rules. In the late 1970s as many as three-quarters of all employees in the UK had at least some of their terms and conditions determined this way. Today, the figure is less than 40 per cent and is mainly confined to those working in the public or ex-public sector (BT, British Airways, British Gas, railways for examples of organisations that used to be in the public sector). However, in mainland Europe, this still remains the most common method by which basic employment terms and conditions are determined and agreed. Indeed in most EU countries the numbers covered by a collective agreement remain at over 70 per cent of the workforce, and in some Scandinavian countries, over 90 per cent (Sweden, Norway).

3 **Legal regulation** – some rules come from legislation, for example health and safety and contract law, but more recently legislation has begun to

directly affect some substantive employment terms. For example the Working Time Regulations introduced a legal maximum for weekly working hours in the UK, minimum rest periods and a legal minimum holiday entitlement. Similarly the National Minimum Wage Act introduced a legally enforceable minimum wage for all workers.

These are the major forms of regulation, although to these we should add 'custom and practice', and unilateral regulation via trade unions. Nowadays unilateral regulation is rare and concerns formal rules made and enforced by workers or their agents (trade unions). However, it is not uncommon to find informal rules operated by workers and colluded with by management (see custom and practice below) and the sociology of work is full of examples of workers 'fixing' output, or maintaining working arrangements in defiance of the formal rules, but examples of formal rules being made this way are very unusual.

Custom and practice

Custom and practice is not a formal mechanism for rule-making but it is very important in employee relations. Such rules emerge informally and normally carry considerable worker support (see the BL 'washing-up time dispute' case study). For example, a contract of employment may state that you have a 15 minute tea-break in the morning and afternoon, but over time this has grown to 20 minutes and this has been tolerated by managers and supervisors. There has been no formal agreement but custom and practice has meant that 15 minutes is now 20. Clearly management could insist on enforcing the formal rule, but it would be advised to proceed with tact and care in changing this given the amount of workforce support there is for the 'customised' rule. An interesting illustration of the significance of custom and practice is provided by the example of the washing-up dispute below. This also underlines the important role played by history in employee relations.

CASE STUDY

British Leyland and the 'washing-up time dispute'

In the early part of 1983 a dispute arose at the company's Cowley plant in Oxford (a plant that today produces the Mini). The dispute concerned workers leaving the production line 15 minutes before the end of their shifts in order to clean up before going home. The company's view was that it was losing production of up to 100 cars a week as a result of this 'early finishing' and announced moves to introduce 'bell to bell' working. The union view was that as the workers got dirty in the company's time they should be able to clean up in the company's time and claimed that there had been an agreement dating back to the early 1920s that established the legitimacy of 'washing-up time', although no such agreement was ever found. From 1980 to 1983 'washing-up' time had been abolished at the company's other factories but Cowley held firm and when the company announced

continued . . . ▶

◀ . . . *continued*

its intention to remove the 'early finishing' at the plant the Cowley workforce of over 5,000 went on strike for a month to resist any changes to this. Eventually the company got its way and Cowley fell into line with other BL car plants although a legacy of distrust continued long after the dispute ended. However, for our purposes, the important point here is firstly, that the practice had operated for so long that most workers regarded it as established by custom and practice and secondly, the dispute illustrates the strength of feeling over an issue that workers had effectively established for themselves and which as a result provoked considerable resistance when attempts were made to remove it.

A more recent example of this concerns the treatment of staff absence from work. It is well-known that in some organisations staff absence is well above the average for the UK, examples include the NHS and the police service. Indeed a recent report revealed that 45,000 NHS workers call in sick every day (NHS Boorman 2009). This may be the result of a number of factors, for example a work environment that tends to encourage high levels of stress, and it would be surprising if this was not important in accounting for recorded absence, but it could also be that over long periods of time high levels of absence have been tolerated by management as 'part of the culture' of the organisation. It has become custom and practice. As with the BL example, a change in the way this is viewed by management, from a normal part of organisational life to an intolerable cost, is likely to challenge the custom and practice that has grown up and provoke a response from the workforce.

It should be emphasised at this point that what we are trying to do here is to understand why things happen in the way they do not to apportion blame to either side. In doing so we are trying to show how difficult it often is to change things, particularly where these have existed informally for such a long time. It also follows that changing these is likely to require careful handling and sensitivity as well as considerable people skills in order that a smooth transition to new working arrangements and understandings can be achieved.

If we accept this definition of the subject area, and note the data in Table 5.1, the past thirty years has seen as major shift in the ways rules are made, changed and administered. We have witnessed a sharp decline in both the extent and scope of joint regulation of terms and conditions particularly in the private sector, reflecting an even greater decline in trade union membership and influence.

In their place we have seen two main developments:

1 A marked increase in managerial regulation of the employment relationship (where managers determine the main terms and conditions of employment and how work is undertaken, as the BL example illustrates).

2 Greater legal regulation of the relationship. In the 1980s this was targeted at curbing trade union power but since the late 1990s has concerned itself more with establishing a further raft of individual employment rights, including a limited number of legally enforceable minimum substantive employment terms for workers.

This focus on employment rules as the main focus of the subject is important and helpful, but there has been an increasing influential view that this fails to capture the breadth of the subject matter and for many there has been a wish to return to 'first principles'. This has meant a shift from collective bargaining as the centrepiece of industrial relations towards the idea of employment relationships and their regulation as being central to employee relations and to an understanding of relations at work more generally (Edwards 2003).

1. Why do you feel that legal regulation of the employment relationship has become more important in recent years?
2. What examples of such legislation can you give?
3. What might be some of the issues for employers and employees in moving away from joint regulation of terms and conditions towards greater legal regulation?

Interlude: The radical perspective

Before proceeding further, a number of readers might at this point raise a concern that what we have discussed so far doesn't adequately capture the many ways in which employment is regulated. Certainly legislation is increasingly important, and collective bargaining remains important for many, particularly those in the public sector but employers do not regulate simply through formal rules. For example, corporate cultures often represent very effective means by which employers control and regulate the activities of staff (Ray 1986) and increasing use is made of CCTV and more subtle forms of surveillance often using teams (Sewell 1998). Moreover, managers as agents of employers have power and authority by virtue of their role and position.

At this point it is worth making reference to more radical perspectives on employee relations particularly those that draw inspiration from the work of Karl Marx. For radical writers, a key feature of employee relations and the world of work is the concept of control. The need for employers to regulate the employment relationship is for radicals about securing control, and for Marxists this is about control over the labour process. Put simply, the means by which employers and managers turn the potential of labour (staff) to produce goods and services into actual output and services. As Richard Hyman (1975) has defined it, industrial relations 'is the study of processes of control over relations'.

Clearly this is about a lot more than employment rules and encompasses broader issues of managerial power and authority as well as style and culture. It follows that for those in the radical tradition, employee relations is less about 'employment rules, how they are made, changed and administered' and much more about a contest for control. These contests, and the shifting of the so-called 'frontier of control' (Goodrich 1920) are for radicals the real stuff of industrial or employee relations.

The radical perspective reminds us that work and employment are infused with issues of power, domination and control. Furthermore, that these are unequally distributed, frequently skewed in favour of employers and that certain groups suffer repeated disadvantages both in work and in seeking and gaining access to work. In the remainder of this chapter we draw on insights from this perspective to help in building up a more complete picture of employee relations in industrial and post-industrial societies. We begin with what many see as a return to 'first principles'.

5.4 Employee relations as the study of the employment relationship

The 'first principles' in question are those surrounding the employment relationship. As Edwards (2003) has helpfully shown, the nature of this relationship carries with it important implications for employee relations. He begins by pointing out that the relationship is made up of two parts: 'Market relations and managerial relations . . . the former covers the price of labour, which embraces not only the basic wage but also hours of work, holidays and pension rights'.

He adds, drawing on the radical tradition, that although this makes labour like any other commodity 'labour differs form all other commodities in that it is enjoyed in use and is embodied in people. The "owner" of labour, the employer, has to persuade the worker . . . the person in whom the labour is embodied, to work. Managerial relations are the relationships that define how this process takes place: market relations set a price for a set number of hours of work, managerial relations determine how much work is performed in that time, at what specific task or tasks, who has the right to define the tasks and change a particular mix of tasks and what penalties will be deployed for any failure to meet these obligations' (2003: 8).

As we have noted at various points in this book, for most of us paid employment is a necessity. Once we have accepted the offer of a job we have entered an employment relationship with our employer. This relationship, is by definition one between employer and employee, potentially mediated by employee associations (such as trade unions) and the state (Edwards 2003), and has a number of dimensions:

1 Economic (pay),
2 Legal (contractual)
3 Social (groups and work colleagues)
4 Psychological (many dimensions but the psychological contract is an important element, includes issues of fairness and justice)
5 Political (with a small 'p' – it is a relationship of power)

The relationship operates both individually and collectively: it is more than just a psychological contract, we share common experiences and often, common terms and conditions. How these dimensions 'play out' at work will clearly have an impact on us as individual workers and as members of a group – a workforce, shaping our identity at work and affecting how we perceive work, colleagues and managers (see discussion of fairness and workplace justice below and in Chapter 8). However, what is important is that once we focus on the employment relationship we broaden the focus of study beyond one just concerned with employment rules, even though a central concern of employee relations is how this relationship is regulated.

KEY TERMS

Individualism Again in the terms used by Purcell (1998) it is directing attention to how employers manage the individual employee. Some have suggested that the term *individualisation* is a better description of a shift away from collective arrangements towards personalised employment agreements and a reduced role for unions in determining the content of employment contracts.

An employment relationship

Imagine that you have been offered a job by an organisation and you have decided to accept it. As soon as you have accepted the job, you have entered into an employment relationship with your employer. That relationship has formal elements, the most important of these being a legal relationship that lays down your basic terms and conditions of employment. Some of these will be determined between you and your employer (normally these are stipulated by your employer and you are formally free to accept these or not, but in general by agreeing to work on the terms stipulated you are deemed to have accepted these), others will be determined in some workplaces by agreements between the employer and recognised trade unions. These elements will also reflect terms in other formal documents, for example those in your job description.

The informal elements of the employment relationship link to the ways rules operate in practice (which of course relates to our earlier discussion of custom and practice), the culture and climate of the organisation and how you *experience* the work environment. Crucially this will be influenced greatly by the relationship you have with and the treatment you receive from your immediate manager. Once inside the organisation you are subject to an *authority relationship* between yourself and your manager who in theory can instruct you to do what he or she wants you to do so long as this is lawful, reasonable and within your job description. How the manager interprets this relationship in terms of style, support and encouragement will clearly have an impact on your motivation and feelings towards the organisation. Of course, other factors will also have a bearing on this including your relationship with your immediate work colleagues, and we should not forget the contribution of the effort bargain (see below) – How hard will I have to work to earn my salary? How will I feel at the end of each day, and each week?

An alternative but related way of looking at this is to view the relationship as one between effort and reward, that once we join an organisation a kind of effort bargain is struck up between ourselves and those we work for. The idea of an effort bargain has been long-established within the sociology of work (Behrend 1957) but has been largely absent from the HRM literature which has tended to focus on the individual psychological contract. Although the latter is important, as we have noted, by its very nature it tends to neglect the collective dimension of work and work contexts.

The value of looking at employee relations through the lens of the employment relationship and effort bargain or wage-effort exchange (Baldamus 1961) is that it allows us to focus on key features of employment and place them into a wider context. This wider context is firstly that employment relationships exist within organisations and are shaped by relationships of power between those who employ people and those they employ. These in turn are affected by broader external factors as well as by an organisation's own objectives and priorities. Second, they are shaped by factors outside organisations: by broader economic, political and legal changes, such as recession, inflation, a change of government or new legislation. Figure 5.3 comes from work on the employment relationship undertaken on behalf of the CIPD. It identifies the dimensions of the relationship, behind which are the range of influences we have identified above.

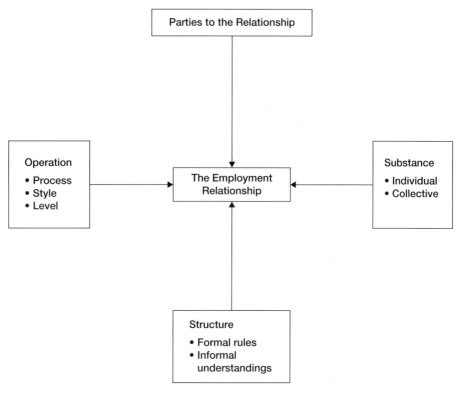

Figure 5.3 The employment relationship (Undy and Kessler 1997, with the permission of the publisher, the Chartered Institute of Personnel and Development, London (www.cipd.co.uk))

Figure 5.3 emphasises that the main dimensions are:

1 **The parties** – normally management, employees and for some, trade unions.
2 **The structure** – the relationship is made up of formal rules (around pay and conditions and other employment rules) and informal understandings that we have identified under the heading of 'custom and practice'.
3 **The operation** – it operates in different ways at different levels and is affected by development and outcomes at these levels as well as being affected by the style of management in terms of how it is viewed and operates.
4 **The substance** – the content of the relationship which has collective elements, for example from collective agreements, and individual elements, linked to rewards, the job and careers.

The main point is these dimensions can change because of external developments or changing priorities within an organisation and these can bring about change in the employment relationship and the 'effort bargain'. For example, pressure to increase sales and profits, or to achieve efficiency savings may lead to those running organisations to seek ways to 'get more from people', and in doing so alter the balance between effort and reward. In terms of our diagram, it may lead to measures to tighten formal rules (on attendance as at Tesco, or charging mobile phones, as at Ryanair), to reduce the scope for custom and practice (as at BL) or to reduce the extent of joint regulation of the employment relationship. In response workers may well seek to redress the balance collectively or individually, to compensate for what they see as an increase in effort by trying to secure improvement in employment terms; improve their pay, work fewer hours, or secure larger bonuses. The important point is that these relationships are dynamic, they change and when they change they have the potential to create issues for the management of staff, both individually and collectively.

What has happened to conflict?

If pluralists are correct in their view about the employment relationship and the potential for conflict how do we reconcile this with the historically low levels of conflict that we witness today? Most of those involved in employee relations would make the distinction between two sets of factors

- Latent conflict (where conflict remains hidden and under the surface) and manifest conflict (where it is observable in terms of open and visible expressions of discontent)
- Organised v unorganised conflict – this links closely with collective and individual expressions of discontent.

In terms of recent developments, as Table 5.1 indicated, there has been a marked decline in organised collective forms of conflict such as strikes but individual expressions of discontent though claims to Employment Tribunals have reached unprecedented levels in recent years. In the context of the decline in collective employee relations, this should not be surprising, but it is striking how the balance between individual and collective forms of conflict has shifted over the past twenty years, particularly in the private sector.

Definition of employee relations

At this point it might be valuable to take stock of where these insights take us in terms of a definition of employee relations. Although he uses slightly different terminology, Rose (2001) provides a definition that is sensitive both to the employment relationship and to the concerns of earlier writers. For him, 'employment relations is the study of the regulation of the employment relationship between employer and employee, both collectively and individually, and the determination of substantive and procedural issues at industrial, organisational and workplace levels' (Rose 2001: 6).

The employment relationship and a life outside work

Although this definition takes us forward it still contains much of the language of a closed system, and therefore concentrates largely on what takes place within organisations. The role of contexts is implicit rather than explicit here but a further concern is that the definition ignores the fact that people have lives outside work and that these lives might impact on what happens in work. Ackers (2002) for example has argued persuasively for a greater appreciation of the impact of the home and non-work factors (leisure, social activities) on employee relations, particularly the connection between work and family. In a world where many more women now work and where the work-life agenda has become an established political concern, Ackers suggests that ignoring what happens outside work, and how individuals balance the demands of work and family is to ignore an increasingly important issue and one that often gives rise to considerable strain and anxiety. His argument is essentially for a broadening out of the influences on the employment relationship and indeed the subject matter of employee relations, one which in his view would allow for a greater understanding and insight into what takes place in the workplace.

To these concerns we would also add a greater awareness and appreciation of other *identities* that enter the workplace. Work may once have been an opportunity for the 'male breadwinner' to express his occupational identity – as a carpenter, joiner, engineer, accountant, technician, teacher – but the 'gender blindness' of this world has been at least partly replaced by a greater sensitivity to the diversity of the contemporary workplace. Gender and work-life balance issues inevitably play out here but so too do issues of race, ethnicity, religion, disability and sexual orientation, and all carry implications for the conduct of employee relations.

 ## What next?

If we accept this reappraisal of employee relations as being about the study of employment relationships how far does this take us in understanding what employee relations is about? Individuals join organisations with certain prior orientations and expectations and whether these are strengthened or violated by their experience of their own employment relationship will owe much to how they are treated, how their concerns are listened to and whether they feel rewards are fair, commensurate with the work they undertake. As we have emphasised already this suggests that management plays a potentially key role in how the employment relationship is experienced by workers and as a result the extent to which they may be interested, loyal, engaged or demotivated and disaffected.

1. Flexible working has become an increasingly important for organisations in discussions about work–life balance. What do you understand by the term 'flexible working' and what are some of the practical employee relations issues that the operation of this is likely to mean for employers?
2. What issues might be raised for the effective management of employee relations by an increasingly diverse workforce?

Conflict and cooperation

One of the central concerns of pluralist and radical perspectives on employee relations has been to acknowledge that both conflict and cooperation lie at the heart of the employment relationship. So that in contrast with the unitarism often associated with HRM, employee relations addresses the messy realities of working relations, that people have different interests and that these interests may lead to conflict, often hidden but sometimes open disagreements and clashes may arise. As we have noted elsewhere, this points to the need for managers to have a broader understanding of the politics of working relations and for a particular skills set that acknowledges different interests and the legitimacy of conflicts that may arise as a result of these differences.

Sophisticated unitarism?

At this point some of you might well counter this by arguing that 'some organisations clearly operate a unitarist approach to managing staff, not a pluralist one', and that in any case unitarism covers a huge variety of different styles of managing staff. Using a typology developed by Purcell (1993), we can distinguish between what he terms the 'traditionalists' (very little HRM and often strong opposition to any union organisation, found in a number of smaller firms), paternalists (family-based organisations with a strong tradition of familial relations with staff) and those he describes as pursuing a 'sophisticated human relations' (investing heavily in people management, enabling trade unions to be kept at bay and promoting a 'one company' view with a very strong culture). We would suggest that in the case of the last category in particular, these organisations are acutely aware of conflicts, but work extraordinarily hard to address them. Examples would include companies like M&S, Virgin and IBM which emphasise not just favourable terms and conditions of employment but also careful and systematic processes of recruitment, selection and induction of staff which help to screen out those with 'less appropriate attitudes and orientation'. To these could be added the attention paid to succession planning, and to training and development.

An important point here is the recognition that although conflicts are a natural and normal product of employment relationships, there is also the hope and expectation that many of these relationships will be long term – what are sometimes called relational contracts. It follows that to stand a chance of securing a long-term relationship requires managers in organisations to recognise the potential sources of conflict and address these, not to ignore them.

It also requires managers to emphasise the positives – to stress the cooperative aspects of the employment relationship, the areas of potential agreement rather than areas of disagreement, something that has become far more common in recent years (Kochan and Osterman 1994). We can see this in government attempts to encourage *partnership* at work, and within the European Union the roles and responsibilities assigned to the *Social Partners*, meaning employers and trade unions. A number of well-known companies have signed 'partnership agreements' with trade unions to try and signify a change in approach to managing employee relations or to underline an approach they wish to promote to staff and customers. These may have attracted the headlines but at the workplace a quieter but perhaps more significant change has been taking place that can be linked to the rise of HRM.

Work in the USA and Britain has helped to develop and refine the AMO framework (Ability, Motivation and Opportunity, Appelbaum et al. 2000) which has provided a rationale for various forms of **employee involvement** (EI) as well as for experiments with high involvement and high commitment management techniques. Of these it is the developments in EI that have probably had most significance.

KEY TERMS

Employee involvement In general it is about the creation of an environment, together with specific initiatives to enable people to have an impact on decisions and actions that affect them in their jobs. This may range from informing staff, through to seeking their views on issues through to sharing of decisions and joint control.

Employee engagement A combination of commitment to an organisation and its values plus a willingness to help out colleagues (CIPD 2009). It is something an employee has to offer, it cannot be required as part of the contract.

Employee involvement (EI)

Returning to our factory of the 1960s and 1970s it would not have been unusual to have turned up for work and if vacancies were available to find a sign outside the factory saying 'Hands Required'. The 'Hands' in question were of course potential recruits but the significant point was that in the factory of the time this was all that was required of the person – manual skills. The vacancy board said it all, we are not interested in the whole person but in a part of that person.

As we have noted at various points in this book, it has been suggested that modern organisations require significantly more than this and that if they are to be successful they need to tap into the thoughts and ideas of their staff. If 'people really are our most important asset' then we need to 'mine the gold in their heads' in order to compete effectively in today's world. It follows that we need to seek ways of securing people's 'buy-in' to their work and to engage them more effectively. One of the major ways in which this takes place in organisations is through what we now term *employee involvement* defined as: 'A concerted attempt by employers to find participative ways in which to manage their staff by investing in human capital' (Marchington et al. 2001).

To try and illustrate this point we will use the example of customer service.

Customer service

As we have noted above, it is often argued that what is different about the world of work today is the importance placed on the customer. At work we are often encouraged to think of everyone as 'our customer' and in an economy where three-quarters of us work in the service sector often dealing directly or indirectly with customers it is easy to see why. Moreover, it is often the front-line staff (check-out operators, customer service staff in banks, receptionists, telephone call operators, teachers, nurses) who have direct contact with customers and receive feedback (positive and negative) who have immediate knowledge of how customers are feeling about products, service, store layout and facilities.

It is clearly in the interests of those who run organisations to try and 'tap into' this knowledge and this is where employee involvement comes in. Some examples of employee involvement are provided on pages 137–8.

Forms of employee involvement

Following the work of Marchington and his colleagues it is possible to identify a number of initiatives that fall under the 'umbrella' of employee involvement.

Figure 5.4 The 'customer' is important

These have a number of elements in common; first they tend to be initiated by managers, second they are what are often termed 'direct' forms of involvement in that they operate directly between management and staff not indirectly through representatives, and third, they tend to operate at the task level, that is the level at which work is actually carried out. The main forms of EI for our purposes are as follows:

- Teamworking – work organised around teams of workers
- Team briefing (cascading) – information cascaded from top to bottom via team meetings
- Direct communication – communication not via a third party, can include one-to-one meetings
- Suggestion schemes – voluntary schemes for seeking employee views on change
- Problem-solving groups
- Quality circles (or quality improvement circles) – linked to continuous improvement of quality

- TQM (total quality management)
- ESOPS (employee share ownership schemes – financial participation)

For example, if we were managing a retail store we may want to build in team meetings at set times in a week, or encourage feedback through suggestion schemes where staff are encouraged to offer ideas for improvement. We may want more face-to-face meetings with staff, introduce a regular staff forum where new ideas for store layout or new initiatives can be discussed and aired and generally consider how we might wish to develop our communications both with staff and with customers. All of these might have the benefit of allowing managers to better understand customer requirements but at the same time provide a way in which staff can feel more involved in the business.

1. From the discussion above, and your knowledge of motivation theory, how do you think employee involvement might contribute to a more motivated, satisfied and productive workforce?
2. In your opinion, why have many of the most recent developments in employee involvement been (a) direct forms of involvement, and (b) targeted at the task level in organisations?

At this point some of you may feel that this amounts to a shift in the effort bargain that changes the nature and terms of the employment relationship. Furthermore, some staff may see this disturbance of the effort bargain as of sufficient magnitude to force a re-evaluation, so that they respond by leaving, absenting themselves or some other form of action. Alternatively, some of you may raise the concern that any ideas that are generated may be completely unsuitable, or that sensible ideas may be ignored. Of course, these things happen and one way managers can reduce the chances of the first happening is by placing clear boundaries on suggestions. Rather than giving staff a 'free rein' to air their views, managers provide a 'steer' on what they expect. In terms of the second, all the evidence suggests that if you invite people to contribute to ideas, you raise expectations and staff understandably assume that things will happen on the basis of their involvement. This is an argument again for careful management of employee involvement and an awareness of some of the dangers involved in such initiatives if managers do not go into these things 'with their eyes open'.

Involvement and engagement?

Currently, one of the biggest issues facing organisations is that of securing engagement from employees. A theme running through much of the HRM literature has been that of organisations seeking to gain loyalty and possibly commitment of their staff. As a number of writers have pointed out, there are considerable difficulties with both of these concepts – loyalty and commitment to what or to whom, whether it is appropriate or reasonable for organisations to ask for either or both of these and the fact that in the case of commitment, there are different types of commitment and it is not always clear what organisations are seeking and from whom.

There has also been a realisation that in a world in which employment relationships are becoming increasingly diverse (varieties of working hours, flexible working arrangements, part-time working, temporary working), that rather than loyalty and commitment, what managers may be seeking are workers who engage with their work. However, this realisation has been tempered by an acknowledgement that the business-driven agenda of much of contemporary HRM has, by putting business needs first, served in some cases to undermine moves to secure **employee engagement** (Truss et al. 2006). As the CIPD put it: 'Engagement is an idea whose time has come . . . it represents an aspiration that employees should understand, identify and commit themselves to the objectives of the organisation they work for . . . For employee relations specialists, it means being more strategic and seeing the "bigger picture". . . but ultimately it may also mean asserting more strongly the employee interest and agenda. This may not fit well with a management culture still based on "command and control": it's a genuinely transformational message' (CIPD 2005).

1. Do you feel it is reasonable for employers to expect people to engage with their work and organisations? Give reasons for your answer.
2. What might be the benefits of doing so for them, their organisations and employee relations? What might be the costs?

And justice in the workplace?

The quote from the CIPD also suggests that there may be considerable resistance to some employee relations initiatives from long-standing and embedded management and workplace cultures. We return to this theme in our conclusion. Here we highlight a related issue that has also come to prominence in recent years.

In a recent study for the Work Foundation, Paul Edwards, a leading figure in academic and policy debates on employee relations has emphasised the importance of workplace justice as a policy objective and the importance of an effective employee voice as a means to contribute to this and to improvements in productivity (Edwards 2007: 40). This view argues that while the trend towards more individualistic management approaches in employee relations may make it easier for managers to manage 'as they see fit', it can neglect the collective dimension of work and the workplace. Furthermore, by potentially neglecting this collective 'voice', workers become disempowered and unable to make an effective contribution to workplace governance.

Edwards' point is that a key issue for organisations has become the promotion of workplace justice – both in terms of the rights of employees but also in terms of the benefits that this can bring to organisational performance. He draws on the work of Budd (2004), arguing that employment relations systems need to balance efficiency, equity and voice. Workplace justice focuses on the last two, defined by Edwards as 'the combination of employment *rights* and effective voice', adding that such a combination is achieved most effectively through consultation arrangements or negotiation with trade unions, or both (2007: 3).

There are a couple of points worth making here. First, there is now a considerable body of evidence that suggests that despite a growing raft of employment rights in the UK, knowledge of these rights and the ability to defend them tends to be mainly confined to unionised workplaces. That is, that in the absence of a collective voice, many of these are ineffective and largely theoretical rights (Brown and Oxenbridge 2004). Second, that the themes outlined by Edwards have been echoed in recent public policy initiatives, both nationally and within the EU. A specific illustration of this has been the passing of the Information and Consultation Directive (2002), and the subsequent UK legislation in the form of the Information and Consultation of Employees Regulations (2004) introduced in phases between 2004 and 2007. Under these regulations employees in organisations with more than 50 employees can, in law, request that their organisations establish or make changes to, arrangements to inform and consult them about issues in their work organisations (BIS 2009). For some, this has the potential to usher in a works council system into the UK (along the lines of systems in many EU countries) and although there is considerable evidence of employers 'reviewing, modifying and introducing voluntary information and consultation arrangements' (Hall et al. 2008) there is currently limited evidence of a European-style transformation having taken place. This should not come as a great surprise, given the history of British management and the general reluctance to embrace initiatives that are felt to be imposed from outside. This is an issue we also return to in our concluding section and suggests that, as with the Edwards' proposals, employers need to see the benefits for them of such initiatives before they 'adapt and adopt' them.

CASE STUDY

Change and the legacy of history: the case of British Airways

Formed as a result of merger and brought under public ownership in 1974, BA was one of a number of national 'flag carriers' that dominated the airline industry in the 1970s. Its flagging reputation (the initials BA were said to stand for 'bloody awful') continued into the 1980s and efforts were made to achieve a major turnaround in performance and culture. The apparent success of these initiatives led the government to privatise a now profitable BA in 1987. However, while there had been much change at BA, this disguised the fact that it continued to operate long-standing features of collective industrial relations – a large number of trade unions, separate arrangements for collective bargaining, complex procedural arrangements for resolving individual and collective grievances and a history of industrial relations that had not always been harmonious.

An expanding market in the second half of the 1980s meant that the company could pursue its 'customer first', quality enhancement strategy based on distinctive customer service, with little disruption. Cabin crew appeared to enjoy the new emphasis, which gave them more responsibility and influence within the company as well as frequent training opportunities. However, by the early 1990s the trading context deteriorated and the company introduced cost cutting measures, targeting staff, which did much to undermine management-staff relations. These problems, and specifically the tension between the 'customer service' strategy and the perceived need to reduce the cost base have continued throughout the 1990s and into the twenty-first century and have intensified since the appointment of the current Chief Executive, Willie Walsh, in 2005.

Walsh came to BA with a reputation for cost-cutting. At his previous company, Aer Lingus, he had cut the workforce by a third and on joining BA pioneered a string of initiatives to reduce what he saw as its high cost base. These have continued since and have included redundancies, pay freezes, new pay and conditions deals for new recruits, attempts to reform the pension scheme as well as a succession of attempts to change working practices. Furthermore, the development of Terminal 5 at Heathrow was seen by Walsh as a key element in removing what he has described as outdated working practices for airport staff, and this was followed in 2008 by the new 'Open Skies' initiative, which allowed BA to fly direct to the US from airlines outside the UK. The potential significance of 'Open Skies' is that it permits the company to use staff in other countries (Spain, Italy for example) but for them not to be covered by UK collective agreements.

In late 2009, as part of its continued cost-cutting, BA found itself in a further dispute with its workforce over attempted changes to working practices and the introduction of new staff rotas. The company made a £298 million loss in the first six months of 2009, and threatened that if a negotiated agreement over changes could not be achieved, it would impose changes unilaterally from the middle of November. In the same month it announced a merger with Iberia, the Spanish airline, although the deal remains dependent on BA dealing with aspects of its pensions deficit (which at year end 2009 stood at over £2,000 million).

1. To what extent do you feel BA is a 'prisoner of its past' in terms of employee relations?
2. Why do you feel that employee relations retain the potential for so much conflict at BA? Does the strategy being pursued by the company make such conflict more likely? Give reasons for your answer.

5.7 Employee relations: change and possible futures

The overtures to commitment, loyalty and engagement that were noted in 5.6 have taken place at the very time that the world has, according to a number of commentators become more insecure and risky. Cappelli (1999, 2008) for example has suggested that the employment relationship has recently undergone change in more fundamental ways. He has talked of a 'new employment relationship' based on the challenges of the new world of work. In his view the traditional relationship relied on employers accepting significant responsibility and risk for the development and career paths of many of their employees which has now broken down. He argues that this is seen most clearly in attempts to redistribute the burden of risk on to employees, a development he sees as associated with growing competition in the global economy and the unwillingness or inability of firms to provide the job security of the past. Others have also picked up on the theme of risk more generally in contemporary society (see Beck 1992, Sennett 1998) and although it is perhaps stretching a point to suggest as Gray does that 'there has been a hollowing out of the business corporation as a social institution . . . (and this) . . . goes in tandem with the further commodification of work. Labour is something that is sold in bits to corporations. Businesses have shed many of the responsibilities that made the world of work humanly tolerable in the past' (Gray 2002: 72).

The significance of the role played by growing competition in employee relations is one that requires more discussion. Before doing so, it is helpful to briefly highlight another feature of contemporary employment which it is suggested is changing the nature of the employment relationship in fundamental ways.

KEY TERMS

Commodification The transfer of goods, services and factors of production into commodities. In essence, it is about turning something into a commodity status, something that can be traded.

Competition and employee relations

In the earlier discussion we noted the contribution of industrial pluralism to the development of industrial relations. A key feature of this perspective is that the workplace is relatively autonomous from the rest of the economy. That is it is an independent space where management and unions can conduct negotiations largely free from interference from external factors. Not surprisingly in view of its influence on the Commission's members, one of the criticisms levelled at the Donovan Report was that there was no real consideration of the wider economic context (Turner 1969) in its findings or its conclusions. That, in terms of Dunlop's model, industrial relations was treated almost as a *closed system* with no impact outside that system. This is somewhat surprising given Dunlop's own emphasis on the importance of context and feedback but some systems were always more open than others.

Significantly, if we can talk about systems of industrial relations in Britain in the post-war period most of these were based around industries, with collective bargaining conducted at the level of the industry and agreements tending to cover most firms in the industry. This system worked reasonably well as long as (a) all the major firms were covered and (b) there was limited competition coming from elsewhere. However, in the cases where (a) did not operate, as in the case of the Port Transport Industry and (b) where there started to be significant overseas competition as in motor vehicles, steel, shipbuilding and port transport, collective bargaining and the industry-based systems of industrial relations started to break down. For some, this heralded the emergence of 'organisation-based employment systems' (Purcell 1991) either based on more local collective bargaining, or a move away from joint regulation altogether.

Whatever the intention, it is hard to avoid the conclusion that competition has played an increasingly important role in shaping employee relations over the past twenty-five years. This is partly because employers have been very effective at 'bringing the outside in', by establishing channels of communication that have permitted them to bring the risks associated with competition and the market into organisations and by dismantling or restructuring established forms of collective representation. More controversially, it may be the case that an absence of competition or a degree of what economists refer to as 'imperfect competition' is necessary for traditional industrial relations institutions and arrangements to survive. If these 'spaces' provided by imperfect competition are eroded away by increased market competition then we should expect to see changes in the way employee relations are conducted (Marchington and Parker 1990).

A number of writers have identified the rise of the service sector and service work as a key feature of post-industrial economies here and elsewhere.

Whether this development changes the nature of the employment relationship in fundamental respects is open to debate but for many engaged in service work a key factor is the presence either physically or virtually of 'the customer'. Marek Korczynski (2002) in particular has highlighted the significance of the customer for certain service work positions and others have noted the 'quasi-managerial' function that customers perform in controlling those in customer service roles. There has also been considerable attention paid to other aspects of 'customer-facing' roles, in particular the importance placed on 'emotional labour' in dealings with customers (Hochschild 1983, Leidner 1993, Ehrenreich 2001). These would suggest that service work and roles might be different from those associated with manufacturing, not least because of the levels of engagement that might be expected of staff who perform them and the role that the customer plays in what now becomes a triangulation of the employment relationship.

Even where workers never see or hear a customer, the ideology and 'cult(ure) of the customer' (Du Gay and Salaman 1992) has been a sufficiently powerful tool to effect change in the employment relationship. In simple terms the customer represents competition (Heery 1993) and the uncertainty that through choice customers could 'go elsewhere'. In his pioneering work on the development of HRM in Britain, Storey (1992) suggests that one of the major shifts he observed was in the ways managers had, through sophisticated forms of communication and involvement, effectively brought the external pressures and risks associated with the market, into organisations and on to workers.

Summary

We began this chapter marking a contrast between two worlds, thirty years apart which in many respects could not be more different. In what has followed we have drawn heavily on a theme of change, of a world that has in many ways disappeared and one which is still revealing itself based on greater international competition and uncertainty. However, despite the evidence for change, question marks remain over the extent of real change and in particular the degree to which management has become more sophisticated in its approach to employee relations. While the changing contexts of the 1980s meant that management could 'deunionise their thinking' (Dunn 1993) and rediscover management prerogative (Purcell 1991), there is far less evidence that this has led to a more strategic view of employee relations. By the early 1990s management could still be described as 'muddling through' (Edwards et al. 1993) and pragmatic. There is also little evidence to suggest that management in the growing service sector is any more strategic than its predecessors in manufacturing. Rather that adopting a strategic approach, management initiatives to employee relations remain tactical with no clear sense of a principled philosophy of people management underpinning them.

These points qualify our discussion in important ways. Managers may want a more engaged, committed and loyal workforce but it is not clear that there is a sufficiently deep understanding of what this means in terms of policies and practice nor a corresponding commitment from senior management to make it happen (CIPD 2006). In their absence, the exhortation to employees to 'go the extra mile' is rather empty. Furthermore, as Edwards (2007) has argued, securing a committed and engaged workforce may well require attention to other things, such as collective voice mechanisms as well as to individualised policy initiatives. In the absence of such attention to the broader aspects of management worker relations, and to parody a famous quote, 'managers probably get the industrial relations they deserve', we shouldn't be surprised that the long arm of history often means lessons are not learned as old conflicts get played out at the workplace.

In their defence, managers frequently find themselves heavily constrained in what they can do. Impatient shareholders, or a raft of imposed Government targets often mean that a wish to build commitment, engagement or high involvement – things that require careful construction over a long period of time – are sidelined for the pursuit of short-term gain. This brings us back to where we started this chapter, with the context of employee relations and reminds us that for all the change and re-regulation, some elements in the environment appear extremely resistant to change, and if they change, do so only slowly. One such area is culture, be this organisational or managerial, another is the ownership and control of organisations (Hutton 1995) and together these continue to exert considerable influence on the nature and conduct of employee relations both now and, in all likelihood, the foreseeable future (Gospel and Pendleton 2005).

KEY IDEAS

Introduction

- As the quotes at the beginning of this chapter show, it is important to understand how we arrived at where we are today. There are few areas of HRM where an appreciation of history is as important as it is in employee relations.

- The particular historical legacy provided by industrial relations: of collective employee relations, constructed on the pillars of industrial pluralism and its artefacts – trade unions, employers associations and collective bargaining. In many places of work this legacy continues to cast a long shadow over how contemporary employee relations are conducted.

- Using the Dunlop framework we introduced the concept of a 'system' of industrial or employee relations and explored some of the ways in which this 'system' broke down or was dismantled during the 1980s and 1990s. We also considered whether a new system has emerged and if it has, what this might be based upon.

What is or are employee relations?

- The shift from industrial relations to employee and employment relations has seen a refocusing of the subject away from 'collective bargaining' towards the employment relationship.

- We explored some of the implications of this shift in terms of both the individual worker and the nature of collective relations at work.

The nature of employment rules

- That employment rules are essentially of two types; *substantive* rules – the 'what' in terms of how much you are paid, how many days holidays, and *procedural* rules – the processes covering rule making and administration. These normally cover procedures around negotiating, discipline, grievance and increasingly attendance and harassment.

- We also considered how rules are made – formally the most common methods are via unilateral action by management alone, or jointly via collective bargaining. Informally, they occur through a process known as custom and practice and tend to emerge out of behaviours and understandings over time.

Employee relations as the study of the employment relationship

- The employment relationship covers market relations (the price of labour), and managerial relations (the authority relationship that persuades or cajoles the worker to work).

- The employment relationship is dynamic because of changing external pressures and changing priorities within organisations, and has a number of dimensions: economic, legal, social, psychological and political.

- When we strip back the employment relationship to its simplest form we are left with an effort bargain, a relationship between effort and reward. In some employment relationships these 'bare essentials' are obvious and often produce a particular form of employee relations. In others this effort-reward relationship is disguised and overlaid by mechanisms designed to go beyond a simple exchange relationship.

What next?

- In this section we considered the role played by management in shaping our experiences of work and employment relationships. It was suggested that management has been

continued . . .

◀ *. . . continued*

encouraged to embrace a less conflictual and more unitarist model of employee relations in recent years, one that has emphasised partnership, non-unionism and HRM.

- It was also suggested that if the potential for conflict is always present in employment relationships then it is likely to be in the interests of managers to recognise this and to address it rather than ignore it.

Employee involvement

- The rise of employee involvement against a backdrop of growing international competition and a renewed managerial confidence, emphasising more individualised, direct and task-based forms of involvement.
- In recent past we have seen a broader concern to secure the engagement of staff in the work they undertake. At the same time there has been a renewed interest in collective voice and the belief that effective involvement, and a sense of justice at the workplace may require collective representation and involvement as well as those based around the individual or small group.

Employee relations: change and possible futures

- The chapter focused on the theme of change in discussing the possible implications of the shift to a service economy, and of growing competition for employee relations.
- Using Korczynski's (2003) argument that industrial relations was located very much within 'a production-centred paradigm' and sits less comfortably with one based around consumption we suggested that competition and the 'cult(ure) of the customer' continue to present challenges for both industrial and employee relations.
- Competition and particularly product market competition is likely to be one of the most important factors in shaping the nature and trajectory of employee relations in the foreseeable future.
- We also noted, following Ackers (2002), that both producer and consumer elements remain important in employee relations and need to be considered in any future refocusing of the subject.

RECOMMENDED READING

A useful background document on the subject of this chapter is the CIPD document *What is Employee Relations?* published at the end of 2005 www.cipd.co.uk/subjects/empreltns/general/_whtemprels.htm It provides an accessible way in to the subject but is also valuable in exploring the theme of *change* which has been a central concern of this chapter.

Those who wish to gain a deeper understanding of many of the elements in this chapter are advised to consult the CIPD texts in this area: Daniels' (2006) *Employee Relations in an Organisational Context* and Gennard and Judge's (2005) *Employee Relations*. The latter is particularly good on the practical aspects of employee relations and on the ways in which law influences the nature and conduct of employee relations.

Rose's (2008) *Employment Relations* is a bigger and more comprehensive text than either of the CIPD offerings and covers all areas in considerable depth and detail.

The Williams and Adam-Smith (2009) text *Contemporary Employee Relations: A Critical Introduction* shares a concern with this chapter of emphasising the importance of the employment relationship as the focus of study. It also has the real strength of being focused on contemporary developments, and covers non-union and issues of unorganised workers in some detail.

Other texts you may find useful to consult include Burchill's (2008) *Labour Relations*, which is particularly valuable for coverage of trade unions, and, for a gentle introduction, Keenoy's (1985) *Invitation to Industrial Relations* is still a very good lead in to what can be a difficult area.

For those who would also like to gain more of a feel for issues 'on the ground' in employee relations you are encouraged to read Ehrenreich's (2001) *Nickel and Dimed* about work in low paid jobs in America, and the more academic *Working for Ford* by Huw Beynon, originally written in the early 1970s. Studs Terkel's *Working*, about the experiences of working people in a range of different jobs also in America is an illuminating work and, like Ehrenreich, provides an interesting journalistic account of working lives that adds to our understanding of aspects of employee relations and the employment relationship.

Finally, and again more academic in their orientation and books to 'work up to', are Andrew Scott's (1994) *Willing Slaves: British Workers under Human Resource Management* and Rick Delbridge's (2000) study of the Toshiba factory near Plymouth in *Life on the Line in Contemporary Manufacturing*, both of which provide interesting insights into how work is experienced under 'new' forms of management.

REFERENCES

Ackers, P. (2002) Reframing employment relations: the case for neo-pluralism, *Industrial Relations Journal*, vol. 33, no 1.

Ackers, P., Wilkinson, A. (2004) Introduction: The British Industrial Relations Tradition – Formation, Breakdown and Salvage, in Ackers, P., Wilkinson, A. (eds), *Understanding Work and Employment*. Oxford: Oxford University Press.

Applebaum, E., Bailey, T., Berg, P., Kalleberg, A. (2000), *Manufacturing Advantage: Why High Performance Systems Pay Off*. Ithaca: ILR Press.

Baldamus, W. (1961) *Efficiency and Effort*. London: Tavistock.

Beck, U. (1992) *Risk Society: Towards a New Modernity*. New Delhi: Sage.

Behrend, H. (1957) The Effort Bargain, *Industrial and Labor Relations Review*, vol. 10, no 4.

Beynon, H. (1975) *Working for Ford*. Wakefield: EP Publishing Ltd.

Boorman, S. (2009) *NHS Health and Well-Being Interim Report*: London: NHS.

Bradley, H. (2008) No more heroes? Reflections on the 20th anniversary of the miner's strike and the culture of opposition, *Work, Employment and Society*, vol. 22, no 2.

Brown, W., Bryson, A., Forth, J., Whitfield, K. (eds) (2009) *The Evolution of the Modern Workplace*. Cambridge: Cambridge University Press.

Brown, W., Edwards, P. (2009) Researching the Changing Workplace, in Brown, W., Bryson, A., Forth, J., Whitfield, K. (eds) (2009) *The Evolution of the Modern Workplace*. Cambridge: Cambridge University Press.

Brown, W., Oxenbridge. S. (2004) Trade Unions and Collective Bargaining: Law and the Future of Collectivism, in Barnard, C., Deakins, S., Morris, G. (eds), *The Future of Labour Law: Liber Amicorum Sir Bob Hepple QC*. Oxford: Hart.

Burchill, F. (2008) *Labour Relations*, 3rd edn. Basingstoke: Palgrave Macmillan.

Cappelli, P. (2008) *Employment Relationships: New Models of White-Collar Work*. New York: Cambridge University Press.

Cappelli, P. (1999) *The New Deal at Work*. Boston: Harvard Business School Press.

Chartered Institute of Personnel and Development (CIPD) (2005) *What is Employee Relations*. London: CIPD.

Daniels, K., (2006) *Employee Relations in an Organisational Context*. London: CIPD.

Delbridge, R., (2000) *Life on the Line in Contemporary Manufacturing: The Workplace Experience of Lean Production and the 'Japanese' Model*. Oxford: Oxford University Press.

Donovan, Lord (1968) *Royal Commission on Trade Unions and Employers' Associations 1965-1968, Report*, Cmnd. 3623 (The Donovan Report). London: HMSO.

Du Gay, P., Salaman, G. (1992), 'The Cult(ure) of the Customer in Retailing', *Journal of Management Studies*, vol. 29, no 5.

Dunlop, J. (1958) *Industrial Relations Systems*. New York: Holt.

Dunn, S. (1993) From Donovan to . . . Wherever, *British Journal of Industrial Relations*, vol. 31, no 2.

Edwards, P. (2003) The Employment Relationship, in Edwards, P. (ed.), *Industrial Relations: Theory and Practice*, 2nd edn. Oxford: Blackwells.

Edwards, P., Hall, M., Hyman, R., Marginson, P., Sisson, K., Waddington, J., Winchester, D. (1992) Great Britain: Still Muddling Through, in Ferner, A., Hyman, R. (eds), *Industrial Relations in the New Europe*. Oxford: Blackwells.

Ehrenreich, B. (2001) *Nickel and Dimed*. London: Granta.

Flanders, A., Clegg, H. (1954) *The System of Industrial Relations in Great Britain*. Oxford: Blackwell.

Gennard, J., Judge, G. (2005) *Employee Relations*, 3rd edn. London: CIPD.

Goodrich, C (1920) *Frontier of Control: A Study in British Workplace Politics*. Cornell University Library.

Gospel, H., Pendleton, A. (2005) *Corporate Governance and Labour Management*. Oxford: Oxford University Press.

Gray, J. (2002) *False Dawn: The Delusions of Global Capitalism*. London: Granta.

Hakim, C. (2004) *Key Issues in Women's Work*, 2nd edn. London: Glass House Press.

Hall, M., Hutchinson, S., Parker, J., Purcell, J., Terry, M. (2008) *Implementing Information and Consultation in Medium-Sized Organisations*, Employment research series No. 97. DTI.

Heery, E. (1993) Industrial Relations and the Customer, *Industrial Relations Journal*, vol. 24, no 4: 284–95.

Hochschild, A. (1983) *The Managed Heart*. Berkeley: University of California Press.

Hutton, W. (1995) *The State We're In: Why Britain is in Crisis and How to Overcome it*. London: Vintage.

Hyman, R. (1975) *Industrial Relations: A Marxist Introduction*. London: Macmillan.

Kochan, T., Osterman, P. (1994) *The Mutual Gains Enterprise*. Cambridge, Mass: Harvard Business School Press.

Keenoy, T. (1985) *Invitation to Industrial Relations*. Oxford: Basil Blackwell.

Korczynski, M (2002) *Human Resource Management in Service Work*. Basingstoke: Palgrave Macmillan.

Korczynski, M. (2003) Consumer Capitalism and Industrial Relations, in Ackers, P., Wilkinson, A. (eds), *Understanding Work and Employment: Industrial Relations in Transition*. Oxford: Oxford University Press.

Leidner, R. (1993) *Fast Food, Fast Talk*. Berkeley: University of California Press.

Marchington, M., Parker, P. (1990) *Changing Patterns of Employee Relations*. London: Harvester Wheatsheaf.

Marchington, M., Goodman, J., Wilkinson, A., Ackers P. (1992) *New Developments in Employee Involvement*. Employment Department Research Paper Series, No. 2. London: HMSO.

Marchington, M., Wilkinson, A., Ackers, P., Dundon A. (2001) *Management Choice and Employee Voice*. London: CIPD.

Marsden, D. (2004) The Network Economy and Models of the Employment Contract, *British Journal of Industrial Relations*, vol. 42, no 4.

McGregor, I., Tyler, R., (1986) *The Enemies Within: Story of the Miners' Strike*. London: Harper Collins.

Purcell, J. (1991) The Rediscovery of Management Prerogative: The Management of Labour Relations in the 1980s, *Oxford Review of Economic Policy*, vol. 7, no 1.

Purcell, J. (1993) The End of Institutional Industrial Relations, *Political Quarterly*, vol. 64, no 1.

Purcell, J., Ahlstrand, B. (1994) *Human Resource Management in the Multidivisional Company*. Oxford: Oxford University Press.

Ray, C. A. (1986) Corporate Culture: The Last Frontier of Control, *Journal of Management Studies*, vol. 23, no 3.

Rose, E. (2008) *Employment Relations*, 3rd edn. London: FT/Prentice Hall.

Scott, A. (1994) *Willing Slaves: British Workers under Human Resource Management*. Cambridge: Cambridge University Press.

Sennett, R. (1998) *The Corrosion of Character: The Personal Consequences of Work in the New Capitalism*. New York: Norton.

Sewell, G. (1998) The Discipline of Teams: The Control of Team-based Industrial Work through Electronic and Peer Surveillance, *Administrative Science Quarterly*, vol. 43.

Sisson, K. (2008) Industrial Relations and the Employment Relationship: Putting the Record Straight, *Warwick Studies in Industrial Relations*, No. 88, Coventry: Industrial Relations Research Unit.

Terkel, S. (2004) *Working: People Talk About What They Do All Day and How They Feel About What They Do*. New York: New Press.

Truss, C., Soane, E., Edwards, C. (2006) *Working Life: Employee Attitudes and Engagement*. London: CIPD.

Williams, S., Adam-Smith, B. (2009) *Contemporary Employee Relations: A Critical Introduction*, 2nd edn. Oxford: Oxford University Press.

6 Role of the manager

'I can no longer obey; I have tasted command, and I cannot give it up.'

Napoleon Bonaparte 1769–1821, Military leader and Emperor of France

CHAPTER OBJECTIVES

- An understanding of the roles that managers perform in organisations and the most common managerial styles
- Knowledge of the ways in which people become managers
- Awareness of a range of managerial skills and why are they important for good management
- An understanding of the key contemporary changes to managerial roles
- Awareness of current trends towards devolving HR responsibilities to first line managers and the benefits for the organisation
- Knowledge of areas of first line mangers' involvement in people management with potential problems between the rhetoric and practice
- Knowledge of core skills for development in future generations of managers

6.1 Introduction

The role of manager has changed significantly over the past years and it varies considerably across industries. One constant, however, is that managers are employed and held accountable by their superiors to make sure they deliver in line with expectations. In order to achieve that, managers need to make sure that people reporting to them also deliver. This requirement places managers in a controlling, decision-making position.

The big change for managers today is how they carry out their responsibilities in managing people. Hoogendoorn and Brewster (1992) propose that line managers are now allocated new responsibilities and held accountable not only for budgeting and allocation of resources, but most importantly for people management issues. In this regard, Storey (1992: 190) argues that line managers may well 'be playing a far more central role in labour management' than HR personnel. Hales (2005) traces the greater involvement of line managers in HR issues to two developments. First, he argues that the spread of HRM and the adoption of more participative forms of management are concerned with securing high performance through commitment rather than control. This has led to line managers taking on the role of 'coach', 'conductor' or 'leader' of a motivated work team. Secondly, he suggests that HR devolvement has led to line managers acquiring middle management functions and becoming 'mini-general managers' accompanied by the loss of supervisory functions downwards to work teams.

6.2 The role approach to management

The role approach to management and leadership examines what the functions of management are. The role approach gained momentum in the early part of the twentieth century when the French industrialist, Henri Fayol, theorised that managers perform five basic functions: planning, organising, commanding, coordinating and controlling (Fayol 1949:3). Fayol was motivated to create a theoretical foundation for a managerial educational programme based on his experience as a successful managing director of a mining company. In his day, managers had no formal training and he observed that the increasing complexity of organisations would require more professional management. Fayol's Five Functions of Management focused on the key relationships between subordinates and managers. (See Table 6.1.)

Although, Fayol's basic functions were based on his own experience rather than sound research, his resulting vision proposed a language to communicate management theory and established a basis for management training. Additionally, the role approach Fayol put forward encourages managers to perceive organisations as living organisms rather than automatic machines.

Management function/role	Activities involved	Fayol's additional remarks
1. Planning and forecasting	• Drawing up plans of actions • Fitting plans with the organisation's resources, type and importance of work • Creating plans according to future trends	• The most difficult of the five tasks • Requires the active participation of the entire organisation • Planning must be coordinated on different levels • Must be both: short-term and long-term
2. Organising	• Providing resources • Allocating workers for the day-to-day running of the business • Building a structure to match the work	• Organisational structure depends entirely on the number of employees. • An increase in the number of functions expands the organisation horizontally and promotes additional layers of supervision
3. Leading	• Optimising the output from all employees in the interests of the organisation	Successful managers have: • personal integrity • communicate clearly • base judgments on regular audits • knowledge of personnel • create unity, energy, initiative and loyalty • eliminate incompetence
4. Coordinating	• Unifying and harmonizing activities and efforts to maintain the balance between the activities of the organisation	Fayol recommended weekly conferences for department heads to solve problems of common interest
5. Controlling	• Identifying weaknesses and errors • Controlling feedback • Conforming activities with plans, policies and instructions	Fayol's management process went further than Taylor's basic hierarchical model by allowing leading functions to operate efficiently and effectively through coordination and control methods. For Fayol, the managing director oversaw a living organism that requires liaison officers and joint committees.

Table 6.1 Fayol's five functions of management (Fayol 1949)

Mintzberg's managerial model

The Canadian academic Henry Mintzberg, who had trained as a mechanical engineer, conducted an empirical research in the1970s that involved observing and analysing the activities of the CEOs (Chief Executive of Organisation) of five private and semi-public organisations. He studied CEOs' calendar of scheduled appointments for a month, collected anecdotal data about their specific activities, made chronological records of activity patterns, a record of incoming and outgoing mail, and a record of the executive's verbal communication with others. Based on the collected data, Mintzberg demonstrated the variety in a manager's work. He first identified six characteristics of the job that together describe the work life of a CEO (Mintzberg 1973):

1 Managers' jobs are never completed as they process large, open-ended workloads under tight time pressure.
2 Managerial activities are relatively short in duration, varied and fragmented and often self-initiated. Half of the managerial activities studied lasted less than nine minutes.
3 Managers prefer action and action driven activities and dislike mail and paperwork.
4 Managers prefer verbal communication through meetings and phone conversations.
5 Managers maintain relationships primarily with their subordinates and external parties and least with their superiors.
6 Managers' involvement in the execution of the work is limited although they initiate many of the decisions.

Mintzberg then identified ten distinctive and interrelated managerial roles, each role defined as a set of activities managers perform (Mintzberg 1973). He then separated these roles into three role categories: interpersonal contact (consisting of three interpersonal roles), information processing (consisting of three information processing roles) and decision making (consisting of four decision making roles) as shown in Table 6.2.

It seems that the carrying out of the suitable managerial activities is not an entirely rational process and, indeed, managers often have to make decisions influenced by 'soft information', including internal and external gossip.

Furthermore, Mintzberg's role typology demonstrated great variety in manager's work as well as regular contradictory work demands. This has been reiterated in some more recent studies of managerial roles and skills required for fulfilling those roles. For instance, Watson found that manager's daily activities are mostly concerned with 'feeling one's way' in confusing circumstances, listening all time and reading signals, struggling to make sense of ambiguous messages, coping with conflicts and struggling to achieve tasks through establishing and maintaining relationships (Watson 1994). It seems that today's managers not only need to master managerial skills and competencies, but he or she also has to be constantly in tune with the complexity of individual situations that require a variety of roles that managers have to employ accordingly.

Role category	Ten roles of the manager	Activities involved
Interpersonal contact	1. Figurehead	Performs ceremonial and symbolic duties, receives visitors, opens
	2. Leader	Gives direction and counselling, motivates and influences subordinates; facilitates training and fosters a productive work atmosphere
	3. Liaison	Develops and maintains a network of contacts within and outside the organisation to gather information
Information processing	4. Monitor	Seek and receive information, scan papers and reports, maintain personal contacts
	5. Disseminator	Forwards information to others: sends memos, makes phone calls, runs meetings
	6. Spokesperson	Represents the organisation to the outside world through reports, speeches and presentations
Decision making	7. Entrepreneur	Identifies the business opportunities, then designs and initiates new projects
	8. Resource allocator	Controls and authorises organisational resources, sets schedules, allocates budgets
	9. Negotiator	Participates in negotiations with unions, suppliers, buyers, and generally represents the department, defending its interests
	10. Disturbance handler	Manages conflict between staff, responds to changing business environment, deals with unexpected events and crises

Table 6.2 Mintzberg's ten roles of the manager (Mintzberg, H. (1973) *The Nature of Managerial Work*. The Free Press)

KEY TERMS

Contingency theory A management theory that is based on the assumption that the best managers consider both their own characteristics and the situation to determine the best way to manage.

Influencing The exertion of control over others in a way that results in changes in behaviour or attitude.

Leadership The ability to persuade a follower to make a commitment to the goals of a group and work toward those goals.

Mentoring A formal or informal relationship in which a more experienced worker helps a less experienced worker develop job-related and career-related skills.

Figure 6.1 The modern manager

This is like balancing on the high wire while carrying a heavy workload, being continuously interrupted and rushing to meet the deadlines (see Figure 6.1).

It is worth remembering that the small sample size of Mintzberg's empirical study (five CEOs in five organisations) means that the results should not be simply applied to all industry, organisations or management positions. However, Mintzberg's managerial roles are often considered common in most managerial jobs, regardless of the functional or hierarchical levels. Additionally, the validity of his model was confirmed in repeated studies and therefore Mintzberg's ten roles created a common language. For instance, Guo's (2003) study of healthcare managerial skills and roles indicates that six out of Mintzberg's ten roles are perceived as very important by senior managers. These six roles are leader, liaison, monitor, entrepreneur, disturbance handler, and resource allocator.

Possibly the most important implication of Mintzberg's model is the challenge of the concept of totally rational management. This puts forward the argument for the practical training of managers in real management experiences, because it rather appears that the management skills cannot be entirely taught in a classroom but can only be enhanced through authentic experiences.

Mintzberg also analysed individual manager's use and mix of the ten roles according to the six work-related characteristics. He identified four clusters of independent variables: external, function-related, individual and situational, that all influence the 'natural' choice and combinations of roles that managers take on accordingly. He concluded that eight role combinations were 'natural' patterns of the job (Mintzberg 1973) (see Figure 6.2).

Figure 6.2 Mintzberg's 'natural' role combinations

Mintzberg's eight role combinations model suggests that although a manager's individual competencies, experience and skills influence his or her success in a managerial role, it is the organisation that determines the need for a particular role. Therefore, effective managers develop certain management procedures according to their job description and individual preference and then match these with the situation at hand.

Managerial styles

Following are the six managerial styles often quoted in the management training programmes, and their meanings:

1 *The coercive management style*
Manager who uses this style is intent on obtaining immediate compliance from employees using tight control and mostly negative feedback. Conversation is one way and he or she is very directive.

2 *The authoritative management style*
The authoritative manager's goal is to provide vision and focused leadership. This manager thinks long term and has a clearly stated direction. Decisions are mainly made by the manager but he or she welcomes some employee input to reality test his or her decisions. This style also relies on the use of influencing skills to gain employee buy-in to decisions. This style could be summed up as a firm but fair approach.

3 *The affiliative management style*
The affiliative manager promotes harmony, cooperation, and good feelings among employees. Affiliative actions include accommodating work-life balance and family needs that sometimes conflict with work goals, quickly smoothing tensions between employees, or promoting social activities within the team. The affiliative manager pursues being liked as a way to motivate people. He or she puts people first and tasks second.

4 *The democratic management style*
The democratic manager focuses on building group consensus and commitment through high involvement and group decision-making processes. This style is normally a hands-off style because employees are trusted to have the skills, knowledge and drive to come up with the best decisions. The manager's role is only to fine tune and approve the plan.

5 *The pacesetting management style*
The manager uses this style to focus on accomplishing a great deal of top quality work him or herself. Employees are thought capable of achieving their own goals with little supervision. When performance is not up to standard, the manager will do it him or herself. The emphasis of this style is on 'Doing it myself'.

6 *The coaching management style*
A coaching manager is mostly concerned with the professional growth of employees. The manager focuses on helping employees identify their strengths and weaknesses, improvement areas and set development plans

that foster individual career goals. The manager creates an environment that supports honest self-assessment and treats mistakes as learning opportunities in the development process.

Most managers develop a personalised managerial style soon after being placed in a position of greater responsibility. The individual managerial style is influenced by formal managerial training, the examples set by other managers or the examples set by role models from manager's life. The other major influence over the managerial style used is the situation at hand; this is called the contingency approach to management styles.

1. What are the most important implications of the managerial role theories of Fayol and Mintzberg?
2. The contingency approach to managerial styles claims that different styles suit different situations. Consider which managerial styles would best suit:
    a) A military exercise
    b) A flat structured advertising agency
    c) Independent expert software developers
    d) Managing a class of 14–16-year-olds on a youth project.

6.3 The balance between specialist and managerial responsibilities

A study of management in local government in UK proposed that rather than simply viewing it as limited number of 'top' or 'leading' positions, management should be defined as a set of competencies, attitudes and qualities broadly distributed throughout the organisation (Local Government Management Board 1993). Effective organisations recognise that 'management skills are not the property of the few and many jobs which have not conventionally borne the tag manager rely none the less on that bundle of actions – taking charge, securing an outcome, controlling – roles that all amount to managing.' (Local Government Management Board 1993: 8).

Most management is done by people who also undertake some kind of specialist work. A manager's way into an organisation is usually through his or her specialism (Rees and Porter 2008). A head of a university department usually has an academic background; a head of a hospital ward usually has some kind of medical training; a tennis coach is often a former professional tennis player. Promotion to management is a way of getting more influence in the organisation. It usually means gaining more power, money or status. However those who are best at the specialism do not necessarily make the best managers. And the best lecturers and most productive researchers may fail in managing other academics. This could be the case when an excellent specialist in a manager's role neglects their managerial responsibilities in favour of the specialist's activity, therefore letting their personal priority clash with an organisational priority.

Equally, the recent CMI survey found that many managers are unhappy with their role in the organisation. Sixty-eight per cent of those surveyed said they had fallen into the role by chance. And forty per cent of managers admitted they had not wanted the responsibility of managing people at all (CMI 2009).

On the other hand, effective managers combine their specialist skills with managerial responsibilities for much of their careers and therefore become and act as *managerial hybrids* (Rees and Porter 2008: 4). On top of their specialist activities, managerial hybrids become more and more involved with various managerial activities such as planning, prioritising, budgeting, resource allocation, liaison, staff supervision and leadership. Rees and Porter propose that people usually have an escalator type progression into management (see Figure 6.3), and the balance between management and specialist work will be determined by their position on the managerial escalator (Rees and Porter 2008: 5).

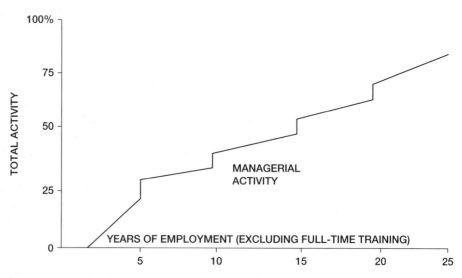

Figure 6.3 The managerial escalator (Rees and Porter 2008: 5)

The formation of managerial hybrids thus starts with a newly employed specialist who usually has some added informal managerial duties after some time of showing competence at their specialist work. They may be involved in showing new recruits around, giving presentations or running projects. After a while (a few years or perhaps even less) a person who has shown competence may be formally promoted to a team leader or a line manager.

For example, a staff nurse may become a charge nurse, an HR assistant may become an HR manger, and a waiter may become a restaurant supervisor or assistant manager. Such line managers often do not have formal management training (CMI 2009). Usually their management responsibilities include people management, managing operational costs, providing specialist advice, work allocation and duty rotas, dealing with clients and quality checks (CIPD 2009). As time passes, people may be carried up the escalator while their managerial activities take over more and more of their role (Rees and Porter 2008: 5).

1. How do people usually become managers?
2. Who are managerial hybrids?

(6.4) Management skills

Katz (1974: 90–102) identified three critical managerial skills. These are technical skills (the ability to perform particular tasks or activities); interpersonal skills (the ability to work well with other people); and conceptual skills (the ability to see the 'big picture').

Some of the basic management skills are outlined next. They include creative problem solving, decision making, planning, managing meetings, delegation, leading, effective communication and personal management.

Creative problem solving

Peter Drucker claims that in a rapidly changing business environment 'An established company which, in an age demanding innovation, is not able to innovate, is doomed to decline and extinction.' Equally, in day-to-day management, different problems and new situations regularly arise and often require innovative solutions. Sometimes logical step-by-step thinking that is based on existing knowledge is simply not enough for finding the best solution. Creative problem solving utilises intuition and imagination, with techniques such as analogies and associations to help produce fresh insights into a problem (Proctor 2005).

Some of the regular problems faced by managers which require creative thinking and innovative problem solving are making effective use of the manager's time, improving staff motivation, cutting costs through more efficient production, identifying new opportunities, retaining highly skilled and trained staff without paying them excessively high salaries.

It is encouraging to know that creative problem solving is a set of skills that can be taught through appropriate training and coaching. For instance, originality is a creative skill and it can be developed by picking one common object and listing many uses for it. Working individually or in a small group, think of 21 original uses for each of the listed objects:

- An electric wire
- A plastic cup
- A toothpick

Now think of 21 ways of combining those three items.

Decision making

Problem solving and decision making are closely linked, and each requires creativity in identifying and developing options. Decision-making skills are utilised to solve problems by selecting one course of action from several possible alternatives. It is often difficult to pick one solution where the positive outcome can outweigh possible losses, because almost any decision involves some conflict or dissatisfaction. Hence, avoiding decisions often seems easier. Yet, managers cannot afford to avoid making daily decisions as it is not only expected of them but it is also the only way to stay in control of the department and business they run.

Managers can be trained to become more confident decision makers. They are usually advised to run each decision they make through a decision-making process (see Figure 6.4).

SWOT (strengths, weaknesses, opportunities and threats) analysis can be used for all sorts of decision making. It is particularly useful because it enables proactive thinking, rather than relying on habitual or instinctive reactions.

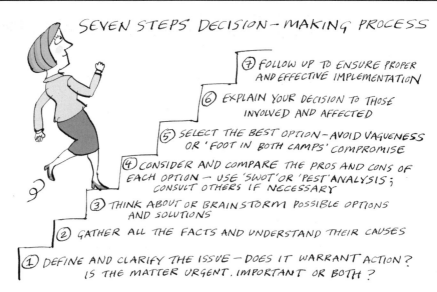

Figure 6.4 Seven steps in the decision-making process

ACTIVITY

Utilising decision-making techniques

The Old Walnut pub chain (currently consisting of five modern and vivacious city gastro pubs and four more traditional country bed and breakfast pub hotels) has been offered the chance to open an outlet in an abandoned local church by a small village council. The remote location has breathtaking scenery and the rent is token, but the investment needed to refurbish the place is significant. The Old Walnut enterprise has suffered significantly during the last recession and three out of seven country outlets had to be closed down. Now with the economy picking up, this is a tempting business opportunity, which could mark the comeback of The Old Walnut. As a general manager of one of the city pubs you are being asked to contribute your expert opinion to the decision making process. Should the company sign a contract with the village council? If they decide to take on this new venture you would be promoted to an area manager (overseeing all the country pubs) and the opening of the new place will be entirely under your supervision. For you personally this would bring higher authority, more responsibility and the doubling of your salary. However, if the venture fails you are likely to lose your job.

SWOT analysis

Using the following table carry out SWOT analysis for this new business opportunity. Many criteria can apply to more than one quadrant. You can identify and add criteria appropriate to your SWOT situation.

Criteria examples	Strengths	Weak-nesses	Criteria examples
• Advantages of proposition • Capabilities • Competitive advantages • Unique selling points • Resources, assets, people • Experience and knowledge • Financial reserves, likely returns • Marketing – reach • Innovative aspects • Location and geographical			• Disadvantages of proposition • Gaps in capabilities • Lack of competitive strength • Reputation, presence and reach • Financials • Own known vulnerabilities • Timescales, deadlines and pressures • Cash-drain • Chain robustness • Plan predictability
Criteria examples	**Opportu-nities**	**Threats**	**Criteria examples**
• Market developments • Competitors' vulnerabilities • Industry or lifestyle trends • Global influences • New markets • Niche target markets • New unique selling points • Business development • Seasonal weather influences			• Local politics effects • Environmental effects • Market demand • New services, ideas • Obstacles faced • Undefeatable weaknesses • Sustainable financial backing • Seasonal weather influences

Pros and cons analysis

Now try to weigh up the advantages and disadvantages for you personally if you were to get involved in this project, by using a simple pros and cons analysis. Use one to five scoring scale where 1 = of insignificant importance, 2 = a little important, 3 = moderately important, 4 = considerably important and 5 = extremely important. Sum up the totals in the last row for aided comparison.

Based on your analysis prepare a short presentation for the board of The Old Walnut directors arguing for or against opening this new pub.

Pros/for (advantages)	Score	Cons/against (disadvantages)	Score
Total:		Total:	

Planning

Planning entails organisational skills and the ability to identify organisational objectives and prioritise tasks by allocating resources and delegating tasks that will be more efficiently performed by other members of staff (short-term planning); adjusting the organisational strategies to competitors' strategies (mid-term planning); and keeping an eye on the future '– trying to identify and forecast future changes in the demand for services and their delivery (long-term planning). Planning entails evaluating the objectives and setting the goals for individual projects and tasks. One of the planning and organising techniques used particularly in project management and in performance management is SMART goals setting.

ACTIVITY

A SMART goal is:

- **S**trategic and specific – answers the questions: who and what?
- **M**easurable – the success toward meeting the goals can be measured in achievement. It answers the question: how?
- **A**ttainable – goal can be achieved in a specific amount of time with available resources
- **R**esults oriented/relevant
- **T**ime bound – goals have a clearly defined time frame including a target date

Set your five short-term (to be achieved within approximately one month), five mid-term (to be achieved within the next year) and five long-term (to be achieved within the next ten years) professional development goals, using the SMART goal setting technique.

Negotiation skills

Situations that require the manager's negotiation skills include:

- Negotiating somewhat conflicting goals between an organisation and its workers. For example: an organisation strives to minimise labour costs, while workers want to maximise their earnings and job security.
- Building effective teams and negotiating team roles and responsibilities.
- Resolution of conflict within the group – negotiating and mediating between the conflicting parties to prevent escalation of the conflict, and possible further cost to both the organisation and employees' well-being.

Figure 6.5 Managers need negotiating skills

Delegation

Delegation is giving an employee tasks to perform with authority to act on the manager's behalf. This is very important as it enables the manager to concentrate on priorities and think ahead. It can also be more cost effective, as those tasks may be performed more quickly by the employee than by a busy regularly interrupted manager, and essentially regular delegation enables the organisation to function smoothly even in the manager's absence. It also means that for performing certain tasks a mix of skills is used.

KEY TERMS

HR specialists HR employees that focus exclusively on specific areas within HR, for example, recruitment or training.
Motivation The conditions that boost, direct and maintain effective work behaviour.
Recruitment The process of attracting qualified job applicants to an organisation.
Selection The process of choosing the person who will be hired.
Stress The physical and psychological response to demands made on a person.
Training Practical education in a skill, job or profession.

The skill of delegation relies on a manager's willingness to invest time to brief or train his staff, and also set standards by which they can effectively monitor the results. It also requires certain coaching skills and confidence in both self and others. Equally, the organisational culture has to be supportive of delegation.

Managing meetings

Meetings can be very productive or they can be a tremendous waste of time. The result will depend heavily on the manager's ability and skill to manage meetings. An effective meeting will be carefully planned, with a clearly defined purpose and agenda, and will be kept within the set time frame. Throughout the meeting the manager will keep focus on the agenda, while allowing contributions from those attending.

Running meetings requires the development of public speaking skills and training in effective presentation skills.

Leading

Leading refers to finding ways of increasing productivity in the workplace through clear and inspirational leadership and motivation of staff. Leading skills are just one of the many assets a successful manager must possess, however a manager cannot just be a leader, he or she also needs formal authority to be effective.

It is important to note here that although they are often used interchangeably, managing and leading are not synonymous, and those terms stand for two different ways of organising people. Richard Pascale made a frequently quoted statement 'Managers do things right, while leaders do the right thing.' (Pascale 1990: 65) This implies that a manager thinks incrementally – using a formal, rational method to get things done through others, while a leader thinks radically, using passion and stirring emotions to inspire people to follow them.

A leader only exists while he or she has the followers; while even if there are no followers a manager may be there. The leader is followed, the manager rules. Managers have subordinates, whom they tell what to do, and the subordinates do this not because they are robots, but because they have been promised a reward (at minimum their salary) for doing so.

Managers are usually people who are experienced in their field, and who have worked their way up the company (as illustrated previously with the managerial escalator model). As a result of that work experience, a manager often knows how each layer of the system works and may also possess a good technical knowledge. A leader can be a new arrival to a company who has bold, fresh, new ideas but might not have experience or wisdom.

Furthermore, managers are appointed and given formal authority by more senior managers whom they are responsible to. On the other hand, leaders are elected; maybe they do, but maybe they do not have any formal authority; however, they receive power directly from their followers.

A manager exercises authority through distribution of rewards and sanctions. For example, he or she can reward employees who contribute towards organisational goals with praise, flexible working time, pay bonuses, company perks or by promoting them. A manager can also assign the negative sanctions for mistakes by withholding promotions or taking disciplinary actions. Motivated by this legitimate 'stick and carrot' sanction system, employees obey managers because it is in their job description; whereas people typically follow a leader on voluntary basis.

Finally, managing exclusively takes place within an organisational context, while leadership can occur anywhere. For example, a crowd can have a leader but does not have a manager. Spartacus was the famous, charismatic leader of gladiators and slaves that fought against the Roman Empire in 73–71 BC; however, he cannot be thought of as the rebels' manager. Nevertheless, leadership in the workplace is common and one of the most desirable managerial assets of the twenty-first century. For instance, work teams often have spontaneously elected leaders that could change roles with other team members according to the requirements of the group tasks, but also an official manger can be a leader at the same time.

Today managers often have to be leaders too. The traditional distinctions between a manager and leader are disappearing. Modern business operates in the uncertainties of the current global slowdown and financial crisis. Consequently, the role of a manager demands flexibility, dynamism as well as leadership quality. Without those leadership qualities an organisation is unlikely to survive in the competitive market for long.

Effective communication

Communication encompasses both transmitting (writing and speaking) and receiving information (listening and reading). A manager who is a good listener will more easily recognise (notice and understand) the problems that employees and customers may have, and therefore address them more quickly and appropriately; he or she will also be explicit and articulate, using illustrations to support arguments and will write and speak clearly, concisely and with confidence. This will all help the manager to stay in tune with the general atmosphere in the workplace as well as to motivate and influence people to do their best working towards the organisational goals.

Personal management

Managing others is hardly possible without adequate self-management. Self-management involves understanding oneself to aid ones understanding of others, assertive behaviour as opposed to a passive or aggressive manner, good time-management, managing ones own emotions and the emotions of others (dealing with stress, or dealing with a difficult customer).

A recent UK study of 3,000 adults by the Chartered Management Institute (CMI) has found that 49 per cent say that under less drastic circumstances, they would rather take a pay cut than work for someone who made bad decisions. According to CMI research (2009) half of workers have resigned from their job due to bad management and almost the same number think they can do a better job than their boss.

UK organisations seem less committed to investing in management skills than their foreign competitors and according to the CMI this lack of investment is taking a considerable toll on the UK economy and people's well-being. This is a wake-up call for UK government and UK businesses to start addressing the lack of managerial skills and reclaim confidence in managers.

1. List the core managerial skills.
2. From the range of managerial skills listed previously, which ones do you identify as your personal strengths, and which ones do you think you will need to develop and improve?
3. How could UK organisations help reclaim confidence in managers?

6.5 Devolving HR responsibilities to front line managers

To add to the number of roles and responsibilities managers have to carry out on a daily basis, there is an emerging trend in the public sector of handing certain human resource management activities from HR departments to front line managers. This emerging trend induced a radical reconsideration of the role of line managers.

The key driving force for this addition to managerial responsibilities is probably commercialisation of the public sector that consequently has led to enhanced customer service and improved employee performance. Getting line managers more involved in HR delivery is a way to achieve a more strategic, value-added approach to managing employees in an ever-changing, competitive business environment. By devolving responsibility for HR practices to line managers, public sector organisations expect a closer relationship between line managers and employees, with speedier decision making and more effective resolution of workplace problems. This delegation of tasks also provides greater freedom for HR specialists to focus more on strategic issues. While line managers engage with day-to-day people management, HR managers with their staff can work on achieving closer alignment of an organisation's policies and procedures with its business objectives, while remaining sensitive to external environmental changes (Brewster and Larsen 1992).

Joint venture between HR specialists and line managers are not only specific to public sector organisations but are becoming widespread. This has been confirmed in a number of studies internationally, for example, Greek findings show that during the past ten years there has been an increasing tendency for collaboration between HR departments and line managers (Papalexandris and Panayiotopoulos 2005). While CIPD (2009) reports that nowadays in many UK organisations front line managers carry out activities which were traditionally the sole responsibility of the personnel department, such as providing coaching and guidance, undertaking performance appraisals and dealing with discipline and grievances. Often, they also carry out recruitment and selection together with the HR department.

HRM as a theory argues that responsibility for the management of an organisation's human resources must be devolved to line managers. Some scholars state this argument differentiates HRM from personnel management (Guest 1987; Kirkpatrick et al. 1992). Guest advocates that, 'If HRM is to be taken seriously, personnel managers must give it away' (Guest 1987: 510). According to HRM theory, it is more appropriate for line managers to take responsibility for people management and development as they are working alongside the people they manage and therefore line managers' actions will be more direct and appropriate (Whittaker and Marchington 2003). As a result, HR departments design processes while line managers deliver it, taking on the HRM ambassadors' role when they carry out performance appraisal, training, coaching and guidance.

HRM theory also stresses that line managers have to treat workers as valued assets, which they have a responsibility to develop, rather than as costs to minimise (Kirkpatrick et al. 1992: 133). In acting upon advice and guidance from the HR department, they need to bring HR polices and practices to life (see Table 6.3).

As the result of the devolving move, it is expected that the organisational performance will rocket. This has been supported by research, for instance, Hutchinson and Purcell (2003) found that line manager involvement in HR activities such as coaching, guidance and communication positively influences organisational performance.

However, the added responsibilities require line managers to have a certain self-confidence, a strong sense of their own security in the organisation, sufficient support from HR departments, extra time in their already busy work schedules and a number of skills. For example, to build good working relationships with their staff line managers have to be effective communicators: they need to ask, listen, decipher ambiguous messages; they need to send clear messages themselves; they also have to be fair; show empathy; help, support and empower their employees. According to some, the first line managers have failed to live up to their new roles and they show reluctance to take on HR responsibilities (O'Donnell 1994; Riemsdjik et al. 2006). This could be explained by a number of reasons (Riemsdjik et al. 2006):

1 Lack of desire – many line managers do not share the enthusiasm about their additional responsibilities, and as a result they give HR tasks low priority. This could be explained by the lack of personal and institutional incentives.
2 Lack of capacity – HR tasks are generally devolved to line managers without reducing their other duties (Brewster and Larsen 2000) and as a result FLM do not have enough time to implement HRM successfully.
3 Lack of skills – few organisations seem to provide formal HR training, and FLM do need HR-related skills for successful HRM implementation (Brewster and Larsen 2000).
4 Lack of support – FLMs needs a support from HR managers. They do not know how to perform HR activities and they need clear advice and coaching. However, some HR managers are either unable or reluctant to abandon their traditional 'interventionist' role and take on a new 'advisor' role.
5 Lack of clear policy and procedures – often there is a lack of clear overall HR policy with accompanying procedures to coordinate, which would guide FLMs' activities on the operational level. As the result of vague policies FLM are pressed to adjust those policies to their own personal understanding.

HRM responsibilities devolved to FLM	Resulting FLM activities
Selection and assessment	• Conducting job interviews • Placing the right person on the right job
Induction	• Orientation of new employees
Staff development	• Developing each individual through appraisal, coaching and training
Building good working relationships with staff	• Effective communication • Securing that employees feel their contribution is recognised
Maintaining the morale	• Securing good working conditions for staff • Application of work-life balance practices • Iintroducing flexible working schemes as a way of keeping employees happy (CMI, 2009)
Creating cooperative and innovative work-climate	• Showing interest in employees' opinions • Encouraging openness • Effective team building
Delivery of HR policies and procedures	• Understanding and interpreting HR policies and procedures • Controlling labour costs • Managing conflict • Early disciplinary actions

Table 6.3 HR responsibilities with consequent day-to-day activities of first line managers (FLM)

Gaining the commitment of line managers and combating the contradictions between HRM polices and practice represent main challenges for organisations (O'Donnell, 1994). Organisational incentives can persuade FLMs to give HR activities serious consideration, for instance by making HR responsibilities an integral part of FLMs' own performance appraisals and their job description (Riemsdjik et al. 2006). HR-related skills could be developed through continual training, while time and clear and proactive support must be available. Equally, HR specialists must give up their traditional interventionist roles and move towards advising, coaching and strategy creating.

1. What are the main driving forces for devolvement of HR responsibilities to line managers?
2. List the HR activities that first line managers are increasingly being asked to perform.
3. What are the main inhibitors of line managers' HR involvement?

 ## Next-generation manager

Hiltrop (1988) predicts that organisations will become more complex and ambiguous places in which to work and consequently the role of the manager will become more lateral, with much more focus on people, customers and processes. He further argues that managers will face more stress, require more dynamic career perspectives, and also need new, more extensive, skills and competences. The future manager will need to demonstrate a wide range of skills and will have to be (Hiltrop 1988):

- *an expert* – a professional showing willingness and enthusiasm for life-long learning and continuous developing of up-to-date knowledge and skills
- *a networker* – with skills in communication, negotiation, problem-solving, project management and open-mindedness
- *self-reliant* – showing initiative and self-motivation, having a vision; using creative techniques in problem solving
- *resilient* – demonstrating stress-tolerance, flexibility, team-working, adaptability, and determination.

It seems that the manager's role is going to get even more demanding and difficult to fill. On top of keeping up with the latest technical skills, the future manager will be particularly focused on developing an array of leadership skills while at the same time the organisations will have to be providing them with a continuous training in HR competencies.

 ## Summary

This chapter began by introducing an array of changes that have affected managers' role in business over the years. This was followed with a detailed exploration of the role approach to management, as represented by its two most prominent pioneers and their work. The chapter went on to examine how people become managers and how managers often struggle to achieve the balance between their specialist and managerial responsibilities. A significant number of management skills were then outlined, guiding the reader to make their own self-assessment of those skills. The devolving of HR responsibilities and the problems this movement has caused for managers in modern business were then outlined and discussed. The chapter concluded by looking at the next generation of managers and the challenges they may have to face in the future.

REFLECTIVE QUESTIONS

1 According to Mintzberg (1973), what are the main managerial roles?
2 Describe and explain the managerial escalator model (Rees and Porter 2008).
3 List core managerial skills.
4 Why is creativity an important manager's asset?
5 What are the main distinctions between leadership and management?
6 How did role of the manager change in the past few decades?
7 Gary Dessler argues that all managers are, in a sense, also HR managers, since nowadays they all get involved in activities like recruiting, interviewing, selecting, and training (Dessler 2007). Yet most organisations also have an HR department. How do the duties of this HR department relate to line managers' human resource duties?
8 Despite the much advertised benefits of participating in HR initiatives, line managers have expressed a number of concerns regarding greater HR involvement. What are the ways of getting line managers to take on HR responsibilities?
9 What are the challenges that the future generation of managers will have to face?

KEY IDEAS

Introduction
As organisations change and develop, so too does the role of the manager.

The role approach to management
Mintzberg (1973) demonstrated in his research that the role of a manager is quite varied and contradictory in its demands, and that it is therefore not always the lack of managerial competence but the complexity of individual situations demanding a variety of roles which troubles today's manager.

Most managers develop their own individual managerial style influenced by the formal managerial training they may have had, the example of other managers at their workplace, or by the example of an authoritative role model in their life. However, the particularity of a work situation often makes managers adopt their style accordingly.

The balance between specialist and managerial responsibilities
The ten managerial roles model imply that managers need to be both organisational generalists and specialists.

Management skills
Managerial skills can be thought and coached, including creative problem solving and leadership skills.

continued . . . ▶

◀ *. . . continued*

Devolving HR responsibilities to front line managers

The move towards shifting responsibility for HR issues is known as devolvement and it refers to giving HRM responsibilities to line managers. While HR specialists work on aligning policies and procedures with organisational objectives and the changing business environment, first line managers bring those policies to life. However, the research shows considerable reluctance of first line managers to take on extra workload.

RECOMMENDED READING

Bevan, S., Hayday, S. (1994) *Helping Managers to Manage People*. Institute of Manpower Studies. London: BEBC.

Child, J., Partridge, A. (1982) *Lost Managers*. London: Cambridge University Press.

Purcell, J. (2004) *Older and wiser? – Reflections on the search for the HRM holy grail,* keynote address at the 3rd Dutch HRM Network Conference, Enschede: University of Twente.

USEFUL WEBSITES

www.managers.org.uk website of The Chartered Management Institute.

REFERENCES

Blake, R., Mouton, J. (1964). *The Managerial Grid: The Key to Leadership Excellence*. Houston: Gulf Publishing Co.

Brewster, C., Larsen, H. (2000) *HRM in Northern Europe: Trends, dilemmas and strategies*. Oxford: Blackwell.

Brewster, C., Larsen, H.H. (1992) Human resource management in Europe: Evidence from ten countries, *International Journal of Human Resource Management*, vol. 3, no. 3: 409–34.

CIPD (2009) The role of front line managers in HR, *The CIPD factsheet*. London: Chartered Institute of Personnel and Development www.cipd.co.uk

CMI (2009) 'Half of workers have resigned due to bed management', *The CMI research report*. London: Chartered Management Institute www.managers.org.uk

Dessler, G. (2007) *Human resource management*. Harlow: Prentice Hall.

Fayol, H. (1949) *General and industrial management*, translated from the French edition (Dunod) by Constance Storrs. London: Pitman.

Guest, D. (1987) Human resource management and industrial relations, *Journal of Management Studies*, vol. 24, no. 5: 501–21.

Guo, K. L. (2003) An assessment tool for developing healthcare managerial skills and roles, *Journal of Healthcare Management*, vol. 48, no. 6: 367–76

Hales, C. (2005) Rooted in supervision, branching into management: continuity and change in the role of first line managers, *Journal of Management Studies*, May, vol. 42, no. 3: 471–506.

Hiltrop, J-M. (1988) Preparing People for the Future: The Next Agenda for HRM, *European Management Journal*, vol. 16, no. 1.

Hoogendoorn, J., Brewster, C. (1992) Human resource aspects: decentralization and devolution, *Journal of Personnel Review*, vol. 2, no. 1: 4–11.

Hutchinson, S., Purcell, J. (2003) *Bringing Policies to Life: the vital role of frontline managers in people management*. London: CIPD.

Katz, R.L. (1974) Skills of an effective administrator, *Harvard Business Review*, vol. 52, no. 5: 90–102.

Kirkpatrick, I., Davies, A., Oliver, N. (1992) Decentralisation: Friend or Foe of HRM, in Blyton, P., Turnbull, P. (eds) *Reassessing human resource management*. London: Sage Publications.

Local Government Management Board (1993) *Managing tomorrow*.

Mintzberg, H. (1973) *The Nature of Managerial Work*. New York: Harper and Row.

O'Donnell, M. (1994) *Decentralized human resource management and reluctant line managers: rhetoric and reality*, New South Wales: University of New South Wales, School of Industrial Relations and Organisational Behaviour, working paper, wwwdocs.fce.unsw.edu.au/orgmanagement/WorkingPapers/WP98.pdf

Papalexandris, N., Panayotopoulou, L. (2005) Exploring the partnership between line managers and HRM in Greece, *Journal of European Industrial Training*, vol. 2, no. 4: 281–91.

Pascale, R. (1990) *Managing on the Edge*. Harmondsworth: Penguin Books Ltd.

Proctor, T. (2005) *Creative problem solving for managers: developing skills for decision making and innovation,* 2nd edn. Abingdon: Routledge.

Rees, W.D., Porter, C. (2008) *Skills of management*, 6th edn. Cengage Learning.

Riemsdijk, M.R., Nehles, A.C., Kok, I., Looise, J.K. (2006) Implementing human resource management successfully: A first line management challenge, *Management Review*, vol.17, no. 3: 256–73.

Storey, J. (1992) *Developments in the Management of Human Resources*. Oxford: Blackwells.

Watson, T.J. (1994) *In search of management: culture, chaos and control in managerial work*. London: Routledge.

Whittaker, S., Marchington, M. (2003) Devolving HR responsibility to the line: Threat, opportunity or partnership?, *Employee Relations*, vol. 25, no. 3: 245–61.

7 Performance management

'We would no more show our performance appraisal to a bunch of outsiders than the Coca-Cola company would let you come in and look over the secret formula for Coke'

(Human Resources Vice President, Grote 2002)

CHAPTER OUTLINE

7.1 Introduction
7.2 What is performance management?
7.3 The performance management cycle
7.4 Performance appraisal
7.5 Measuring performance
7.6 Managing underperformance
7.7 Key roles in performance management
7.8 Summary

CHAPTER OBJECTIVES

- A better understanding of the meaning and importance of performance management
- Knowledge of the role of performance appraisal in managing performance and the different methods of appraising performance
- Awareness of the various approaches to measuring performance
- Knowledge of action, both formal and informal, which can be taken to manage underperformance
- An understanding of the critical role of line managers in the practice of performance management
- Awareness of the potential problems that face organisations in designing and operationalising performance management and the role of HR and senior managers in providing support

Introduction

Recruiting and selecting good quality people for the job does not necessarily guarantee that those individuals will perform to their best ability. Employees need to know what the job entails and the expected standards of performance, they will require training and development, and there may be times when factors outside their control (at home or work) adversely impact on their performance and they need support. Performance management is the means by which organisations can help encourage, support and guide employees to achieve their best performance, with a view, ultimately, to delivering high organisational performance. The term 'performance management' is often mistakenly used to refer to performance appraisal or a practice which revolves around measurement and objective setting. While these are integral components of managing performance, performance management should be viewed as a holistic and integrated approach to managing the business. It is a process which starts as soon as an individual joins the organisation, and incorporates many HR activities such as induction, training and development, performance appraisal, reward and handling capability procedures. Interest in performance management has grown considerably over the last few decades, and a recent survey estimated that 87 per cent of organisations had a formal performance management process for some or all of their employees (CIPD 2005). However, while the benefits are potentially great, performance management is a complex process, often misunderstood, difficult to implement effectively and an area 'ripe for interpersonal conflict' (Latham et al. 2007). It also embodies the dichotomy between 'hard' and 'soft' HRM. This is clearly illustrated by the two distinct perspectives on performance management. The traditional view, which is based on the belief that managers need to establish clear standards for employees to comply with, is associated with measurement and control, with a focus on poor performance. The alternative approach focuses on continuous improvement and gives emphasis to performance management as a tool to train and develop individuals as a means of enhancing performance. These tensions run through any performance management process and present difficulties for both those managing the process and employees.

What is performance management?

There is no one widely accepted definition of performance management but two descriptions which capture some of the key features are:

'It is now commonly agreed that performance management as a natural process of management contributes to the effective management of individuals and teams in order to achieve high levels of organisational performance. As such, it establishes shared understanding about what is to be achieved and an approach to leading and developing people which will ensure that it is achieved' (Armstrong and Baron 2005, p. 2).

'A continuous process of identifying, measuring and developing the performance of individuals and teams and aligning performance with the strategic goals of the organizations' (Aguinis 2009, p. 2).

Fundamentally, performance management seeks to encourage, support and sustain high performance at individual, team and organisational level. The key characteristics of any performance management process are that it is:

- Strategic
- Integrated: vertically and horizontally
- Flexible
- A continuous process, not a discrete event
- A tool to communicate the organisation's strategy and objectives to all employees, and facilitate a dialogue between employees and management
- **Line manager** owned and driven rather than being the sole responsibility of a specialist HR function.

Performance management is strategic, in that it seeks to directly link individual, team, and departmental objectives to the organisation's goals, and thus develop a shared understanding of how to improve organisational effectiveness. A recent CIPD discussion paper considered that performance management was 'about creating a line of sight between what the individual does and what the organisation needs' (CIPD 2009a, p. 2). It is therefore both a communication tool and means of engaging employees with the organisational goals. If an individual can identify and understand the contribution their job makes then they are more likely to be committed to the organisation and 'go that extra mile'. The implication, therefore, is that performance management must be designed and implemented within the context of the organisation. It must be tailor-made, and cannot be bought 'off the shelf' or borrowed from another organisation. A well designed performance management process should be flexible and enable the organisation to respond to the changing economic and competitive environment. In recessionary times it is a vital tool to maintain motivation and efficiency and deliver messages about how the organisation is performing and what might be done to improve performance. It is also a holistic approach to managing people and brings together many interrelated HR activities to help support and deliver effective performance such as induction, training and development, reward and recognition, performance appraisal, and capability procedures. Although often portrayed as a formal process with a series of stages and one-off events, performance management should operate as an ongoing, <u>continuous</u> cycle incorporating informal as well as formal activities. Line managers should be regularly managing and monitoring the performance of their employees, having informal discussions about progress and problems and providing regular feedback, rather than waiting for the annual performance review to take place. Performance management is, therefore, also a key mechanism to help managers manage, and it is the responsibility of the line to implement HR policies and practices which support the performance management process.

KEY TERMS

Line manager A line manager is someone who is responsible for supervising and managing employees and this will include conducting performance reviews/appraisals. Line managers are at all levels of management and at the first level these managers are typically referred to as team leaders, supervisors or front line managers.

Strategic performance management

The starting point in designing a performance management process should be a clear articulation of the organisation's strategy and goals, and this will be framed by the values and beliefs of the organisation (see Chapter 13, Strategic HRM). Organisational objectives, based on the strategy, cascade down through the organisation to departmental, team and individual levels, as shown in Figure 7.1, thus emphasising the importance of vertical integration. The upward arrows highlight the importance of feedback in setting objectives. One of the early challenges in designing an effective process is therefore showing this linkage in a way which is meaningful and relevant and there are a variety of approaches to this. One popular method is the 'balanced score card', developed by Kaplan and Norton (1992), which provides a framework for measuring and managing performance. It assesses performance on four perspectives – the customer (how do customers see us?), financial (how do we look to shareholders?), internal (what must we excel at?) and learning and innovation (how can we continue to improve and create value?). All the perspectives are equally weighted and integrated. Organisations choose a small number of key interrelated measures for each perspective to illustrate its goals and vision. This 'balanced' approach avoids overemphasis on the financial aspects of performance and allows managers to make connections between changes in one area to another. For example, improved financial results could

Figure 7.1 The performance management process

have an adverse impact on the customer if achieved through cutting staffing levels.

Tesco, the UK-based supermarket, has converted the scorecard into a graphic called the 'steering wheel' which covers four areas of the business: finance, operations, people and customers (IRS 2000). Objectives relating to these areas are drawn up for each store and displayed in staff areas. The people quadrant, for example, might include targets for recruitment and retention; finance could include targets for sales and profit. Many organisations use **key performance indicators** (KPIs), as shown in the example of the Nationwide.

KEY TERMS

Key performance indicators Key performance indicators, often referred to as KPIs, are performance measures used by organisations to set targets and evaluate their success. KPIs are sometimes linked to the organisation's strategy using the balanced scorecard approach.

CASE STUDY

The Nationwide Building Society's commitment to its status as a mutual organisation (meaning it is owned by its members rather than shareholders) underpins its corporate strategy and influences its relationship with customers, employees and other stakeholders. This approach to business and ownership is seen to distinguish the organisation in the financial services market place and offer a competitive advantage. The commitment to mutuality is translated into operational level through key performance indicators (KPIs). In 1999, for example, these were expressed as:

- Nationwide is my first choice
- Nationwide has the best ratings
- Nationwide is where I want to work

A number of KPIs (which have equal value and are not weighted) are used to measure performance against these criteria. Employee satisfaction and competences are some of the measures used to capture 'Nationwide is where I want to work'; mortgage share and complaints are indicators of 'Nationwide is my first choice'; capital ratios and costs are measures of 'Nationwide has the best ratings'. These KPIs are set annually at corporate level and cascade down to divisional, departmental and individual level. A traffic light system of red, amber and green is used to monitor performance on a monthly basis.

(Adapted from Purcell et al. 2003, with the permission of the publisher, the Chartered Institute of Personnel and Development, London (www.cipd.co.uk))

1. In 2009 Tesco's core purpose was stated as 'to create value for customers to earn their lifetime loyalty'.
   Provide some examples of measures that might be used (qualitative and/or quantitative) for each quadrant of the steering wheel to help Tesco deliver this vision.

Managing individual performance: The AMO theory

Designing a performance management process also requires an understanding of the factors which influence employee performance, and, in particular, what encourages people to exhibit positive **discretionary behaviour** and 'go that extra mile' for the organisation.

KEY TERMS

Discretionary behaviour This refers to the degree of choice people have over how they perform their tasks and responsibilities (Purcell et al. 2003), and is something which is given voluntarily and cannot be forced.

Positive discretionary behaviours are associated with working beyond the basic requirements of the job (as outlined in their employment contract and job description), for example covering for an absent colleague or helping new employees learn the job, and it is this which can give an organisation a competitive advantage. The AMO theory, developed to explain the link between HRM and performance, is helpful in understanding how to manage individual performance and encourage positive discretionary behaviours. It also explains the connection between HR policies. This model states that job performance is a function of ability, motivation and opportunity (Applebaum et al. 2000; Boxall and Purcell 2008). In other words employees perform well and utilise their discretion when:

- **A** – they have the *ability* to do so, meaning the necessary skills and knowledge. This is influenced by recruitment and selection, training, learning and development.
- **M** – they have the *motivation* to do so. This is influenced by performance reviews, feedback, reward and recognition, training and development, flexible working and promotion.
- **O** – their work environment provides the necessary support and *opportunities* for people to deploy their skills and be motivated. HR policies and practices such as team briefings, involvement initiatives, team working and job design are important influences.

Managing employees at the individual level therefore brings together many different HRM policies and practices which need to be mutually supportive and reinforcing, in other words, horizontally integrated.

Think about a job you have had:

1. What motivated you to put effort into your work and work 'beyond contract?
2. What factors might influence the 'opportunity' to use your skills and be motivated?
3. What HR policies and practices will influence your 'motivation' and 'opportunities'?

(7.3) The performance management cycle

At the individual and operational level performance management can be viewed as a cycle (Figure 7.2) and this emphasises that it is a continuous process, with sequential activities. For new starters this begins with induction (Marchington and Wilkinson 2008) a vital stage to ensure that new employees not only understand the nature of their job, and the required standards of performance

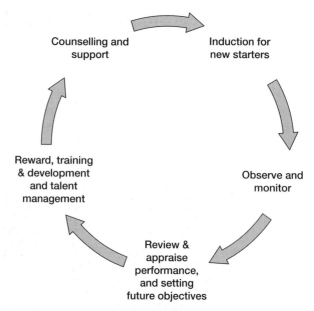

Figure 7.2 The cycle of performance management

but also the organisation's culture and strategic objectives and how they might contribute to this. It is also an opportunity to communicate company policies and procedures, orientate employees so they know where everything is located, and socialise them into the workplace so that they don't feel isolated or alienated. Some organisations allocate a 'buddy' to new employees to offer advice and guidance, perhaps provide on the job training, and help with the socialisation process. Nevertheless, the importance of induction is sometimes overlooked by organisations, and even where it is offered it may come too late to be of any benefit. Data on labour turnover (CIPD 2009b) shows that a fifth of new starters leave the organisations within the first six months, highlighting the importance of a good induction process and the potential costs of getting it wrong.

For all employees there must be ongoing observation and monitoring of an individual's performance, both formal and informal, tasks usually performed by the line manager and/or team colleagues. Regular team meetings, project reviews and one-to-one meetings between a manager and his or her staff can facilitate this process. This will feed into a formal review or appraisal, often an annual event, where past performance can be assessed, problems of underperformance can be identified and objectives set for the future. The review will identify training and development needs and possibly other reward outcomes. Finally counselling and support must be offered to those who fail to meet the required standards of performance. These elements are considered in further detail.

Figure 7.3 Regular team meetings help to monitor performance

(7.4) Performance appraisal

Performance appraisal is often seen as the central pillar of performance management and focuses on reviewing an individuals' performance against an agreed set of criteria, providing feedback, and assessing an individual's potential and development needs. There may also be a link with reward. As ACAS explain: 'The appraisal is an opportunity to take an overall view of work content, loads and volume, to look back on what has been achieved during the reporting period and agree objectives for the next' (ACAS 2008: 3).

Typically performance appraisal is presented as a formal event, often undertaken annually, between an employee and his or her line manager. However, managers should be regularly reviewing and providing feedback on performance on an informal basis too, so that any issues or problems can be dealt with when they arise.

ACAS (2008) recommends that for appraisal schemes to operate effectively the following supportive conditions are necessary:

- Senior managers should be committed to the idea of appraisals and ensure that training, time and resources are available to those conducting the appraisals.
- Consultation takes place on the design and implementation of the scheme with the relevant parties, such as managers, employees and employee representatives.
- A timetable is fixed for the implementation of a scheme.
- All managers who carry out appraisals should receive appropriate training.
- Schemes should be monitored regularly to ensure that interviews take place and are carried out effectively and all forms completed. Schemes should be checked to see if they need modifying to meet the changing needs of the organisation.
- Appraisal schemes should be kept simple, clear and straightforward.

Employee involvement is also important in any performance appraisal, so that the review can be constructive and open, and future objectives are agreed that are relevant, achievable and owned by the individual. This will help employee buy-in to the process and commitment to achievement of any objectives set. Conducting formal reviews can, however, be challenging and requires managers to have good communication and listening skills, particularly when dealing with underperformance since negative feedback can be damaging to an employee's self-confidence and demotivating. All managers who conduct performance appraisals should receive training and some organisations make this a mandatory requirement. This should cover the skills of performance appraisal (the 'how' to do it), including instruction on how to complete the necessary forms, and the reasons for performance appraisal and how it fits into the organisation's performance management strategy, in order to gain understanding and commitment to the process.

A key outcome from the review is an assessment of training and development needs and potential, and many organisations use personal development plans (PDPs) to formally record what action is to be taken. Outcomes can cover a variety of activities such as formal courses, coaching and mentoring, work shadowing, on the job training, and distance learning. Collated information can also be used to gain an overview of employees' skills and potential gaps and analyse the training needs across the organisation. At Cheltenham Borough Council (IDS 2009) copies of each employee's personal development plan is sent to the learning and development department to inform the council's training plan for the following year. Increasingly organisations are using the performance appraisal as a talent management tool to identify and retain talent, and fast track those suitable for promotion.

Who does the appraising?

Choosing who does the appraising depends on the context and consideration should be given to what fits with the organisational culture, the aims of the performance management process, the groups of employees (such as managers) and the type of job to be appraised. There are a variety of approaches which are summarised in Table 7.1. The most common form of appraisal is a review by the immediate line manager, sometimes referred to as **downward appraisal**, which is conducted on a one-to-one basis. This is often combined with some form of self-assessment which allows the person being appraised to have some input into the review. The rationale for downward appraisal is that line managers are normally in close and regular contact with their employees, aware of factors which many influence their performance and the business needs and thus best placed to perform appraisals. Other options include **peer appraisals**, **upward appraisal**, **customer appraisal** and **multi-source feedback**, often referred to as **360 degree feedback** which involves collecting feedback from a number of stakeholders. Multi-source feedback provides a broader view on an employee's performance and can dilute any potential bias and subjectivity. Whichever approach is adopted, it must be ensured that whoever does the assessment understands what constitutes good, acceptable and poor performance, gives honest and frank feedback, receives support and training in the role and respects confidentiality.

CASE STUDY

Kimberly-Clark, the multinational paper manufacturer who produce Andrex toilet paper and Kleenex tissues, have introduced a global approach to managing and measuring performance which covers all of its white collar employees working in 68 countries. This includes a 360 degree process with feedback from customers, peers and direct reports. However, because some cultures, particularly in Asia and South America, find it difficult to make critical comments about their bosses, especially if they could be identified, the feedback is anonymous. In North Asia, which covers China and Korea, attitudes towards this approach revealed a generation gap. Younger employees were positive about the process and more willing to give honest feedback, especially about their bosses, compared to older employees. Training at the implementation phase has encouraged all employees of all ages to see the benefits of this type of feedback.

(Arkin 2007)

1. What types of appraisal scheme would you recommend for the following jobs?
   a) Football coach
   b) Doctor in local GP practice
   c) Sales assistant in retail shop
   d) Project manager
   e) Journalist on local newspaper

Type of appraisal	Key characteristics	Strengths	Weaknesses
Downward appraisal	Conducted by immediate line manager. Can be combined with self-assessment.	Strengthens relationship between line manager and subordinate. Facilitates communication.	Relies on good line management skills. Subject to bias.
Self-appraisal	Individual assesses self. Often used in combination with other methods.	Research suggests can be accurate. Suited to jobs with high levels of discretion, specialised skills or work in isolation from the manager.	Inaccurate assessment. Prone to overrating or underrating. Women, for example, tend to underrate themselves in comparison to men.
Upward appraisal	Employees appraise their manager or superior. Usually anonymous.	Involving employees may be motivating and improve their commitment. Subordinates in close and regular contact with their manager. Supports an open style culture.	Employees may feel intimidated and not give an accurate response. Can be undermining for manager.
Peer assessment	Assessed by peers and colleagues.	Suited to team working environment.	Colleague may not understand individual's job. Reluctance to be honest. May be influenced by jealousy or rivalry ('Screw your buddy').
Customer appraisals	Customer surveys. Mystery shoppers.	Helpful in customer facing environment.	High surveillance and control.

Type of appraisal	Key characteristics	Strengths	Weaknesses
360 degree appraisal	Ratings from colleagues, self, direct report, line manager, customers (internal and external). Often anonymous	Multiple reviewers should ensure a more balanced perspective. Higher validity. Useful for more senior managers.	Time-consuming. Costly to administer. Analysis of information can be complex.

Table 7.1 Types of appraisal

Problems with performance appraisal

One of the major problems with all appraisals is the potential for distortion in the assessment of performance, raising questions about the validity of the process. Some of the most common distortions are outlined by Grint (1993) in his critique of performance appraisal:

- The 'halo' or 'horns' effect – one specific criteria or characteristic distorts the assessment of others. For example, a serious mistake can mean the appraiser lowering the ratings in all other areas.
- Crony effect – distortion caused by closeness of the personal relationship between appraiser and appraised.
- Doppelganger effect – rating reflects the similarity of character or behaviours between appraiser and appraised.
- Veblen effect – this is the problem of central tendency and named after Veblen's habit of giving all students 'C's irrespective of their quality. Arises when appraisers are reluctant to rate individuals at the outer ends of the rating scale, and rate on the middle scale.

Another distortion is the 'recency' effect where recent events influence the assessment. Research has also shown that an individual's gender, age, ethnic origin and race may affect the appraisal. Males, for example, are usually rated as more effective than females (Latham et al. 2007). To minimise the problems of bias and help achieve consistency in reporting standards, ACAS recommends that senior managers have the opportunity to comment upon and sign the report, managers keep running records of the performance of their employees and suitable training is offered to the appraisers (ACAS 2008).

Performance appraisals can also be time consuming, often involve a lot of form filling and bureaucracy and are frequently considered an administrative burden.

Critics of performance appraisals also claim it is a means of management control leading to resentment and even resistance from employees (Redman 2009). This is particularly so in a customer serving environment, such as a call centre, where the constant presence of measurements and use of technological monitoring gives the impression of high surveillance. Multi-source feedback where 'every customer, peer, subordinate and colleague is now also a potential appraiser' (Redman 2009: 180) also increases the potential for management control.

Linking with pay

In some organisations individual performance is directly linked to pay on the basis that pay will motivate people to perform well. Typically percentage increases or lump sum payments (which are not consolidated into the salary) are awarded according to the performance rating of an individual. Table 7.2 shows how this could apply to pay increases.

Performance rating	Pay increase/cost of living plus percentage
Outstanding	5%
Highly effective	3.5%
Effective	2%
Less than effective	0%

Table 7.2 Example of performance-related pay

Another approach is to supplement 'across the board' increases for all staff with additional increases for exceptional staff. However there are difficulties with paying for performance and research suggests it does not always motivate employees and, indeed, can have the reverse effect. The amount of pay linked to performance may be too small to make a difference in terms of encouraging people to perform better and of course not everyone is motivated by pay. The system can also be very divisive with employees not receiving any reward complaining of favouritism, (particularly where the performance factors to be assessed are subjective) and can inhibit teamwork because of its individualistic character. In relation to the performance appraisal, it is unlikely that the person being appraised will admit to developmental needs if their salary or part of their salary depends on a good appraisal. For this reason it is recommended that organisations that choose to pay for individual performance should keep the pay review separate from the developmental review (see Chapter 4, Reward). Non-monetary rewards can also be linked to performance at individual and team level, through for example recognition, skills development, career opportunities. John Lewis Partnership, the retail organisation, have a scheme called 'One Step Beyond' which provides line managers with the opportunity to reward employees in a personal and immediate way by giving, for example, a bottle of champagne or voucher (Hutchinson and Purcell 2007). Some organisations have 'employee of the month' schemes which publically acknowledge individual or team success.

Figure 7.4 Individual performance is sometimes directly linked to pay

7.5 Measuring performance

In order to assess how an individual or team is performing and make decisions about what is needed to improve performance or develop an individual, some form of measurement is needed to define the required standards. However, finding measurements that are meaningful, accurate and not subject to bias is difficult, and can be a source of employee discontent. Some organisations are criticised for choosing measures that are not necessarily the most important but the easiest to measure and clearly some aspects of performance, and some jobs, can be more easily measured than others. Compare an assembly line worker producing standard quality goods to a laboratory scientist testing potential new drugs. The assembly worker could be measured on the number of goods produced per hour, but how do you assess the scientist, especially when a new drug may take years to develop? The starting point for any organisation is to define the desired job performance it seeks as action and/or behaviours and this should be relevant to the attainment of an organisation's goals (Latham et al. 2007). Only then can instruments or measurements be developed for assessing the required performance. These should be valid (in other words, does the method actually measure what it is supposed to measure?), objective, meaningful and fair.

Many organisations use the **SMART** acronym (Table 7.3) to describe the key requirements of good target setting, and reduce subjectivity. The Crown Prosecution Service, for example, advises its employees and line managers that objectives set in the performance development review process should be SMART and each objective should address the following questions:

- Why are we doing this?
- What is going to be different?
- Will it help to achieve the overall corporate objective?

(IDS HR Study 2009: 28)

Essentially there are two broad approaches to measuring performance: objective-based and competency-based assessments, although in practice a combination of methods can be used.

Specific	Outcomes need to be clearly defined, using a language which can be easily understood by employees and managers.
Measurable	Outcomes should be capable of measurement on a quantitative and/or qualitative basis.
Agreed	Although managers may set the objectives they should be agreed with the employee to ensure buy-in.
Realistic	Targets should be set within the capabilities of the individual, but be challenging and offer the opportunity for development. They should also be in line with the job description and appropriate to the role.
Time-bound	Target dates or timescales should be set for achievement of the objectives rather than be open ended.

Table 7.3 Ensuring objectives are SMART

Objective-based assessments

KEY TERMS

Objective-based assessments These are focused on outcomes or results, and usually expressed as targets to be met over a period of time (such as x sales a year), and are often easily quantifiable.

This type of assessment may also include some quality control measures, such as customer satisfaction index, or level of accuracy, to ensure that product and service quality is not compromised at the expense of quantity. One common approach is management by objectives (MBO) whereby objectives are agreed between the employee and his or her line manager at the beginning of the appraisal or review period, often with the aid of the job description. Subsequent appraisals are based on looking at how far the objectives have been met and setting future objectives to be achieved within a set time period (normally short term). The advantages with this output-based approach are that it is objective, clear to understand, the appraisee can have input into the targets set, and objectives can be linked to team/departmental targets. However there are disadvantages. Not all jobs can be easily measured in this way, and it does not take account of factors outside a person's control (such as the economic environment, or the input of others), which may result in a person receiving a high or low evaluation undeservedly. It also ignores the process by which achievements are made, which is important if we need to understand what and how improvements can be made.

Performance measurements for a customer advisor in a call centre (just taking inbound calls) may include a combination of quantitative and qualitative objectives:

- Number of calls taken per hour
- Length of calls
- Length of time customer is waiting
- Customer satisfaction

Competency approaches

More recently organisations have moved towards a focus on a competency-based approach. Competencies are behaviours that are necessary to perform a job well, and competency frameworks are used not only in performance management but also recruitment and selection and assessing training and development needs. Competency approaches are particularly helpful in identifying areas for improvement and providing an appropriate language

Figure 7.5 Quantitative and qualitative objectives measure performance in call centres

for feedback (Redman 2009), but assessing competencies is complex, time-consuming and prone to subjectivity and thus bias.

One common method of assessing competencies is behaviourally anchored rating scales (BARS), which are based on the assumption that it is helpful to give the appraiser 'a frame of reference in the form of behavioral illustrations of what constitutes unacceptable, acceptable and highly acceptable behaviour' (Latham et al. 2007: 367). Thus specific and usually detailed examples or 'anchors' are given to illustrate each behavioural criteria. The key features of this method are:

- Raters (normally managers or job experts), this may include, list the key aspects of the performance of a particular job. For example, adaptability/ flexibility for a project manager (see Table 7.4).
- The same group provides examples of excellent/good, average and poor/ unsatisfactory performance for each aspect of the job.
- These examples are assembled along a numerical rating scale to indicate a range from excellent to very poor (e.g. 1 to 3, 1 to 5 or 1 to 7).
- This process is repeated by another group to check the validity of the process.
- Once the process is completed appraisers use it to evaluate and rate individuals on the basis of each job holder's typical behaviour on each scale.

Key behaviour: adaptability/flexibility

Unsatisfactory	Needs improvement	Meets expectations	Exceeds expectations	Exceptional
Able to focus on only one task at a time	Easily distracted from work activities	Handles a variety of work activities without difficulty	Handles a variety of work activities concurrently	Easily juggles a large number of activities
Avoids changes	Complains about changes	Accepts reasons for change	Understands and responds to reasons for change	Encourages and instructs others about the benefits of change
Refuses to adapt to new or changed policies	Makes only those changes with which they agree	Adapts to changing circumstances and attitudes of others	Adapts to changes and develops job to assist others	Welcomes change and looks for new opportunities it provides
Only considers own options when seeking a solution	Occasionally listens to others but supports own solutions	Listens to others and seeks solution acceptable to all	Ensures everyone's opinions are considered in reaching a solution	Actively seeks input and facilitates implementation of solution

Table 7.4 Example of behaviourally anchored rating scales for project manager: key behaviour: adaptability/flexibility (adapted from Aguinis 2009: 110)

The advantage of BARS is that anchor scales are directly relevant to the job being assessed and the approach has the potential to be objective. The main drawbacks, however, are that job experts must be used to design the scheme and it is complex, time-consuming and costly. A variation of this approach is behaviourally observed scales (BOS) which require appraisers to rate the frequency with which they have observed an employee demonstrates specific behaviours (Latham et al. 2007).

Performance ratings

Most performance management schemes use some form of performance rating to indicate the overall level of performance achieved, grading employees on a scale which covers the range excellent to very poor. A grading scale can have 3, 4, 5 (as in the example above) 6 or 7 levels to differentiate performance, which is particularly important in informing pay decisions or developing talent. While easy to understand, ratings can be highly subjective and it is common for appraisers to rate people around the average. Partly to overcome this some organisations use forced rankings, whereby appraisers rate along a distribution curve and must use the full range of scales. Typically a small percentage of people are at the top and bottom of the curve and the majority in the middle. This forces managers to differentiate between performers and take difficult decisions about who are the best and poorest performers. The approach seeks to ensure greater consistency in marking between managers and, if linked to pay, is an aid to budgetary control. It also enables organisations to identify the top performers who need to be retained and invested in. There are, however, problems with this approach, in particular it can be demotivating for those not receiving high rankings, it can be divisive, particularly in a teamworking environment, and penalise teams made up of mostly high performers. Nevertheless, many high profile organisations in the United Sates use or have used this approach including General Electric, Microsoft, Sun Microsystems, Ford and Hewlett Packard. In the UK the civil service use a distribution curve to rank its senior civil servants into a top rank (top 25 per cent), middle rank (next 65–70 per cent) and a bottom rank of 5–10 per cent. Basic pay and bonus awards are linked to these rankings.

Some organisations use this approach to systematically remove the bottom performers (e.g. 10 per cent) each year. Referred to as the 'ranking and yanking' approach (Redman 2009), this controversial approach is claimed to raise the overall calibre of employees in an organisation but on the downside can create a 'culture of fear'. Although only about 4 per cent of UK organisations are believed to adopt this approach, a survey of 562 UK managers found that 77 per cent felt that sacking a fixed amount of underperforming employees each year would boost financial performance and productivity (Arkin 2007).

Design a performance measurement system to rate:

1. The performance of the lecturers at your university
   or
2. The job of assistant manager profiled in Chapter 2 (on recruitment and selection).

7.6 Managing underperformance

Whilst the emphasis in performance management should be on creating a positive climate, encouraging and supporting success, it also provides the opportunity to identify and address those who are underperforming. It is therefore particularly beneficial for organisations who have traditionally overlooked poor performance, perhaps because of their culture, management style or simply a reluctance to confront problematic people.

The IRS 2008 performance management survey of 139 UK organisations identified that underperformance is a widespread problem and four-fifths of respondents experienced the issue to 'some extent', and one in ten claim it is a problem to a 'considerable extent' (IRS 2008). Underperformance is most commonly associated with poor standards of work but can manifest itself in other ways such as poor timekeeping, regular absence from work, failure to follow instructions or poor attitudes/behaviour towards work colleagues or customers. It is important to recognise that, although poor performance is commonly attributed to capability issues, it may be affected by factors outside the work environment, such as personal relationships and commitments. A recent CIPD survey (CIPD 2009c) on absence found that 43 per cent of respondents cited home and family responsibilities as a major reason for short-term absence for non-manual employees and 39 per cent for manual employees. However, even if work related, poor performance may not always be solely the fault of the individual. An employee may lack the necessary training or resources, may be unclear about what the job entails, may know what is required but not know how to achieve it, or lack influence over factors that would enable them to achieve higher levels of performance. Poor performance may also arise because of bullying or stress in the workplace. Critical to managing underperformance is, therefore, a diagnosis of the problem – what is the nature of the problem, its causes, and how can it be resolved? The formal performance appraisal provides the opportunity to perform this analysis, but informal and regular communication between managers and employees also enables problems to be addressed early and 'nipped in the bud'. It is also important that underperforming employees understand and recognise that there is a problem and take ownership for resolving it.

Appropriate action to resolve the problem may include:

- *Training, learning and development* interventions for individuals who lack the necessary skills and experience.
- *Counselling and support* – this may be formal, such as occupational health or counselling services, or informal, for example coaching and guidance from the line manager.
- *Adjustment to work duties or redeployment* – where the employee is unable to improve and reach the required standards, or alternative work can be considered or the job may be redesigned or adjusted.
- *Disciplinary procedures*

Some organisations choose to place emphasis on the probationary period of employment to try and identify performance issues early on and during this period (for example three or six months) progress is regularly reviewed. Formal performance improvement plans, sometimes referred to as capability procedures, can be developed to help not only those who underperform, but the managers managing the problem. The aim is to provide a supportive and consistent process to deal with capability issues which is distinct from the formal disciplinary procedure which can be perceived of as more punitive and used as a last resort.

Counselling approaches are particularly relevant where employees have personal problems, whether at home or work, and may be informal with the line manager listening and/or offering advice, or more formal through the provision of specialised services such as occupational health and/or employee assistance schemes (EAPs) (Taylor 2008). An employee, who has medical reasons for underperforming such as a back injury, might call upon the services of occupational health to facilitate a return to work or advice on improvements to the work environment. EAPs usually deal with personal matters relating to finance, relationships, health and emotions, stress, and addictions, and would be expected to employ trained counsellors. A person who is persistently off sick or late for work for alcohol-related problems may, in the first instance be referred to occupational health or EAP for advice and support rather than resort to use of the disciplinary procedure, particularly where that individual has a history of good or effective performance. Organisations consider these facilities worthwhile investing in because, in the long term, they can positively impact on employees performance but are obviously expensive to offer and therefore tend to be found in larger organisations.

Formal disciplinary procedures should normally only be used when performance has not improved following a performance review and the chance to improve has been given. When formal procedures are initiated they should follow best practice as outlined in the ACAS Code of Conduct. However ACAS stress that disciplinary procedures should not be seen simply as a punishment and means of imposing sanctions but as means of encouraging improvement in performance.

CASE STUDY

At Novartis Vaccines and Diagnostics (IDS Study 2009) a performance improvement plan (PIP) is used to address underperformance at any time in the year. This is essentially a set template for line managers to follow and clarifies the issues to be addressed. If it results from the performance management process then the PIP has to be initiated by the operational manager within 30 days of the review meeting. Managers meet employees on a PIP at least fortnightly to assess progress and are advised to consult their HR business partner for guidance on the particular issue. When satisfactory performance is achieved the PIP closure form is signed and logged on the individuals' personal file. In the event that performance does not improve after 90 days, the line manager is advised to discuss options with HR. This may include extending the PIP, changing an individual's role, initiating the capability proceeding or, where appropriate, dismissal. A similar approach of monitoring underperformance is often used in secondary schools although of course pupils are rarely expelled for poor performance unless it's a case of gross misconduct!

ACTIVITY

Consider the case of Emma, who has recently become seriously demotivated at work and whose standard of performance has dropped. Emma has worked for the organisation for three years and has in the past been a good employee. However she now regularly arrives late for work in the morning (five or ten minutes), often phones in sick on Mondays and doesn't always complete her work on time. Several work colleagues have complained about her, particularly as they have to cover for her work. As her line manager what action would you take?

(7.7) Key roles in performance management

The role of line managers

Performance management has traditionally been an area in which line managers have had direct and extensive involvement and one of the key characteristics of performance management is that 'it is owned and driven by the line' (Armstrong 2008: 2), rather than being the responsibility of a specialist HR function. Indeed it seems quite logical that line managers should be involved for they are directly responsible for the performance of a work area, normally in close and regular contact with their employees and should be aware of factors which may influence employees' performances. This practice is confirmed in recent survey findings. An IRS survey found that 95 per cent of respondent organisations expected line managers to monitor and review the performance of their direct reports (IRS 2008), and a CIPD survey (2005) showed that 75 per cent of respondents agreed/strongly agreed that line managers own and operate the performance process. In essence: 'Performance management is the means by which many firms ensure that managers do what good managers ought to do, ensure people know what they ought to be doing, have the skills to do it and complete it to the adequate standard' (CIPD 2009a, page 2).

Recent research highlights the vital role line managers play in the delivery of HRM by the way in which they implement HR policies and practices or 'bring policies to life' (Purcell and Hutchinson 2007). Line managers are critical to the implementation of the AMO model of performance, referred to earlier, for they impact on individuals' ability and motivation to perform and provide opportunities for individuals to develop and use their skills. In operationalising performance management these managers are involved in a range of HR activities including induction, reviewing and appraising performance, identifying training needs, providing coaching and guidance, allocating rewards, handling capability issues, dealing with grievances and providing counseling and support. In induction, for example, line managers need to ensure new starters understand what their job entails and 'the way things are done around here'. They may also arrange for a 'buddy' to guide and support new recruits or arrange work shadowing. Typically line managers will conduct appraisal interviews, and motivate employees by providing positive feedback and recognition and perhaps allocate rewards. In dealing with underperformance they are expected to conduct 'difficult conversations' with employees, investigate problems informally, conduct return to work interviews for absent employees and can often discipline up to the first level of warning.

However involving line managers in the practice of performance management can be problematic, and research points to variability in the behaviour of line managers and a gap between intended policies and those practised by the line (McGovern et al. 1997; Hutchinson and Purcell 2003). In researching the link between people management and performance, Purcell and colleagues found that even within organisations that employed 'best practice' HRM policies, the frequency of, and quality of performance appraisals varied quite markedly due to variations in line management behaviour (Hutchinson and Purcell 2003). The aforementioned IRS survey on performance management found that two thirds of HR professionals did not consider line managers to be competent or confident in managing underperformance (IRS 2008). A range of factors can inhibit line manager ability to manage performance effectively including lack of skills and knowledge, work overload, and lack of role clarity (Table 7.5). Performance appraisals are a notorious area for 'impression management' leading to distortion and bias in making judgements, referred to previously. At a practical level appraisals are often associated with excessive paperwork and form filling and can be very time-consuming to undertake. At John Lewis a 'good' appraisal can take up to three hours, plus additional time to write up and record the outcome of the meeting (Hutchinson and Purcell 2007). Where appraisals have both a reward and developmental function there is a tension for line managers in fulfilling the dual role of coach (for developmental purposes) and judge (in allocating reward) – roles which may be difficult to reconcile and involve different skills (Leopold 2002).

Clearly line managers need to be provided with resources, time and training so that they can effectively manage and support the performance of individuals in their team. They have to be committed to, and take ownership of performance management which requires an understanding of the importance of performance management and the impact it can make on the team and organisational performance and service delivery. Reinforcing this through the way in which they themselves are performance managed, and by monitoring and rewarding their people management skills, can ensure buy-in. Support and advice is also required for senior managers and the HR function.

- Lack of interpersonal skills such as communication, coaching and listening.
- Lack of knowledge on policies and procedures, legislation and 'best practice'.
- Work overload and lack of time.
- Too much administration and 'bureaucracy'.
- Making subjective judgements ('impression management').
- Lack of commitment – performance appraisal often relies on manager's own motivation for fulfillment (McGovern et al. 1997).
- Conflict of personalities between appraisee and his/her line manager.
- Tension between manager's role as 'judge' and 'coach'.
- Dislike of having 'difficult' conversations with poor performers.
- Lack of accountability in allocating rewards.

Table 7.5 Line management difficulties in managing performance

Senior managers

Senior managers have a role to play in not only establishing strategies and targets which underpin performance management but also in developing a strong performance management culture and providing support and active commitment through positive role modelling (Hutchinson and Purcell 2007). By demonstrating, through their own behaviour, that performance management is taken seriously in the organisation, senior managers can encourage line management buy-in to performance management. Bad habits as well as good ones are copied, and it is hard for line managers to be motivated and committed to effective performance management if their own manager is not. Senior managers can also comment on appraisal reports which allows them to check on the progress of staff and ensure consistency in approach.

HR function

The HR function is responsible for the design of performance management policies and processes and needs to work closely with line managers in providing support and advice, in particular in developing their skills and knowledge (through training and development) so that they can manage performance effectively. They also need to clarify that performance management is a key element of what managers do, through job descriptions and providing handbooks and guides which set out their responsibilities and provide advice on 'how to', for example coach, or hold a 'difficult conversation'. HR should also ensure that systems are not overly bureaucratic and cumbersome, and regularly monitor performance management processes. Increasingly organisations are relying on delivering online tools to assist line managers in managing the appraisal process by easing the completion of forms, reminding managers of the need to conduct formal appraisals, tracking reviews and improving management information. HR specialists are often criticised for designing policies which are good in theory but hard to implement in practice and need to involve line managers in the development of performance management policies to make sure that the goals and targets are understood, relevant and deliverable.

CASE STUDY

John Lewis Partnership is one of the UK's top ten retail businesses, and the largest and best known examples of worker ownership in the UK. In 2006 the organisation made a conscious effort to include line managers in both the formulation and communication of their new performance management strategy. Working parties were set up comprising line managers – and non-management partners – to consider the development of a new reward system. These addressed a range of issues such as performance measures, competencies, pay banding working groups and the appraisal system. This facilitated management buy-in to the new strategy and meant that a language was developed on levels of performance which was readily understood in the stores. Line managers also play a key role in communicating any new system to their staff and receiving feedback. The organisation also introduced an IT based payroll and management system call 'partner link' to alert managers when they need to conduct a review.

(Hutchinson and Purcell 2007)

Providing criticism is difficult. Criticisms should be constructive, focus on an individual's actions or behaviours, rather than their personality, and aim to concentrate on how future improvements can be made rather than look back at the past. For example, you would not want to say 'you are lazy' or 'you are simply not up the job' as this can be demotivating and does not suggest what action needs to be taken to improve.

1. Provide examples of how a line manager can give criticism effectively, through action and/or words.

 ## Summary

Performance management is essentially a tool for organisations to encourage, support and sustain high performance at individual and team level and ultimately improve the organisational effectiveness. Performance management can be seen as the embodiment of 'HRM', with its clear emphasis on vertical and horizontal integration, and the role of the line manager. As an integrated approach to managing the business, it connects individual and team objectives with the corporate strategy, and is a means of promoting employee engagement with organisational goals. It also brings together a range of interrelated HR activities, such as induction, training and development, reward, performance appraisal and capability management. Line managers have the responsibility for the day to day delivery of these practices and should be regularly reviewing the performance of their team, formally and informally. These managers can significantly impact on individuals' ability and motivation to perform and therefore play a critical role in the performance management process. Performance management is now widespread and while the benefits are clear, its operationalisation is problematic. Multiple tensions are inherent in the process because of its conflict in purpose. In this chapter we have given emphasis to performance management as a tool to motivate, train and develop individuals and elicit positive discretionary behaviours, but the need to have measurements, and monitor and assess performance means performance management can be perceived of as a management tool for control and surveillance. Identifying training and development needs and allocating rewards have also been shown to be incompatible and for line mangers this presents the dilemma of being 'judge' or 'helper'. In addition the potential for distortion in the assessment process, difficulties in developing measurements and problems of bureaucracy and time means that performance management is a challenging process for organisations to manage effectively.

KEY IDEAS

Some of the main points addressed in this chapter are listed below. If you feel unsure about any of them revisit the appropriate section. The recommended reading list provides additional material on the topics you might wish to explore further.

What is performance management?

- Performance management seeks to encourage, support and sustain high performance at individual, team and organisational level.
- It emphasises the need to link individual and team goals to the organisation's objectives and connects many interrelated HR activities. Performance management thus highlights vertical and horizontal integration in HRM.
- Inherent in any performance management process are tensions between its use as a tool to motivate, support and develop individuals versus its use as a means to measure and control employees.

The performance management cycle

- At individual and operational levels performance management can be viewed as a continuous process, with sequential activities.
- These activities include induction (for new starters), observing and monitoring, reviewing and appraising performance, identification of training and development needs and possibly reward, support and counselling for those who underperform.
- The cycle incorporates formal and informal activities and processes.

Performance appraisal

- The appraisal focuses on reviewing individual performance against a set of criteria, providing feedback and assessing potential and development needs.

continued . . . ▶

. . . continued

- There are a variety of approaches to appraising depending on who does the appraising. Options include downward appraisals, peer appraisals, upward appraisal, customer appraisal and 360 degree appraisal.
- Performance appraisal can be problematic. It can be highly subjective and therefore prone to distortion, time-consuming and bureaucratic. There are also difficulties in linking performance to pay and it is recommended that organisations who pay for performance should keep the pay review separate to the developmental review.

Measuring performance

- There are two broad approaches to measuring performance: objective-based and competency-based assessment. Many organisations rank overall performance on a scale to differentiate between good, acceptable and poor performance.
- Measurements should be valid, objective, meaningful and fair.

Managing underperformance

- Performance management provides the opportunity to identify and address underperformance, formally and informally.
- Formal approaches to resolving underperformance include training, learning and development, counselling and support, adjustment to the role or redeployment and capability procedures. Formal disciplinary procedures should only be used as a last resort.

Key roles

- Line managers should own and operate performance management, although they often lack the competence or confidence to manage performance effectively.
- HR and senior managers can support line managers in variety of ways, including designing performance policies that can be implemented, acting as role models, and offer advice and training.

RECOMMENDED READING

If you would like to learn more about some of the key issues addressed in this chapter you might like to consider the following books and articles:

What is performance management?
Michael Armstrong's book *Performance Management* provides more detail on the aims, characteristics and guiding principle of performance management. The CIPD publication, *People Resourcing* by Stephen Taylor, also devotes a chapter to performance management strategies, which includes a discussion on the different perspectives of performance management and examines some contemporary thinking.

The performance management cycle
In their chapter on Performance Management in *Human Resource Management at Work*, Mick Marchington and Adrian Wilkinson consider the various elements of the performance management cycle in some detail and go beyond traditional definitions of performance management to include the induction of new staff.

Performance appraisal

Tom Redman provides a critical and comprehensive review of key developments in performance appraisal in *Contemporary Human Resource Management*. The ACAS guide on *Employee Appraisals* also provides practical advice and guidance on appraisals, including designing an appraisal system and examples of different types of appraisal schemes. Detailed advice is also given on conducting an appraisal interview.

Measuring performance

Herman Aguinis's book on *Performance Management* and *Managing Employee Performance and Reward* by John Shields both provide detail on choosing a measurement approach and how to measure results and competencies, with numerous case study examples.

Managing underperformance

Managing underperformance, including particular issues associated with absence management, are considered by Pilbeam and Corbridge in their book *People Resourcing: Contemporary HRM in practice* and by Mick Marchington and Adrian Wilkinson in *Human Resource Management at Work.* Both books also have chapters on discipline procedures.

Key roles in performance management

Recent research on the role of line managers in reward and training, learning and development by Sue Hutchinson and John Purcell, published by the CIPD, *Line managers in rewards, training learning and development*, considers the difficulties line managers face in delivering these aspects of people management, and the importance of performance management as a tool to help managers manage. The article 'Human resource management on the line' by McGovern et al. examines the role of line managers in performance appraisals.

USEFUL WEBSITES

www.acas.org.uk Website of the Advisory, Conciliation and Arbitration Service
www.cbi.org.uk Website of the Confederation of British Industry
www.cipd.co.uk Website of the Chartered Institute of Personnel and Development
www.incomesdata.co.uk Website of Incomes Data Services
www.xperthr.co.uk Website of XpertHR – online HR Intelligence

REFERENCES

ACAS (2008) *Performance Appraisals*, March 2008.
Arkin, A. (2007) From soft to strong, *People Management*, September.
Aguinis, H. (2009) *Performance Management,* 2nd edn. Pearson International Edition.
Appelbaum, E., Bailey, T., Berg, P., Kallebergh, A. (2000) *Manufacturing Advantage: Why high performance systems pay off.* Ithaca, NY: ILR Press.
Armstrong, M. (2008). *Performance Management: Key strategies and practical guidelines*, 3rd edn. London: Kogan Page.
Armstrong, M., Baron, A. (2005) *Managing Performance: Performance Management in action.* London: CIPD.

Boxall, P., Purcell, J. (2008) *Strategy and Human Resource Management*, 2nd edn. Basingstoke: Palgrave.

CIPD (2005) *Performance Management survey report*. London: CIPD.

CIPD (2009a) *Performance management: Discussion paper*. London: CIPD.

CIPD (2009b) *Survey on recruitment, retention and turnover*. London: CIPD.

CIPD (2009c) *Absence Survey*. London: CIPD.

Grint, K. (1993) What's wrong with performance appraisal? A critique and suggestions. *Human Resource Management Journal*, vol. 3, no. 3: 61–77.

Hutchinson, S., Purcell, J. (2003). *Bringing Policies to Life: The vital role of line managers*. London: CIPD.

Hutchinson, S., Purcell, J. (2007). *The role of line managers in reward, and training, learning and development*, Research Report. London: CIPD.

IDS HR Studies (2009), 886, January.

IRS Employment Trends (2000), 703, May.

IRS Employment Review Survey: Managing Employee Performance (2008), 890

Kaplan, R.S., Norton, D.P. (1992) The balanced scorecard – measures that drive performance, *Harvard Business Review*, vol. 70, no. 1.

Latham, G., Sulsky, L.M., MacDonald, H. (2007) Performance management, in P. Boxall, Purcell, J., Wright, P. (eds) *The Oxford Handbook of Human Resource Management*. Oxford: Oxford University Press.

Leopold, J. (2002) Human resources in organisations, London: FT/Prentice Hall.

Marchington, M., Wilkinson, A. (2008) *Human Resource Management at Work*, 4th edn. London: CIPD.

McGovern, F., Gratton, L., Hope Hailey, V., Stiles, P., Truss, C. (1997) Human resource management on the line? *Human Resource Management Journal*, vol. 7, no. 4: 12–29.

Purcell, J., Hutchinson, S. (2007). Front-line managers as agents in the HRM–performance causal chain: theory, analysis and evidence, *Human Resource Management Journal*, vol. 17, no. 1: 3–20.

Purcell, J., Kinnie, N., Hutchinson, S., Rayton, B., Swart, J. (2003). *Understanding the people and performance link: unlocking the black box*. London: CIPD.

Redman, T. (2009) Performance appraisal in Redman, T., Wilkinson, A. (eds.) *Contemporary Human Resource Management: text and cases*. 3rd edition. Harlow: FT/Prentice Hall.

Shields, J. (2007*) Managing Employee Performance and Rewards: Concepts, Practices, Strategies*. Cambridge: Cambridge University Press.

Taylor, S. (2008) *People Resourcing*, 4th edn. London: CIPD.

8 Employment law

'Most workers want no more of the law than that it should leave them alone'

Wedderburn 1986: 1

'Protection at work increasingly rests on individual statutory rights . . . It is not simply a question of there being more law twenty-five years on. The nature and scope of legal regulation has also shifted decisively, going to the heart of the employment relationship and providing more universal coverage.'

Dickens and Hall 2009: 332

CHAPTER OBJECTIVES

- Appreciate the changing nature of employment law in Britain, and in particular the reasons for the growing importance of individual statutory employment rights
- Understand the main sources of employment law, together with the options available to the parties to seek legal redress through the Courts
- Appreciate the shifting concerns of employment law and the growing importance of European law in shaping the priorities in UK employment law
- Appreciate the impact of law on the work of the HR function from recruitment through to termination of employment
- Appreciate the significance of the contract of employment for an understanding of modern HR work and in dealing with many of the legal issues affecting HR work

8.1 Introduction: nature and sources of employment law

When Wedderburn – widely regarded as one of the leading figures in labour law in Britain over the past fifty years – wrote the words that preface this chapter many would have agreed with him. As the principal architect of the employment legislation of the previous decade, he was writing in a period of profound change, although the magnitude and extent of this was barely discernible at the time. From the vantage point of the second decade of the twenty-first century, it is clear that at the time many of the traditional supports and regulatory mechanisms provided by trade unions and collective bargaining to cushion and protect workers were being eroded by a combination of factors and in their place management was able to restructure employment and employment relationships largely unchallenged. As we shall see, the law played an important role in helping to bring about this transformation, but it has also subsequently played a significant role in filling the gap in regulation left by the retreat of collective bargaining.

In this chapter we focus upon the growing importance of employment law in regulating employment and the employment relationship as identified by Dickens and Hall. The fact that it merits a separate chapter at all in a book on human resource management reflects the changing concerns and priorities of policy makers, the growing significance of Europe in regulating work and employment and, to an extent, the failure of other forms of regulation to achieve the results both governments and organisations desire.

KEY TERMS

Contract A legally binding agreement between two or more parties.
Trade union immunities These are particularly important in respect of industrial action where unions are afforded some immunity from prosecution under the law. In such cases unions are protected from legal claims for damages from an employer. There is no 'right to strike', only certain immunities from prosecution so long as the industrial action 'is in contemplation or furtherance of a trade dispute' and that it has been sanctioned through an approved ballot where the majority have voted in favour of action.
Statutes Any authoritatively declared rule, ordinance, decree or law.

The role of law in employment is both broad and complex and in this chapter we have deliberately chosen to concentrate on those areas which are of particular importance to those working in personnel and HR. Our main focus will be on the **contract** of employment and how this has evolved with the growth of employment legislation. This will necessarily involve consideration of the impact of equality legislation, so-called 'family friendly' laws as well as more traditional concerns around employment protection and termination of employment. Before embarking on this we begin by distinguishing between various forms of law, the sources of law and the ways in which the law is used to affect employment relationships.

At the outset, it is important to point out that although labour or employment law is a subset of law generally, and draws heavily on established legal principles, it is also different in important respects – its own **statutes** (see below), and its own court structure (employment tribunals for breaches of statutory rights) and within this legal subsystem, a distinction between collective and individual law that is not found outside this area of law. For many lawyers, it is also seen as a rather indistinct area of law, one that is often best suited to those who have spent time working in industry and commerce rather than 'pure lawyers'. Indeed this view heavily influenced those who designed what is now the employment tribunal system in England and Wales. We will return to this issue later in the chapter but at this point it would be useful to establish some definitions and make some distinctions.

A useful starting point is to note that the law we discuss in this chapter is UK law, and this law comes some a number of sources which are detailed below.

Sources of law

In many countries a key source of law is the *constitution* but in the UK, in the absence of a written constitution, we rely on the following:

- *Case law* – judicial decisions that add to the body of common law (see below).
- *Legislation* – statute law, Acts of Parliament. What we most commonly think of as a source of law.
- *Delegated legislation* – some statutes give the relevant Secretary of State power to make **regulations** that normally add to a particular Act. These generally have to be approved by Parliament and are termed *statutory instruments*.
- *Codes of practice* – although not strictly law, legislation permits a minister or a statutory body to issue codes of practice. The most important of these in the employment field are issued by ACAS, and the best known is the Code on Disciplinary and Grievance Procedures revised regularly and which is used as a guide to organisations as to how to devise and operate such procedures. Where these have been developed and followed by organisations, they are taken into account by tribunals when making judgments relating to cases involving unfair **dismissal**.
- *European Union law* – in the employment field these are normally in the form of **directives** which are then transposed into national laws through the Parliaments of the Member states. Also important are decisions of the European Court of Justice, the supreme European Court, which has cases referred to it by member states (see for example the 2009 *Heyday Case* concerning the legality of statutory retirement ages). Note also that Community law takes precedence over national laws – so that national laws must be consistent with the EC Treaty.
- *Human Rights Act (1996)* – this has added significantly to the scope of law in the UK and supplements the long-standing role of the European Court of Human Rights (linked to the Council of Europe not the EU).

KEY TERMS

Directive A legislative act of the European Union which requires member states to achieve a particular result without dictating the means of achieving that result.

Dismissal The termination of employment of an employee and can be with or without notice. Where it is without notice this can give rise to a common law claim of wrongful dismissal.

Transposition The process of transferring, normally an EU Directive, into National Law.

As well as the sources of law, a distinction is normally made between *civil* and *criminal* law.

Civil law

Law that generally relates to individual rights and normally involves individuals taking action against other individuals or organisations to 'right some civil wrong'. That is, where a private individual has suffered some harm and chooses to bring an action against the person who committed the wrongful act that produced the harm. The law of contract and the law of **tort** are both significant in employment law and both are firmly grounded in civil law.

Criminal law

A crime, a criminal offence, is one against the state, against society generally and it is normally the state that enforces this branch of law (Lewis and Sargeant 2009: 1). To use an example outside employment law: dangerous driving potentially causes danger to everyone, it is not an act against a particular individual by another. It is possible therefore for the police to seek criminal proceedings against someone in this situation.

The normal sanctions under criminal law are fines and/or imprisonment, whereas under civil law actions are normally pursued with a view to some sort of compensation, often in the form of **damages**.

KEY TERMS

Damages Monies awarded by a court where there has been held to have been a breach of contract or as compensation for a tort.
Tort A civil wrong, for example negligence or nuisance. In employment law, personal injury claims are often made where the alleged negligence of an employer has given rise to some sort of physical or psychological injury. In collective law, trade unions may be liable for damages where they commit economic torts against an employer.

In practice most employment law normally involves civil law rather than criminal, but there are some exceptions. The most common of these are aspects of health and safety law that can give rise to criminal action and some aspects of the regulation of industrial disputes can lead to 'breaches of the peace' and criminal sanctions.

A further distinction in employment law is one between collective and individual law, one that closely parallels a distinction between public and private law which is more familiar to lawyers.

Collective versus individual law

As its name suggests, *collective employment law* concerns itself with relations between associations of **employees**, such as trade unions, and employers and associations acting on their behalf. This includes the law relating to trade unions and their immunities, and the law on industrial action. *Individual employment law* focuses, at its name suggests, on the individual worker and is largely concerned with employment protection through *regulatory law*.

Finally, and most important, is the distinction between statute and common law.

Statute law

This is law that is enacted by Parliament in the form of legislation, for example Acts of Parliament. These may be initiated by the Government of the day – for example the National Minimum Wage Act (1998) – or by the European Union through a directive (for example the Working Time Directive 1998), with Parliament required to enact legislation to bring the European Union Directive into operation in the UK (for example, the Working Time Regulations 1998).

KEY TERMS

Employee Someone who works under a contract of employment.
Precedents A judicial decision that may be used as a standard in subsequent similar case.
Regulations A legislative act of the European Union which becomes immediately enforceable as law in all member states simultaneously.

Common law

This is often commonly referred to as case law or 'judge-made' law. It is extremely important in this country, and employment law is no exception. When courts make judgments about particular cases they do so on the basis of past judgments, of **precedents**. These precedents are judicial decisions that help provide legal guidance to those deciding any new cases.

What is sometimes difficult for non-lawyers to appreciate is the importance of the common law. While statute law often provides the basis for a decision in law, frequently areas of law require interpretation. That is, where no statute exists, or where a statute does not always provide a clear answer, or where the circumstances of a particular case are unusual and require a particular interpretation we often have to rely on case law to provide the basis for judgment. One example of this is the law relating to unfair dismissal, where there have been many illustrations of where aspects of this law have been interpreted and reinterpreted by the courts. These judgments in effect, create new law, new *common law*. A further example is that of the contract of employment, where the impact of common law, notably in the development of *implied terms* (implied into a contract rather than expressly stated) lay down legal obligations on the parties to the contract and to this day 'remain the most powerful instrument available to the courts to regulate contracts for work' (Collins 2003: 35).

The distinction between statute law and common law is closely mirrored in the differences in the enforcement methods for pursuing claims for breaches of contract and breaches of statutory rights. Although not as clear-cut as it once was, the former start off in the county or high court, whilst the latter are pursued through the tribunal system. Both processes are detailed in Figures 8.2 and 8.3.

A note on European law

We have noted the contribution of European law to sources of law in Britain but it is important to emphasise the various ways in which the European Union has influenced the development of employment law since the mid-1970s. Indeed, European law has been the major influence in establishing a 'floor of employment rights' over the past thirty years. This influence has grown significantly since the late 1990s when the New Labour government in the UK signed up to the Social Chapter of the then Maastricht Treaty. An initiative that has opened up the UK to a significant tranche of new legislation in areas such as parental and paternity leave, protection for part-time, fixed-term and now agency workers, the establishment of arrangements to inform and consult staff, and to new areas of discrimination law, specifically, religion, age and sexual orientation.

Figure 8.1 European law has had a major impact on employment law

In any analysis of European law the original Treaty of Rome (1957) and its subsequent revisions is a sensible place to start. The Treaty is made up of articles or chapters that cover specific areas of policy (for example equality of opportunity) and which provide the legal basis for specific pieces of legislation in these policy areas. On occasions they can also be used instead of a directive in pursuing an action where the Treaty article is broader in scope. An example would be the case of Equal Pay legislation and the scope afforded by Article 141 of the Treaty which covers equality of pay between men and women. On a number of occasions in the UK the Article was used because it had a broader scope than that afforded at the time by the Equal Pay Act 1970.

Normally, the Treaty article forms the basis for subsequent legislation which takes the form of regulations or directives. Regulations tend to be fairly broad and have direct effect in all member states, but as we noted above, it is directives that are most common in the employment field. Directives are legislative instruments and are drawn up by the Council of Ministers and the Commission and, once passed, member states are required to transpose them into national law within a specified time period, normally two to three years. How individual countries do this is very much up to them but any law introduced must operate to achieve the same result, that is to be consistent with the intended effect of the directive. Where a member state fails to implement a directive into national law or transposes it inadequately, an individual citizen may rely on EU law in the absence of an appropriate national law. Thus a directive may have *direct* effect, but normally only what is termed *vertical* effect. That is it can 'only be relied upon against the state or emanations of the state' (Lewis and Sargeant 2009: 6) – this rather quaint term includes local authorities, schools, hospitals as well as central government but it excludes private companies and organisations.

A note on the role of Commissions

Equalities and Human Rights Commission (EHRC)

Established under the Equality Act 2006, the EHRC came into existence in October 2007 and provides for one statutory body with responsibility to protect, enforce and promote equality across the seven 'protected' grounds – age, disability, gender, race, religion and belief, sexual orientation and gender reassignment. The EHRC replaced the individual Commissions (Equal Opportunities, Race Relations, Disability) that had previously had responsibility for the protection and enforcement of specific areas of law.

The EHRC has extensive legal powers and like its predecessor Commissions can issues codes of practice and take legal action on behalf of individuals although generally, it tends to do this only where there is some significant issue of legal principle at stake. It also acts as a significant pressure group in influencing government policy and legislation in the equalities field, and in promoting good practice among organisations in their handling of equality issues.

The background to the establishment of the Commission was a growing concern in some quarters that the existing Commission and legislative system was failing to deliver the desired improvements in equality of opportunity. In 1997 the Government had set up the Women and Equality Unit which took a particular interest in gender and pay and followed this in 2004 with the establishment of the Women and Work Commission (*Shaping a Fairer Future* 2006 and a review of this in its final report in 2009) which highlighted persistent inequalities for women and paved the way for a more wide-ranging *Equalities Review* (2007) which painted a similar picture across the whole equalities field. At the same time (2005) the Government launched its *Discrimination Law Review* which focused on the fragmented nature of equality law in the UK and made recommendations to unify this area of law in a single equality bill (*Discrimination Law Review* 2007). The Government took the recommendations on board and in April 2009 introduced the Equality Bill to the House of Commons. The expectation is that this will become law in 2010 and will go some way to addressing on-going problems associated with multiple discrimination, which is suffered by some individuals.

8.2 Legal enforcement: the court structure

In general, claims for a **breach of contract** follow the route set out in the flow diagram in Figure 8.2.

The majority of cases are heard in the County Courts but where a claim is in excess of £50,000 then it will generally be brought to the High Court. If the Court makes a decision and this is appealed on legal grounds, then the decision would be reviewed in the Court of Appeal, and if appealed again, the UK Supreme Court. The European Court of Justice (ECJ) is a referral court, this means that a national court can refer a case to the ECJ if it involves some issue of European Law.

In contrast, claims for a breach of a statutory right such as a claim for unfair dismissal, or sex discrimination follow the procedure detailed in Figure 8.3.

Employment tribunals

As a result of the growth of statutory rights in Britain over the past thirty years, employment tribunals have become one of the key elements in the enforcement of employment law in Britain. Originally set up in 1964 and known as industrial tribunals, they were established with a view to reflecting the real world of the

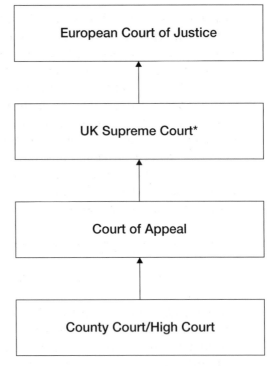

Figure 8.2 Breach of contract route

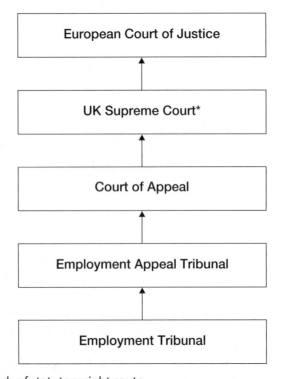

Figure 8.3 Breach of statutory right route

workplace. Consisting of three people, a legally qualified chairman and two lay members, one appointed from a list representing employee organisations (normally trade unions), the other from a list representing employer organisations. Despite the affiliations of the two lay members, these are set aside in a tribunal hearing and cases are judged on the merits of the case having regard to relevant case law. In recent years the main concern about the tribunal system has been that because the volume and scope of its jurisdiction has expanded significantly with the growth of statutory employment rights, the system has now become over-burdened, with cases taking longer to get to court and in some instances longer to resolve. Table 8.1 below details the growth of claims to tribunals and documents the main areas of law that provide most of the focus for tribunal activity.

From the table a number of key themes stand out.

1 A steady increase in the number of claims alleging discriminatory treatment by employers.
2 The significance of unfair dismissal claims but at the same time their declining share of the total claims to tribunals.
3 The importance of equal pay claims, accounting for over a fifth of all claims in 2006/07. The particular reasons for this lie with changes in pay arrangements and job evaluation in parts of the public sector, notably local authorities and the NHS.
4 The growing importance of employment tribunals for dealing with cases alleging breach of contract.
5 Not surprisingly, the importance in 2008/09 of redundancy issues, particularly claims alleging failure to inform and consult over proposed redundancies.

KEY TERMS

Breach of contract A situation where one party to a contract does not comply with the terms of a contract. Normally gives rise to a claim for damages.

At this point we should stress that not all claims to tribunals are accepted and many of those that are accepted are not successful. A large number of claims are withdrawn or dismissed every year on the grounds that they are frivolous or stand little or no chance of success. From April 2006 until the end of March 2009, these accounted each year for between 36 per cent and 45 per cent of the total number of tribunal applications. Furthermore, ACAS (the Advisory, Conciliation and Arbitration Service) can be engaged in individual **conciliation** where there is a potential or actual Employment Tribunal case. That is where an employee has submitted an ET1 claim against an employer under employment rights legislation (for example, claiming they have been unfairly dismissed,

Nature of claim	1998/99	2004/05	2006/07	2007/08	2008/09
Sex discrimination	6203	11,726	28,153	26,907	18,637
Pregnancy	765	1345	1465	1646	1835
Equal pay	5018	8229	44,013	62,706	45,748
Race discrimination	2746	3317	3780	4130	4983
Age discrimination	-----	-----	972	2949	3801
Religious discrimination	-----	307	648	709	832
Sexual orientation discrimination	-----	349	470	582	600
Disability discrimination	1430	3664	5533	5833	6578
Unfair dismissal	37,034	39,727	44,491	40,941	52,711
Unauthorised deductions	16,689	37,470	34,857	34,583	33,839
Working time	636	3223	21,127	55,712	23,976
Breach of contract	8986	22,788	27,298	25,054	32,829
Written statement T&C	1061	1992	3078	4955	3919
Redundancy (pay and failure to consult)	4812*	10,541	12,494	11,793	22,210
Total	**85,380**	**144,678**	**228,379**	**278,500**	**252,498**

Table 8.1 Applications registered by employment tribunals (including multiple claims) (Tribunals Service Annual Reports 2008/09; 2006/07; 2004/05; 1999/00)

or had unlawful deductions made from pay or been unlawfully discriminated against) ACAS can get involved in helping to conciliate between the parties (so-called pre-claim conciliation to try and secure an agreement without going to tribunal) prior to a case being heard. In 2005/06 of the 160 000 tribunal claims dealt with, 119,000 did not reach a tribunal hearing with 42,000 settled by ACAS and 55,000 withdrawn, many through the influence of ACAS (Gibbons 2007: 32).

The impact of the growth of statutory employment rights for the tribunal system has been mirrored for HR practitioners. These rights, together with the impact of the tribunal system in driving and shaping the nature and volume of internal procedures, and how these operate, have done much to change the way HR operates today. The importance placed on disciplinary and other procedures, and – critically in terms of **natural justice** and legal compliance – ensuring that these are adhered to and operated fairly and reasonably is a key concern and one we return to later in the chapter. Before doing so, we provide some background to account for how we arrived at where we are now in terms of legal regulation of employment.

KEY TERMS

Conciliation A form of dispute resolution where two sides are in dispute and a third party, a conciliator, tries to help reach a settlement between the parties.
Natural justice Relevant to cases involving claims for unfair dismissal in particular, natural justice includes the requirement that an employee should be given full notice of charge(s), has a right to be represented and to have a full opportunity to offer a defence of charges, has the right of appeal, and that any penalty should be proportionate to the offence.

1. Employment or labour law often distinguishes between collective and individual law. What is the basis of this distinction and what examples can you give of each?
2. What actions in the employment field could give rise to criminal action and why?
3. Statute law has grown considerably in importance in the employment field since the mid 1970s and again since the late 1990s. What do you understand by statute law and why do you feel it has become more important in employment law in recent years?
4. If an individual wished to challenge a decision made against her either in a tribunal or a county court, on what basis would such an appeal from a lower court to a higher court be accepted?
5. What are the essential features of a European directive and how does it become law in individual Member States?

8.3 The development of employment law in Britain

According to one of the leading authorities on labour law in the post-war period the principal purpose of labour law is 'to regulate, to support, and to restrain the power of management and the power of organised labour' (Kahn-Freund 1972). Like Wedderburn, Kahn-Freund's perspective influenced and reflected the importance of collective relations between management and labour and the joint regulation through collective bargaining, which was so dominant at the time. In this view, collective bargaining encouraged a high degree of self-regulation, with the law providing the broad framework within which the parties would operate – the ground rules and the boundaries on the parties' scope for action – intervening only as and when necessary. However, with the decline in collective bargaining in the UK, it may be more fruitful to view labour law more broadly, as 'the way labour legislative rights regulate managerial decisions' (Anderman 2000: 2).

While the breadth of this definition is helpful, it is also useful to distinguish between different types and functions of law. Again, Kahn-Freund is valuable here. In his view labour law could achieve its purpose in three ways; through regulatory law, restrictive law and auxiliary law.

Regulatory law

Legislation that is largely protective in nature and frequently involves establishing rights for employees or workers which are enforceable and which serve to regulate the behaviour of employers or trade unions towards members. Examples would include equality legislation such as the Sex Discrimination Act (1975), Race Relations Act (1976), Equality (Age) Regulations (2006), the legislation protecting employees against unfair dismissal, and the Working Time Regulations (1998). Recent European legislation has greatly extended the scope of regulatory law in this and other EU countries, but it should be remembered that in many developing countries such law is less comprehensive and where it does exist is often enforced less effectively.

Restrictive law

Where the law operates to determine the rules within which relationships are conducted. More specifically this tends, as its title suggests, to restrict the scope and influence of one or both parties within employment relationships. The best examples of these are to be found in the 1980s where, through a series of Acts of Parliament (Employment Act 1980, Employment Act 1982, Trade Union Act 1984, and the Employment Acts of 1988, 1989 and 1990) the governments of Margaret Thatcher attempted to curb the activities and influence of trade unions.

Auxiliary law

This is where the law is designed to promote or support particular forms of behaviour. Examples would include encouraging and supporting collective bargaining or more recently requiring companies to provide rights to information and consultation for employees (Information and Consultation of Employees Regulations 2004).

The balance between these three functions of labour law has altered over time. For much of the twentieth century the impact of the law on employment was limited. Although there had been regulatory law covering hours of work, and the employment of women and children for over 150 years, these had tended to be piecemeal and largely secondary to the protection afforded by collective agreements. By the 1960s some change was evident with legislation covering contracts of employment (Contracts of Employment Act (1963)), and redundancy payments (Redundancy Payments Act (1965)). From the early 1970s these were greatly extended through statutory legislation covering equal pay, sex and race discrimination and for the first time, pregnancy and maternity. Since then, these have been enhanced and extended further by developments in European law, developments that have mainly been in the area of regulatory law.

In contrast to the 1980s which witnessed significant developments in restrictive labour law, it would probably not be an exaggeration to say that in the past twenty years it has been regulatory law that has grown most rapidly. People entering work for the first time today have considerably more in the way of statutory employment rights than those of their parents and grandparents. This said, it is still the case that many of the most significant of these legal rights are only available to employees (those working under a contract of employment) and only become available after a specific time period (in most cases this is currently one year) working for the same employer.

Law and the regulation of the employment relationship

In the remainder of this chapter we examine the ways in which the law impacts upon the employment relationship, from initial recruitment into the organisation through to termination of employment. In locating the role of law in terms of the employment relationship we extend a theme of previous chapters (see Chapter 5) and make our main preoccupation and focus, the contract of employment: the essential legal relationship governing the rights and responsibilities of employer and employee.

The decision to focus the chapter around the contract of employment is based on a number of factors;

1 Most people at work are employed by someone else, that is they work under a contract of employment or 'contract of service'. Such contracts can be for fixed or indefinite periods, for full-time employment (normally 35 or more hours a week) of for some fraction of this.
2 The existence of a contract of employment imposes important legal duties and obligations on employers and employees, in addition to specific statutory rights, breach of any of which can lead to a claim for damages.
3 Those who do not work under a contract of employment are deemed to be self-employed, that is working for themselves, in business on their own

account, such as an independent contractor. They have what in law is described as a 'contract for services'.

4 Although in most cases the differences between (1) and (3) are reasonably clear, in some cases they can be blurred. This has often been the case in some industries, such as building and construction, and because the distinction matters in terms of legal duties and employment rights, has given rise to a considerable amount of case law (see below).

For those working in the area of people management, the employment contract is the basic reference point. It is normally the first stage in clarifying what an employee can reasonably be asked to do, and what can reasonably be expected of them.

8.4 Trying to enter employment: recruitment, selection and the law

Notwithstanding the importance of the contract we have also outlined a broader aim of identifying the impact of the law on the various stages of employment, beginning with recruitment into the organisation. As we discussed in Chapter 2, employment law has come to play an important role even before people enter an organisation and are offered a contract of employment. If the view is taken that recruitment involves 'finding applicants', and selection involves 'choosing between applicants and identifying who would be most suitable for the job', the key factors are trying to ensure the best candidates for the posts apply and that they are then subjected to a rigorous but fair process of selection. In both cases considerations of equality of opportunity are of great importance.

Legally, the major concerns here relate to the concepts of **direct** and **indirect discrimination** and cover issues of sex, race, age, sexual orientation, religion and nationality. These issues of discrimination apply to many areas of employment, not just to recruitment and selection but we focus on them here because they have particular importance for this area and protect those who apply for jobs even where they are not recruited or selected.

Issues of discrimination law have a particular significance in terms of recruitment and selection and it is not difficult to see why. If those who make key recruitment and selection decisions in organisations deliberately choose to ignore certain groups when recruiting, or more commonly are unaware that by using certain sources of recruitment or certain language in job adverts they are closing off opportunities for these groups, then they leave themselves open to claims of discrimination. Moreover, if they continue to rely on person specifications that

KEY TERMS

Direct discrimination Where a person is treated less favourably than someone else is, has been or would be treated in a comparable situation.
Indirect discrimination A condition of employment introduced by the employer – and not a necessary condition – that will disproportionately discriminate against a particular group.
Victimisation Refers to situations where people are targeted with abuse, suffer detriment to their employment conditions or are dismissed as a result of bringing a claim for another form of discrimination.

emphasise non-job related criteria or are insensitive to the potential problems of certain selection techniques (for example some personality tests may indirectly discriminate against certain nationalities or ethnic groups) then the same problems may arise.

Irrespective of the potential damage to an organisation's reputation that may arise as a result of tribunal cases being brought against it, there are also the monetary costs that could follow if a tribunal decision goes against the organisation. Unlike some claims (such as unfair dismissal) where compensation is capped, discrimination cases have no limit and although compensation relating to discrimination in recruitment and selection is often modest, this is not always the case and successful prosecutions on the grounds of sex discrimination and harassment relating to promotion and constructive dismissal (where an employee resigns as a direct result of the conduct of the employer) have on occasions brought with them a very high level of compensation for the individuals concerned.

Forms of discrimination

Direct discrimination

To take the example of sex discrimination, a person is directly discriminated against where someone 'discriminates against a woman if . . . on the ground of her sex he treats her less favourably that he treats or would treat a man' (SDA 1975). There are similar definitions found in the Race Relations Act (1976), the Disability Discrimination Act and the Employment Equality (Age) Regulations. European law has developed the concept of 'less favourable treatment' so that the 2000 Race Directive defines direct discrimination as occurring when a person is treated 'less favourably than another is, or would be treated in a comparable situation on grounds of racial or ethnic origin' (in Fredman 2002: 94).

Indirect discrimination

The concept of indirect discrimination extends the scope and impact of discrimination law considerably. As the Race Equality Directive puts it, indirect race discrimination is where 'an apparently neutral provision, criterion or practice would put persons of a racial or ethnic origin at a particular disadvantage compared with other persons, unless that provision, criterion or practice is objectively justified by a legitimate aim and the means of achieving that aim are appropriate or necessary' (Race Equality Directive 2000).

This definition was also applied in the EU Framework Directive on Discrimination (2000) to religion and belief, disability, age and sexual orientation and has now been extended to sex discrimination. In practice the definition is not without its problems, in some areas of discrimination – such as age and religion – it can be difficult identifying a group with whom a meaningful comparison can be made (Deakin and Morris 2009: 546).

However, in terms of recruitment and selection, it follows that certain forms of recruitment such as 'word of mouth' (in a workplace where the vast majority of workers are white and male), while 'apparently neutral', could have indirect discriminatory effects by reducing the pool of suitably qualified non-white applicants. Furthermore, the example illustrates the scope for case law to modify or extend the impact of statute. Important issues in discrimination law have been the areas of 'objective justification' or 'proportionality'. Certain forms of discrimination may be objectively justifiable by reference to some legitimate aim. In the area of age discrimination an example could be the use of pay schemes that reward seniority. As seniority is often linked to age, there is a potential for such schemes to be held to constitute indirect discrimination (*Wilson v HSE* (2009), *Cadman v HSE* (2006)). In such cases an employer would have to show that the schemes are objectively justified in terms of a legitimate aim – the employer could argue that this could be retaining scarce skills, or retaining those with high levels of human capital as a direct result of company training, or those with specific organisational knowledge.

Discrimination law also encompasses the concept of **victimisation** where an individual is singled out for unfair, and usually unlawful treatment (Willey et al. 2009: 428)

Implications for HR

The implications of discrimination law for HR clearly extend beyond the area of recruitment and selection, but in all areas they carry a similar message. HR need to pay attention to both the *content* of policies and initiatives and the *process* by which these policies are carried out. In terms of the content of initiatives and policies – such as job and person specifications, job adverts, selection methods, reward policies and succession planning – HR need to ensure these are monitored and updated to reflect legal changes and 'best practice'. In terms of process the focus is upon *how* these are carried out, which leads to a concern with the education and training of those with responsibilities for recruiting, selecting, appraising, promoting and disciplining staff. Clearly, having good 'discrimination proofed' policies is vital for an organisation, but if those in the organisation are unaware of the policies, unwilling to cooperate with them or the culture is unsupportive of them, then they stand little chance of success and the organisation remains vulnerable to tribunal claims.

ACTIVITY

ABC is a small engineering company that employs around 75 people in a small suburb of Birmingham. Many of the staff have worked for the company for many years, and when it has recruited new staff it has often relied heavily on the networks of its existing staff as a source for new recruits.

The company has a strong informal culture and it remains keen to preserve the culture which it feels gives it a family feel with everyone prepared to 'muck in' and support one another. Because the company has relied on strong links with its employees and their networks, it has a number of employees who are related to one another or are near neighbours.

You have recently joined the company as a member of its newly formed HR department and have been asked to look at the issue of recruitment and selection of staff. In the brief time you have been with ABC this issue has already begun to give you cause for concern. What problems do you see with the current recruitment practices and what arguments might you use with your new employers to try and get them to change their approach to recruitment and selection of staff?

1. Using examples from the chapter and others you can think of, where is discrimination law likely to be important in recruitment and selection decisions?
2. What are the recruitment and selection methods that might be particularly vulnerable to claims about possible discriminatory effects?
3. A job advert for bar staff in a pub is placed only in the ladies' toilets. Is this a case of discrimination? If so, is it direct or indirect?
4. Where might discrimination law be particularly relevant in other areas of HRM?

Taking up employment: the contract

Once we have gone through the recruitment and selection process and been offered employment with an organisation, which we have accepted, a contract of employment comes into existence. In many respects this is similar to other contracts: there is an *offer* of work, of employment and if there is *acceptance* of that offer, and some *consideration* – that is something of value for each side – we can talk of a contract existing. Also like other contracts it is not required to be in writing, although it is clearly preferable that it is. Indeed in employment law it has been a requirement for some time that an employee should receive a *written statement of terms and conditions* within one month of starting work. The written statement, we should add, is not the contract of employment, for reasons that we will explore later in the chapter, but it is normally held to be evidence that such a contract exists.

The formal assumption in law is of 'freedom of contract', that a contract is freely entered into by both sides, employer and employee. However, this is where the similarities with other contracts starts to break down and you might reasonably ask whether the employment contract is not fundamentally different from say, buying a washing machine. As we have noted in Chapter 1, for most of us work is a necessity and although we may be fortunate enough to have a choice of who we work for, we do not generally have a choice of whether or not to work. In contrast, we may be able to exist without a washing machine, and many people still do. Although laborious, we could clean our washing by hand or we could choose to use the services of a laundrette. Furthermore, when we buy a washing machine we are not only able to specify very clearly the terms of the contract but a number of additional statutory rights have developed over the years relating to the sale of goods, and particularly consumer protection legislation that minimise many of the risks associated with entering into such a contract.

The employment contract is rather different. Although we can specify many of the terms of the contract in advance (so called *'express terms'* because they are expressly stated), as we noted in Chapter 5, the employment relationship is imprecise and subject to change. Furthermore, getting people to perform to the level that an employer requires necessitates certain duties or obligations to be placed upon the employee and employer to 'give effect to the contract'. These are what are commonly referred to as *'implied terms'* and as their name suggests are not expressly laid down in a contract but implied into the contract. This is so because they are seen as so obvious as to not need explicitly stating. An example is the duty placed on the employee to 'obey lawful and reasonable orders', something that gives legal force to the idea of managerial prerogative

Figure 8.4 A contract of employment

(management's right to manage) that we have already encountered in Chapter 5.

We now explore the concepts of express terms and implied terms further. As we noted above, express terms are those expressly stated and are specific to the contract, they are drawn up by the employer alone or negotiated with the potential employee, some come from statute and some from collective agreements (between employers and trade unions) where these exist. They include hours of work, weekly pay or salary, holiday entitlement, any bonus entitlements, location and any mobility requirements (whether required to work at different locations for example) and normally take precedence over implied terms. The implied terms in contrast are of two types: those that may be implied by a court where there is a gap in the contract and it is felt necessary to do so in the circumstances of a case, and the more common case where terms are not expressly stated but are implied into all contracts of employment. These implied terms are duties and obligations on the parties to the contract: the employer and the employee. The main implied terms are listed below.

A number of duties and obligations apply to the employer:

- **To pay wages**
  The duty applies if an employee is available for work, unless there is an express term to the contrary (see above). Deductions from wages by an employer are *unlawful* unless these have been sanctioned by an employee and are covered under the 1986 Wages Act or required by statute.
- **To provide work**
  Employers are not generally obliged to provide work but in some cases, such as individuals who depend on piecework (payment according to the amount produced), failure to provide work may amount to a breach of contract.
- **To cooperate with the employee**
  This has become more significant in recent years as cooperation has been extended to encompass the notion that the employee should not destroy or undermine the 'mutual trust and confidence' upon which cooperation is built (Lewis and Sargeant 2009: 28). A particular example of this relates to the operation of mobility clauses (see *United Bank v Akhtar*). Also covers a duty to treat employees with respect (see *Wood v WM Cars* (1981), *BT plc v Ticehurst* (1992))
- **To take reasonable care of the employee**
  This covers such issues as having a personal duty of care to each employee, and to provide a safe system of work, which includes safe work colleagues as well as safe premises and equipment.
- **To provide references**
  The duty is to provide a reference that is 'in substance true, accurate and fair' (Lewis and Sargeant 2009: 33).

The corresponding duties on the employee are as follows:

- **To obey lawful and reasonable orders**
  Often described as the duty to cooperate with the employer, and is the corresponding duty on the employee to that placed on the employer. It also extends to a duty not to impede the employer's business. The latter is important in relation to forms of industrial action such as strikes which clearly breach this duty because they conflict with the presumption in contract law that the employee is ready and willing to work in exchange for remuneration. In cases of industrial action by an employee, an employer may lawfully withhold pay, either in full or in part, for the period of action (*BT v Ticehurst* 1992, *Wiluszvnski v Tower Hamlets Council* 1989).
- **A duty of fidelity**
  There is a general duty of 'faithful service' placed on an employee. This covers areas such as the obligation not to disclose confidential information, not to

compete with the employer (for example, working for a competitor in the employee's spare time).

- **To take reasonable care**

  This is the corresponding duty on the employee of that imposed on the employer. In effect it means that 'employees must exercise reasonable care in the performance of their contracts' (Lewis and Sargeant 2009: 37).

To these is often added a further duty:

- **To adopt new working practices (or adapt to new practices)**

  Following the decision in *Cresswell v IRC* (1984), it was held that where there was a change in the way in which the job was performed rather than a change in the job itself, it was reasonable that employees would adapt to the change. The case involved the computerisation of a filing system and it is likely that in such situations a duty would also be placed on the employer to ensure adequate training or retraining was available for employees.

To reiterate, for employees – those working under a contract of employment – as well as the express terms of their contract there are common law duties that apply to both parties. In addition there are statutory rights that apply to employees, which in some cases have been extended to the broader category of workers. As we have already seen, some rights, such as those covering discrimination, apply even before entering employment, while others become effective after periods of continuous service. These key statutory rights, providing a degree of additional employment protection above and beyond common law rights and responsibilities are identified in the insert below and have led some to argue that they have substantially strengthened the contract in favour of employees and constitute a 'new model employment contract' (Nairns 2004).

Implications for HR (1)

When legal and specifically contractual issues arise with an employee, the normal starting point is *'What does the contract say'*? In many cases the legal implications of a situation can only be deduced once we know this. For example, can an employee be asked to take on a particular task? If they can, when should we consult with them? Do they require training to perform this task and if so, when should this take place?

ACTIVITY

1. John is employed by CostLess Supermarkets as a check-out operator. He has worked for them for six months and in that time has only served on the tills. His manager has now told him that he needs him to replenish the shelves on two days for this and next week and that from the end of next week he will need him to work at one of the company's other stores, seven miles away for the following month.

    John has come to you for advice on what rights he may have in respect of this request.

2. Safina is employed by a major high street store as a beautician. She has worked for them for 18 months and her work involves serving customers, advising on make-up and tone, and on occasions, 'mock ups' with customers. She has an express term in her contract which states that she 'may be required to undertake other appropriate duties from time to time at the request of her manager'. She has now been asked to promote the company's new storecard and has formally objected to this saying, 'It is not part of my job and I won't do it'. Advise Safina on her legal position.

The issue of employment status

In this chapter we have assumed that the issue of whether someone is an employee or not, that is working under a contract of employment, is a relatively straightforward one, but it may not be. Take the example below:

Sara is 18 and has been hired by a beauty salon as a hairdresser and has been told that her work will involve her working with other people in the firm on hairdressing and other beauty treatments. It has been made clear to Sara by the owner, Barry that he wants Sara to be self-employed, to pay her own tax and national insurance but that her hours will be 8.30 to 5.00, five days a week. Sara agrees to this because she wants the job and because she understands that it is normal in parts of the industry. She soon discovers that she is often working overtime and on occasions Saturday mornings in addition to her normal hours. She works in one of Barry's salons, and although she has her own equipment regularly makes use of Barry's equipment when she needs it. After three years she is asked by clients if she would do their relatives' hair privately at a discount rather than through Barry's salons. Sara thinks about this, decides that as she could do with the extra money and agrees to do this in her evenings. She informs Barry of this and that, as a self-employed contractor, she would like to take these jobs on, assuring Barry that they would not interfere with her 'day job'. Barry then threatens that if she does she will have no work to come back to as Barry would dismiss her and give the work to someone else. Sara decides that she cannot afford to lose the job and so does not take the additional work, but decides to seek legal advice as to whether Barry would be within his rights to dismiss her.

What advice would you give Sara?

For something that would appear quite straightforward, this is a complicated area of law. There are a number of 'tests' that can and have been applied to try and determine whether someone is an employee or not. For example, the Inland Revenue has a comprehensive set of criteria that is helpful in defining self-employment and the Courts have used these as well as common law tests (e.g. the control test). In Sara's case, she agreed to be self-employed and a number of the arrangements set up between Sara and Barry would suggest that she was operating as an independent contractor, but others would not. Today the key test applied by the courts tends to be that of 'mutuality of obligation' – is there an obligation to provide work, and if so, is there an obligation to accept such work (see *Clark v Oxfordshire Health Authority* (1998), *Carmichael and Leese v National Power* (2000)). For Sara, the problems arose when she wanted to do work for others, something she was perfectly entitled to do if her status was genuinely that of a self-employed person. Clearly if she was an employee her working for another employer could have breached the implied duty of fidelity. The fact that Sara tried to establish the position with Barry before taking on the work would probably be viewed favourably by any court as would the fact that this kind of arrangement – getting people to accept self-employed status when it is not clear that they are – where employers have considerable bargaining power, is increasingly common in parts of the service sector.

Workers and employees

Although as we have seen, much of employment law applies to employees rather than to those defined as self-employed, the influence of European Law has extended the scope of some laws to the broader category of *worker*. This is defined under section 230 of the Employment Rights Act 1996, and includes those working under a contract of employment but also 'any other contract, whereby the individual undertakes to do or perform personally any work or services for another party to the contract, whose status is not . . . that of client or customer'. This includes so-called 'casual workers' who are employed 'as and when required' rather than having sufficient 'mutuality of obligation'. Many rights established since the late 1990s, including the application of the minimum wage, controls over working time and protection from arbitrary deductions from pay extend to this group rather than to employees alone. We would add that these issues are particularly important at the present time in respect of agency workers.

Employment rights for those working under a contract of employment

Rights that do not require a qualifying period of service	Rights that require periods of continuous service

• Not to be discriminated against on the grounds of:
  – sex
  – race
  – disability
  – age
  – religion
  – sexual orientation
  – membership of a trade union
• The right to equal pay
• The right to maternity and paternity leave
• The right to claim for a breach of contract
• The right to be paid at least the national minimum wage
• The right to minimum rest periods and 28 days paid leave (latter for full-time staff)
• The right to an itemised pay statement
• The right not to have unlawful deductions from pay
	Those that require continuous service include:
	• A claim for unfair dismissal (one year)
	• The right to additional maternity leave (one year)
	• The right to take parental leave (one year)
	• Right to request flexible working (26 weeks)
	• The right to guarantee pay (one month) – (pay if work unavailable)
	• The right to a written statement of terms and conditions (one month)
	• The right to claim for a redundancy payment (two years)

Table 8.2 Employment rights for those working under a contract of employment (Nairns 2004; Lewis and Sargeant 2009; Willey et al. 2009)

Employment rights: part-time, temporary and agency workers

As we noted above, some statutory employment rights apply not just to employees but also to workers. Furthermore, following decisions under European Law, there is no distinction made between rights for full-time as opposed to part-time employees other than that some rights (as with holiday entitlement) operate on a pro-rata basis. It is worth remembering that the majority of those working part-time are women, so any difference in provision between full and part-time staff would constitute indirect sex discrimination (see case law here). Temporary workers also have the same statutory rights as other employees so long as they have the necessary qualifying periods of service (Lewis and Sargeant 2009: 52). There are some limited exceptions to this but one area that has remained controversial is where an organisation uses agency workers. In theory it has been assumed that any contractual arrangement that exists in respect of agency staff, does so between the agency and the worker and the organisation and the agency. Indeed, many organisations use agency staff precisely because they do not want to employ staff directly and have the obligations associated with employees. However, if the worker engaged by the client organisation is under an obligation to perform work, and has done so for some considerable time, it may be inferred that a contract does exist between the client organisation and the agency worker (*Motorola Ltd v Davidson* (2001)). In any event this is likely to be clarified when recent European legislation (temporary (agency) workers Directive 2008/104/EC) is implemented in the UK in 2011.

Managing change (1): changing contractual terms

Before we leave discussion of the contract of employment we need to consider what happens when an employer wishes to change terms – variation of the contract. On the face of it, this is straightforward. As with the setting up of a contract in the first place, any variation can only take place through agreement. That is, it is not possible for one side to vary the contract without agreement from the other side.

In practice, the question as to whether a change has been consented to (agreed) is often controversial. Normally, such consent can be gained through individual or collective negotiation (collective bargaining) and in terms of best practice, this is clearly what an employer – and an HR department – would want. It is also possible to *imply consent* – that is through the conduct of the parties. For example, if an employer has changed certain contractual terms but there has been no formal negotiation and agreement, where employees continue to come to work and work 'normally' for some considerable time after the changes have been imposed, they are normally assumed to have accepted the changes.

In some cases an employee may continue to work, but does so 'under protest', and it will then be a question for the courts to establish in fact whether a variation has been accepted. It is important to remember that where one side, normally the employer, makes a unilateral variation to a contract and this is not accepted, this will constitute a breach of the contract and could bring the contract to an end. If the employer has behaved in this way and the employee accepts this breach as having brought the contract to an end they could resign within a brief period following the breach and make a claim for constructive dismissal, one that is in all probability likely to be successful.

However, a note of caution applies here. First, as we have seen, the common law has established a duty to adapt to new working practices, and second, the law of unfair dismissal (see below) makes it difficult for an employee to resist a unilateral variation by an employer where the variation can be justified by 'a sound business reason' for a change. Indeed in a competitive context that requires businesses to make frequent changes to the work environment, resistance may very well provide grounds for dismissal: 'So long as a minimum amount of consultation has taken place, it is relatively easy to satisfy a tribunal, particularly where the majority of employees has been prepared to go along with the employer's proposals, that an employer has acted reasonably in treating a refusal to accept a variation as a sufficient reason for dismissing' (Lewis and Sargeant 2009: 197).

Implications for HR (2)

The changes in operating environments that many organisations now experience place a premium on staff displaying flexibility in various forms. Employees perform tasks within what are now broader job roles, and where organisations retain job descriptions these often include flexibility clauses to minimise the extent to which formal contractual variation needs to take place. This clearly requires thought as to the precise nature of the express terms in contracts. It also throws into sharp focus the importance of process, and places a responsibility on management to consult, both through formal collective information and consultation forum (with trade unions or elected employee representatives), and directly with the individuals likely to be affected.

As well as varying the contracts of existing staff, many organisations have sought to achieve greater flexibility through the employment of part-time and temporary staff. As we have already seen, for those on non-standard contracts (part-time and temporary staff), employers cannot discriminate in the terms and conditions offered between these groups and those on full-time, indefinite contracts, other than the pro-rating of benefits for part-time staff. Case law also suggests that HR departments need to be very clear about the contractual implications of hiring agency staff, particularly if they believe that they are likely to have to maintain the services of such staff for an indefinite period.

8.6 Terms and conditions: pay and hours of work

Until recently the direct impact of statute law on terms and conditions of employment was limited. We have seen the common law duty on employers to 'pay wages', and there was some protection afforded to employees historically through the Truck Acts – to avoid payment in 'kind'. Furthermore, legislation has applied to specific groups of employees where it was felt they were particularly vulnerable in the labour market. This included groups of employees who had hours of work regulated (Shops Act 1950) and for some, the establishment of minimum pay and conditions, through Wages Councils (for example for those employed in agriculture, retail, hotels and catering, until the majority of these were abolished in the 1990s). More recently the Wages Act 1986, formally recognised problems associated with unlawful deductions from pay in certain areas (a particular issue was staff at petrol filling stations who were having pay deducted because of cars driving off without paying), and it is now the case that any deductions from pay must be by prior agreement with the worker concerned. Note that this includes such things as trade union subscriptions as well as season ticket loans, car allowances, and additional pension contributions.

Since 1998 two major pieces of legislation have been passed which have changed this approach significantly. We now have law that has a direct impact on express terms in the contract of employment. Both the Working Time Regulations (1998) and the National Minimum Wage Act (1998) lay down minimum requirements for all workers. The former regulates working time, rest periods and holiday entitlements, the latter provides for minimum basic hourly rates of pay, while including a facility for different rates to apply to different age groups.

The Working Time Regulations (1998) have been the subject of some controversy both before and after their introduction. The originating legislation (the EU Working Time Directive 1993) was passed under the umbrella of health and safety legislation and is part of a general concern to 'adapt the work to the worker' and the 'humanisation of work'. The hope of those designing the legislation was that it would bring about significant changes in the organisation of working time, but the evidence for this in the UK has been limited (Barnard et al. 2003). Part of the problem has been the weakness of the key element of the legislation – the 48-hour week averaged out over a 17-week reference period. The UK government managed to secure from the EU agreement for an individual 'opt-out' from the 48-hour week (one of three so-called **derogations** from the Regulations), that is individuals could agree not to be covered by this if they so wished. This has been further weakened by the large numbers of workers (such as managers), deemed to have what the Regulations have termed 'unmeasured working time'. Furthermore, as a health and safety initiative it is enforced by the Health and Safety Executive but resource constraints on its officers have meant enforcement has been uneven.

In contrast, the National Minimum Wage Act (1998), was established following a manifesto commitment by the New Labour Government that came to office in 1997. The government established a Low Pay Commission (LPC), which recommended the establishment of a National Minimum Wage (NMW), something that brought the UK in line with a number of other EU states. The LPC continues to report annually to parliament and makes recommendations as to the level at which the NMW should be set. The Act is enforced by Her Majesty's Revenue and Customs, with inspectors visiting premises with the authority to impose sanctions against employers that fail to comply. They can serve an enforcement notice on an employer that is held not to be complying with the terms of the Act and if the employer fails to respond to such a notice, the inspectors can take civil proceedings to recover the money or serve a penalty notice on the employer requiring a fine to be paid within four weeks.

Implications for HR

The main implications for HR relate to issues of compliance and the maintaining of records. In both cases there is the threat of sanctions for non-compliance and again there is the potential damage to reputation if an action is brought against an employer. In terms of the Working Time Regulations there is a need to identify those in the workforce who are covered by the various provisions, how the Regulations affect contractual terms and what derogations the company may be able to take advantage of, in particular the costs and benefits of individual opt-outs. Finally, there is a need to decide what record systems are likely to be most appropriate to cover the maximum working week, night-work patterns and the assessment of night workers.

In respect of the national minimum wage, the Act 'places a clear obligation on employers to pay workers remuneration which is not less than the national minimum wage in any pay reference period' (normally one month, Willey et al. 2009: 290). To aid this, any employer of a worker who qualifies for the national minimum wage has a duty to keep records to ensure that they are being paid correctly (Willey et al 2009: 293).

As well as these recent pieces of legislation, it is also important to remember the continuing significance of discrimination law for the development and operation of payment systems generally. The impact of equal pay legislation remains important, particularly in those areas where equal value claims (equal pay for work of equal value based on the evaluation of an analytical job evaluation scheme) have been successful as has been the case recently in a number of local authorities (*Bainbridge v Redcar and Cleveland B.C* (2007)). There has also been evidence that some payment systems, such as PRP schemes have the potential to discriminate against women (e.g. City bonus cases: *Barton v Investec Henderson Crosthwaite Securities Ltd* (2003)), because the nature of the work they undertake makes it less likely that they can earn as much through bonuses as male colleagues. Finally, pay systems that reward long service/seniority may be susceptible to claims of age (and possibly sex) discrimination unless these can be 'objectively justified' in terms of a legitimate aim. For example, an employer could argue that this could be retaining scarce skills, or retaining those with high levels of human capital as a direct result of company training, or those with specific organisational knowledge.

KEY TERMS

Derogation A waiver from the provisions of a statute, permitted under that legislation. See individual opt-out under the Working Time Regulations 1998.

ACTIVITY

1. Your company has a number of workers who work on a casual 'as and when required' basis. Many have worked for over a year and regularly work four or five nights a week. You have been asked to advise on what entitlements, if any, they might have to holidays.
2. Your company has recently contracted out its catering business to an outside company. You have recently heard allegations that the contract staff receive pay that is only £5.20 an hour. You have decided to investigate further and want advice on how you should proceed.

8.7 The management of the employment relationship: legal issues

Once established in employment, the focus shifts to maintaining levels of performance, interest, motivation, engagement and possibly commitment. Other chapters in this book have examined the various ways in which HR policies can endeavour to address these issues, but as we have noted at various points in the book it is not just the '*what*' of policy but also the '*how*' of implementation that is critical to the success of any policy initiative. One way of exploring this further in terms of the impact of law on the management of the employment relationship is through the concept of the 'framework of organisational justice' (Torrington and Hall 1998). The central purpose of the framework is to identify the ways in which organisations endeavour to ensure 'mutual satisfaction with the employment contract'. As the diagram below shows, it draws attention to areas that are key to ensuring such satisfaction, and are under the direct control of the employing organisation. However, the law underpins many of these by helping to shape the boundaries and content of the framework and by influencing the nature and operation of rules and procedures: discipline, grievance and attendance, as well as those relating to equal opportunities, harassment, flexible working, part-time and temporary working and redundancy.

The framework of organisational justice

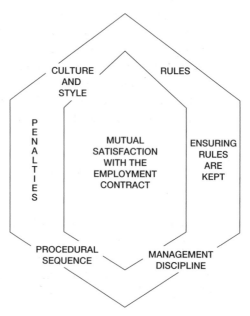

Figure 8.5 The framework of organisational justice (Source: Torrington and Hall 1998, Pearson Education Ltd)

The Torrington and Hall framework is valuable for a number of reasons. It allows us not only to see how the law might impact on the management of the employment relationship and organisational justice – through its influence on rules, procedural sequence (the ACAS Code) and on penalties, but also how the impact of law might be 'watered down' in practice through organisational practices and weak enforcement of procedures. In the framework, they draw attention to the potential influence of organisational culture, and of management, in either enforcing rules or by ignoring or bending them and through their consistency (or lack of it) in the application of rules and procedures. The framework therefore has immense practical value for those in organisations and reminds us that the effectiveness of the law in regulating the employment relationship, together with how people feel about their contract, has as much to do with how rules and procedures are operated and enforced as much as with the rules and procedures themselves.

Leaving aside for the moment the importance of contract, the main areas of law that have an impact upon the framework of organisational justice are those relating to the operation of procedures and the penalties associated with these. Specifically this includes the laws relating to dismissal, redundancy, health and safety, the protections afforded to employees when their organisations are taken over by another (Transfer of Undertakings Protection of Employees Regulations 2006) and the provisions relating to the provision of regular consultation and communication with employees laid down by the Information and Consultation of Employees (2004) Regulations. Limitations of space prevent a detailed coverage of these areas and readers who would like more information are encouraged to look at the final section and the recommended reading at the end of this chapter, but the law relating to dismissal is sufficiently important to merit further discussion and this forms the basis of the next section.

8.8 Termination of employment: fair and unfair dismissal

Dismissal is defined as the termination of an employee's employment, with or without notice (Willey et al. 2009: 422). They add that 'The law requires that a fair reason is given for the dismissal, that the disciplinary process leading to the dismissal conforms with standards of fairness and natural justice; and that the decision to dismiss is reasonable in all the circumstances' (Willey et al. 2009: 422).

In practice dismissal is commonplace in the UK, with an estimated million workers losing their jobs every year (DTI 1999) and can occur in one of three ways: where a contract under which a person is employed is terminated by the employer, where a fixed-term contract ends and is not renewed and where an employee terminates the contract in circumstances in which they are entitled to terminate it by reasons of the employer's conduct (so-called 'constructive dismissal') (see s. 95 and 136 of ERA 1996). There are six areas that are normally held as constituting fair reasons for dismissal:

1 Capability
   The 'skill, aptitude, health or other mental or physical quality' (s. 98(3) ERA 1996) and Qualifications – any educational or vocational qualifications relevant to the position the employee held.
2 Conduct of the employee
   An employee's conduct at work may constitute grounds for a fair dismissal.

Normally the issue is whether an employer acted reasonably in dismissing an employee, given the facts of the case.

3 Redundancy

Where an employer's business has ceased or the specific work that an employee was engaged in has ceased or diminished (Willey et al. 2009: 53).

4 Contravening a statutory duty or restriction

For example where a job might require a valid driving licence but an individual has been disqualified from driving.

5 Dismissal on the grounds of retirement

It remains lawful under the Employment Equality (Age) Regulations to dismiss employees on the grounds of 'retirement' provided that the employer has complied with procedural requirements (Willey et al. 2009: 255).

6 Dismissal for some other substantial reason

A number of cases have permitted some clarity around what 'some other substantial reason' might mean. For example it has been held that dismissing employees who refuse to agree to a change in working practices or restructuring where such a change is deemed necessary (*Scott & Co. v Richardson* (2005)) could constitute a substantial reason, as could a situation where an employer has been able to argue for an economic, technical or organisational reason connected with the transfer of an undertaking. Other examples have included the dismissal of an employee convicted of a criminal offence outside work and an employee with a 'difficult personality' dismissed on the grounds that their conduct justified their dismissal (*Perkin v St George's Healthcare NHS Trust* (2005)).

In all of the above, there is still a requirement to follow procedure, except in the case of gross misconduct which normally justifies summary dismissal. Cases that fall under (1), (2) and (6), are in most cases likely to require warnings through staged disciplinary procedures before dismissal. It should also be remembered that even in the case of gross misconduct there normally remains the need to investigate cases thoroughly before a dismissal is effected.

The following constitute the areas where dismissal is automatically unfair

- For family reasons – pregnancy, taking of maternity leave, flexible working (ERA 1996)
- For a health and safety reason
- For exercising rights under the Working Time Regulations or National Minimum Wage Act
- For asserting statutory rights generally
- For pursuing or attempting to enforce rights under Part-time Workers Regulations and Fixed-term Employees Regulations

- For taking part in lawful, official industrial action within 12-week protected period
- For trade union membership or participation in trade union activities
- For acting as an employee rep in relation to redundancy and transfer of undertakings or as trustee of an occupational pension scheme
- Where sole or main reason is a transfer of an undertaking or a reason connected with a transfer that is not an 'economic, technical or organisational reason

Willey et al. (2009); Lewis and Sargeant (2009)

Before the arrival of unfair dismissal legislation in the early 1970s, the common law was the only protection against dismissal and this relied on claims for **wrongful dismissal** or **frustration**. Wrongful dismissal relates to situations where an employer has dismissed an employee but where the employee has not been given the required period of notice. The latter arises 'where because of an event outside the control of the employer or employee, it becomes impossible to perform the contract' (Willey et al. 2009: 245). In the past this has included situations such as imprisonment and long-term illness but with the arrival of unfair dismissal law it has become much more difficult to argue for incapability as a justification for frustration of the contract.

This said, unfair dismissal law has significantly extended the scope and strength of law in this area and has done much to encourage the development of procedures (e.g. *Polkey v A E Dayton Services* (1987)) and curb inconsistent management behaviour in respect of dismissals. Moreover, even where an employer has established that a reason for a dismissal was fair, it is still necessary to show that the decision to dismiss was reasonable (*Iceland Frozen Foods Ltd v Jones* (1992), Willey et al. 2009: 258). This is not as straightforward as it might appear and establishing whether an employer acted reasonably in the circumstances in treating an action as sufficient reason for dismissal, has become one of the most controversial questions in modern employment law. One of the problems has been the so-called 'range of reasonable responses test' where tribunals are required to ask 'whether the decision to dismiss was within the range of actions that an employer could have been reasonably expected to take in the circumstances' (Willey et al. 2009: 260).

The important point is that individual employers may take a different view of what is reasonable in a particular situation. This means reliance on case law, which has played an important part in determining outcomes. The problem for employers is in the lack of guidance that the case law provides. Because the circumstances of cases are often very different, this makes the application of case law particularly difficult and creates uncertainty for employers in guiding their actions.

KEY TERMS

Frustration Occurs where it becomes impossible for the performance of the contract to occur through no fault of either party (e.g. death of the employee).
Wrongful dismissal Wrongful dismissal is based on contract law. Any claim for wrongful dismissal will therefore mean looking at the employee's employment contract to see if the employer has broken the contract.

Implications for HR

Two dominant themes run through the area of unfair dismissal law, first, the need for fair and effective procedures, ideally drawn up according to ACAS guidelines and second, proper adherence to these procedures. The ACAS Code also provides valuable guidance on handling disciplinary issues in the workplace (ACAS 2004, Lewis and Sargeant 2009). These further underline the importance both of procedural fairness and the principles of natural justice – to act consistently, to have an issue thoroughly investigated, to have a right of accompaniment, and to have a right of appeal. These go to the heart of issues of organisational justice and the maintenance of 'trust and confidence' as integral to the continuing vitality of the contract of employment.

1. Claims for unfair dismissal rose significantly in the 1990s and have continued to dominate the work of the tribunal system. What if anything does this tell us about the state of management-worker relations in the UK at the present time?
2. Joy is a PA who has been with the company for four years. After a period of good performance and attendance, in the last six months she has begun getting in to work late, having days off and the standard of her work has declined. She was spoken to and given a verbal warning three months ago, but the problem has continued and last week she received a written warning for persistent lateness. Earlier this week a colleague found her in tears and she has not been into work since. You have been asked to speak with her and want some advice as how best to proceed.

ACTIVITY

Your organisation has tried a number of policy initiatives to combat problems of lateness and absenteeism. At the present time it has an attendance policy, which includes the monitoring of absence, and covers a number of specific areas including sickness absence. The attendance policy involves an on-going review of employee attendance using absence data, and operates on a rolling 12-month cycle. It is triggered when an individual has eight or more days absence in any rolling 12 months, three or more separate periods of absence, continuous absence of more than twenty days or repeated absences on specific days, for example Mondays or Fridays. Any period of absence involving more than 20 days absence automatically triggers a referral to the Occupational Health department or the employee's doctor. In the event that a problem of ill-health is unlikely to be resolved through an individual continuing in their present job, the procedure provides in such cases for the possibility of redeployment.

Where there are occasional absences, the procedure provides initially for informal resolution and takes the form of a counselling interview. However where improvement in attendance does not improve within the 12-month period this can trigger the formal procedure which provides for three stages of absence interviews culminating in a final stage after which any failure to improve would lead to a dismissal.

A problem has come to light of significantly higher levels of absence among the van driver fleet in the company, one that is alleged to have been going on for some time. The allegation is that an informal 'rota' of absence has been operating which has been largely ignored by management. This has led to absence levels some 20 per cent higher than other departments and seems to have been concentrated on certain days, particularly Fridays. Of particular concern is the fact that an employee in another department who has recently been dismissed by the company for repeated levels of absence has indicated his wish to take the company to an Employment Tribunal, claiming a lack of consistency in the operation of the policy. He has the backing of his trade union, which is also threatening to publicise the alleged problems with the inconsistent application of the procedure and others like it, more widely.

As a newly appointed HR Officer this issue has been given to you to investigate further. What should you do to progress the issue and assuming that you find that the allegation of a 'rota' of absence and of inconsistent application of policy to have foundation, what should you do about this?

What guidance, does the law provide here in helping you to resolve the issue?

8.9 The issue of redundancy

Redundancy is defined under Section 139(1) of the ERA 1996 as a situation where:

- An employer has ceased, or intends to cease, to carry on the business *for the purposes the employees were employed*
- The employer has ceased or intends to cease to carry on that business *in the place where the employees were employed*

- That the requirement of that business for employees to carry out work of a particular kind, or for them to carry out work of a particular kind in the place where they were so employed, has ceased or diminished or is expected to cease or diminish.

Following a House of Lords ruling in *Murray v Foyle Meats Ltd* (1999), the issue for the Courts has focused upon (a) whether the requirements of the employer's business for employees to carry out work of a particular kind have really ceased or diminished or are likely to, and (b) whether the dismissal was wholly, or mainly attributable to this state of affairs (see Lewis and Sargeant 2009).

Assuming that an employer has satisfied a tribunal of (a) and (b) he will also need to show that he has consulted with trade unions or employee representatives (unless fewer than 20 people are to be made redundant) and with the individuals likely to be affected. The employer will also need to show that the selection criteria for redundancy has been based on fair and objective criteria and applied fairly. In practice it remains common for organisations to use a 'last in first out' policy, partly to protect seniority and expertise, and partly to minimise cost (lower redundancy payments) but it is likely to be indirectly discriminatory on both age and sex grounds and an employer would need to provide objective justification for its continued use.

The consultation process, particularly the collective consultation needs to take place 'in good time' (TULRCA 1992, s. 188(1A)) and is likely to focus on alternatives to redundancy. This might include voluntary rather than compulsory redundancies, natural wastage, leaving vacancies unfilled, early retirements, cutbacks on overtime, recruitment bans, the operation of short-time working as well as retraining and redeployment. In cases where a downturn in trade is experienced by an organisation and this is seen as temporary, it is likely that many of the alternatives to compulsory redundancies will be introduced. Where a downturn is seen as being more permanent, the avoidance of compulsory or voluntary redundancies is likely to prove more difficult.

Assuming that redundancies are inevitable those affected are entitled to statutory redundancy pay if they have been continuously employed for two years or more. Although employers can and do provide redundancy payments above the statutory minimum, most individuals made redundant have to rely on this minimum. Since 1967, anyone who has the necessary qualifying period of service is entitled to a statutory redundancy payment based upon age and length of service (ERA 1996 s. 162). For example someone aged 45 at the time of redundancy and who had worked for the same employer for eight years this is equivalent to ten weeks' pay. In contrast, someone who is 25 and has worked for the same period for the same employer would receive six-and-a-half weeks' pay.

Implications for HR

The implications of redundancy are much the same as with other areas of dismissal. The emphasis on fairness in handling redundancy issues, particularly in terms of due process and natural justice mirrors that in unfair dismissal law. What is different here is the requirement for an employer needing to make redundancies to engage in collective consultation and, that where those affected have relevant periods of continuous service, the requirement to provide at least the statutory minimum redundancy payment.

 ## 8.10 A brief overview of other relevant areas of employment law

Inevitably in what is an introduction to the legal issues that are important for HR practitioners we have had to be selective in what we have chosen to examine in detail. There are of course many areas that we have had to either ignore or deal with in limited detail. In this final section we attempt to address this by drawing attention to three areas of employment law that also have important implications for HR.

The law relating to transfers of undertakings

A difficult and complex area of law, one that seeks to provide a degree of protection to employees in the event that their employer is taken over, merges with another or where work is subcontracted. It does so by enabling 'the contract of employment of an employee to be transferred over to the buyer of a business' (Willey et al. 2009: 90) in the event of it being sold. That is, 'the pre-existing contractual terms and conditions are preserved' (ibid.: 90), and that such a transfer takes place without any break in service. It follows that any dismissal that is directly connected with the transfer of the business is deemed to be automatically unfair.

The law relating to health and safety at work

We have already seen that the common law provides for some protection for employees under the implied duty of care. However, developments in health and safety law have significantly strengthened and extended the scope of health and safety protection. The Health and Safety at Work Act 1974 remains the primary legislation in this area and covers all employers and all aspects of work. It provides for a statutory duty on employers who have the primary responsibility, to ensure 'the health safety and welfare of all his employees' (HASWA 1974 s2(1)), with associated duties on employees. More recently the Management of Health and Safety at Work Regulations 1999 has strengthened this further by placing a requirement on employers to carry out risk assessments in their place of work. This does not mean the elimination of risk, but that

Identifying risks is seen as the first step towards 'the reduction of risks to the lowest acceptable level' (*New Southern Railway Ltd v Quinn* (2006)).

The law relating to family leave and work–life balance

This area has become one of the most important for HR in recent years following a number of developments in European Law. For example, the Parental Leave Directive provided rights to both parental and dependent leave, the Paternity and Adoption Leave Regulations (2002) applies to employees and provides for two weeks leave for fathers. Under the Work and Families Act (2006) there is a provision to extend this by an additional six months although the Government is currently looking at this again. Since 2003 there has also been a right for employees with at least 26 weeks service to request flexible working to enable the employee to care for his/her child. It is likely that this area of law will remain important but will also continue to court controversy. More than any other area this is the one where employers have argued that developments impose unacceptable burdens on them. The pressure from them to resist or 'water down' developments in this area of law is unlikely to dissipate in the foreseeable future.

The law and best practice HR

As a final note to this chapter it cannot be emphasised enough that in general the law is no substitute for good or best practice. Although in many areas the law is leading on developments, in practice many of the largest and best run organisations are well ahead of the minimum protection laid down by statute. It follows that many of the initiatives of the past ten years have been to 'raise the floor' and ensure that all employees, and in many cases workers, have a minimum entitlement to basic employment rights.

The 'floor of rights' argument, one that increasingly extends into human rights more generally, has been driven by a number of concerns both in the UK and Europe. Fears of social exclusion and 'social dumping', concerns to ensure the humanisation of work and improved work/life balance have spawned a range of initiatives that as we have seen, have changed significantly the work of the HR function. However, behind these developments is also a concern for effective enforcement. Ideally, this comes from organisations adopting, adapting and extending these developments (assuming they have not done so already) and to embed them in their policy and practice. It follows that the most effective form of regulation is through self-regulation. The law provides a framework with minimum standards but it is up to organisations, in the context of a broad enforcement regime, to ensure that these work 'on the ground'. It also follows that a good deal of the responsibility for such effective self-regulation lies with those in HR departments.

8.11 ## Summary

Throughout the chapter a concern has been to underline the central importance of the contract of employment but also to emphasise how this has been significantly added to with the growth of statutory employment rights. Many of the latter have come to the UK from European law and many apply not just to those working under a contract of employment but also to workers. Overall, the end result of these changes has been a greater legal regulation of the employment relationship and one that has required HR practitioners to have a far greater working knowledge of employment law and to ensure that their knowledge in this area remains as current as possible.

KEY IDEAS

Introduction: nature and sources of employment law
- The main sources of law: case law, legislation, delegated legislation, codes of practice, European Union law and the Human Rights Act (1998).
- Distinguishing between criminal and civil law, collective and individual law and between statute and common law.

Legal enforcement: the court structure
- The route for pursuing a claim for breach of contract.
- The route for pursuing a claim for a breach of a statutory employment rights.
- The main impact of law at various stages in the employment cycle, including employment tribunals and the different types of claims that are made.

The development of employment law in Britain
- The significance of collective bargaining and trade unions in shaping employment law.
- Kahn-Freund's view of labour law: regulatory law, restrictive law and auxiliary law.
- The changes that have taken place with the decline of unions and the development of the contract of employment.

Trying to enter employment: recruitment and selection and the law
- Direct discrimination.
- Indirect discrimination.
- HR departments need to be aware of the potential for both types of discrimination in these and other areas of the employment cycle.

Taking up employment: the contract
- The significance of the contract of employment both in regulating the employment relationship and in terms of employment status.
- Express and implied terms in the contract.
- The factors that need to be borne in mind when an employer wishes to vary contractual terms.

continued . . . ▶

. . . continued

- The growing importance of statutory rights for those working under a contract of employment.
- Employment status is an important issue and there are difficulties in some cases of making a clear distinction between an employee and someone who is classified as self-employed.

Terms and conditions: pay and hours of work

- The legal regulation of pay and hours of work.
- National Minimum Wage Act (1998).
- Working Time Regulations (1998).
- Discrimination issues around pay and conditions.

The management of the employment relationship: legal issues

- Using the concept of the 'framework of organisational justice' (Torrington and Hall) to consider the significance of law in shaping the content and the management of employment procedures.

Termination of employment: fair and unfair dismissal

- The role of unfair dismissal legislation in the development and management of procedures.
- The role of ACAS and the tribunal system in helping to sustain a commitment to procedures.
- The role of HR in ensuring procedures are adhered to.

The issue of redundancy

- The definition of redundancy.
- The consultation period.
- Selection procedure for redundancy and the problem of discrimination.
- Alternatives to redundancy such as natural wastage, early retirement, redeployment.
- Statutory redundancy pay.

And finally: a brief overview of other relevant areas of employment law

Three other areas of law of particular relevance to HR practitioners:

- Transfers of undertakings.
- Health and safety at work.
- The increasingly important area of work-life balance.

RECOMMENDED READING

There are a large number of textbooks covering employment and labour law but many are written for people who are aspiring lawyers rather than those who are seeking an understanding of the law to help them develop their careers, be this in HRM or some other area of management. For those wanting a more detailed but accessible treatment of the materials dealt with in this chapter we would suggest looking at any of the following:

Janice Nairns' (2007) book, *Employment Law for Business Students* (3rd edition, Longman) provides a helpful introduction and notwithstanding recent developments is particularly good on the sources of law as well as the Court structure.

The CIPD text by David Lewis and Malcolm Sargeant, *Essentials of Employment Law*, now in its tenth edition, is designed for those studying for CIPD qualifications and is targeted more at postgraduate students in HRM – as such it is something that needs to be worked up to. Fortunately the two authors have also produced a text more geared to undergraduate students (Sargeant and Lewis (2008), *Employment Law* (4th edition, Longman)) and which provides a thorough coverage of all areas of employment law. It is particularly good in its treatment of discrimination law and the contract of employment generally.

Like Lewis and Sargeant, two other texts are geared mainly to a CIPD market and are useful if you want more detailed treatment of particular areas. Taylor and Emir (2009), *Employment Law: An Introduction* (2nd edition, Oxford University Press) also has extensive treatment of discrimination law, while Willey et al. (2009) *Employment Law in Context* (3rd edition, FT/Prentice Hall) is particularly useful for detailed treatment of areas such as discipline and dismissal, work-life balance and discrimination law and in helping us to understand why law has developed in certain areas in the first place.

Many of the main texts cited here also provide online support, which extend to updating of materials where new case law has become available. A further way in which you can check on recent developments is through publications such as *People Management* which is published twice monthly and contains a law update section which details recent case law and statutes in the employment field.

In addition to the above, there are a number of specialist texts covering specific areas of employment law. Malcolm Sargeant's (2004) book on *Discrimination Law* is a case in point, as is the same author's detailed treatment of age discrimination in *Age Discrimination in Employment* (Gower).

STATUTES

Disability Discrimination Act 1995
Employment Rights Act 1996
Equal Pay Act 1970
Health and Safety at Work Act 1974
Human Rights Act 1998
National Minimum Wage Act 1998
Race Relations Act 1976
Sex Discrimination Act 1975
Shops Act 1950
Trade Union Act 1984
Wages Act 1986
Work and Families Act 2006

STATUTORY INSTRUMENTS

Employment Equality (Age) Regulations 2006 (SI 2006/1031)
Employment Equality (Religion or Belief) Regulations 2003 (SI 2003/1660)
Employment Equality (Sexual Orientation) Regulations 2003 (SI 2003/1661)
Fixed-term Employees (Prevention of Less Favourable Treatment) Regulations 2002
Flexible Working Regulations 2006 (SI 2006/3314)
Information and Consultation of Employees Regulations 2004 (2004/3426)
Management of Health and Safety at Work Regulations 1999 (SI 1999/3242)
Part-time Workers (Prevention of Less Favourable Treatment) Regulations 2000
Paternity and Adoption Leave Regulations 2002 (SI 2002/2788)
Transfer of Undertakings (Protection of Employment) Regulations 2006 (SI 2006/246)
Working Time Regulations 1998 (SI 1998/1833)

CASES

Bainbridge v Redcar and Cleveland (2007) IRLR 494
Barton v Investec Henderson Crosthwaite Securities Ltd (2003) EAT
BT plc v Ticehurst (1992) IRLR 219, CA
Cadman v HSE (2006) IRLR ECJ 1969
Carmichael and Leese v National Power plc (2000) IRLR 43, HL
Clark v Oxfordshire Health Authority (1998) IRLR 125, CA
Cresswell and Others v Board of Inland Revenue (1984) IRLR 190, HC
Iceland Frozen Foods Ltd v Jones (1992) IRLR 439, EAT
Motorola Ltd v Davidson (2001) EAT
Murray v Foyle Meats Ltd (1999) HL
New Southern Railway Ltd v Quinn (2006) IRLR 266
Perkin v St George's Healthcare NHS Trust (2005) IRLR 934
Polkey v A E Dayton Services Ltd (1987) IRLR 503, HL
Scott & Co. v Richardson (2005) EAT
United Bank v Akhtar (1989) IRLR 507, EAT
Wilson v HSE (2009)

REFERENCES

Anderman, S. (2000) *Labour Law: Management Decisions and Workers' Rights*, 4th edn. London: Butterworths.

Barnard, C., Deakin, S., Hobbs, R. (2003) Opting out of the 48-hour week: employer necessity or individual choice? An empirical study of the operation of article 18(1)(b) of the Working Time Directive in the UK, *Industrial Relations Journal*, vol. 32, no 4.

Collins, H. (2003) *Employment Law*. Oxford: Oxford University Press.

Deakin, S., Morris, G. (2009) *Labour Law*, 5th edn. Oxford: Hart.

Dickens, L., Hall, M., (2009) Legal Regulation and the Changing Workplace, in Brown, W. et al. (eds), *The Evolution of the Modern Workplace*. Cambridge: Cambridge University Press.

Discrimination Law Review (2007) *A Framework for Fairness: Proposals for a Single Equality Bill for Great Britain: A Consultation Paper*. London: Ministry of Justice.

Equalities Review (2007) *Fairness and Freedom: The Final Report of the Equalities Review*. London: Communities and Local Government Publications.

Fredman, S. (2002) *Discrimination Law*. Oxford: Oxford University Press.

Gibbons, M. (2007) *Better Dispute Resolution: A Review of Employment Dispute Resolution in Great Britain*. London: DTI.

Kahn-Freund, O. (1972) *Labour and the Law*. Oxford: Oxford University Press.

Lewis, D., Sargeant, M. (2009) *Essentials of Employment Law*, 10th edn. London: CIPD.

Nairns, J. (2004) *Employment Law for Business Students*. 2nd edn. Harlow: Pearson.

Torrington, D., Hall, L. (1998) *Human Resource Management*, 3rd edn. London: FT/Prentice-Hall.

Tribunals Service (1999-2009) *Annual Reports* (various years). London: Ministry of Justice.

Wedderburn, K. (1986) *The Worker and the Law*, 3rd edn. Harmondsworth: Penguin.

Willey, B., Murton, A., Hannon, E., Mison, S., Sachdev, S., (2009) *Employment Law in Context: An Introduction for HR Professionals*, 3rd edn. Harlow: FT/Prentice Hall.

Women and Work Commission (2006) *Shaping a Fairer Future*. London: WWC.

Women and Work Commission (2009) *Shaping a Fairer Future: A Review of the Recommendations of the Women and Work Commission Three Years On*. London: WWC.

9 Equality and diversity in the workplace

'Man was born free, and he is everywhere in chains. One man thinks himself the master of others, but remains more of a slave than they.'

(Rousseau (1762) *The Social Contract*)

CHAPTER OUTLINE

9.1 The background to equality and diversity
9.2 Why bother about workplace equality and diversity?
9.3 Key terms in discrimination
9.4 Workplace discrimination in the UK
9.5 The role of the Equality and Human Rights Commission
9.6 The role of HRM
9.7 Equality and diversity in operation: case study of the Kent Fire and Rescue Service
9.8 Summary

9.1 The background to equality and diversity

Historical perspective

The debates and laws about equality of opportunity are not new. But we do not have to go too far in the past, to find serious examples of individual and society prejudice against minority groups. For instance, think about how easy or difficult it was to register with your place of study or work, and contrast it with an incident which happened in the 1960s, and which is summarised below.

Equal access to university?

On June 11, 1963, State Governor Wallace personally barred the path of two black students attempting to register at the University of Alabama. The governor was flanked by armed state troopers. He defied federal Justice Department orders to admit the students, James A. Hood and Vivian J. Malone.

President Kennedy federalised the Alabama National Guard and ordered some of its units to the university campus. Wallace stood aside and the black students were allowed to register for classes

Pearson (1998)

In other words, the fight to give equal opportunity to all members of society has been comparatively recent. In this case, an American state governor was using the police to block black students from attending a university. In response, the American President of the time, John F. Kennedy, sent the army to protect the two students and enable them to register.

Within the UK, fights to establish the rights of all member of society to have equality of opportunity have been equally important, although arguably less potentially confrontational as in the American example. For instance, in the fight for equal pay for women, a group of women machinists went on strike in 1968 for three weeks at the Ford factory in Dagenham, claiming that they were being paid 15 per cent less than men for doing the same work. Their action became the starting point for a long journey towards laws and policies to introduce equal pay for women: Barbara Castle, Labour's Employment Minister at that time became involved and subsequently steered through the introduction of the Equal Pay Act of 1970.

Figure 9.1 Women machinists striking at the Ford factory in Dagenham

But despite these and many other cases, and supporting legislation, there is still considerable inequality within UK society. With the publication of a proposed change in UK legislation on discrimination, the UK government (2009) highlighted the following shortcomings which it is considered still demonstrated that inequality existed in the UK.

CASE STUDY

Why the UK still needs to tackle discrimination in the workplace and service provision

The view of the Government Equalities Office

- Women still earn, on average, 22.6 per cent less per hour than men.
- The gap between the employment rate of disabled people and the overall employment rate has decreased from 34.5 per cent to 26.3 per cent since 1998, but disabled people are still more than twice as likely to be out of work than non-disabled people.
- If you are from an ethnic minority, you were 17.9 per cent less likely to find work in 1997 than a white person. The difference is still 13 per cent.
- Six out of ten lesbian and gay schoolchildren experience homophobic bullying and many contemplate suicide as a result.

(Government Equalities Office (2009: 8–9))

 9.2 ## Why bother about workplace equality and diversity?

The terms equality and diversity may be used interchangeably in everyday use, but it is important that the student of HRM recognises that there are important differences between the two concepts, and the management actions which may then follow from them.

Figure 9.2 Equality and diversity

Equality is regarded as 'sameness' but there are a range of different approaches about what this may mean. For example, we may consider 'equality' as everybody having the same opportunity (so, equal opportunity), without regard to gender, disability, ethnicity, and so on. Alternatively, it may be regarded as equality of outcome (for example, equal pay). The focus on 'equality' within the workplace has been developed since the late 1970s, alongside the introduction of laws such as the Equal Pay Act 1970, the Sex Discrimination Act 1975, and the Race Relations Act 1976. However, a criticism of the equality and equal opportunity approaches are that they assume that because people may be different, that the differences may be disadvantages. The terms equality/equal opportunity also may be seen as a negative perception, in which organisations which fail to comply with legal requirements incur financial penalties, rather than organisations which positively wish to promote diversity for the business and social justice reasons which it brings.

On the other hand, the term diversity has become more widespread in UK usage over the last twenty years. Here, diversity may be defined as valuing everyone irrespective of their differences as individuals – whether they are employees, customers, or clients. The focus on diversity, rather than equality, has been advocated for the focus it brings on emphasising the benefits to the organisation of being different (for example, Kandola and Fullerton 1994, Cornelius et al. 2001). But while the term diversity has a widespread appeal and is publicly embraced as a goal by many organisations, the concept of diversity, just like equality, has been criticised as being potentially naïve, since it fails to recognise that it de-emphasises workplace conflict and problems in implementing organisational policies (Prasad et al. 1997).

ACTIVITY

Look for policies for equality and diversity in your places of study, and/or work. What evidence is there that these are based on 'equality' or 'diversity'?

Business case arguments

As part of society-wide discussion to justify equality and/or diversity in the workplace, a 'business case' rationale has been developed. The arguments for a diversity (non-discriminatory) business case relate to human capital considerations (including, a wider recruitment selection pool, and maximised use of a wide range of different skills and outlooks). For example, Cornelius et al. (2001) summarise the business case as

1 Taking advantage of diversity within the labour market, so as to reduce problems associated with recruitment difficulties.

2 Maximising employee potential, so as to maximise the capabilities of diverse groups in order to maximise organisational performance, and reduce the negative impact on morale which may be caused by the perceived unfairness of prejudice and discrimination.
3 Enhancing the ability to manage across cultures and borders.
4 Create opportunities and enhance creativity, with access to new customers and new markets, accessing the knowledge of a culturally diverse workforce.

In the example of age, the 'business case' was developed during the 1990s to include both wider pool of labour arguments, and avoiding the loss of skills to the organisation and the economy as a result of early exit (through retirement) of the workforce (Duncan and Loretto 2004).

However, as laudable as the non discrimination business case may appear in its presentation, it has been criticised. For example, Dickens (1994) and Kaler (2001) see the rationale as being essentially narrow and short term in nature. In particular, economic experience in the final years of the first decade of the twenty-first century set a context of increasing unemployment and worker lay-off rather than the perceived need for recruitment from a previously over-heated labour market, as is indicated by the increase by 1.1 per cent in the UK unemployment rate of 6.3 per cent, as at December 2008 (ONS 2009). Similarly, the perceived narrow business case need not necessarily embrace all types of minority group, especially if some groups are seen as less economically productive or necessary than other groups (Kirton and Greene 2005: 203).

Noon (2007) also challenges the 'fatal flaws' of the diversity business case. Noon's argument is that the business case is short term; that the business case purports to develop an over-rational, and potentially unobtainable, cost–benefit approach to diversity; is based on flawed assumptions of management rationality; and that the arguments are based on an underlying assumption that the right to fair and equal treatment needs to be justified on the contingency that equality needs to be good for business and the organisation, rather than any social justice arguments. Noon also notes that, to assume that managers will behave rationally in pursing the business case for diversity, is to ignore that managers are equally capable of reacting with prejudice. For these reasons, a wider interpretation of the diversity business case is required, which goes beyond legislative compliance, and considers the social, ethical, and environmental arguments, even if short-term business benefits are less obvious (Dickens 1994, 1999).

Social justice

The social justice rationale for workplace equality or diversity is based on the moral argument that employees should be treated fairly, and with appropriate dignity. Therefore decisions and behaviours should be taken which are both within the law, but also without recourse to stereotypical judgments about individuals, or prejudices.

The social justice argument may be more persuasive then the business case argument, but it too may be criticised. For example, whose assessment of what is 'social justice' should be considered here? It may also be that managers who may believe in the social justice of diversity in their everyday lives actually see their role in business as different, and so apply different standards of social justice or see the requirements of the business as being different from social justice reasoning.

1. Consider the arguments for equality and diversity policies in an organisation for which you are the HR Manager. Which out of the business case and the social justice case are you most likely to apply to your organisation, and why? Which is likely to be most persuasive to our work colleagues?

Legal requirement

We have already seen some examples of where discrimination is unlawful. In fact, there are currently nine major pieces of discrimination legislation, around 100 statutory instruments setting out rules and regulations and more than 2500 pages of guidance and statutory codes of practice (Government Equalities Office (2009: 8–9).

The frequency of legal cases submitted for consideration by Employment Tribunals, together with average compensation awarded is shown in Table 9.1.

The table shows that the most cases referred to Employment Tribunals are for unfair dismissal. However, where cases are referred to tribunals for discrimination, average awards are higher and maximum awards may be considerably higher than for unfair dismissal.

Why organisations manage diversity

Having considered the differences between 'equality' and 'diversity', and the differing approaches of the business case, the social justice case, and the legal reasons for workplace opportunities for otherwise minority groups, exactly why do organisations seek to promote equality and diversity? A survey for the Chartered Institute of Personnel and Development in 2007 (see Table 9.2) suggested that most organisations (68 per cent) adopted diversity policies in response to legal pressures, and to recruit and retain the best talent (64 per cent). However, the table does show that corporate social responsibility and moral arguments follow closely at 63 per cent and 60 per cent respectively. Based on this research, we may conclude that organisations have a mixture of both business reasons and social justice reasons for adopting equality and diversity in the workplace.

Claim Type	Numbers of claims	Average (mean) award (£)	Highest award (£)
All claims, including unfair dismissal	266,542	7,959	84,005
Sex discrimination	18,637	11,025	113,106
Disability discrimination	6,578	27,235	388,612
Equal pay	45,748	Not available	Not available
Race discrimination	4,983	32,115	1,353,432
Part-time workers regulations	664	Not available	Not available
Discrimination on grounds of religion or belief	832	10,616	24,876
Discrimination on grounds of sexual discrimination	600	63,222	23,668
Age discrimination	3,801	8,869	90,031

Table 9.1 Claims made to UK employment tribunals, April 2008 to March 2009 (Tribunals Service, Employment Tribunal and EAT Statistics (GB) 1 April 2008 to 31 March 2009)

In summary, organisations have a variety of motives for addressing workplace diversity. These have been summarised by Kirton and Green (2005) as negative, minimalist, compliant, and comprehensive proactive (see Table 9.3).

9.3 Key terms in discrimination

So far, we have seen that a lack of equality or diversity awareness may lead to a range of discriminatory and similarly inappropriate behaviours and practices. The reasons and backgrounds as to why these behaviours and actions are inappropriate are discussed below. Those which are most relevant to the HRM student include:

Why diversity management?			
Percentage rating of importance			
Driver	Most/very important	Important	Less/least importance	Overall rating
Legal pressure	45	6	17	68
Recruit/retain best talent	30	19	15	64
Corporate social responsibility	30	26	18	63
Employer of choice	30	14	17	61
Makes business sense	31	14	15	60
Morally right	24	15	21	60
Improve business performance	16	15	17	48
Help recruitment problems	19	12	15	46
Belief in social justice	20	12	14	46
Improve customer relations	13	15	13	43
Improve products and service	19	13	12	44
Improve creativity and innovation	14	14	15	43
Desire to reach diverse markets	13	11	15	39
Improve corporate branding	12	13	12	37
Enhance decision making	11	15	9	35
Trade union activities	7	8	17	32
Respond to market competition	12	10	8	32
Respond to global competition	9	8	13	30

Table 9.2 UK organisations' rationale for diversity management (CIPD 2007: 7, with the permission of the publisher, the Chartered Institute of Personnel and Development, London (www.cipd.co.uk))

The negative organisation	• No EO or diversity policy • May be unlawful/discriminatory
The minimalist organisation	• Self declared as EO employer • But low profile for diversity • May now have EO policy
The compliant organisation	• Narrow but compliant business orientation • Emphasis on recruitment practice • Adopt EO codes of practice
The comprehensive proactive organisation	• Proactive and promotes EO business case • Broadens the debate to include social justice case • May include positive action • Senior management endorsement

Table 9.3 Organisational responses to equality and diversity (Kirton and Greene 2005: 207)

Direct discrimination

This is unlawful in employment and occurs when an employment decision is made on unlawful grounds because of an individual's sex, ethnicity, disability, age, sexual orientation, religion or belief.

CASE STUDY

Direct discrimination

Noone applied unsuccessfully for a job, where the selection criteria were training, qualifications, experience and personality. Born and educated in Sri Lanka, Noone was better qualified, and had more experience and more publications than the successful candidate. The Court of Appeal decided that she had been discriminated against on racial grounds

Noone v North Thames Regional Health Authority [1988] IRLR 195

Indirect discrimination

This is unlawful under discrimination legislation and occurs in employment when the same conditions are applied to all people, but the effect is such that the impact on a minority group is that they are disproportionately disadvantaged. Indirect discrimination is unlawful under each of the laws for sex, race, disability, age, sexual orientation.

CASE STUDY

Indirect discrimination: Care advised when advertising to 'recently qualified' graduates

Graduates and 'recently graduated' recruitment policy could be considered as potentially direct and/ or indirect discrimination and unlawful, since it will tend to recruit people aged in their twenties and disadvantage older graduates.

ACAS (2006) *Age and the Workplace: Putting the Employment Equality (Age) Regulations into practice*

1. In view of the advice on avoiding age discrimination, how would you phrase advertising for graduate entrants?
2. What other systems would you need to put into place in the recruitment process to ensure that age discrimination was avoided when recruiting graduates?

Harassment

This is usually defined in terms of being any conduct related to gender, ethnicity, disability, age, sexual orientation or religious belief, with the purpose of creating an intimidating, hostile, degrading, humiliating, or offensive environment. The concept is important in UK antidiscrimination law, where an employee may complain in law both against the conduct of fellow employees as well as the organisation for permitting an environment in which harassment occurs and may have been regarded as part of the work culture. The case study below shows how Employment Tribunals deal with proven cases of harassment.

CASE STUDY

Harassment

Porcelli was a laboratory technician. Over a period of time, two of her male colleagues made suggestive remarks, removed personal belongings, failed to pass on information to her, brushed against her physically and stored equipment where it was difficult for her to reach.

Porcelli was forced to leave her job. In a subsequent Employment Tribunal case, it was found that she had been the victim of sex discrimination and harassment, since her male colleagues would not have behaved the same way towards a male colleague

Strathclyde Regional Council v Porcelli [1986] IRLR 134

Victimisation

This occurs when an employee brings a claim against his/her employers (for example, for sex, racial, sexual orientation, religious belief or age discrimination), and the employer then treats that employee in disadvantageous terms because of the claim.

You may hear the terms harassment and victimisation used interchangeably – but they are *not* the same thing: harassment may occur from any employee towards another employee; victimisation is when the employer mistreats the employee once a formal claim has been submitted.

CASE STUDY

Victimisation

Nagarajan was of Indian racial origin. Over several years, Nagarajan brought a variety of successful and unsuccessful race discrimination claims against his employer, London Regional Transport (LRT). He applied unsuccessfully for a job and then claimed that he had been victimised. The House of Lords found that Nagarajan had been victimised since LRT had consciously or subconsciously had in mind previous claims against LRT in rejecting him for the job vacancy.

Nagarajan v London Regional Transport (LRT) [1997] IRLR 572

KEY TERMS

Direct discrimination – when an employment decision is made on unlawful grounds because of an individual's sex, ethnicity, disability, age, sexual orientation, religion or belief.
Indirect discrimination –when the same conditions are applied to all people, but the effect is such that a minority group is disproportionately disadvantaged.
Harassment – any conduct related to gender, ethnicity, disability, age, sexual orientation or religious belief with the purpose of creating an intimidating, hostile, degrading, humiliating or offensive environment.
Victimisation – when an employee brings a claim against his or her employer and the employee is treated in disadvantageous terms because of the claim,

---

Genuine occupational qualification or objective justification

In exceptional and very limited cases, the law does recognise that there may be circumstances where discrimination in employment may be justified. In sex and racial discrimination, this is known as genuine occupational qualification (GOQ), and in the case of age discrimination it is objective justification. However, the case example below underlines how stringently the law interprets exceptions such as the GOQ.

CASE STUDY

Genuine occupational qualification

Rowan, a man, applied for a job as a sales assistant in a shop selling girls' and women's clothing. Rowan was not considered for the vacancy, and claimed that he had been directly discriminated against because of his sex. The shop (Etam) claimed genuine occupational qualification and said that Rowan could not be considered because the job required personal contact in measuring customers and with female customers in the changing rooms of the shop.

The Employment Appeal Tribunal found that Rowan should have been considered for the job and GOQ did not apply because Rowan could have undertaken most other parts of the job without inconvenience or embarrassment to customers.

Etam plc v Rowan [1989] IRLR 150

Equal pay

Women in the UK typically receive less pay than men. The average (mean) percentage pay gap between men and women is estimated as 17.1 per cent while for women working part time the mean gap is 35.6 per cent (EHRC 2009b).

Under the Equal Pay Act of 1970, a woman may claim the same terms and conditions of employment as a man doing similar work, where she can show that she is performing like work, the work is rated as equivalent and the work is of equal value.

CASE STUDY

Equal pay

Hayward was a cook who worked at the Cammell Laird Shipyard. She successfully claimed that her work was of equivalent value to joiners and insulation engineers at the shipyard.

Hayward v Cammell Laird [1984] IRLR 463

In the second example, Enderby was a speech therapist working at Frenchay Health Authority. She claimed that her qualifications and work were of equal value to male colleagues working in pharmacy and as clinical psychologists in other parts of the Health Authority, but whose pay was negotiated with different negotiating bodies. This case eventually was decided at the European Court of Justice, which ruled that the Health Authority could not rely on different negotiating bodies to justify different rates of pay for like work.

Enderby v Frenchay Health Authority [1993] IRLR 591

In addition to this outline of key issues in UK discrimination law, it is important to be aware of the following concepts.

Stereotype

This describes how individuals may be biased in perception of another person. The term is first attributed to Lippmann in 1922, and refers to the way in which we tend to group people together when they appear to us to share similar characteristics.

Stereotypes have been defined (Cuddy and Fiske 2002: 4) as 'cognitive structures that store our beliefs, and expectations about the characteristics of members of social groups'.

To stereotype another person is not unlawful in itself, but may easily lead to bias in how we perceive others and see only their negative or positive attributes, rather than seeing the 'whole person' for what he or she actually is. As a result, stereotyping is often at the root of discriminatory behaviour towards other people.

For example in age discrimination, McCann and Giles (2002) argue that stereotypes do not occur in isolation, but reflect stereotypes, both negative and positive, about older people which are widespread within society. Greller and Stroh (1995) found that many people look for cues and role definitions from others in society about how they should respond, and age and attitudes towards older workers were no different. Therefore Greller and Stroh proposed that older employees internalised the types of stereotypes which were appropriate for their ages and that this inevitably influenced their willingness and ability to learn, even to the extent of resistance to new challenges 'even though they would rather continue to work' (Greller and Stroh 1995: 239).

1. What are your personal stereotypes of other people? What are the sources of these stereotypes?

Horizontal and vertical segregation

This refers to the effect that women, ethnic minority and disabled workers are likely to hold jobs within an organisation which are of lower status and lower paid (Kirton and Greene 2005: 54). This may also apply to lower opportunities for promotion, employment benefits (such as pensions), training, and other ways in which employees may progress within the organisation. Horizontal and vertical segregation is considered to be inequitable and may often indicate that unlawful discrimination occurs within an organisation but it is not unlawful in itself.

Similarly, gender occupational segregation refers to the disadvantages (including overall pay disadvantage) which women experience in accessing particular occupational roles – not because they are prevented from doing so (since this would be unlawful) but because it may be considered to be unusual for women to be considered for such roles.

Institutional racism

This has been defined by Macpherson as:
'The collective failure of an organisation to provide an appropriate and professional service to people because of their colour, culture, or ethnic origin. It can be seen or detected in processes, attitudes and behaviour which amount to discrimination through unwitting prejudice, ignorance, thoughtlessness and racist stereotyping which disadvantage minority ethnic people' (Home Office 1999: paragraph 6.34).

This landmark definition followed a judicial enquiry and heavy criticism of alleged racist conduct by the police, after a young black adult, Stephen Lawrence was stabbed to death in 1993 at a bus stop in South London in an unprovoked racist attack. In the subsequent police enquiry, the police were collectively criticised for the manner in which the criminal investigation was conducted and the effect which this had on the attempts to prosecute suspects in the case.

KEY TERMS

Genuine occupational qualification – exceptional circumstances in sex and racial discrimination where discrimination in employment is justified.
Occupational qualification – exceptional circumstances in age discrimination where discrimination in employment is justified.
Horizontal and vertical segregation – the effect where women, ethnic and disabled workers are likely to hold lower status, lower paid jobs within an organisation, with lower opportunities for promotion, employment benefits or training.
Gender occupational segregation – the disadvantages women experience in accessing particular occupational roles because it is considered unusual for women to be considered for such roles.

Positive action, but not positive discrimination

UK law recognises that minority groups may need special support in order to enable them to progress in the workplace but that it should remain unlawful to make a decision on employment based only on their minority membership.

Lawful positive action ensures that support is given to minority groups such as a particular ethnic group or gender, when those groups are under-represented in the workplace. For example, the provision of careers support or development workshops to encourage women to apply for more senior roles, or to occupations where women are under-represented would be lawful positive action. On the other hand, positive discrimination – such as appointing women to roles solely on the basis of gender and not on their ability to do the role would be considered as unlawful under UK law, but some types of positive action may be permissible in the USA.

1. Consider occupations where you feel women may be under-represented in the workforce. What action could be taken by way of positive action to encourage the participation of women in the workforce? What and why are the limitations of positive action in this case?

 ## Workplace discrimination in the UK

This chapter will now consider individual areas where minority groups may be marginalised within the workplace. The reasons for marginalisation are complex: behind each group below there are different historical and social reasons for the disadvantages which they experience. It is not possible to explore these in any detail but the aim is to give some insight into the complexity of workplace discrimination; the roles of gender and age are explored in further detail below.

Gender

Women are taking an increasing role in paid occupational employment but still lack equality in the opportunities and rewards compared with their male colleagues. The National Statistics Office, Social Trends 31, (2002) shows:

- An increase in the number of women employed, from 10 million in 1971 to 13 million in 1999 and is forecast to be 14.1 million by 2011.
- The increase in this period has been greatest among women aged 25–44.
- In contrast, the number of men employed rose from 16 million in 1971 to 16.2 million in 1999 and is forecast to reach 16.5 million by 2011.

The many differences between the workplace experiences of men and women have been the subject of a UK legislation programme dating back to the mid 1970s. The Sex Discrimination Act 1975 and Equal Pay Act 1970 were intended, respectively, to eliminate gender discrimination in selection and employment and to achieve equality of pay between men and women. Subsequent legislation (for example, The Maternity and Parental Leave etc. Regulations

1999 and The Part Time Workers (Prevention of Less Favourable Terms) Regulations 2000) have sought to refine and further develop women's rights in the workplace. However, despite the existence of this legislation for over thirty years, there remains extensive evidence of gender based discrimination within the workplace.

The gender gap for pay also widens with advancing age. Leaker shows that, while men and women may have comparable rates of pay when they enter the labour market at the ages of 18–21, the gender pay gap starts to be evidenced from ages 30–39, and then the gap increases for the 40–49 year age group (Leaker 2008: 21). Furthermore, there are gender pay differences between occupational groups. Leaker notes that the widest pay gaps among full-time employees are for skilled trades (25.4 per cent). The narrowest gender pay gaps are for professional occupations (3.8 per cent) and sales and customer services roles (5.9 per cent) (Leaker 2008: 22).

The glass ceiling for women's careers

Women are less often in managerial roles than men. It is estimated that in 1974 only 2 per cent of managers were women (Equal Opportunities Commission 2006) and that by 2006, the proportion had increased to 34 per cent. Even so, women's progression to more senior roles is often obstructed by a 'glass ceiling'. This term has been used for about twenty years to describe the 'invisible barrier for women and minority groups, preventing them from moving up the corporate ladder' (Weyer 2007: 483). Morrison and Von Glinow described the glass ceiling as a barrier which was 'so subtle that it is transparent, yet so strong that it prevents women and minorities from moving up in the management hierarchy' (Morrison and Von Glinow 1990: 5). Oakley (2000) proposed that the glass ceiling could be accounted for on the basis of corporate practice, such as procedures for advancement or recruitment; culture and behaviour, such as leadership styles and (gender) stereotyping, and structure and culture, based on feminist theory. By 2007, the UK EHRC reported that women were still under-represented in managerial roles, with 11 per cent of FTSE 100 directors female and 18 per cent (2005) of small businesses having a majority of women directors.

This raises the question of how the UK glass ceiling continues to be a significant factor in UK organisations. Broadbridge and Hearn noted that women have similarly high levels of education as their male counterparts, and a desire to advance in their personal careers. However, they are unlikely to reach comparable levels of management or to achieve pay equality with their male counterparts (Broadbridge and Hearn 2008: S44). Broadbridge and Hearn suggest that 'male homosociality' may contribute to this, in which emotional detachment, competitiveness and viewing women as sexual objects form a masculine work environment with a 'pecking order' amongst the men

Figure 9.3 The glass ceiling

(Broadbridge and Hearn 2008: S44). Similarly, Charles and Davies (2000), cited in Mavin (2008) suggest that male culture associations of power fail to align with women managers' gender identity. So, women may be less likely to aspire to more senior roles, but if they do aspire to more senior roles they may do so with stereotypical masculine traits which are not acceptable to either their male or female colleagues (Mavin 2008: S76). Furthermore, Mavin also notes that 'forms of sexism mean that women are harder on other women than men are' (Mavin 2008: S77), and that women may find it harder to deal with senior women (rather than senior men) because the strategies they use to deal with men (being flirtatious, generally supportive, admiring) do not work with senior women (Mavin 2008: S77).

With such inequalities in opportunity for women in the UK, academic research in the role of women in the workplace has been extensive, including consideration of how 'sex' and 'gender' should be defined. Oakley (1972) defined 'sex' as biological differences, while 'gender' reflected social and cultural differences. It is not for this chapter to examine the detailed arguments on what constitutes sex and gender, but it is important to be aware of the underlying social construction of gender and the impact this may have on workplace relations. Much of the literature on women's careers has been from the perspective of women as sexually heterogeneous, although some (for example, Pringle 2008) have also considered women managers who may be lesbians. Here, the conclusion is that the challenges facing all women managers in the workplace are similar, and that 'strategies for success are represented by tactics for navigating the labyrinth of heterosexual attributions and innuendos'. (Pringle 2008: S118)

In a review of how management may be considered to be gendered, Broadbridge and Hearn conclude that gender is 'not one thing, but is 'contested, complex, differentiated' (Broadbridge and Hearn 2008: S40) and they categorise the research which has been undertaken as falling within the following headings:

- The valuing of organisations and management themselves over work in private domains, so valuing men's work over women's work.
- Gendered divisions of labour in management, so that men and women tend to specialise in particular roles, with consequent vertical and horizontal segregation of labour.
- Gendered divisions of authority in management, so that women and men's formal and informal authority may be valued differently within organisations, especially since organisations often reflect masculine values.
- Gendered roles between the organisational centre and the organisation margins or boundaries so that 'central' functions tend to be male and margin functions (frontline roles) tend to be female.
- Gendered relations of organisational participants to domestic activity, so that women typically undertake domestic roles of child care, and care of older relatives.
- Gendered processes in sexuality.
- Gendered processes in violence, such as bullying and harassment.
- Gendered processes in interactions between individuals and individuals' internal mental models.
- Gendered symbols, images and forms of consciousness, such as advertising, media and corporate logos (Broadbridge and Hearn 2008: S41).

Disability

Despite improvements over the previous two decades, disabled people remain disadvantaged in the workplace. According to the Equality and Human Rights Commission (2009a), under half of disabled people are in paid work and 40 per cent of disabled adults do not have a formal qualification. For disabled people aged 19, unemployment rates are three times higher than for non-disabled people of the same age (Equality and Human Rights Commission 2009a: 8).

However, it is wrong to focus on a person's disability and make wider judgements (stereotype thinking) about their wider ability to work. Firstly, the disability may not actually be linked to their capability or otherwise to work; and secondly the individual may be quite able to work if employers were to make adjustments to working practices within the workplace. For this reason, employers are required by law (Regulation 3A(2) Disability Discrimination Regulations 2003) to make reasonable adjustments to enable a disabled person to work. Such adjustments may include reallocation of duties or working hours, making adjustments to the premises or working equipment and time off for disability assessment, treatment, or rehabilitation. Therefore the emphasis is on enabling a 'disabled' person to work, rather than finding ways to exclude them from the workplace.

Figure 9.4 Disabled people remain disadvantaged in the workplace

1. As the HR manager of an organisation, what adjustments would you expect to make to continue to employ an individual with the following disabilities?
   a) Diabetes
   b) Profound deafness, but with a need to speak regularly to colleagues by telephone
   c) Back pain or musculoskeletal pain from sitting too long at a workstation
   d) Visual impairment, with difficulties reading visual display screens

Ethnicity

Within the UK, minority ethnic groups remain disadvantaged in employment, both in accessing paid employment and in progressing within the workplace. This is in spite of laws making direct and indirect discrimination and other forms of race discrimination unlawful (for example, the Race Relations Act 1976).

Women from ethnic minorities have even worse representation in managerial roles, despite them having similar aspirations at age 16 as white women: as a result, 11 per cent of white British women are in management roles, for black Caribbean the number is 9 per cent and for Pakistani women it is 6 per cent (EOC 2007: 9). Grant Thornton International (2009) estimated that 21 per cent of senior positions in UK organisations were filled by women managers, leaving the UK ranked below the global average of 24 per cent and below Hong Kong (28 per cent), People's Republic of China (31 per cent), Russia (42 per cent) and the Philippines (47 per cent).

Furthermore, the experience of those of different race origins varies considerably.

1. How do organisations monitor differences in race origin?
2. Go to the job vacancies site of a large employer, and see their application form process.
3. How do employers monitor the ethnic origin of candidates for different jobs?
4. What steps do they take to ensure that applications are considered on a candidate's ability to do the job, rather than other factors such as their ethnic origin?
5. How do organisations say they use the information from these monitoring forms?

Age

Age is an important source of potential workplace discrimination in the UK and one that is seen to be increasingly important as people live for a longer time and face the prospect of longer working lives. Further information about age in the UK is shown below.

Figure 9.5 Age is a potential source of workplace discrimination

Macnicol suggests that age discrimination may be a more complex and challenging form of employment discrimination to engage than sex, race, or disability, since it is problematic to define, quantify, and counter (Macnicol 2006: 6).

The UK government reported in 'Framework for a Fairer Future' (2008: 7) that 62 per cent of people aged over 50 believe that they are turned down for employment on the grounds of age. Walby et al. (2008) estimate from the UK Citizenship Survey 2005, that 4.9 per cent of the UK workforce believe that they have experienced age discrimination in the workplace, which is twice the rate estimated for sex discrimination. Based on Walby et al. (2008), a 4.9 per cent rate of the UK Workforce of 29.42 million (Office of National Statistics 2008) suggests that 1.2 million UK workers will have experienced some form of workplace age discrimination. Furthermore, in a survey conducted on a business to business basis by Chiumento (2003), 38 per cent of employers acknowledged that it is more difficult for candidates aged 50–54 to be shortlisted for interview, while 27 per cent of employers candidly acknowledged that ageism starts to be an issue for candidates in their 40s.

There are 19.7 million people aged 50 and over in the UK, of which 8.9 million are age 50 to State Pension Age (SPA). The over-50 age group represents 25.1 per cent of those aged 16 to SPA. 71.6 per cent of those aged 50 to SPA are in employment, which is lower than the 81.5 per cent rate for those aged 25 to 49, and higher than the 56 per cent of 16-24 year olds employed.
Older workers are more likely (24.6 per cent) to be in part-time employment than those aged 25 to 49 (20.8 per cent). Across the UK, employment rates of older workers vary by region, from 77.8 per cent in the South East to 64.9 per cent in Inner London.
Self-employment is more common among older workers, with 17.8 per cent of older workers self-employed compared with 12.3 per cent of those aged 25 to 49.
Older people have lower qualifications than younger workers and 20.1 per cent of older people have no formal qualifications.
Older people's ILO* unemployment rates are lower than those for their younger counterparts. (Aged 50 to SPA 3.3 per cent; aged 25–49 3.9 per cent; 16–24 14.5 per cent) * International Labour Organisation (ILO) definition of unemployment, defined as aged over 16, seeking a job over the previous 4 weeks, and able to start work within 2 weeks, or out of work, have found a job, and due to start within 2 weeks. Those who are not actively seeking work are defined by the ILO as 'economically inactive'
Older people are likely to remain unemployed for a longer period than their younger counterparts – 39.5 per cent of those unemployed aged 50 and above have been unemployed for more than a year.

Table 9.4 Key Facts and Figures on Older Workers in the UK, Quarter 2 2007 (ONS Labour Force Survey Q2 2007 – Great Britain and DWP (2007: 5))

The UK Department for Work and Pensions (DWP 2007) commented that pressures to find workers with appropriate skills gaps appeared to encourage organisations (70 employers interviewed in 2006) to adopt more age-friendly HR policies. Ominously, in the light of the subsequent downturn in the UK economy from late 2008, the report offered the view that 'if this apparently positive climate is to survive an economic downturn, it may be necessary to reinforce messages about age discrimination in areas like redundancy and early retirement' (DWP 2007: 3).

Sexual orientation

For this section of the chapter, sexual orientation refers to the sexual preferences of lesbian, gay and bi-sexual (LGB) people; in addition, we may consider transgender individuals within this category. It is unlawful (Employment Equality (Sexual Orientation) Regulations, 2003) to discriminate on the grounds of sexual orientation. There are no reliable statistics for the numbers of LGB workers in the UK, although one estimate (Stonewall 2007) puts the figure at 1.7 million. Ellison and Gunstone (2009) found that about 40 per cent of lesbians and gay men had been bullied and suffered low self-esteem, and that about two-thirds of gay men and lesbians have experienced name calling. One of the challenges for organisations in tackling discrimination against the LGB group is in the difficulties in collecting data on who is actually affected within this population, with evidence that organisations have been slow to collect data and individuals themselves reluctant to declare their LGB status.

Within occupational employment, Ellison and Gunstone (2009) have noted that there have been some improvements in employment rights and experiences for gay and lesbian workers, but that the evidence is less clear for bisexual men and women.

Religious belief

It is unlawful under the terms of the Employment Equality 2003 (Religion or Belief) Regulations to discriminate against workers on the grounds of religion or similar belief. Bond, Hollywood and Colgan (2009) note that 71 per cent of the population in 2001 described themselves as Christian in the UK, with 15 per cent declaring no religion. Of the remainder, 3 per cent are Muslim, 1 per cent are Hindu, 0.6 per cent are Sikh, 0.5 per cent are Jews and 0.3 per cent are Buddhists.

There is limited evidence of how religious belief affects employment and it is difficult to separate discussions on religious belief from ethnicity – for example, Muslims have higher unemployment than Sikhs and Hindus (Beckford et al. 2006).

(9.5) The role of the Equality and Human Rights Commission

The Equality and Human Rights Commission (EHRC) was established on 1 October 2007. The vision of the EHRC is to establish 'A society built on fairness and respect. People confident in all aspects of their diversity' (EHRC *Interim Business Plan 2007–08*, Executive Summary: 3). The Commission's remit covers age, disability, gender, gender reassignment, race, religion or belief and sexual orientation. The early objectives of the EHRC are set out in Table 9.5.

- Promote understanding of equality and diversity
- Encourage good practice in equality and diversity
- Promote equality of opportunity
- Promote awareness and understanding of rights under the equality laws
- Enforce equality laws
- Work towards elimination of unlawful discrimination
- Work towards elimination of unlawful harassment
- Promote understanding of human rights
- Encourage public authorities to comply with Human Rights Act 1998

Table 9.5 EHRC Objectives (EHRC *Interim Business Plan 2007–08*, Executive Summary)

When you have read this chapter, it is well worth visiting the EHRC website www.equalityhumanrights.com for more information on the state of equality in the UK today.

 ## The role of HRM

This chapter has shown that there are business, social and legal reasons why organisations will wish to avoid discriminatory practices. Human Resource Managers therefore have an important role in ensuring all people management policies and practices, including the way employees work with each other, are non-discriminatory. These requirements therefore apply to policies ensuring equal treatment in recruitment, reward (pay and benefits policy), opportunities for career advancement, access to training and learning opportunities, and how employees' performance is reviewed.

Typically, human resource departments are seen as having a key role in the development, implementation, and management of polices to eliminate inequality and lack of diversity in the workplace. But there is mixed evidence about their capability to monitor or police those policies. For example, despite the activity which many HR functions undertake to develop diversity policies, there is less evidence that those policies are actually monitored and corrective actions are taken. Kersley et al. (2006) found that organisations were comparatively weak at monitoring HR practices, and even in recruitment and selection, only 20–24 per cent of organisations actively measured this. In other areas of potential discrimination (promotions and pay reviews), the proportions of organisations actually monitoring the effects of policies was even less (see Table 9.6).

Percentage of workplaces monitoring equality policies					
	Recruitment and selection	Recruitment and selection procedures	Monitor promotions	Review promotion procedures	Review relative pay rates
Gender	24	19	10	11	7
Ethnicity	24	20	10	11	5
Disability	23	19	9	10	4
Age	20	16	7	9	3

Table 9.6 Percentage of UK workplaces (with 10 or more employees) monitoring workplace equality policies (Kersley et al. 2006: 248)

Furthermore, even when diversity polices are monitored, this is not to say that HR specialists feel empowered to address the issues arising. For example, Lyon and Pollard found that personnel departments were often unable to resist line managers' ageist behaviour (Lyon and Pollard 1997: 253). But in considering the role of HRM and good diversity practices in the workplace, the responsibility for doing this does not rest with HRM alone. Bond et al. noted in their research commissioned by the Equality and Human Rights Commission on integration of employment practices on age, sexual orientation and religion or belief in the workplace that 'organisations felt that it was essential to have support from managers at the most senior levels in order to pursue an equalities agenda effectively' (Bond et al. 2009: 29). For the HR manager, this underlines the importance of working closely with all managers to promote workplace diversity.

Overall, we may conclude that in the absence of further research on the impact of HRM in managing diversity in the UK workplace, the evidence from the CIPD surveys and the WERS reviews suggest that:

- Diversity policy and interest at the organisational level are more likely to be related to legal compliance, rather than changes in culture, values, or behaviours.
- Policy development and process are infrequently supported by meaningful policy review and action.

9.7 Equality and diversity in operation

So far, the chapter has looked at key issues in equality and diversity in the UK. To conclude the chapter, this case study of Kent Fire and Rescue Service has been written to enable you to consider the wide range of stakeholders which need to be considered in developing a workplace – and in this case a community service – which can truly be described as achieving objectives in equality and diversity. In reading the case study, consider the breadth of actions which need to be taken, both within the workplace and in the community it serves. Note also that this is not only about compliance, but involves extensive development of training and workplace cultures if the diversity objectives are truly to be achieved.

CASE STUDY

Diversity at Kent Fire and Rescue Service (KFRS)

Figure 9.6 Kent Fire and Rescue Service logo

About Kent Fire and Rescue Service

Kent Fire and Rescue Service (KFRS) provides fire and rescue services to more than 1.6 million people in Kent and Medway, from sixty-six fire stations and four fire safety offices.

With 2000 staff, it works closely with HM Coastguard and the Royal Air Force in land- and water-based fire and rescue. It is also responsible for safety and rescue in the Channel Tunnel, where it works with its French counterpart, the Service Departmental D'Incendie et de Secours du Pas-de-Calais.

KFRS was the first fire and rescue service in the South East region to achieve level three of the Local Government Equality Standard, recognising its achievements in promoting fairness in all areas of its work.

continued . . . ▶

◀ *. . . continued*

This case study shows why and how Kent Fire and Rescue Service strives to make real progress in its commitment to deliver fair employment practices and equal access to the service it provides, free from prejudice and unlawful discrimination.

Why is effective diversity management important at KFRS?

Acting Deputy Chief Executive Ann Millington said:

'By working with groups and associations and understanding the needs of all the community, we have been able to develop a better response to incidents, protect those who may be at an increased risk of fire and helped spread the message KFRS is a great place to work, with excellent career opportunities for everyone.

The assessment highlighted many areas of good practice which contributed towards KFRS's level three rating. These include targeting and engaging with hard to reach groups, effective partnership working, strong and committed leadership at all levels, enabling and supporting staff with diverse needs to develop within the organisation and strong investment in training and development for staff around the equality and diversity agenda.'

Equality and Diversity with Kent Fire and Rescue Service

To meet these needs, KFRS developed the following key equalities priorities to help meet the equality agenda. They also form part of changing the Service's culture and business practices to enhance service to Kent's residents.

'KFRS Operational Diversity Plan (2010–2013)

We have reviewed our key equality priorities to more accurately reflect how we believe our equality agenda can be delivered.

- Monitoring and knowing our community – We need to ensure that we understand our community profile and its diversity and where it is changing. This is fundamental to how we shape our services and establish targets.
- Consultation and engagement – Understanding our community also includes taking time to involve our stakeholders as we develop our policies and procedures which affect them. This also includes working closely with our partners.
- Measurable improvement and celebrating success – We need to identify where we are making an improvement and building on our good practice which we can do through self and peer assessment. We can learn from others by sharing best practice and bench marking with others as well as promoting what we have done well.
- Our equality duties – Our commitment to diversity and equality is supported by general and specific legal duties that require us to promote equality and eliminate discrimination towards people based on their, race, gender (including transgender), or disability in everything that we do in delivering services and in our role as an employer. We also have obligations under other legislation around age, sexual orientation and religion/faith. We understand that discrimination

continued . . . ▶

◀ *. . . continued*

can also take place because of other factors such as where some one lives or their background. We have a duty to promote good relations in these areas.

- Development of people skills and diversity – We will ensure that we continually equip our workforce to be sensitive to the needs of other and have the skills that they need build good relationships with people in the workplace or delivering services in the community.
- Internal leadership – KFRS performance on operational diversity will be managed through strong internal leadership, transparency and open to scrutiny. Resources will be targeted to ensure efficiency and value.'

How does KFRS monitor diversity impacts?

Each fire station in the county has produced a People Impact Assessment which identifies community make up, the specific needs and risks within that community, including people with disabilities, harder to reach groups and other matters unique to that area.

This process has given KFRS further evidence that communities are made up of many different groups which require services tailored to their specific needs. Following each assessment an action plan has been produced to address specific impacts identified. It also considers proactive ways to both identify and overcome any accessibility barriers that exist to the services we offer to the community.

An example of this is KFRS work with the travelling community, where a DVD has been produced specifically designed to raise awareness of the dangers of fire, focused around candle and electricity safety within trailers, caravans and the sites occupied.

Within days of the DVD being distributed site managers saw examples of the advice being taken, like caravans being moved further apart and gas cylinders removed to safe distances.

Diversity training

Training programmes include:

- Operational briefings for all staff will incorporate aspects of impact on individuals or groups in the community.
- e-learning on operational aspects of diversity.
- Training for all staff with staff management responsibilities which will include the General and Specific Duties set out in the Race Relations (Amendment) Act and the tools necessary to undertake an Equalities Impact Assessment. This will be supplemented with discussion and formal training courses and conferences. Training will help people to identify policies and procedures that need to be addressed, carry out Impact Assessments and report on results.
- Focused equality skills training for staff undertaking service specific tasks which require enhanced understanding of need, for example education staff working with young people.
- A range of self-managed learning resources such as the Authority's Valuing Difference – Diversity Workbook and computer-based learning resources and the testing of knowledge following the use of such resources.
- Understanding and Complying with Equalities Legislation – a programme to enhance managers' capabilities and confidence in working across diversity and progressing equalities in the

continued . . . ▶

◀ *. . . continued*

workplace, including antidiscrimination legislation and the Authority's role as a provider of high quality services and being an employer of choice.

● Focused seminars for managers on raising Awareness of Gay Lesbian, Bisexual and Transgender (LGBT) issues – includes understanding of how to provide a service that is responsive to the needs of LGBT customers and to combat discrimination and harassment on grounds of sexual orientation.

Neugebauer (2009) Prepared in consultation with Kent Fire and Rescue Service

ACTIVITY

Kent Fire and Rescue Service gives an opportunity to consider diversity policies in action. So think about the following questions and how you can use the evidence from the case study to support your conclusions.

1. What kinds of issues would you expect a fire and rescue service may face in diversity?
   (a) In employment?
   (b) In the provision of its services?
2. To what extent does the KRFS action plan address:
   (a) The business case for diversity?
   (b) The social justice case for diversity?
   What evidence can you give to support your argument?
3. How would you categorise KFRS's diversity and equality approach (see Kirton and Greene (2005) above)
4. Which areas of the KFRS have been designed to meet employment law requirements?
5. Which of the KFRS plan goes beyond strict legal requirements? Why has KFRS undertaken these additional actions?
6. How does KFRS track progress on its diversity policy? What additional monitoring might you recommend?
7. What employment measures would you expect KFRS to use to monitor the employment impacts of their service?

(For more details about the KFRS see www.kent.fire-uk.org/Work_for_us/Equality__Diversity_in_KFRS/Equality_and_Diversity.html)

9.8 Summary

The chapter has demonstrated that discrimination in the workplace occurs for multiple reasons, whether based on gender, ethnicity, disability, religious beliefs, age or sexual orientation. In the UK, laws have been developed to tackle this discrimination but there continues to be widespread evidence that discrimination continues. According to the Government Equalities Office if we do not make quicker progress in eliminating workplace discrimination, the pay gap between men and women will not close until 2085; and it will take almost 100 years for people from ethnic minorities to get the same job prospects as white people (Government Equalities Office 2009: 8–9).

Organisations may have business reasons or social justice reasons for establishing equality or diversity polices. However, there is more limited evidence that these polices are effectively monitored, and that follow-up action is taken.

Students of business studies, and, in particular, human resources, have an important responsibility to develop their understanding of workplace equality and diversity. In particular, human resources specialists must be equipped to develop non-discriminatory workplace cultures which not only comply with legal requirements, but establish workplace fairness where each person's contribution is valued, irrespective of any minority group to which they may otherwise belong.

KEY IDEAS

Having read this chapter, you should have a good idea of the concepts listed below. If you are unsure about anything, please have another look at the chapter. If you want to read more about diversity, please see the bibliography and further suggested reading.

The background to equality and diversity
- The terms 'equality' and 'diversity' have different meanings - you should be able to explain these different terms

Why bother about workplace equality and diversity?
- Organisations have different reasons for how and why they wish to manage workplace discrimination. The HRM student therefore needs to understand the key differences between the 'business case' and the 'social justice' arguments

Key concepts of discrimination
- Inequalities in UK workplaces may be obvious (for example, direct discrimination, or harassment) or less obvious (for example, indirect discrimination or horizontal and vertical segregation). The HRM student must be familiar with both obvious and less obvious causes.

Workplace discrimination in the UK
- UK law offers a range of protections against workplace discrimination, including discrimination based on gender, ethnicity, disability, age, sexual orientation and religious beliefs.

The role of the Equality and Human Rights Commission and the role of HRM
- The EHRC and HRM seek to confront discrimination and promote workplace diversity: despite their efforts, and the UK law, significant obstacles to workplace diversity continue to exist.

Equality and diversity in operation: case study of the Kent Fire and Rescue Service
- The Kent Fire and Rescue Service case study demonstrates the breadth and depth of activity required to promote workplace diversity.

RECOMMENDED READING

Statutes
Equal Pay Act 1970
Sex Discrimination Act 1975
Race Relations Act 1976
Disability Discrimination Act 1995

Regulations
Equal Pay (Amendment) Regulations 1983
Disability Discrimination (Meaning of Disability) Regulations 1996 (SI 1996/1455)

The Maternity and Parental Leave etc. Regulations 1999
The Part Time Workers (Prevention of Less Favourable Terms) Regulations 2000
Fixed-term Employees (Prevention of Less Favourable Terms) Regulations 2002
Disability Discrimination Act 1995 (Amendment) Regulations 2003
Employment Equality (Sexual Orientation) Regulations 2003
Race Regulations Act 1976 (Amendment) Regulations 2003
Employment Equality (Age) Regulations 2006

Codes of practice
ACAS (2006) Age and the Workplace Putting the Employment Equality (Age) Regulations into practice
ACAS (2006) Bullying and harassment at work: a guide for managers and employees, found at www.acas.org.uk/index.aspx?articleid=794
ACAS (2003) Disciplinary and Grievance Code of Practice 1
Commission for Racial Equality (2005) Code of Practice on Racial Equality in Employment
Disability Rights Commission (2004) Code of Practice Employment and Occupation
Equal Opportunities Commission – Equal Pay Review Kit
Equal Opportunities Commission – Code of Practice on Equal Pay
Equal Opportunities Commission Code of Practice – Sex Discrimination

USEFUL WEBSITES

Equality and Human Rights Commission www.equalityhumanrights.com – more detailed information on the state of equality in the UK today.
Chartered Institute of Personnel and Development www.cipd.co.uk for more information on the HR managers' perspective.
You should particularly see CIPD (2005) Managing Diversity: People Make the Difference at Work – But Everyone is Different, also at http://www.cipd.co.uk/subjects/dvsequl/general/divover.htm?IsSrchRes=1.
It is also well worth looking at trades unions' websites to understand more about the role which they have in developing and supporting workplace equality and diversity.

REFERENCES

Austin, M. and Droussitis, A. (2004) Cypriot Managers' Perceptions of Older Managers in Cyprus, *European Business Review*, vol. 16, no 1, 80–92.
Beckford, J. A., Gale, R., Owen, D., Peach, C., Weller, P. (2006) *Review of the Evidence Base on Faith Communities*. London: Office of the Deputy Prime Minister.
Bond, S., Hollywood, E. and Colgan, F. (2009) *Integration in the workplace: emerging employment practice on age, sexual orientation and religion or belief*. Manchester: Equality and Human Rights Commission Research Report 36.
Broadbridge, A. and Hearn, J. (2008) Gender and Management: New Directions in Research and Continuing Patterns in Practice, *British Journal Of Management*, vol. 19, no s1, S38–49.
Charles and Davies (2000) in Mavin, S. Queen Bees, Wannabees and Afraid to Bees: No More 'Best Enemies' for Women in Management? *British Journal of Management*, March 2008, vol. 19, supplement 1, S75-S84(1).

Chartered Institute of Personnel and Development (2007) Diversity in Business A Focus for Progress. London: CIPD.

Cornelius, N., Gooch, L., Todd, S. (2001) Managing Difference Fairly: An Integrated Partnership Approach, in Noon, M. and Ogbanna, E. (eds) *Equality, Diversity, and Disadvantage in Employment*. Basingstoke: Palgrave.

Cuddy, A.C., Fiske, S.T. (2002) Doddering But Dear: Process, Content, and Functioning in Stereotyping of Older Persons, in Nelson, T. (ed) *Ageism: Stereotyping and Prejudice Against Older Persons*. Cambridge, Mass.: MIT Press, 1–26.

Department for Work and Pensions (2007) *Older Workers: Statistical Information Booklet*, Quarter Two, April–June 2007.

Duncan, C., Loretto, W. (2004) Never the Right Age? Gender and Age-Based Discrimination in *Employment, Gender Work and Organization*, vol. 11, no 1, January.

Ellison, G., Gunstone, B. (2009) *Sexual orientation explored: a study of identity, attraction, behaviour and attitudes in 2009*. Manchester: Equality and Human Rights Commission.

Equality and Human Rights Commission (2009a) *Priorities and Work Programme, 2009/10*. Manchester: Equality and Human Rights Commission.

Equality and Human Rights Commission (2009b) *Equal Pay Position Paper*. Manchester: Equality and Human Rights Commission.

Equality and Human Rights Commission (2008) Sex and Power Report taken from http://www.equalityhumanrights.com/media-centre/sex-and-power-report-reveals-fewer-women-in-positions-of-power-and-influence/.

EOC Equal Opportunities Commission (2007) *Sex and Power: Who Runs Britain?* Manchester: EOC.

Government Equalities Office (2009) *Towards a Fairer Future*. London: HMSO.

Greller, M.M., Stroh, L.K. (1995) Careers in Mid-Life and Beyond: A Fallow Field in Need of Sustenance, *Journal of Vocational Behavior*, vol. 16, no 5, 457–468.

Home Office (1999) *The Stephen Lawrence Inquiry: Report of an Inquiry by Sir William Macpherson of Cluny*, Cm 4262-I, February 1999.

Hornstein, Z., Encel, S., Gunderson, M., Neumark, D. (2001) *Outlawing Age Discrimination: Foreign Lessons, UK Choices*. Bristol: Policy Press.

Kandola, R., Fullerton, J. (1994) *Managing the Mosaic – Diversity in Action*. Trowbridge: Cromwell Press.

Kersley, B., Alpin, C., Forth, J., Bryson, A., Bewley, H., Dix, G., Oxenbridge, S. (2006) *Inside the Workplace Findings from the 2004 Workplace Employment Relations Survey*. Abingdon: Routledge.

Kirton, G., Greene, A.M. (2005) *The Dynamics of Managing Diversity. A Critical Approach*. Oxford: Elsevier Butterworth Heinemann.

Leaker, D. (2008) The gender pay gap in the UK, *Economic and Labour Market Review*, April 2008, vol. 2, no 4, 19–24.

Lewis, D., Sargeant, M. (2007) *Essentials of Employment Law*. London: CIPD.

Lyon, P., Pollard, D. (1997) Perceptions of the Older Employee: Is Anything Really Changing? *Personnel Review*, vol. 26, no 4, 245–257.

Mavin, S (2008) Queen Bees, Wannabees and Afraid to Bees: No More 'Best Enemies' for Women in Management? *British Journal of Management* vol. 19, ss75–84.

McCann, R., Giles, H. (2002) Ageism in the Workplace: A Communication Perspective in Nelson, T. (ed.) *Ageism, Stereotyping, and Prejudice Towards Older People*, 163–200. Cambridge MA: MIT Press.

National Statistics Office (2002) Social Trends 31 Available at http://www.statistics.gov.uk/downloads/theme_social/social_trends31/ST31(final).

Noon, M. (2007) The Fatal Flaws of Diversity and the Business Case for Ethnic Minorities, *Work Employment and Society*, vol. 21, no 4, 773–784.

Noon, M., Ogbonna, E. (2001) (eds) *Equality, Diversity, and Disadvantage in Employment*. Basingstoke and New York: Palgrave.

Oakley, A. (1972) *Sex, Gender, and Society*. London: Temple Smith (and 1985 revised edition Aldershot: Gower).

ONS Office of National Statistics and DWP (2007) *Labour Force Survey Q2 2007 Great Britain*

ONS Office of National Statistics (2009) Source: http://www.statistics.gov.uk/downloads/theme_labour/WebTableA2.xls Taken from the web 21 July 2009.

Patrickson, M., Ranzijin, R. (2004) Bounded Choices in Work and Retirement in Australia, *Employee Relations*, vol. 26, 422–32.

Pearson, R. (1998) Former Alabama Governor George C. Wallace Dies, *Washington Post*, 14 September, PA1. Taken from the web on 2 October 2009 www.washingtonpost.com/wp-srv/politics/daily/sept98/wallace.htm

Prasad, P., Mills, A., Elmes, A., Prasad, A. (eds) (1997) *Managing the Organizational Melting Pot: Dilemmas of workplace diversity*. Thousand Oaks, CA: Sage.

Pringle, J.K. (2008) Gender in Management: Theorizing Gender as Heterogender, *British Journal of Management*, vol. 19, S110–19.

Rousseau, J. J. (1998) *The Social Contract*. Ware: Wordsworth Editions.

Stonewall (2007) *Sexual Orientation Handbook* taken from the web on 27 October www.stonewall.org.uk/workplace/1473.asp

Walby, S., Armstrong, J., Humphreys, L. (2008) *Review of Equality Statistics*, Research Report No 1. Equality and Human Rights Commission.

10 Ethics

'Ethics begins only when the good is revealed to consist in nothing other than a grasping of evil...'

(Giorgio Agamben 2007, 1 p IV)

CHAPTER OUTLINE

CHAPTER OBJECTIVES

- Locate ethics as a way of thinking
- Introduce some basic concepts
- Outline the relationship between business ethics and philosophy
- Consider some ethical consequences for Human Resource Management
- Examine the relationship between individuals and organisations

10.1 Introduction

This chapter will look at business ethics, considering contemporary business issues and particularly those of concern to the human resources field. After reading this chapter you should be familiar with ethical challenges inherent in the following:

- The power of human language
- Utilitarianism in a corporate world
- Globalisation and diversity
- The financial sector in the aftermath of the credit crisis
- Organisational behaviour

The theoretical models that will be explored in connection with these issues will include:

- Act and rule utilitarianism
- Ethics of duty and stakeholder theory
- Corporate social responsibility
- Corporate governance

Ethics – a starting point

The term 'ethics' comes from the ancient Greek word '*ethos*', meaning character, manner or habit. The way of thinking about actions involved in ethics identifies something which is unique to us as human animals. It is important to understand what ethics is not: it is not the same as feelings – many people feel good even when they are doing something ethically wrong. It is also not about religion – many people are not religious but ethics involves everyone, whether they are religious or not.

In everyday usage we are fairly clear that ethics relates to morals, to the rules of conduct, for instance, recognized in certain areas of human life. In the medical profession as well as amongst legal professionals, teachers and social workers we expect high standards of ethical behaviour. Ethical considerations must be at the forefront in all these sorts of professional dealings. We have strong intuitions about what counts as right and wrong behaviour. However, some grey areas exist just beyond the scope of these clear-cut definitions. The area of politics, for example, often challenges our intuitive thinking, and business has sometimes claimed a place for itself outside of the ethical domain. We think we know when something is wrong – a politician fiddling his or her expenses allowance for instance, a ponzi scheme (pyramid fraud such as Bernie Madoff's) a disaster such as the gas leak at the Union Carbide factory in Bhopal, India, which in 1984 killed 20,000 people (Sinha, 2009). (See, for example, http://www.guardian.co.uk/environment/gallery/2009/nov/30/bhopal-anniversary-union-carbide for further details on this.)

Sometimes ethical questions involve conflicting claims that make things more complex. Ultimately though, we come to consider questions of character and choice in relation to our lived experience amongst other human beings, and we do so from one basic starting position: that of our own individual character.

 ## Ancient origins

Returning to the ancient Greeks, we see how this subjective aspect of experience and decision was crucial in the thinking that founded western civilization. According to the philosopher Socrates (428–348 B.C.), what we most need to learn if we are to discover truth is how we ourselves ought to live. Ethics, in this regard, defines us as human animals: we have language, the capacity to self-reflect, the ability to give voice to the choices we make. In contrast to Christian moral theory (where the notions of an afterlife dictate the ultimate consequences of moral choice), the classical philosophical tradition connects recognising truth with living a successful and therefore happy life.

For Aristotle (385–322 B.C.), being virtuous involved a personal disposition that unfolded through practical actions. Discovering virtue is the same as performing well. Avoiding extremes of behaviour means choosing to be happy and successful, even though to do so often means turning away from what seems immediately pleasurable: 'When pleasure is at the bar the jury is not impartial' (Aristotle, Ethics Book 2). The point here is that ethics in this Aristotelian sense is *active*. It is not only reasoning about truth but also living truthfully and therefore fruitfully. This is related to that unique factor in humans: we have language and therefore can have an impact on the world.

 ## The justice approach

We can see that language is essential to our reckoning about ethics when we consider how our laws are written down, created from thoughts that occur in speech, in language. Justice is another way of approaching ethical decision, and again has been greatly influenced by Aristotle and other Greek philosophers. The originating idea is that all equals should be treated equally. In current situations this principle founds ethical actions that treat all human beings equally, or if unequally, then fairly based on some standard that is defensible. This may seem obvious, a truism in Western societies based on democratic freedoms and equality, but if we consider issues such as bonus culture or CEO salaries that are thousands of times greater than the earnings of most others in these companies we sense injustice. We might also consider the continuing disparity between women's and men's pay in our own society. Looking further afield, we can think about the huge wealth imbalance between industrial 'first world' nations and the rest of the world. Can such disparities be defended? Are they due to an unfair imbalance of power?

10.4 The common good approach

The Ancient Greek philosophers also established the notion that life is lived not in isolation but in community. They saw this aspect of human society as a good in itself and thought that our actions should contribute to that life, not take away from it. This idea has come under attack many times, not least by politicians. Consider, for example, Prime Minister Margaret Thatcher's infamous statement made in the 1980s: 'There is no such thing as society'. The common good idea holds that the interconnecting relationships of society are the basis of ethical reasoning and that respect and compassion for all others are therefore essential.

Hobbes' Choice

In the seventeenth century the British philosopher Thomas Hobbes famously described life without such an awareness of our interdependence as a return to animal conditions: 'Life in a state of nature is solitary, poor, nasty, brutish and short' (Leviathan, 1651). Hobbes proposed the social contract. In broad terms this means that people concede some personal freedom in order to have a viable means of living together. It is a founding principle of democratic government. This approach also calls attention to the common conditions that are important to the welfare of everyone. From the system of laws that maintain the conditions for business to flourish, to healthcare provisions or environmental protection, all citizens depend on the stability of these social agreements.

Hobbes' vision of life without society:

'Bellum omnium contra omnes' (the war of all against all)

ACTIVITY

What are your top ten beliefs?

1. Make a list of the beliefs you consider most important to who you are as a person. They might be spiritual or religious, philosophical, gender-focused, practical, artistic or creative, humanistic, political, family-oriented, sociological or economical. They should be the beliefs that structure the choices you make in your life, from the trivial to the serious decisions you make.

2. Do any of your beliefs seem to contradict each other?
3. Do some of them make your life uncomfortable at times?
4. How have your beliefs changed over the last ten years?
5. How do you put your beliefs into practice?
6. Consider some famous or infamous influencers on human experience: Martin Luther King, Joseph Stalin, Bill Gates, Aung San Suu Kyi, Bernard Madoff. Consider their connectedness to our world. How has each of these people used language to change people's perceptions?

 ## Man knows, man speaks

As the contemporary philosopher Giorgio Agamben puts it: 'Man does not merely know nor merely speak; he is neither Homo sapiens (knowing) nor Homo loquens (talking), but Homo sapiens loquendi, and this entwinement constitutes the way the West has understood itself . . . The unprecedented violence of human power has its deepest roots in this structure of language' (Agamben 2007, 2, pgs. 7 - 8). This is to say more than that a person's choices can affect the lives of others. Our unique identity means that through our capacity to create meaning in language, we as individuals can radically change the nature of human experience. The importance of ethics in business practice cannot be exaggerated when we consider the enormous influence and the power of our capitalist system, of multinational or transglobal corporations and of consumerism. Of course there is no antithesis between making money and ethics per se. As human beings we need to make money in order to flourish. And much of what goes on in business depends on trust. The conventions that make trading possible, whether it is in international financial transactions or the production and distribution of goods, all are dependent on a shared and normative sense of right and wrong. While there can of course be conflicts between moral questions and the making of money in certain instances, it is possible to work out the best way of proceeding according to ethical precepts.

 ## Normative ethical theories

Ethical questions can be highly complex, affecting many individuals or groups, perhaps from a wide range of cultural and ethnic backgrounds. Culture affects how we see things. This is of particular relevance to those working in the human resources field. In diverse groups of people there may be very different ideas and attitudes towards whatever moral issues are affecting them. Arriving at ethical conclusions and resolving the complex conflicts of interests is not going to be easy. So we look for clearly thought-out arguments based on sound principles to back up our ethical approaches. We find there is a range of theories to help us think more clearly.

Relativism

As Aristotle noted, 'Fire burns both in Hellas and in Persia; but men's ideas of right and wrong vary from place to place' (Nicomachean Ethics). This notion points to the importance of the social environment in determining how people think about both what is, and about what ought to be, the case. Diversity in our global interactions has had the major consequence of broadening our thinking about human values. The relativist position holds that there are no universal standards of good and bad, right and wrong. We can have a more concrete sense of this in business terms if we look at the contemporary issue of globalisation. A predominant outcome of globalisation has been the need for much greater sensitivity and understanding of difference in relation to cultural systems of values or ethics. This often raises many complex issues for businesses when making decisions and especially when those decisions can radically change people's lives. For Human Resources workers difficult situations such as redundancy, dismissal or discrimination tribunal hearings are all part of professional life. The issues underlying such dilemmas send us back to the theoretical drawing board so as to be clear about our viewpoints.

KEY TERMS

Relativism: The view that beliefs and their underlying principles have no universal or timeless validity but are relative only to the age in which they are held, or the social group or even individual person by which, they are held.

CASE STUDY

Perspectives on global marketing

Nike Recall: In 1997 Nike had to recall a range of trainers because of a logo found offensive by Muslims in America. The concern was that the flame logo used resembled the word 'Allah'. Nike withdrew the product.

France Télécom Staff Suicides: An alarming 23 suicides and 13 attempted suicides over 18 months provoked furious criticism in France in 2009. Critics pointed to desperation spreading through the company as France Télécom pushed forwards a modernization program designed to make it competitive in the global market. A total of 10,000 staff had changed jobs over the last three years. (*Times Online*, 14 September 2009).

Nestlé Boycott: In the late 1970s a boycott was launched on this Swiss-based corporation's products. It was prompted by outrage over the company's marketing of breast milk substitutes (infant formulas) in less economically developed countries (LEDCs). UNICEF has estimated that a non-breast-fed child living in the unhygienic, disease-ridden conditions often common to such regions is 6–25 times more likely to die of diarrhoea than a breast-fed infant. The boycott continues. (Moorhead, 2007).

Consequences

The relativist position is found in **consequentialist theories**. These focus on intended outcomes of actions. If an outcome of an action is desirable then the action is morally right; if the outcome is not desirable then the action is morally wrong. The ends, therefore, can justify the means. This is the bare bones of an approach that emphasises goals as the main factor to be considered in ethical decision-making. It is found in the different forms of **utilitarianism**. We will consider aspects of this thinking more closely later in this chapter but before doing so we must examine the opposite position to relativism.

KEY TERMS

Consequentialist theory – where the ends justify the means. If the outcome of an action is desirable then the action is morally right; if the outcome is not desirable then the action is morally wrong. So, rightness, in this view, is not an intrinsic property of actions but is dependent on the goodness or badness of the consequences.
Utilitarianism – The theory that takes the ultimate good to be the greatest happiness of the greatest number and defines the rightness of actions by gauging their contribution to the general happiness.

Absolutism

By contrast the **absolutist** approach sees itself derived from eternal, universally applicable moral principles. In this view, therefore, right and wrong are objective truths applicable to actions or events. They are rationally determined; that is to say the right action can be understood through rational thinking, as can the wrong action. The ancient Greek philosophers pursued such reasoned thinking. This means that the ethical choice is made for reasons important beyond the immediate outcome of the action taken as it relates to the doer. A non-consequentialist position does not factor in as its top priority the pay off to the person performing the act. As we saw in the introduction, Socrates held that there *was* a logical consistency between virtuous living and happiness or flourishing, even if not immediately apparent.

KEY TERMS

Absolutism – The opposite of relativism, this very complex term has within it the idea that unconditional truth exists beyond contingent instances or experiences. For instance, much about me now was contingent: that my parents met and made me is one obvious contingency on which I depended. Absolutism attempts to describe a necessary and complete wholeness of being beyond the collections of conditionals making up our world.

KEY TERMS

Non-consequentialist – ethical choice is made for reasons important beyond the immediate outcome of the action taken.

CASE STUDY

A Western-based multinational clothing company has been discovered using children in India to make their garments. In their defence they point out that this sort of employment situation is normal in this culture; that although the wages being paid to 10–13 year olds are meagre they fund food for these children and their families that would not otherwise be affordable. The implications of stopping children working in their factories are grave. The company acknowledges that such low labour costs put it in a position to sell its clothing range at cheaper prices in the West and still increase profit margins. They point out that greater numbers of customers can enjoy these garments at cheap prices. This also provides more employment both in the company's Western stores and in the impoverished villages of India.

1. What are your intuitive responses to this problem? Try to think about it from your own understanding of right and wrong according to your cultural upbringing.
2. Now try looking at the problem from the local perspective. How might that perspective be different from ours? What might revoking employment contracts mean for local people in this situation? Do these considerations change your views on the theories you have read?
3. What about in the terms of absolutism? Are there necessary ethical truths involved here?

Ethics of Duty: Kant's Three Principles of Categorical Imperative

A philosopher of the Scientific Enlightenment, Immanuel Kant (1724–1804), thought that if a rule can be made universal without contradiction then it is morally good; if a rule cannot be made universal without contradiction then it is morally bad. He wrote that humans have a *categorical imperative* to choose virtue. He proposed three principles underlying ethical choice in human life. These principles have had a major influence on Western civilization. They are found in many humanistic approaches to understanding behaviour, particularly in the workplace as well as in the forms of modern **stakeholder theory** currently shaping much of the thinking around corporate responsibility and governance. Stakeholder theory has been developed through looking at how corporations affect the various groups beyond shareholders who have a legitimate interest in their activities (Edward Freeman, 1984). This area of theoretical development concerns human resources departments, as it is increasingly their role to shape company policies and contribute to future strategies. Rafts of legislation derived and influenced by stakeholder theory developments directly affect these undertakings.

Kant's Three Principles of Categorical Imperative

1 To act consistently in accordance with universal law.
2 To act in such a way as to treat humanity always as an end, never as a means.
3 To act so that your action could be regarded universally as lawgiving.

Kant is a notoriously complex philosopher. To simplify his principles and their meaning we could think of his aims as being thus:

- Logical thinking founds us as rational animals; ethical actions can only be ethical, i.e. right actions, if everybody can follow their underlying principle in the same way. One way to think about this is that an idea of truth can only be possible if it is wrong to lie. In the meaning of truth we encounter the wrongness of lying. If we did not know that it was wrong to lie we would have no sense of truth, it would not exist. It does exist, however. This is known as the **first imperative**. It therefore sets up the need for ethical action to have consistency across the whole range of human experience.
- Of the three principles making up Kant's famous imperative, the most familiar is the maxim to treat a person always as an end only, and never as a means to an end. Simply put, this principle says that the dignity of a human life should never be ignored. An employee, for instance, is more than just a unit of labour used to achieve what an employer wants to achieve; that employee has their own wants and needs and this must never be forgotten or ignored. We might associate the Christian maxim: 'Do not do to others what you would not like done to you' with Kant's second category.
- The universal aspect returns in a different way in the third principle: it might be simply understood as the maxim 'don't do anything to others that would make your family or friends ashamed of you'. That is to say, look outside of your own subjectivity and test whether every human being would find your action ethical or unethical. In this light we might look at lesser acts of deceit – politicians' fraudulent expenses claims for instance. While these acts are not as serious as, say, murder is, they are acts that are highly embarrassing for all concerned when they come to light (Kant 1977).

There are criticisms that can be made of the theory, as of all theories. But the ethics of duty principles have been, and are still, highly influential in Western thought. They underlie many of the attempts through laws, conventions, treaties and regulations to conduct fair or just relations between humans engaged in our economic processes.

Consider some examples of professional dilemmas from within the Human Resources sphere:

1. You are newly appointed to deal with promotion bundles being processed through your organisation. One employee makes a complaint to the effect that they have been repeatedly passed over for promotion because of an incident involving health and safety violation where they whistle-blew to the relevant authorities. On enquiry from your line manager you are informed 'off the record' that this is indeed the case and that the employee in question will never receive promotion on instruction from the CEO. How do you go about thinking this problem through?

2. You realise that the database on your company's workforce of 30,000 people you have been asked to update is to be sold to a medical insurance firm. You register your concerns to your line manager who tells you it is not the concern of the HR department but relates to company strategy. Is this your concern?

3. You are conducting appraisals with members of your company's sales team. The highest selling salesman refuses to take on board the minor changes you have been instructed to gain his agreement on. To your testimony of complaints by admin staff over his verbal abuse he tells you to 'get over yourself'. As he is the highest earner he will behave as he pleases or leave for a competitor. What do you do?

In thinking about how to approach these problems try to gauge your thinking against Kant's principles (see above). Does having a notion of universal principles bring any clarity to your understanding of these dilemmas?

Utilitarianism

Often a good way to see whether we agree with a theory is to look to its opposite. Utilitarianism takes a different position from the Kantian view. There are a number of different sorts of utilitarian approaches. They all share a defining characteristic of focusing on outcomes of actions as the primary measure for ethical decision-making. We tend to associate classic utilitarianism with the British philosophical tradition of Jeremy Bentham (1748–1832) and John Stuart Mill (1806–1873). Simply put, 'the greatest happiness principle' sees that man's ultimate goal in life is to maximise pleasure and minimise pain. The theory came out of the massive social changes brought about by the Industrial Revolution. The rule of utility judges goodness in terms of the amount of happiness that an action produces. Utility is the goodness scale, as it were, by which to measure the product, happiness.

As with so much else of what we think of as modern thought, if we look to the ancient Greeks we see this theory originating in approximately the fifth century

BC in the writings of Epicurus, among others. In this guise utilitarianism is again an effort to respond to the overarching question for the ancients: how ought a man to live? How should he act? Practical wisdom was what the Greeks sought. One version of an answer to the problem was that a man should act in such a way as to produce the best outcome possible. Thus we can think of the ethical corporate action as that which produces the greatest good and does the least damage for all those who are affected: shareholders, customers, employees, suppliers, the local community and the local and wider environment. Such thinking is found in policies to create **corporate social responsibility** initiatives. This term refers to a widely accepted understanding that businesses have social responsibilities beyond increasing their profit margins. For some this responsibility is only justified by the business case; being socially responsible can increase or maintain profits. For others, there are moral arguments for CSR: as corporations cause social problems, they have a responsibility to resolve or prevent them. The immense size and power of many transglobal businesses makes the moral imperative all the more urgent (McWilliams and Siegal, 2000).

Types of Utilitarianism

This form of ethical reasoning has developed widely since the eighteenth century. It was divided into different forms that emphasised different aspects to be focused on when considering utility:

- **Act utilitarianism** considers the likely consequences of potential actions. The action that we believe will generate the greatest happiness is then chosen. The stark directness of this approach can lead to some outlandish outcomes, as has been shown by critics.
- **Rule utilitarianism** focuses on potential rules of action. In deciding whether to follow a rule, we should consider what would happen if a rule were constantly followed. This allows us to consider wider implications of the choices we make than just the direct consequences of an action. Thus we can reject actions that would entail dramatically bad outcomes for some, though still weighing in favour of utility for the majority.

Consider the ethical dilemmas below, using these two different theories as your guide.

1. In your role as Liaison Officer you interview an employee who has been flagged up by their line manager for frequent late arrivals at work and failure to meet deadlines. During the interview the employee tells you in confidence that they are in recovery from alcoholism. While they were drinking their work was satisfactory. They are no longer drinking but in recovery they are dealing with many changes and expect it will take some months before they fully return to their former efficiency. Do you report them?

2. The accounts manager for a large company agrees to give you a payroll servicing contract (their first to your company), expecting you to agree to make a £1,000 donation to his favourite charity, a local youth sports team. How do you respond?

3. You are newly employed as an assistant sales director for a large recruitment agency specialising in supplying financial services executives. You are the first female to join the sales team. Your manager entrusts you with entertaining a group of potential clients with a dinner engagement followed by a West End cabaret show. On reaching the venue you realise it is a lap-dancing club. What do you do?

4. You and your team are required to draw up a list of suitable candidates for redundancy in a restructuring drive. You know many of those chosen personally and one in particular is a close friend. You are required to maintain strict confidentiality until the company is ready to announce its decision to cut the workforce. Do you?

Economic utility

Utilitarianism has been very successfully inducted into capitalism and been adopted by the corporate world of work. This is because it puts at the centre of moral decision-making a variable which is very familiar to economics. Utility in the science of economics is a commonly used parameter for measuring the purely economic value of actions. In the language of economics, utility is as familiar a term as is love in the language of religions such as Buddhism. The emphasis on utility is often at odds with the more human-centred approaches advocated by human resources specialists and requires some analysis when dealing with the day-to-day issues met by personnel professionals.

Corporations

Begun in America in the early 1800s, the legal conventions licensing companies to amalgamate so as to become gigantic have resulted in the phenomenon of corporatism shaping our entire world and experience. Over the last 30 years a predominating ethos developed in corporate dealings. The Nobel Laureate economist, Milton Friedman, maintained that the only social responsibility of business was to increase the profits of its shareholders (*New York Times Magazine*, 13 September 1970). This has been termed the **'bottom line'** approach. It called for government non-interference in a free market economy. Taken to the level of absurdity it could lead to a *carte blanche* climate in which commercial interests override any ethical consideration whatsoever. Corporations have a history that includes the disastrous mistakes of Bhopal, Exxon Valdez, Enron, Nestlé, WorldCom, and more recently, Northern Rock and Bear Stearns. The free market view has been severely shaken by the recent credit crisis. Increased government regulation on global business trading is being introduced following the meltdown. The EU is drawing up legislation to ensure that corporate responsibility (CR) is adopted. Critics have pointed out that it may simply lead to evasive action being taken: corporations moving their operations to areas beyond the boundaries of such laws, or threatening to do so should governments impose restrictions they find anti-commercial (Legge, 2000).

Certain political and ethical codes are being developed to try to deal with the many criticisms and issues associated with the power of transglobal corporations, many of which have annual turnovers greater than some nation States' GDPs. Of the FTSE 100 companies surveyed, 90 per cent can produce an ethical code written into their mission statements. However, only 45 per cent of these companies provide any training in ethics. Research into the efficacy of such codes is made difficult by the variety of differing definitions of key terms in use (O'Sullivan, 2008). What is often forgotten in such considerations is that organisations, however large, are made up of people. Without its people there is no organisation. Human resources departments focus on organisational behaviour in much of their work. From recruitment through induction and training to exit interviewing or redundancies, human resources policy seeks to promote and shape human behaviour. Many human resources departments offer **Employee Assistance Programs (EAPs)**, a confidential service including professional counselling. As we have seen in the France Télécom example (see case study above) the processes engaged in by organisations can have profound and unpredictable impacts on people's lives (O'Sullivan, 2008).

 Confidentiality

The introduction of Employee Assistance Programs to the range of services provided by HR departments involves ethical codes of behaviour and confidentiality that require increased sensibility. Serious issues such as mental illness in employees may need to be dealt with. Many mental conditions are stigmatised in society and especially in the workplace. Statistics indicate that 13 per cent of the population experience severe mental illness at some stage in their lives. Twenty-five per cent of woman and 12 per cent of men experience severe depression at some stage. One per cent of the population experience psychotic episodes at some stage. Dr. Liz Miller has highlighted the difficulties faced in the workplace by those with mental illness. (drlizmiller.co.uk) Ironically, workplace stress may be significantly affecting mental health in employees (www.mind.org.uk). For HR professionals involved in providing counselling in the workplace it is crucial that a strongly defined code of conduct and understanding of confidentiality is in place. Who is the HR professional loyal to in maintaining confidentiality? Is it the employer or the client? Jenny Summerfied suggests that in order for EAPs to be successful on behalf of the whole organisation, they must maintain the *client's* confidentiality as their top priority. Senior management must understand and agree upon this code of conduct in order for trust to be in place and the EAP to function properly (Summerfield 1995).

 ## The financial crisis

'Over the last 18 months. . .the world financial system – and particularly but not exclusively the world banking system – has suffered a crisis as bad as any since the stock market crashes of 1929.' (Adair Turner, Chairman, FSA, 21st January 2009).

With American losses estimated at $8.3trillion dollars (www.imf.org) and British public sector debt pushed to at least £1.5trillion (Office for National Statistics, 2009), the world financial crisis has ushered in a climate for regulation and scrutiny of global trading that is unprecedented. A consequence of the crisis is unemployment. Those in the human resources field will have direct and increasing engagement with these realities in the aftermath of this disaster.

 ## The future of work

A term familiar to human resources theory, the **psychological contract** is 'a set of implicit and unwritten understandings between employee and employer which each would abide by.' (O'Sullivan 2008) The understanding of the term has developed to encompass more employee-determined values. This includes working hour's flexibility and opportunities for development (Porter, Bingham, Simmonds 2008). Induction is seen as crucial to setting out a reciprocal good faith relationship. This includes a sense of perceived organisational support (POS). Periods of recession bring increased pressures on employees. Objections have already been raised about developments under the banner of **organisational citizen behaviour**. This has been described as a phenomenon wherein employees contribute to their organisations beyond the strict obligations of their job descriptions.(O'Sullivan 2008) It relates to our more theoretical study of ethics in this way: studies have shown that employees with high ethical standards also rate highly in their contribution to OCB. This disposition has been termed **good soldier syndrome.** (Organ, 2006) The dark side of this syndrome has increasingly been highlighted as 'the exploitative and abusive tendency of supervisors and managements to impose so-called "voluntary" or "extra-role" activities via compulsory or coercive mechanisms in the workplace.'(Vigoda-Gadot, 2006) When recession brings increased redundancy and unemployment such coercive tendencies in management can increase. (McGregor, 2006)

In 2004 UNESCO produced a major report looking at the globalisation of work. It found that 'the future of work is now no longer an affair of States but a **governance** of a global system. . .operating in a network and, amongst which the **firm** has a privileged place' (UNESCO, 2004). The activities of human resources management are fundamental to the creation of ethical practice and humane policies, carried within corporate strategy, and effectively managed in the daily interactions of the human beings making up our organisations.

 ## Summary

This chapter began by looking at the origins of ethical thought in the ancient world and how certain ideas that were important to early philosophers have shaped our civilisation. It then analysed two opposing takes on ethics, that of relativist consequentialism and the absolutist ethics of duty of Immanuel Kant. Drawing on the contemporary developments from these foundations, the chapter focused on utilitarianism and stakeholder theory.

The ways in which such theoretical approaches can be relevant in the human resources field were explored through case studies. Aspects of corporate responsibility, governance, diversity issues and the future of work were highlighted.

The chapter found that increasing globalisation and the growth of power and influence of transglobal corporations in a boundary-less environment makes ethical practice all the more crucial in the business world.

KEY IDEAS

What is Ethics?
- Ethics is one of the most complex, often deeply troubling forms of thinking about how a person should live and what a person ought to do.
- Thinking ethically and the capacity to speak and act self-consciously according to ethical principles define us uniquely as human beings.
- We are also uniquely capable of immense violence.

Philosophical Approaches
- Relativism is the general idea under which ethical theories involving consequentialism congregate (see below).
- Absolutism is a complex philosophical approach that funds non-consequentialist theories in opposition to relativistic and consequentialist ones (see below). It is the idea that there are inviolable principles beyond the variables of human desires.

continued . . . ▶

. . . continued

Two Contrasting Ethical Theories

- Consequentialist theory – where the ends justify the means. If the outcome of an action is desirable then the action is morally right; if the outcome is not desirable then the action is morally wrong.
- Utilitarianism is a consequentialist form of ethics in which outcome is focused on when deciding action. In Act Utilitarianism the action that we believe will generate the greatest happiness is chosen. Rule Utilitarianism considers what would happen if a rule were constantly followed.
- Non-consequentialist ethics of duty: Kantian ethics involving the 'inescapable, binding requirements of the categorical imperative' (Blackburn, 2008). Stakeholder theory is derived from this form of thinking. Its ultimate perspective is to view all humans as ends not means.

Ethics at Work

- Psychological contract: a set of implicit and unwritten understandings between employee and employer by which each would abide.
- Employee Assistance Programs: services on offer to employees where health issues, personal or work-based problems may be discussed in a supportive environment. Many types of counselling offered and confidentiality is essential.

RECOMMENDED READING

If you would like to learn more about some of the issues in the sections within this chapter you might like to consider the following books and articles:

Appadurai, A. (2001) *Globalization* Durham: Duke University Press delves into many of the most pressing issues of globalisation as it affects developing countries. *Fear of Small Numbers* Durham: Duke University Press. Anxieties held by Western nations in relation to boundaryless minorities are also analysed.

Bauman, Z. (2008) *Does Ethics Have a Chance in a World of Consumers?* Cambridge, MA: Harvard University Press attempts to find new and adequate ways of reframing our thinking about our consumerist societies.

Crane, A. and Matten, D. (2006) *Business Ethics* Oxford: Oxford University Press provides a rigorous examination of the European approaches to some of the most pressing ethical problems of our age.

Davis, M. (2006) *Planet of Slums*, London: Verso. A gripping vision of the urban future.

Plato, *The Republic of Plato*, Books I and II, www.classics.mit.edu. The fundamental text for understanding the origins and development of Western democratic society.

USEFUL WEBSITES

www.gutenberg.org/etext/3207 free books for download including Aristotle's *Ethics* and Hobbes' *Leviathan*.

www.ciaonet.org/journals. Contemporary essays in ethics fields for free download.

www.classics.mit.edu. Ancient philosophical texts in translation for free download.

REFERENCES

Agamben, G. (2007) *The Coming Community,* Minneapolis: University of Minnesota Press 2, *Infancy and History*, Verso 2007

Aristotle (350BC) *Nicomachean Ethics* www.gutenberg.org

Blackburn, S. (2008) *Oxford Dictionary of Philosophy* Oxford: Oxford University Press

Coyle-Shapiro, J. and Conway, N. (2005) 'Exchange relationships: examining psychological contracts and perceived organizational support' *Journal of Applied Psychology* vol. 90, no. 4, 774–781

Freeman, R.E. (1984) *Strategic Management: A Stakeholder Approach.* Harlow: Pitman

Friedman, M. (1970) *New York Times Magazine* 13 September 1970

Hobbes, T. (1651) *Leviathan* www.gutenberg.org

Kant, I. (1797) *Fundamental Principles of the Metaphysics of Morals*, www.gutenberg.org

Legge, K. (2000) 'The Ethical Context of HRM: The Ethical Organization in the Boundaryless World' in D. Winstanley and J. Woodall (eds.), *Ethical Issues in Contemporary Human Resource Management*, Basingstoke: Macmillan

McGregor, D. (2006) *The Human Side of Enterprise* New York: McGraw-Hill Books

McWilliams, A. and Siegel, D. (2000) 'Corporate Social Responsibility and Financial Performance: Correlation or Misspecification?' *Strategic Management Journal* vol. 21, no. 5, 603–9

Miller, L. (2008) 'Doctor's Orders' *The Guardian*, 11 June 2008 www.drlizmiller.co.uk

Moorhead (2007) *Milking It* feature article http://www.guardian.co.uk/business/2007/may/15/medicineandhealth.lifeandhealth

Office for National Statistics (2009) www.statistics.gov.uk

Organ, D. (2006) *OCB: Its Nature, Antecedents, and Consequences* London: Sage Publications

O'Sullivan, N. (2009) 'The Future of Work' in Matthewman, L., Rose, A. and Hetherington, A. (eds.) *Work Psychology*, Oxford: Oxford University Press

Porter, C., Bingham, C. and Simmonds, D. (2008) *Exploring Human Resource Management* New York: McGraw Hill

Sandell, M. (2009) 'A New Citizenship' *The Reith Lectures* www.bbc.co.uk/radio4/features/

Sinha, I. (2009) 'On the Continuing Scandal of Bhopal 2009' *The Guardian* http://www.guardian.co.uk/environment/gallery/2009/nov/30/bhopal-anniversary-union-carbide

Summerfield, J. and Van Oudtshoorn, L. (1995) *Counselling in the Workplace* London: Institute of Personnel Development

Turner, A. (2009) 'The Economist's Inaugural City Lecture' *The Economist's Inaugural City Lecture* www.fsa.gov.uk (accessed 21 January 2009)

UNESCO (2004) 'The Future of Work in Europe: Ethics and Globalisation' http://unesdoc.unesco.org/images/0013/001347/134775eo.pdf

Vigoda-Gadot, E. (2006) 'Theorizing Some Dark Sides of The Good Soldier Syndrome' *Journal for the Theory of Social Behaviour*, vol. 36

11 Culture

'*There is nowhere you can go and only be with people who are like you. Give it up.*'

(Bernice Johnson Reagon, composer, song leader, scholar and producer)

CHAPTER OUTLINE

CHAPTER OBJECTIVES

- Understanding of different aspects of culture in the modern work environment
- Awareness of the influence of time and circumstances on creating generation cultures with generation specific core values and beliefs
- Comprehension of the meaning of organisational culture and its origins
- Awareness of contemporary cultural issues in the workplace, such as breaking through a glass ceiling and work–life balance trend
- Understanding the role of HRM in managing corporate culture
- Knowledge of how HRM is able to participate in strategic cultural changes in the workplace

11.1 Introduction

In today's global environment, all business is international business. Culture pervades and radiates meanings into every aspect of enterprise (Trompenaars 1993). These aspects of enterprise range from culture-specific product demand, for example whitening facial creams in Thailand as opposed to self-tanning range of cosmetics in Western Europe, to challenges in achieving an effective interpersonal communication in multicultural working environments (Guirdham 2005).

If you ask a British or American colleague, 'How are you today?' you can expect with much certainty a standard answer, something along the lines of, 'Fine, thank you,' or 'Jolly good'. While this could be true reflection of their current mood sometimes at least, it is more likely to be the culturally ingrained forced jollity and the Anglo-Saxon famous stiff upper lip cover up. Finns, on the other hand, are recognised as being more honest and direct, so do not be surprised if you get this kind of answer to your greeting question, 'I have a stiff neck'. And if you can handle both kinds of answers on the same corridor between the offices, award yourself a tick on the highly-sought cross-cultural interpersonal communication competencies list.

Figure 11.1 Communication and cultural differences

Modern organisations are finding themselves confronted with many diverse beliefs, behaviours and ways of conducting business, equally internally and externally. In order to survive in the modern workplace both domestic and international managers have to become open to and flexible in working with different cultures and abandon the premise that 'my way is the only way'. Rosalie Tung (1994) identified three core cultural competencies that organisations need to seek, develop and nurture in their workers.

1 An ability to balance conflicting demands of global integration on one hand and local responsiveness on the other, captured in a phrase: *Think global – act local.*
2 An ability to work in multidisciplinary, multifunctional and multicultural teams – Felix Adler offered a helpful metaphor of people diversity that could be used for promoting this ability in the workplace: '[People] may be said to resemble not the bricks of which a house is built, but the pieces of a picture puzzle, each differing in shape, but matching the rest, and thus bringing out the picture'.
3 An ability to work with and/or manage people from diverse racial and ethnical backgrounds. National histories, identities and politics are universally complex and multilayered. Therefore, assumptions should be dropped and questions asked instead of expecting confirmation of an understanding people may have formed about other cultures.

Rising issues of managing individuals in multinational and multicultural organisations are of a particular importance to international human resource management (IHRM). One of the hot IHRM topics is expatriation/repatriation and helping international employees cope with culture shock that develops from those major relocations, international career development as well as achieving the work–life balance in a multicultural setting. Other important area of interest for IHRM is the relationship of culturally different employees with their employer. Understanding the cultural differences is of particular importance to managers in multicultural organisations. For example, a German employee might regard open criticism of weaknesses as acceptable, even helpful; while in order to avoid likely defensive reaction, American or British employees need more kid glove handling and may respond better to **sandwich feedback**: packing (disguising) the criticism inside other positive remarks.

The sandwich feedback technique enables a manager to restructure feedback aimed at more sensitive employees, so it is easier to deliver, reinforce good behaviour and ask for improvements to the employee's behaviour. It's even more effective if it's structured as praise, criticism and helpful advice or suggestion of alternative (desired) behaviour in future.

IHRM should take a lead in the development of organisations' intercultural competence as well as in managing multicultural groups and teams (Tung, 2008).

Figure 11.2 Sandwich feedback

Finally, whether an organisation is seeking the best suited recruitment process in a multicultural environment or opening a new office in a different country, its HR department will have their hands full facilitating the intercultural awareness.

 ## 11.2 The meaning of culture

As a whole, culture is a pattern of thinking, feeling and acting that is learned throughout a person's life, beginning in early childhood (Trempenaars 1993). Indeed, an individual's cultural programming starts from the moment he or she is born. For instance, the custom to dress newborn babies in either pink or blue cues everyone who interacts with the baby to treat the child as either a 'girl' or a 'boy', according to that group's norms. Whenever people form a group of any size they develop and teach social norms that help them carry on together. Most of these norms are unconscious 'rules' that impact every level of each person's life, including behaviour, values, norms and basic assumptions.

Morgan (1997) defines culture as a social system of knowledge, ideology, values, laws and day-to-day rituals. Since it is produced by shared history and experiences of people who represent a certain culture, national boundaries are often used as a synonym for a culture (Guirdham, 2005). However, nations are made up of diverse peoples and are often multicultural themselves. So, Hofstede (1981) proposed using the word culture in the sense of the *collective programming of the mind*, which distinguishes the members of one group of people from another. He suggested that people share a collective national character that represents their cultural mental programming. This mental programming shares values, beliefs, assumptions, expectations, perceptions and behaviour. Such a group of people can be a nation (national culture), but also a regional or ethnic group; women or men (gender culture), old or young (generation culture), poor or rich (social class culture), HR managers or ophthalmologists (occupational culture), private doctors or public health doctors (type of business culture), or members of a work organisation (organisational culture) (Guirdham, 2005).

Mix of generation cultures in the workplace

Several generations with differing values, ambitions, views and mindsets overlap in today's workplace. The different generations of workers tend to have some common values that came from growing up in the same circumstances marked by that particular time. Zemke at al. (2000) define four generational groups and the characteristics they tend to display at work (See Table 11.1).

	Born		Work Assets	Work Liabilities
Veterans	1922–1943	Early influences are associated with the Great Depression and World War II	Stable Detail oriented Thorough Loyal to the organisation Hard working	Resistant to change Unwilling to challenge the system Uncomfortable with conflict Unforthcoming when they disagree
Baby boomers	1943–1960	Raised in an era of extreme optimism, opportunity and progress	Service oriented Driven Willing to 'go the extra mile' Good interpersonal skills Compliant Team players	Not 'budget minded' Uncomfortable with conflict Reluctant to go against peers May put process ahead of result Overly sensitive to criticism Judgemental of those who see things differently
Generation X	1960–1980	Came of age in the shadow of the boomers	Flexible Techno-literate Autonomous Unintimidated by authority Creative	Impatient Weak people skills Sceptical

	Born		Work Assets	Work Liabilities
Nexters, Generation Y or Millennials	1980–2000	Born into the current high-tech economy	Work well in teams Optimism Tenacity Multitasking capabilities Digital natives (Palfrey and Gasser, 2008)	Need for supervision and structure Inexperience, particularly with handling difficult people issues Oversensitive to criticism Low organisational commitment

Table 11.1 Generation culture impacting work behaviour (Adapted from Zemke, Raines, and Filipczak, (2000))

KEY TERMS

Organisational commitment The degree of an employee's desire to remain with an organisation.
Organisational culture A set of core values and common perception shared by the members of an organisation.
Recruitment The process of attracting qualified job applicants to an organisation.

A positive outcome of the generational blending in the workplace could be talents of all ages, higher creativity and broad insight into customer base. People with different perspectives always have the potential to bring different thoughts and ideas to problem-solving and future opportunity. However, an unfortunate and more common outcome may be generation gap and conflict. While younger workers may believe their older colleagues are rigid, technological dinosaurs, to older professionals who more often than not value structure and hierarchy, their younger colleagues may seem unreliable. To make the matters worse different generations are motivated in a very different way. Xers are motivated by overtime and cash incentives, they have a desire to work and do not take employment for granted; while Millennials are typically not motivated by money but by change, challenge, improved work conditions and workplace satisfaction. They expect promotions, flexible work schedules, lots of holiday time, better pay, as if those benefits are their right not something to be earned. Managing this mixture of human resources with dissimilar retention methods required for each generation group is an increasingly difficult task (See the activity *Millennials in the workplace*).

Equally, changing cultural values have an impact on HRM activities and procedures. For example, younger men's aspirations are different to previous generations and fathers are now spending more time with their children. This has been already recognised and addressed by Sweden, Iceland and Australia, which all have progressive paternity leave provisions, with legislation allowing parents to share their leave entitlement. Changes in traditional gender roles and new lifestyles where achieving the 'work–life balance' is becoming increasingly important to individuals in western societies, change the way workers are motivated and managed in the workplace (Bratton and Gold 2003).

ACTIVITY

Millennials in the workplace
When born in 1985, Stephen was driven in a car with a 'baby on board' sign from the baby-friendly suite at a local hospital in Dublin to a newly decorated baby room in his parents' home, fully fitted with baby safety devices. He wore a 'Daddy's champ' bib, over an 'Aren't I cute?' babygrow. Stephen has been given a lot of praise for any step he took, any burp he uttered. Stephen's parents were deeply devoted to their son; they did basically everything for him, strongly believing that their most important role was to foster Stephen's self-esteem. During his school days Stephen proudly collected a number of special awards and trophies for various achievements, ranging from the most creative essay in the first term of 1995 to the best team player in one of the school's projects. Upon completion of his secondary education, Stephen took a gap year to travel the world, which was mostly the English-speaking world. On his travels he was working a bit as a diving instructor, waiter and a street entertainer while his parents happily picked up the rest of the bill. When he got back to Dublin he was a new man with a new piercing and a new tattoo; however, he couldn't decide whether to get another job or enter a post-secondary education, so he took some more 'finding himself' time. Finally, Stephen graduated in computer science last year and landed a job at an IT firm in Brighton.

The HRM department of his new employer managed to break through the tattooed shell and they spotted the immense talent, the natural way with information technology, willingness to learn, openness to challenge and optimism Stephen had to offer. They got him to sign a three-year exclusive contract with them and they slipped in a free iPod as a welcome gift. On his first day at work the HRM department received a curious phone call from Stephen's mum, who wondered how her little software designer was doing and if they were treating him well.

Stephen's entrance to the firm has not gone unnoticed since. In the first year he created numerous software solutions for his firm and dated a few young women that he met on Facebook. He was equally as happy behind his computer as he was to work in project teams on applications development.

Meanwhile the HR department learned to address Stephen's shortcomings such as tardiness and lack of respect for more experienced team members gently, as he has been proven to be very sensitive to criticism and short on corporate loyalty.

Keeping in mind that there are almost twice as many Millennials (Generation Ys) compared to their Generation X predecessors, the HR managers could not avoid hiring Millennials altogether. They endeavoured to get to know and understand them, learn how to manage them, retain them and change corporate policies to cater for a new generation's culture at work.

You have been offered the post of HR manager at Stephen's firm

1. How would you make sure that he doesn't leak important work information to your competitors?
2. How would you handle complaints from Stephen's colleagues, concerning his brash way of communicating?

National cultures and HRM

The internet and widely accessible information technology, international music, worldwide television with uniform reality programmes, talk shows and quizzes, alongside more affordable travel have been reducing differences in values between people living on different parts of our planet. However, significant differences in national values remain noticeable and much of them are based on socioeconomic situation and predominant religious beliefs.

So, countries continue to differ along a number of dimensions that influence the attractiveness of direct foreign investment in each country. Moreover, in global markets, the most important factor influencing international human resource management (IHRM) is the culture of the country in which a facility is located. First, national culture greatly affects a country's laws, in that laws are often the codification of right and wrong as defined by the culture.

Secondly, culture also affects human capital, because if, for example, education is very much valued by the culture, then members of that community strive to increase their human capital. A country's human capital may profoundly affect a foreign company's desire to locate there or enter that country's market. While countries with low human capital attract companies that are looking for low-cost production, requiring low-skill jobs with low wage levels, countries with high human capital are attractive to companies looking for a highly skilled labour force.

In addition, cultures have an important impact on approaches to managing people, because cultural characteristics influence the ways managers behave in relation to subordinates and the perceptions of the appropriateness of various HRM practices. For instance, in some parts of India a job candidate may be accompanied by a family member at a selection interview whereas this would be thought inappropriate in organisations located in North America or Europe. On the other hand, cultures differ strongly on such things as how subordinates expect leaders to lead, how decisions are handled within the hierarchy and how individuals are motivated. For example, in Germany, managers focus on demonstrating their high technical skills so employees look to them to assign their tasks and resolve technical problems. While, in the Netherlands managers encourage others to participate in decision making.

Some cultural distinctions between different nations were highlighted during the latest recession that called for major shake-ups and strategic change in national and multinational companies. Many companies responded with restructuring, reengineering and redundancies – in other words job cuts – which not only affected those who had lost their jobs, but also the workers who survived those lay-offs, leaving them with an extra workload but no extra reward. It is interesting that, unlike most other G20 countries, France well-known for its industrial strike culture, had seen social unrest in response to the global downturn, with millions of workers taking industrial action at the beginning of year 2009 in protest at the government's handling of the economic crisis. Nonetheless, France became one of the first European countries to exit recession, together with Germany, when official data showed the French economy grew by 0.3 per cent between April and June 2009. Meanwhile, although undoubtedly affected by the global recession, by the end of March 2009, the Indian economy grew 6.7 per cent in a year. It is also interesting that, during recession, instead of implementing major job cuts, the Indian government increased spending on their scheme to help the urban poor find employment.

KEY TERMS

Culture A socially constructed system of knowledge, ideology, values, laws and day-to-day rituals.

Feedback Provision of information about how an employee is doing in the job.

Human capital A nation's resources in terms of the economic and social abilities and skills of its people.

Masculinity Cultural values that give priority to assertiveness, competition and aggressive success over compromise and cooperative success.

Matrix organisations Organisations which join together two different groupings, for example, a human resource department is superimposed on a functional grouping.

Dutch psychologist, Geert Hofstede had a particular interest in values in the workplace and how they are influenced by culture. He conducted comprehensive research looking for similarities and differences among national cultures. In the late 1960s and early 1970s, Hofstede issued questionnaires to 80,000 IBM employees in 66 countries across seven different occupations in order to conduct a cross-cultural research. Based on all the data collected, Hofstede (1981) suggested a four-dimensional model of national culture, widely used in multicultural management research. The four dimensions are:

1 *Uncertainty avoidance index (UAI)*: the extent to which members of society are culturally programmed to feel comfortable or uncomfortable with the unknown, the uncertain and the ambiguous. Cultures that are high on this dimension (Greece, Portugal, Guatemala, and Uruguay) prefer rules and set procedures to contain uncertainty, while those with low UAI (Singapore, Jamaica, Ireland) tolerate greater ambiguity and have higher tolerance for deviation and innovative ideas. High UAI people are also more emotional and driven by inner-nervous energy, as opposed to low UAI society members who are more phlegmatic, contemplative and generally do not show their emotions easily.

2 *Power distance index (PDI):* the extent to which less powerful members of institutions (with family being the smallest) and organisations accept and expect that the power is distributed unequally. This represents society's level of inequality, but is endorsed by the followers as much as by the leaders. Cultures with high PDI (Malaysia, Philippines, India, France, and Belgium) have companies that are usually organised in rigid vertical hierarchies, where information flow is formalised and restricted and relations between different power groups are strictly formal. While cultures with low PDI (Scandinavian countries, New Zealand, Israel, Ireland) tend to have flat and matrix organisations, with open communication and informal relations.

3 *Individualism (IDV):* the relative importance of individual goals compared with group or collective goals. Members of individualist cultures primarily operate as individuals and their tasks prevail over the personal relationships. Therefore, in individuals' societies the social ties are loose and everyone is expected to look after themselves and immediate members of their family; while in collectivist societies people are from their very birth integrated into strong, cohesive in-groups, often extended families, including grandparents, uncles and aunts who offer them protection in exchange for unquestioning loyalty. Among top individualist countries in Hofstede's research were USA, Australia, United Kingdom, Canada, Netherlands and New Zealand, while collectivist cultures include South American countries, Pakistan, Greece, Serbia and Portugal. It is interesting that countries with individualist cultures are often wealthier than more collectivist cultures. Whereas, Hofstede found that collectivistic cultures with high power distance all had less developed economies.

4 *Masculinity (MAS):* the extent to which the life goals of men dominate those of women. Highly masculine cultures, which have wider gap between men's values and women's values (Japan, Austria, India, Venezuela, Italy and Switzerland) are competitive – they approve assertiveness, aggressiveness and success by any means – while more feminine cultures prefer compromise, cooperative success and modesty (Finland and Sweden).

In his later work with Chinese scholars, and based on Confucian dynamism, Hofstede added a fifth cultural dimension to his model: short-term versus long-term orientation (LTO), or willingness to postpone payback or satisfaction against wanting or needing quick returns and rewards (Hofstede and Bond 1988). This construct acknowledges that in many Asian countries a longer time horizon is considered for planning and decision-making. This has also been represented in the inclusiveness and over-employment in India as mentioned before, against seemingly ruthless lay-offs in the USA in particular during the latest global recession.

Cultural values as described by Hofstede strongly influence the nature and suitability of HRM practices. In individualistic cultures companies often design selection procedures to focus on assessing an individual's technical skills, while in collectivistic cultures the focus is more on assessing how well an individual will perform as a member of the work group. When a person raised in an individualistic culture has to work closely with those from a collectivistic culture, communication problems and conflicts often appear. HRM should have strategies in place to manage conflicting work practices and communication styles, as well as strategies for raising awareness of cultural differences in the workplace.

It must be stated that Hofstede's dimensions are not comprehensive in explaining cultural variations, and religion, gender equality, ethnocentrism and high/low context communication are also significant variables that have been identified in cross-cultural research (Guirdham 2005). Hofstede's model is also criticised for oversimplification of a concept that is too vibrant and complex to be constricted into few dimensions (Tayeb 1996). However, Hofstede's model remains popular in management research probably because of its large sample size; codification of cultural characteristics; and emphasis on attitudes in the workplace.

1. What is culture?
2. How does culture affect the modern workplace?
3. What cultural issues are of particular concern to HRM today?
4. Name five of Hofstede's cultural dimensions with examples of value differences between different nations.

11.4 Organisational culture

Organisational culture is comprised of behavioural expectations that become unspoken 'rules for survival and success' within the organisation. It often stands for an imperfectly shared system of interrelated understanding, values, beliefs, norms and assumptions that shape the ways in which people behave and things get done (Schein 1988; Armstrong 2003; Guirdham 2005). In other words: 'the feel of the place'. What is believed to be important along with the unwritten rules of behaviour may never be articulated or even observed, but together those common organisational values and norms set the way in which 'we do things around here' (Furnham and Gunter 1993). Therefore, organisational culture determines the way the organisation carries out business, treats its human resources and customers, manages conflicts and makes decisions about the future. In addition, organisational culture sets the manner of communication that takes place within the organisation and the means by which that communication is conducted (Martin and Nakayama 2000). It includes both organisational self-image and the concept of the organisation's mission. It also includes physical manifestations of the organisation's activities, or artifacts of the culture such as 'the way we dress here', 'the way we greet each other' and 'the volume we use to speak to each other at corridors', and even the décor of the offices.

Organisational culture varies widely. Schein (1988) described dimensions that he used to differentiate between organisational cultures in different organisations as follows: what is valued; the dominant leadership styles; the language and symbols, the procedures and routines; the definitions of success that characterises an organisation; the habit of thinking; people's mental modes; the climate; the group norms. He further suggested that organisational culture could be divided into three levels, similar to those of Hofstede stated for national culture (Schein 1988). The most visible level of organisational culture: **behaviour and artefacts** consists of behaviour patterns and outward manifestations of culture: privilege granted to executives, dress code, level of technology utilised, and the internal office decoration. All may be visible indicators of culture, but difficult to interpret. Artefacts and behaviour also may tell us what a group is doing, but not why. Staff of a small Serbian Health Centre predominantly whisper when talking on corridors – it seems unusual for a fairly busy place, and most workers are aware of this peculiarity but cannot tell when and why it all started.

The next level consists of **organisational values and beliefs** that underlie and to a large extent determine organisational behaviour, as they express preferences for certain behaviours or certain outcomes. However values are not directly observable, as behaviours are. There are two types of values:

KEY TERMS

Artefacts are culturally influenced non-verbal communication messages based on the way employees are dressed or the way objects around them are designed.

Low-context communication Assumes low level of shared knowledge and uses verbally explicit speech.

Power distance Cultural value dimension which contrasts acceptance that power is distributed unequally with its opposite.

Uncertainty avoidance Cultural value dimension referring to how a culture resolves ambiguity, uncertainty and change.

terminal values or desired outcomes that people seek to achieve, for instance commitment to the company; and **instrumental values** that are desired modes or patterns of behaviour, such as unofficial working hours that go to support the organisational commitment (Brown 1995). In other words, terminal values are 'what we want to be' (highly committed workers) and instrumental values are 'how we're going to get there' (by staying late at work and long after an official end of the working day).

Finally, the deepest level of organisational culture is the level of **assumptions**. Schein (1988) argues that underlying assumptions grow out of values until they become taken for granted and drop out of awareness. People within an organisation are often unaware of or unable to articulate the assumptions forming their deepest level of culture. An example of assumption is a general attitude toward risk taking and aggressiveness in working practices, or moral principles that prevail.

ACTIVITY

Describe the dominant culture of an organisation with which you are familiar.

1. What are the main characteristics of an organisational culture?
2. How does organisational culture differ from national culture?
3. Describe Schein's three levels of organisational culture.
4. Illustrate the differing cultures with the type of work or industry you think would adapt best to that culture.

The formation and fostering of organisational culture

Schein (1988) suggests that an organisation's culture develops to help it cope with its environment. It is formed by a variety of organisational characteristics, such as characteristics of people within the organisation including their personalities, cultural background, gender, age, occupation, social class. Organisational culture is also shaped by the particular line of industry, size of the organisation and organisational structure. A lot of organisational culture originates from the founder of the organisation. In the early 1970s Richard Branson founded Virgin Records (a chain of record stores), later known as Virgin Megastores. His Virgin brand grew rapidly in 1980s, while his strong, flamboyant personality became part of the organisational culture in over 360 Virgin companies today, including Virgin Atlantic Airlines, Virgin Mobile, Virgin Trains, Virgin Fuels and Virgin Galactic (his Space Tourism Company founded in 2004). People that were hired by Virgin companies had a similar drive to Branson and they thought that creativity and competitiveness were rewarded. For many years, Virgin products and services grew around those core values established by the founder. All the employees know the story of Richard Branson's enterprise and how the company was founded, and they share a common perception and values that continue to be their basis for understanding and interacting with each other.

Like Virgin Companies, most organisations sustain their original culture through selection procedures and socialisation of new workers. Socialisation is the process by which members learn what is expected of them and how the reward system is structured, so that they can internalise the values and norms of an organisation's culture. Some companies include socialisation in the induction training. New employees are made aware of the core values, the company's vision of the future, expected work behaviours and other important aspects of organisational culture, and they are also shown how to effectively fit in with the established culture.

Therefore, selection and assessment practices followed by induction training are commonly used as tools for socialising newcomers in a particular role orientation, depending on what the organisation desires from its members. Role orientation is the characteristic way in which newcomers respond to a situation.

There are two basic types of role orientation: An institutionalised role orientation results when individuals are taught to respond to a new context in the same way that existing members respond to it. An individualised role orientation results when individuals are allowed and encouraged to be creative and experimental when responding to a new situation. Often a job applicant's ability to fit into organisation's culture is assessed during the selection interview. Equally, the potential employee uses the entrance interview to assess whether the organisation suits them and offers their preferred work environment, as well as extracting clues as to what role orientation to take should they get the job. In addition to formal HRM procedures, organisations also use stories, ceremonies, symbols and language to convey cultural values (Trice and Beyer 1984).

ACTIVITY

Organisational culture largely determines whether a person will be satisfied working for a company. Consider what kind of organisational culture would suit you best.

1. Where does an organisation's culture originate from?
2. How do organisations usually sustain and nurture their culture?

11.5 The growing culture of work–life balance

Work–life balance is not a new phenomenon, but has recently been high on Western governments' and corporate agendas, partly because of the changing needs and demands of the workforce (i.e. Millennials claim flexible working conditions that fit around other needs and interests they have in life), and partly as an initiative to produce a healthy, happy and productive labour force. Much work–life balance discussion has focused on 'family-friendly' policies and the challenges faced by people with young children. Traditionally the emphasis of work–life balance has been on women but many men also stand to benefit in their roles as fathers (CIPD 2008). A recent CIPD study in the United Kingdom (2005) found that almost half of those surveyed believe that they have struck the right balance between work and life outside work. However, for those with children, 35 per cent claim that working long hours get in the way of their relationship with their children and among men the issue was particularly acute. Organisations have recognised the emerging trend and they are looking for ways to meet the changing needs of their employees.

Flexible working initiatives are a direct product of the work–life balance agenda. They include a wide range of arrangements, from part-time work, flexible days and hours, compressed workweeks, job sharing, working from home and career breaks, to maternity and paternity provisions.

Creating an organisational culture that supports the work–life balance with flexible working and family-friendly workplaces makes good business sense and needs to be an aim for those organisations that want to remain competitive in the future. Flexible organisations are more attractive to employees and foster better motivation and retention of staff, which are the key goals of HRM. Such organisations also boast higher productivity and cost savings. British Telecom, for example, claims that every year it adds £8 million to its bottom line purely as the result of allowing more people to work from home, while their productivity increases by an average of 20 per cent.

11.6 Predominant male culture at work

Corporate culture with 'supremacy of male values', male-dominated senior management teams and widespread negative attitudes towards women managers with children, has been blamed for the lack of women at senior management level also known as a **glass ceiling** (Wirth 2001: 53). A study in 2007 found that there were only 100 women directors in FTSE 100 companies making 11 per cent of total directorship in FTSE 100, even though this was up 0.7 per cent on the 2006 figures (Vinnicombe et al. 2008: 38). Further evidence of a glass ceiling in businesses lies with Veale and Gold's (1998) study where nine out of ten women questioned claimed they would be unable to move upwards in their careers. In fact, there is still a significant difference in the number of women and men achieving senior management roles even in some cultures that rate low on Hofstede's masculinity scale (Wood 2003).

KEY TERMS

Glass ceiling this is the place in the organisational structure above which employees who are discriminated against cannot be promoted.

In most organisations, predominant male culture at work manifests itself through 'old boy' networks where men display a preference to work alongside other men (Beck and Davis 2005) and subsequently exclude women from their networks (Klenke 1996; cited in Cooper-Jackson 2001). Also, when it comes to decisions about promotion, men typically prefer more aggressive behavioural traits to the more friendly style of management which women tend to believe is important to success (Wood 2006). Interestingly, when men demonstrate these 'male traits' in business environments, they are labelled 'leaders', whereas if women demonstrate them they are labelled 'bossy' and 'pushy' (Davidson and Cooper 1992; cited in Cooper-Jackson 2001). This undoubtedly is holding back women from effectively climbing up the career ladder because if they display typical female traits they are undervalued, but if they demonstrate typical male qualities they are criticised.

What is more, it seems that the 'think manager – think male' attitude is strong and stable across time and different national cultures since men consistently perceive women as less well qualified for managerial positions (Schein 2007). Such attitudes reinforce the corporate social stereotype that manager equals male (Cruz, Mbinkar-Gondo and Honma 2004).

On a more positive note, there is some evidence that the stereotypical view of women is beginning to fade and perhaps there is hope that changes can be made in the arena of 'women in management'. For example, in the United Kingdom there has been a positive shift in employers' and employees' attitudes towards women as managers (Cruz et al., 2004). This positive change is influenced by the growing formation of an all-inclusive organisational culture (starting with education and awareness of business leaders and HR managers) so that the talents that women bring to business are recognised and valued in the promotion process (Vinnicombe et al. 2008: 39). However, in many other countries, such as Japan, Switzerland and China women managers' capabilities continue to be perceived negatively.

ACTIVITY

You are working as an HR manager in a busy, medium-sized chain of real estate agencies in London, with a prevailing highly competitive culture. Recently you received an email reporting discrimination at work from one of the company's employees, Amanda, a sales agent, working in Highgate Village branch. The team of sales agents in Highgate Village consists of seven people, six men and Amanda – the only woman. The manager of the agency is also a man. Your investigation of the case shows that Amanda uses slightly different tactics to her male colleagues to achieve property sales. She uses a less aggressive and more accommodating style in dealings with potential buyers. However, she generally gets the same results as others. In her email she objects to the fact that all the team members, including the boss, often make jokes about her soft approach and that occasionally they go behind her back to pinch her deals. She has not spoken to her manager about the issue, but has addressed her complaint directly to your office.

What action will you take?

(11.7) Managing culture: role of HRM

Multinational companies are increasingly interested in promoting corporate culture and organisational ideology to improve control over, coordination of and integration with their subsidiaries.

Harrison (1972) identified four organisational ideologies:

1 *Power-oriented* There is a central source of the power and control is exercised mainly through selecting loyal key individuals, rather than following set procedures or relying on the logic. Many small enterprises and large conglomerates display the characteristics of a centralised power culture.
2 *People-oriented* Consultants both within organisations and freelance, workers co-operatives, barristers' chambers.

3 *Task-oriented* Organisations that display such a culture are: **network organisations** when many separate organisations co-operating together to deliver a project; and **matrix organisations** which are project-oriented with ever-changing project or contract teams. Team or cell technologies fall into this mode of organising.

4 *Role-oriented* Departmental functions are defined and empowered with their role, for example, the HRM department or the finance department. The work within and between departments is controlled by procedures, role descriptions and authority definitions.

Similarly, Hofstede (1981) identified six cultural dimensions to differentiate between organisational cultures.

1 Process-oriented versus results-oriented (organisations differ in the ways they prioritise how things are done and what gets done).

2 Job-oriented versus employee-oriented (job-oriented organisations unconditionally focus on the work that is being done while employee-oriented organisations are primarily concerned with workers' satisfaction).

3 Professional versus parochial (in professional organisations, individuals' identities are based on individual expertise while in parochial organisational culture individuals' identities come from being in the organisation).

4 Open system versus closed system (it is generally easy to join an open system, and a new employee can quickly get up to speed in the new environment, whereas it is difficult to join the closed system organisation and only certain kinds of people can fit in).

5 Tightly versus loosely controlled cultures (tightly controlled cultures are characterised by seriousness, punctuality, strict procedures and high discipline, whereas, loosely controlled cultures have a more casual work climate, less rules and generally tolerate improvisation).

6 Pragmatic versus normative cultures (pragmatic cultures are predominantly market-driven, while normative cultures are more ideologically driven).

Moreover, the subsidiaries of multinational companies are embedded in local national cultures wherein the underlying basic assumptions about people and the world may differ from those of the national and corporate culture of the mother company. These differences may hinder the acceptance and implementation of human resource practices, such as career planning, appraisal and compensation systems, in addition to selection procedures and the socialisation process.

ACTIVITY

As an HR manager of a multinational bank that has opened a new subsidiary in Goa, India, you have been asked to draft an induction week plan for new recruits, all of them locals, and trained accountants, whose job will be to promote and sell a variety of the bank's products (ranging from loans, mortgages and insurance policies to current, saving and credit accounts). How would you welcome new recruits and how would you make sure that their first week at work effectively socialises them into the organisation? How would you decide whether to make any changes to the company's existing induction protocol?

HRM is concerned with developing and implementing practices at the same time as partnering with managers to align these practices with the business strategies in a particular environment of local culture. HRM also plays an important role in managing transition of multinational business to its new location, therefore from one cultural environment to another. Additionally, HRM has the role of representing local employees' concerns to senior management, as well as maximising employees' contributions to increase efficiencies and lower costs.

1. Why has the work–life balance become high on the agenda of many organisations?
2. What are the reasons behind the glass ceiling many women find in their careers?
3. How can HRM facilitate organisational culture management?

A high-performance culture

The components of high performance organisation cultures, independent of the company's size, type of business or other conditions are (Shinazy 2006):

- A clear and inspiring shared vision that drives the organisation's mission and is woven throughout all business practices, including HRM procedures and policies.
- Leaders who act as role models and exemplify the culture in their daily professional behaviour.
- Employees who identify leaders as leaders, informally if not by title or rank.
- Celebrating small demonstrations of key aspects of the culture, for example taking pride in working for the company by using its product in your own household or wearing a T-shirt with the company's logo even when not working.

However, qualities of a high level of business performance culture vary according to context. Consider the three companies described in the case study on page 323.

Organisational cultures, like all cultures, adapt to the group and circumstances that created them. Besides, they evolve over time, for example, a culture of multitasking, leaderless team organisation may be appropriate for the corner

CASE STUDY

'Cash cow' organisation

Pizzeria Mamma Mia – an established European restaurant chain. This organisation has an established hierarchy and promotes itself with a recognisable brand, colours, uniforms, way of delivering service and food quality. Job roles and the division of labour are well-defined. Newcomers are expected to fit into the existing culture and new ideas are neither sought nor encouraged.

Figure 11.3

Growing enterprise

The Green machine – a local, and very popular secondhand bicycle repair and sale shop. This organisation is run by friends or family members, employees have multifunctional job roles, there is an informal atmosphere at work; it is a learning organisation, open to new ideas and new ways of doing things.

Figure 11.4

Troubled organisation that is rapidly losing its market share

Balkan Railway Services – hit by a combination of mounting dept, latest recession and lack of consumer confidence. When a serious crisis hits an organisation, the status quo and the relevance of existing culture are challenged . In order to survive, along with assessing the damage, such an organisation is likely to be undergoing deep changes such as replacement of the top management, redefining the nature of the business – possibly from transportation to service, restructuring and a reduction in hierarchical levels followed by job cuts. HRM can play an important role in facilitating those transformational changes.

Figure 11.5

bicycle shop, but once it starts growing it will probably evolve in more structured, centralised and hierarchical system. Therefore, organisational culture serves a function that may actually become obsolete over time. As business conditions change, so too does organisational culture. The question that organisations face is whether this change will be conscious and deliberately strategic or not.

The positive impact of consciously created organisational culture radiates in every aspect of an organisation, including employee performance, selection and recruitment, and retention of staff. For instance, the organisation with a clearly defined and articulated culture is more attractive to potential employees because it clearly answers the question **What's in it for me?** Such an organisation has an equal appeal to the younger generation of employees looking for 'great places to work' as well as to older workers looking for organisations with clarity and consistency of culture.

 ## HRM and culture change

Strategic culture change involves creating a new vision of the future and the organisation's ideal culture. A vision is a statement about what an organisation wants to become. It gives shape and direction to the organisation's future. In other words, a vision answers the core questions *where this organisation is going* and *how it is going to get there*. It should resonate with all members of the organisation and help them feel proud, excited and part of something much bigger than themselves. A vision stretches the organisation's capabilities and image of itself. This is then a ground for new norms and desired behaviour, which must be reinforced by management. Visions range in length from a couple of words to several pages.

Here are some examples of vision statements:

'Our vision is to create a profitable restaurant with an exciting atmosphere, great food and excellent service where people truly enjoy coming to eat. We also aspire to provide a safe, healthy and rewarding workplace for all our employees.'

'Growing from strength to strength, "Garden Tools" is dedicated to improving the quality of life, making it better, safer and easier.'

'We aim to provide high quality products that combine performance with value pricing, while establishing a successful relationship with our customers and our suppliers.'

'We intend to stay ahead of the competition by innovating new products and services based on the needs of our customers and market demand.'

'IT Wizards have become a profitable provider of high quality software solutions and services that offer strategic value to our customers and create a company that can attract, recruit and retain smart and talented employees.'

ACTIVITY

Where would you like to see yourself in five years' time and how do you plan to get there? Create your personal vision statement.

The biggest challenge for HR managers is to shift their focus from current operations to strategies for the future. Successful HRM is about developing an atmosphere within the organisation, which allows for these highly desirable policies to flourish.

(11.9) Summary

This chapter began by introducing what is usually meant by culture and how different meanings relate to business and HRM in particular. This was followed by a detailed exploration of national cultural differences, with a special focus on the effect that such differences have on organizational behaviour and management in today's highly diverse work environments. The mix of different generations and cultures, the growing work–life balance culture and predominant male culture in the workplace were then presented and discussed. The chapter went on to examine the role of HRM in managing various organizational cultures, outlining the components of a high performing organizational culture. It concluded with a discussion of HRM's role in managing culture change.

REFLECTIVE QUESTIONS

1 Why is culture important to organisations and HRM in particular?
2 Name Schein's three levels of culture.
3 What is organisational culture?
4 List three differences of generation-specific values influencing different behaviour and attitudes between generations at work.
5 What are the common ways of nurturing and sustaining organisational culture?
6 What are the possible applications of Hofstede's cultural dimensions to HRM?
7 How can organisations incorporate work-life balance into HR practices and procedures?
8 What are the positive aspects of consciously created organisational culture?

KEY IDEAS

Introduction

A growing number of multinational and multicultural organisations are interested in the relationship of culturally different employees with their employer, and understanding the cultural differences is of particular importance to international human resource management (IHRM).

The meaning of culture

Culture is defined as a group of people who share common core values, beliefs, assumptions, expectations, perceptions and behaviour.

Organisational culture

Organisational culture is defined as a group of people working in an organisation sharing a common perception and core values and beliefs. It dictates many aspects of the working environment, such as general attitude toward creativity and innovation, attitude toward risk taking and aggressiveness, formalisation of disciplinary and other HR procedures as well as unspoken rules and control, people orientation, attitude toward woman and minorities, unofficial working hours and commitment to the company, dress code, interior office decoration, acceptance of fun and jokes at work, communication style, and moral principles. Organisational culture changes over time and with changing business conditions. Managing strategically these changes is the best option an organisation can make. Strategic culture change entails creating a vision of the organisation's ideal culture. The differences between national and corporate culture of the multinational company may hinder the acceptance and implementation of human resource practices.

The range of different generation's cultures in today's workplace require careful management of HRM policies so to prevent problems that differences of generation-specific values may cause.

The growing culture of work–life balance

Organisations that support the work–life balance of their employees, providing flexible working hours and creating family-friendly workplaces are finding it easier to recruit and retain their workforce, which is one of the key goals of HRM.

RECOMMENDED READING

Bennett, M.J. (1998) *Basic concepts of intercultural communication: Selected readings*. Maine: Intercultural Press.

Hickson, D.J., Pugh, D. (2002) *Management worldwide: Distinctive styles amid globalization*. Harmondsworth: Penguin Business.

Markoczy, L. (2000) National culture and strategic change in belief formation, *Journal of international business studies*, vol. 31, no. 3, 417–42.

Van Oudenhoven, J.P., Askevis-Leherpeux, F., Hannover, B., Jaarsma, R., Dardenne, B. (2002) Asymetrical international attitudes, *European Journal of Social Psychology*, vol. 32, no. 2, 275–89.

USEFUL WEBSITES

www.flexibility.co.uk/issues/WLB/index.htm Links to a number of interesting articles on the emerging culture of work-life balance.

www.geert-hofstede.com Useful website for added insight into practical applications of Hofstede's cultural dimensions as well as for checking out cultural dimension scores of different countries.

www.worldbusinessculture.com Provides the culture-focused profiles of 39 countries.

REFERENCES

Beck, D. and Davis, E. (2005) EEO in senior management: women executives in Westpac, *Asia Pacific Journal of Human Resources,* vol. 43, 273–88.

Bratton, J., Gold, J. (2003) *Human Resource Management: Theory and Practice,* 3rd edn. Basingstoke: Palgrave Macmillan

Brown, A. (1995) *Organizational culture and leadership.* London: Pitman.

CIPD (2005) *Flexible working: impact and implementation – an employer survey.* CIPD survey report.

CIPD (2008) *Work–life Balance.* CIPD Factsheet.

Cooper-Jackson, J. (2001) Women middle managers' perception of the glass ceiling. *Women in Management Review,* vol.16, 30–41.

Cruz, A., Mbinkar-Gondo, I., Honma, B. (2004) *Breaking Through the Glass Ceiling: Women in Management.* Geneva: ILO Publications.

Guirdham, M. (2005) *Communicating across cultures at work,* 2nd edn. Basingstoke: Palgrave Macmillan.

Hofstede, G. (1981) *Cultures and organisations: Software of the mind.* London: Harper Collins.

Hofstede, G., Bond, M. (1988) The confusion connection: from cultural roots to economic growth, *Organizational Dynamic,* vol.16, 4–21.

Martin, J.N., Nakayama, T.K. (2000) *Intercultural communications in context,* 2nd edn. Mountain View, CA: Mayfield.

Morgan, G. (1997) *Images of Organisation,* 2nd edn. London: Sage Publications, 119–52.

Palfrey, J., Gasser, U. (2008) *Born Digital: Understanding the First Generation of Digital Natives.* New York: Basic Books.

Schein, E. H. (1988) *Organizational Culture and Leadership.* San Francisco: Jossey-Bass.

Schein, V. (2007) Women in management: reflections and projections, *Women in Management Review,* vol. 22, 6–18.

Shinazy, M. M. (2006) *Shaking off the dust: Designing an organization culture for strategic advantage.* Paper presented at Western Region IPMA-HR Conference, Portland, Oregon – May 3–5, 2006.

Tayeb, M.H. (1996) *The management of a multicultural workforce.* Chichester: John Wiley

Trempenaars, F. (1993) *Riding the waves of culture.* London: Nicholas Brealey.

Trice, H. M., Beyer, J. M. (1984). Studying organizational culture through rites and ceremonials, *Academy of Management Review,* vol. 9, no. 4, 653–69.

Tung, R.L. (1994) *Managing Human Resources Diversity for Global Competitiveness.* Keynote speaker at the International Conference on Managing Human Resources/Labor Relations Diversity for Global Competitiveness, McMaster University (Canada), 22–24 May.

Tung, R.L. (2008) The Cross-Cultural Research Imperative: The Need to Balance Cross-National and Intro-National Diversity, *Journal of International Business Studies,* vol. 39, 41–6.

Veale, C., Gold, J. (1998) Smashing in the glass ceiling for women managers, *Journal of Management Development,* vol.17, 17–26.

Vinnicombe, S., Singh, V., Burke, R.J., Billimoria, D., Huse, M. (2008) *Women on corporate boards of directors: International Research and Practice.* Cheltenham: Edward Elgar, 37–8.

Wirth, L. (2001). *Breaking Through the Glass Ceiling.* Geneva: ILO Publications.

Wood, G. (2003) What does it take to get to the top: do middle and senior managers agree? *Women in Management Review,* vol.18, 122–31.

Wood, G. (2006). Career advancement in Australian middle managers: a follow-up study, *Women in Management Review,* vol. 21, 277–93.

Zemke, R., Raines, C., Filipczak, B. (2000) *Generations at Work: Managing the Clash of Veterans, Boomers, Xers, and Nexters in Your Workplace.* New York: AMACOM Books.

12 Communication

'*The problem with communication . . . is the illusion that it has been accomplished*'

George Bernard Shaw

CHAPTER OUTLINE

CHAPTER OBJECTIVES

- Understand the purpose of communication
- Knowledge of the means of communication
- Appreciate the significance of theoretical models of communication
- Understand the role of non-verbal communication and symbolism in effective communication
- Knowledge of cultural influences
- Understand work and communication
- Appreciate the importance of the employee voice
- Awareness of miscommunication, both inadvertent and deliberate

12.1 Types of communication

Living in a multimedia age we have adapted personally and professionally to a wide range of communication formats.

We are able to deal with communication directed at all of us (Underground announcements, traffic lights, advertisements and television programmes) and filter out what we have no interest in. We wait for the green man at the traffic light paying little attention to who is standing beside us, or tune out an announcement for a train on a different line to our journey. Personal communication has also become more complex as we text, email and skype directly to a specific person tailoring our communication so that the recipient will understand and unconcerned whether others can decipher our message or not.

We can cope with communication happening directly and **synchronously** (telephone calls, meetings, or one to one sessions) as well as the convenience of the **asynchronous** but remote and indirect (letters, reports, emails or texts). Advantages of the direct and synchronous communication are that ideas can be developed and spontaneously enhanced. It is also easier to understand the intentions of the speaker when we are there as we have so many more cues to work from. Not only the context of the communication but the eye contact, voice inflection and body language: both deliberate and **leaked**. We are able to assess a communication from a range of inputs. A simple 'It'd be nice to have something on that for the meeting' is interpreted appropriately as a direct order, a nice to have or a sketched outline, according to how the comment is delivered. This is much more ambiguous when we rely on indirect communications which are asynchronous, not least because situations can alter between the time they are sent and when the receiver accesses them.

KEY TERMS

Asynchronous Does not happen at the same time for both parties.
Leaked body language Unintentional body language cues revealing inner feelings.
Synchronous Happening simultaneously at the same time.

Before reading on, think of:
1. A direct form of impersonal communication that is synchronous.
2. An indirect form of personal communication that is asynchronous.

Communication within organisations

Organisations have prided themselves on improving their internal communication and much of this has fallen to the HR department. HR deal with a bewildering array of communications from sending out information to new recruits to briefing managers on changes in labour laws. HR devises the tailored health and safety policies in line with the legal requirements as well as defining practices and processes in staff handbooks and online resources. When it comes to examining the current situation HR runs diversity audits, satisfaction questionnaires, job analysis and training needs analysis. It also falls to HR to be the keepers, educators and enforcers of diversity and ethics policies (Lucas et al. 2007). The HRM function has also kept pace with modern developments using e-recruitment and e-learning. As well as vetting candidates via traditional routes, the use of Facebook information and their feedback on ebay or paypal accounts also help to create a composite picture of a candidate. The ethics for this are still evolving and HR is creating the blueprint as it works.

Within an organisation communication is used to:

- Inform: reports, team briefings, disciplinary, policy notices, legal presentations, intranet, annual accounts, newsletters, grapevine and informal rumour.
- Engage: induction training, informal meetings, guidance interviews, interim appraisals, preformance review, brainstorming, away days, departmental meetings.
- Develop: mentoring, coaching, performance reviews, appraisals, goal setting, shadowing, specialist training and development opportunities, secondment briefings and support.
- Feedback: focus groups, surveys, suggestion boxes, union meetings, works councils, quality circles.
- Promote: mission statement, press releases, public relations exercises, corporate sponsorship, industry awards.

12.2 The purpose of communication

Communication is used to engage employees, to communicate the organisation's mission and its strategic direction. Good communication is the sharing of information between two or more individuals or groups to reach a common understanding (Jones and George 2007).

Skilful communicators take into account their target audience, level of previous knowledge, attitude to the information and any inherent bias or prejudice of the communicator themselves. Messages are clear, compelling and positive.

The persuasive communicator is able to defend by attack since they understand their opponent's argument and engage with rather than dismiss it.

This sounds intuitive yet within our own disciplines and areas of expertise we develop codes, short cuts, convenient abbreviations and cultural jargon that can render our communication impenetrable to outsiders. HR, as the gatekeeper of much of the organisation's structural and procedural knowledge is as guilty as any of her sister departments of using elitist terms and unintentional barriers to communication.

ACTIVITY

By way of illustration, try to decipher this short piece which was sent internally to HR practitioners only, but serves to illustrate how quickly our discipline can estrange us from others and create a common mode of communication which others are unable to understand.

'HRM, IHRM and SHRM are expected to encompass L&D (including CPD), RM, MD, ER, PM, EV and an awareness of OCB and CSR should feature in all ethics policies. R&S requires a knowledge of GOQs and relevant ERRs together with updates in EO legislation and the organisation's DM potential.'

1. How much of this can you decipher?
2. Is it reasonable for professionals to use such extensive abbreviations?
3. What are the advantages of this type of communication?
4. Can you think of any disadavantages?

(For the full unabbreviated version see the end of this chapter.)

In oral communication **active listening** has been shown to improve communication and minimise miscommunications. Active listening requires more skill from the listener than the communicator. Devised by Carl Rogers as a therapeutic technique he asked the listener to suspend their own position and particularly stressed the need to 'fix' what they were listening to and to try to see the situation from the speaker's perspective (Rogers 1957).

Active listening requires:

- Concentration for a long time
- Understanding of another's point of view
- Ability to read between the lines
- Ability to elicit information by probing

- Probing questions which should be open
- Ability to feedback clearly without framing

Influencing also relies on listening but it is more concerned with reframing the content that is heard or received to the influencer's advantage. Political spin and advertising use this technique effectively and skillfully.

KEY TERMS

Active listening Attending not only to what is said but what is not being said; may also involve open questioning or reflecting back what a speaker has said.

CASE STUDY

2 a T

Milan and Sine met at university and set up a T-shirt printing company called '2 a T' together. Initially they used their own designs or quickly devised customer ideas at festivals and street parties. One year they went to Ibiza and worked successfully on the beaches running customer surveys with every order.

After only two years they had settled into an informal but generally effective way of working, dividing up the interesting and creative tasks and the dull, mundane ones. Milan tended to deal with suppliers and Sine dealt with buyers and retailers. Sine had extended into children's sports teams as well as school uniform T-shirts. Communicaton was informal but immediate and they texted or left scribbled notes for each other. Due to the expanded business they had recruited more workers: Milan's sister, Sonya, Sine's flatmate Dylan and Amelia who used to work for their T-shirt supplier. Training took a sitting-by-Nellie approach and relied on newcomers asking questions and working out their own way of fitting into the work pattern at 2aT.

Amelia arrived promptly at 9 and left at 5 as she had in her old job while Dylan arrived later and worked as long as he needed to and Sonya liked to take tasks home to fit in around her three-year-old twins. Deliveries of plain T-shirts were missed on occasion and recently an important festival pick-up deadline was missed resulting in the payment of a penalty and no repeat business from a client of four years' standing.

Milan is looking at outsourcing some of the larger projects to a large manufacturer in Delhi but was troubled when he witnessed the working conditions of the local workers there. He set up some guidelines based on EU labour laws which were adhered to while he was there but a recent visit showed that the staff were still not getting breaks or working to the standards agreed in 2aT's contract with the owner, Niral Saini. Niral claims these are just teething problems and that he is putting them right but when Milan suggested a works council or representatives to liaise with him in London he was told that this would be 'totally unnecessary'.

Sine has just won a major account with a large political party and huge numbers of T-shirts are required for rallies, demonstration and nationwide visits prior to the General Election and they are keen not to repeat any of their earlier mistakes.

ACTIVITY

Sine and Milan have engaged you as a HRM consultant to improve their internal communication.

1. Analyse the current situation and identify mistakes made.
2. Make suggestions for their communication within the home team.
3. Make suggestions for their overseas subcontractor communication.

 ## Early models of communication

Table 12.1 outlines some of the early attempts to define the communication process. As you can see, many are linear and inclined to look at communication as **mechanistic** or **robotic**, with its focus on one-way influencing. The role of the listener is passive and the responsibility of the communicator ill defined in terms of their target audience. Although noise or interference, via perceptions or culture are noted, no adjustments are made to accommodate them. The responsibility for decoding the message appears to lie with the receiver and not the sender.

By the 1960s, Berlo's model had moved from the mechanistic to the **psychological** approach. This psychological approach included an awareness of the need to accommodate differing levels of understanding within the communication and that there could be a variety of perceptions of the same message. For example, when briefing a team of cleaners as opposed to a team of infection control experts, the level of the communication would differ to address the needs of the different listeners. There was a growing awareness that culture, attitudes, feelings and perceptions coloured our ability to receive a communication in its originally intended form. The budding mass media of the day meant that accessibility and appropriateness of different methods of communication were also taken into account.

 ## KEY TERMS

Mechanistic Like a machine that runs efficiently although without thought.
Psychological approach An approach to communication that recognises the need to accommodate the recipient's level of understanding.
Robotic More like a human than a machine but still unable to think or feel.

The authoritarian leader and **autocratic** system relied on a **top-down communication** model where information was issued in the form of instructions and questions or feedback were neither invited nor tolerated. However, it was not until this century that the role of the top-down communication as the most influential was deposed.

A **social constructionist** model emerges with the communicators creating a shared meaning. The social constructionists were aware that communication evolves and is organic and susceptible to being influenced by its environment. Carey (2006) promotes the use of ritual which was so well illustrated by Nelson Mandela (RWC 1995) when he chose to use support of the previously white-dominated sport of rugby and the Springbok team to unite a fractured South Africa behind the One Team One Nation successfully. When they won it was noted that it was not the mixed group in the Ellis Park Stadium that had provided the support but the 43 million South Africans who were behind them as one. A similar approach was adopted by the Reuters Thomson HRM department when merging the two major publishing companies under the One Company banner (2008).

Lasswell formula (1948)	● Basic communication model: sending a message to a receiver ● One direction of communication, with no opportunity for feedback ● Of its time: mass communication for propaganda was first widely used and is still the basic 'selling' model for information
Shannon and Weaver (1949)	● The Transmission Model ● Described by Johnson and Klare (1961) as 'the most important' model ● Communication is a one-way process ● Takes into consideration who the message is going to and how it is sent ● Aware that messages can get distorted if the sender and receiver perceive them differently ● Does not deal with the meaning of the message; only concerned with communicating its content ● An example is a policy which is refined and edited until it is clear and accessible
Berlo (1960s)	● The medium matters: transmission model is source-message-channel-receiver (SMCR) ● Source: the sender and the message rely on the source's knowledge, communication skills, attitudes and culture ● Message: can be broken down into areas like content, structure, code and treatment to analyse how to make it more successful

▶

◄

	• Channel: considered for clarity, accessibility and which senses it appeals to • Receiver: recipient can only receive it successfully if the knowledge communication skills, attitudes and culture are aligned with the sender • Useful for sending differing versions of the same message, for example to management, overseas posts, shop floor workers and HR staff
Carey (1975; 2006)	• Communication takes place in a context • Ritual or repeated communications are important • Ritual in songs, plays, sermons, journalism, dance, architecture • Ritual to create a sense of community and shared experience • Ritual influences by encompassing and representing shared beliefs • Can be created by HR by having rituals around Away Days or briefing meetings, coffee clubs and Christmas parties

Table 12.1 Definitions of the communication process

KEY TERMS

Autocratic Authority which is not to be questioned or challenged.
Social constructionist Groups create a shared meaning within a social environment which evolves as the environment changes.
Top-down communication Strategic or board level communication of decisions or ideas to the rest of the organisation.

 Match these models to their model type choosing from the descriptions below the table.

Model	Model type
Shannon and Weaver (1949)	
Berlo (1960)	
Carey (1975; 2006)	

Social constructionist   **Mechanistic**   **Psychological**

12.4 Recent approaches to communication

The **systematic** approach is more concerned with how messages are processed and how the message evolves as it is interpreted. Galloway and Thacker (2007) are aware of the necessity of feedback and interaction to ensure that the original message is not distorted as it is passed along the communication chain.

The **critical** approach brings us almost full circle to the early mechanistic models which viewed communication as a means of influencing. The critical approach considers communication as a source of power and potentially a force that can be used to oppress both individuals and whole social groups. This darker side of communication is often glossed over within organisations (Li and Roloff 2004). Li and Roloff (2004) argue that strategic negative communication has a role in some negotiations.

However the current way forward as recommended by Cornelissen (2004) and Grunig and Grunig (2007) with its focus on a resource-based approach owes much to Argenti's (2007) model. All emphasise the importance of key relationships at all levels to deliver successfully.

Argenti (2007) focuses on internal benchmarking as well as frequent levels of consultation, feedback and a mindfulness of how a communication will be delivered and its impact on the receiver. The model acknowledges the importance of attitudes and knowledge with an eye on fostering a closer identification with the organisation. This more progressive approach to internal communication has proven successful for mergers, restructuring and communicating for change.

KEY TERMS

Systematic approach An approach to communication which tries to create a perfect system so that the message can be easily sent and clearly received as intended.

Critical approach An awareness of communication as a means to influence and manipulate others. It includes spin to obscure the facts and negative negotiating tactics where the negotiator is artificially negative to influence a more positive outcome for themselves on a win-lose model rather than the cooperative win-win.

Galloway and Thacker (2007)	• Feedback from receiver to sender. This could be represented in satisfaction surveys or post-training testing or simply a team member asking a clarifying question about an instruction. • Interaction between communicators in team meetings or briefings. There is a two-way dialogue just as there would be in an appraisal so that unforeseen messages emerge from the spontaneous discussions.
Cornelissen (2004)	• Corporate communication: whether externally communicating the corporate social responsibility agenda or internal policies on the HR site. • Communication activities. Having a meeting or an away day, sending an email or writing a report.
Grunig and Grunig (2007)	• Amalgamate resources. This involves concentrating efforts across boundaries as when quality circles, matrix teams or focus groups are set up. • Align communication to strategy. There is a corporate strategy and a business strategy as well as a departmental strategy and all should be cohesive so the communication strategy should be able to fit within all.
Argenti (2007)	• Strategic approach of messaging. Aware of the impact of sending messages out and being more conscious of the effect you want to achieve. • Responses consider the feedback you get whether direct or indirect. • Analyse organisational strategy: what does this organisation want to say about itself today? • Derive communication objectives, resources and reputations. • Build on strengths and use communication to keep or gain a foothold both in how the HR department is perceived and the organisation as a whole: 100 best employer listings or how recruitment advertisements are phrased or placed. • Analyse for attitude to and knowledge of organisation. Attune communication to the current situation with a view to improving it. Paul Pressler apologising for Gap's working practices and winning an ethics award (2004) because of their honest reporting. • Select channels and approaches for messages how should this be delivered e.g. not emailing redundancies but perhaps communicating change with a board level roadshow. Maybe the best approach for communicating effectively is to pick a popular worker to convey the news.

▶

◀

	• Develop with feedback: learn from communication what works and what doesn't for your organisation. • Foster identification with organisation – encourage staff to become a part of the organisation. John Lewis, Johnson and Johnson and White Stuff have all managed this very effectively.
Li and Roloff (2004)	• Strategic negativity in negotiation.

Table 12.2 Approaches to communication

Match these models to their model type, choosing from the descriptions below the table.

Theorists	Concepts
Galloway and Thacker (2007)	
Cornelissen (2004)	
Grunig and Grunig (2007)	
Argenti (2007)	
Li and Roloff (2004)	

Strategic negativity
Feedback and interaction

Resource-based and strategic
   alignment
Corporate communication
Analyse for attitude; develop with feedback; foster organisational
   identification

(12.5) Non-verbal communication

The models above consider direct explicit communication but communication is more than the exchange of words. It is cultural; it is interactive. It draws on how we learned to speak and give non-verbal cues (LeBaron 2003).The models effectively analyse what can be seen or easily perceived. Situations, skill sets and disposition or sympathies are often open and declared while perceptions, assumptions, attributions as well as our individual motivators and emotions are not (Guirdham 2005). Mehrabian (1967) went as far as to say that only 7 per cent of what we pick up on from a verbal communication is in the words but he later went on to explain that this is only when the content is emotional. However Marie Dasborough (2006) found that when delivering appraisal feedback that was positive in a negative manner the appraisee felt demotivated and upset whereas a negative appraisal outcome delivered positively had an uplifting impact.

Silence is another form of non-verbal communication which cannot be assumed to simply indicate polite listening. Van Dyne et al. (2003) identify three types of employee silence depending on the motivation for the silence. **Acquiescent silence**, **defensive silence** and **prosocial silence**, each having a corresponding type of voice. Silence is more ambiguous with less guaranteed outcomes.

In acquiescent silence there is an agreement and compliance which goes unvoiced whether through compliance or resigned disengagement.

Defensive silence is self-protective and fear based. There is reluctance to speak out in case it has unfavourable repercussions for the individual.

Pro-social silence is silence to protect others. It is not motivated by personal interest or gain but by an awareness that speaking may harm or put others at risk. There is a level of altruism to this silence since it is both cooperative and focused on the needs of others (Van Dyne et al. 2003).

KEY TERMS

Acquiescent silence A silence which yields to what has been decided although it may still not be agreed with.
Defensive silence A hurt or self-protecting silence to prevent further harm or abuse.
Pro-social silence Silence to protect others as to speak out may damage or endanger them.

Body language

We have each evolved our own personalised set of gestures, postures and expressions which help to communicate who we are as well as what we mean. However, some of these are attributable to body leakage or unintentional cues to our inner intentions.

It is often said that 'the eyes are the windows of the soul', but research has provided evidence that other parts of the body can provide clues about a person's state of mind, motivation and thought processes.

Ever since Bandler and Grinder (1979) took neurolinguistic programming to the masses with their book *Frogs into Princes*, interest in body language and reading body language has mushroomed. They discovered that visual memory is accessed as the eyes move up: either to access created material or remembered material. To determine which side of the brain is responsible for remembered visual memory, a simple checking question such as 'what is the colour of your front door?' could be used. This should establish whether visual memory is right or left. By implication, the other side is responsible for created material (including lies). If I find the colour of my front door by moving my eyes up and to the right, then it can be relied on that that is where my visual memory is, whereas my creative visual information is on the opposite side. So, if I am stopped in the corridor and asked how my report is progressing, my eyes may move up to the left as I say that I only have to print it out, but I know that it is not even written yet! Lies are created material and thus associated with the left side.

When two people sit together, if their legs are crossed in towards the centre space they are forming a private group which will be respected by others. Similary, if the two people sitting at each end of a larger group cross their legs inwards it will create a group space which will also be respected by others who will not intrude on it. Those familiar and comfortable with one another often mimic each other's body language unconsciously. The flexing of a foot indicates disagreement while liars often find they have an itchy nose or fall prey to the Pinocchio Effect (Pease and Pease 2004).

Body language experts watch international politicians to see who pats the other's shoulder last to achieve higher status, while walking with the hands behind the back and forming steeples with the fingers also count as high status gestures. A self-hug or reassuring tummy pat, often disguised as the straightening of a tie is a sign that the person is feeling uncomfortable and in need of reassurance.

Open gestures for interview include sitting square without crossing legs or arms; sitting straight and leaning slightly forward both communicate interest; making eye contact but moving the eyes when speaking; returning a handshake evenly and looking back to the questioner once the question has been answered to ensure that the interviewer has all the information required.

Body language can be described as:

- *Engaged* – when a person is visibly listening and part of what is happening.
- *Disengaged* – when a person is clearly disinterested or seeking to distance themselves from what is happening.

ACTIVITY

Body language and non-verbal communication

Keepers is a successful online retail organisation and is now in a position to promote some of its existing staff due to recent expansion. As they want to send the message that there is a career here for all backgrounds they have called three different candidates to the upgrade interview. They are looking for people who could successfully lead and influence the new teams.

Maya has a postgraduate degree in computer science, she is bright but nervous – sitting forward in her chair her eyes dart between the three interviewers. When asked a question she colours visibly and becomes flustered although she answers well. When challenged on a technical point she initially looked away and bit her lip to think but responded accurately. Maya puts her head on one side to listen and stays focused on the questioner when answering. As Maya stands to leave she is visibly shaking.

Frasier has an undergraduate degree in media and has had some disciplinary issues around teamworking although his work is always in by the deadline. Frasier moves his chair closer to the table and leans his elbows on it. He looks relaxed and comfortable but in his first two-part question he answers only one section of it. When he is asked again he rubs the back of his neck and tuts but answers appropriately. When asked where he sees himself in five years' time he leans back, resting his head in his interlocked fingers before answering. Frasier smiles and waves as he leaves.

Mercy began work one summer and left school at 16 when offered a full-time job with Keepers. Mercy has always made a point of getting to know everyone and is keen to ask questions and help out in new areas of the business. Smiling when she arrives Mercy greets everyone by name and sits down. She crosses her arms and waits for the first question. Less articulate than the other two she asks questions to get clarification and answers with examples. Mercy gesticulates as she speaks and stops to make eye contact and check how they are receiving her responses. At one stage she says, 'That's probably not what you want to hear but. . .' Mercy responds to the query around her lack of qualifications with a silence before letting her gaze drift out of the window as she says that she learnt all she needs to know here.

1. Give examples of engaged and disengaged body language in these three candidates.
2. Is there any single gesture that would decide you against any candidate?
3. Which candidate would impress you most and why?
4. Write a profile for a fourth candidate including the body language they might exhibit.
5. Two of the three panel members want to offer a post to Mercy, suggest how they could persuade the third member based on Mercy's interview and body language indicators.

Symbolism

Symbols vary between cultures and generations can reinvent what has symbolic value. At Hewlett Packard the Golden Banana Award was instituted when a company engineer went to his manager with a new solution to a difficult problem. The manager was so impressed that he wanted to reward him straight away but all he could find to give him was a banana. This became the golden banana award and spawned the catch phrase 'close, but no banana' for work that was on track but not prize winning yet. This shows that even the humblest fruit can be endowed with meaning if the organisation choose to elevate it to a symbol. At Hewlett Packard the banana became a symbol of excellence, but this would be meaningless when seen out of context in another organisation, where no symbolism had been attached to it.

Brand recognition identifies the user/wearer with what the product symbolises. Such identification is not always in the brand's interest as when Burberry became associated with football hooligans and C-list celebrity after enjoying a reputation for English elegance. It stopped manufacturing a particular cap that had become the football hooligan's headwear of choice. Similarly disgraced organisations (Enron, Nestle, Exxon, etc.) can have a stigma for their workers who might not want to identify with the morals of the organisation (Koh and Boo 2000).

Symbolism varies from the elusive prestige of a corner office to the images we obey without question: exit notices and symbols to let us know which toilets to use stop signs and hazard symbols, or where the delete button is.

Culture and context

Cultures can be divided into **high** and **low context cultures** (Edward T. Hall 1993).

In a high context culture, less is explicitly articulated and more is understoood implicitly. Relationships have many levels and are long term. This type of communication relies on clear rules and norms to function. It also relies on all participants being aware of what is happening. On the diagram it is clear that Japan is a high-context culture where rules are not explicit as they would be in the low-context Swiss–German culture. Therefore it would be more difficult to integrate into a Japanese culture with its unwritten rules and social etiquettes than in the explicit rule declarations of Switzerland. These cultural styles impact on communication and perceptions of that communication. A catastrophic example of problems in communication between high- and low-context cultures occurred when Korean pilots attempting to land a plane in New York stated to air traffic control that they did not have much fuel. However owing to their high context culture the pilots were neither aggressive nor extreme

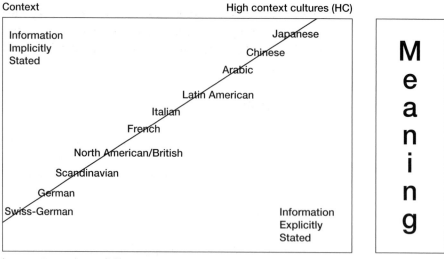

Figure 12.1 Context and communication (Hall 1998)

in their language and air traffic control left them circling, assuming that the siutation was not as urgent as it was. This resulted in a fatal crash. The flight recording when it was played back demonstrated a quiet diffident tone with no urgency behind the words and no emphasis placed on the immediate danger.

The receiving low context culture – the air traffic controllers – were not equipped to take in all the nuances of the communication, since low context cultures codify knowledge and are explicit in what they want and expect from the situation they find themselves in. They separate between work and personal relationships and interpersonal exchanges are shorter in duration.

KEY TERMS

High context culture The culture has many rules in context but you might have to have grown up there to understand them. Nuances and etiquette are not explained.
Low context culture Little background knowledge is required to understand the rules since they are all explicit.

12.6 Employee voice

In order to facilitate the feedback recommended by the researchers above it is necessary to have communication channels in place. The choice of approaches ranges from two extremes: the soloist, which may favour some individuals over whole groups depending on their status within the organisation, and at the other end of the spectrum, the collectivist, where the good of the group is most important.

KEY TERMS

Collectivist A culture where each individual strives for the good of all and not for personal gain or status.

Collectivist

In order to enable communication between workers and management a number of strategic approaches have developed (Purcell and Sisson 1983 in Porter et al. 2008: 224).

The **traditional** approach features a **unitarist** managerial perspective which is hostile to unions. Unitarists adopt an underlying belief that all share common goals and should conform to work in harmony towards them. Those who dissent or challenge the managerial prerogative are seen as deviant and any conflict is viewed as interpersonal rather than an organisational concern.

The softer face of unitarism is illustrated by the **sophisticated paternalist** approach where management, while still maintaining a unitarist perspective, focuses on employee well-being, doing away with the need for union representation.

In the **standard modern** approach there is a pragmatic recognition of a **pluralist** environment where goals which are shaped by individual motivations. Line managers recognise unions and work with them to reconcile the varied interests both within the workforce and management.

Sophisticated moderns also take a pluralist approach but, rather than the defensive strategy of the standard moderns, the sophisticated moderns not only recognise unions but have developed bargaining procedures to aid consultation and conflict resolution.

Unions and management attitudes towards membership have waxed and waned throughout the last century with an American drive towards a hybrid of the sophisticated paternalist and the standard modern wherein HRM took on the mantle of benfactor and peace keeper. Currently UK management attitudes are broadly in favour of union membership (60 per cent) with only 5 per cent against and the rest are neutral or haven't decided (Kersley et al. 2005). As an endorsement of the union presence in organisations, 83 per cent of managers who bargain with trade unions are in favour.

KEY TERMS

Pluralist A belief that all have differing motivations and values when working towards a common goal.

Sophisticated modern Where the management recognises a pluralist work-force and the benefits of unions but also puts processes in place to facilitate consultation and conflict resolution.

Sophisticated paternalist Where the management caters to employee needs to render unions or outsider interference unnecessary.

Standard modern Where the management recognises that workers have differing goals and values and welcomes union assistance in reconciling these goals to achieve a productive workforce.

Traditional A unitarist management approach hostile to interfering influences.

Unitarist A belief that all are working towards the same goals in harmony.

In countries such as Norway and Sweden, union membership runs at a stable 90 per cent of the workforce (Sparrow et al. 2004). Yet trade union membership has been in sharp decline in the UK since the 1980s after the crippling strikes which afflicted the country during the winter of discontent (1978–79). Around 29 per cent of employees are members of unions (Grainer 2006, in Porter et al. 2008: 221) and the figure is higher in the public sector and much lower in the private sector. Some UK organisatons even go as far as to request new employees to sign a contract stating that they will not join a union. However in the USA union membership runs at an average 12.4 per cent although it is growing slowly annually. Lowest are the southern states with 3.5 per cent in North Carolina while New York, Hawaii and Alaska were all over 20 per cent (Bureau of Labor Statistics 2009; 2008 data).

Without a union presence representation can devolve to **works councils** which have been effective in Europe but are less prevalent in the UK and have in some cases been reduced to token bodies with little opportunity to communicate or negotiate. Stirling and Fitzgerald (2001) questioned whether a body so inextricably linked with management could operate as an independent voice.

Other mechanisms for involving employees include surveys and focus groups. **Quality circles** across departments and disciplines to discuss common problems and share best practice have proven useful for interdepartmental relations as well as sharing of best practice. Adopting a matrix structure where teams are created for projects and bring differing skills to each new team they join also serves to foster communication across team, disciplines and departments. Using shared training or cross-departmental mentoring can also offer insights giving better view of the whole organisation.

KEY TERMS

Quality circle A group of similar level interdepartmental managers who meet to discuss problems with a view to improving processes and practices and establishing a quality approach within their professional dealings with others.
Works councils Often found where unions are discouraged these are approved worker groups which may act as representatives communicating workers' needs to the board or more strategic decision making levels.

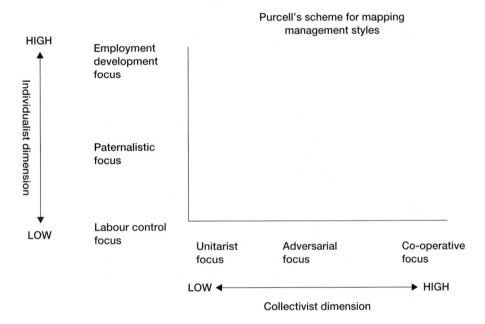

Figure 12.2 Mapping managerial styles (Purcell 2007)

Which of the following is not a management approach?

a Standard modern
b Traditional
c Sophisticated paternalist
d Postmodernist
e Sophisticated modern

12.7 Personality and personal style

Personality and personal styles also impact on our willingness to engage in communication and our innate communciation styles. Passive people are more likely to take a laissez faire attitude and avoid confrontation. They may choose not to engage in the debate and are keen to avoid reaching decisions. An aggressive person would seek out confrontation while a passive aggressive person would exhibit symptoms indirectly (Chowdhury 2009) . Thus a passive aggressive may show up for meetings late and leave early as they did not want to attend: in this way their anger is expressed non-verbally. An assertive person is capable of playing a mature role in procedings by articulating their own position; while encouraging others to express their perspective.

All of our communication is influenced by a range of personal experiences and deliberate inputs such as education or training, and adherence to beliefs, myths and stereotypes. From 1961 Milgram ran a 'pain' experiment wherein he would ask participants to act as a teacher and administer electric shocks to an unseen learner if their answers were incorrect. In fact the learner was an actor and was never shocked but the teacher participant believing that they were would still continue to administer shocks up to 450 volts if instructed to do so. Even when the participant was uncomfortable complying they would still continue when instructed to do so by the experimenter. However, if the experimenter left the room or was connected only by phone contact the compliance levels diminished. This appears to have implications for overseas communication between parent and daughter plants of multinational corporations (MNCs). Longatan (2009) suggests that organisations should train in crosscultural teams to prepare for overseas secondments. Mead (2005) found that the more preparation prior to a foreign secondment the more likely the candidate was to appreciate and succeed in the placement.

CASE STUDY

Alja was keen to promote the new accessories line in her boutique. She called a training session for Fergal, the Saturday boy who had a flair for marketing, Ayesha who was the customers' favourite because of her helpful nature and Hema who had been there the longest and liked to think she was in charge.

As the training was on Saturday evening and unpaid Alja was surprised that only Ayesha was there on time. She had brought her knitting and was chatting away about her niece's baby, making no effort to even look at the new accessories. Fergal breezed in complaining about the cold and Alja's timing as he had a date later. "Let's get on with it then!" he laughed but Alja could see he wasn't really attending to the merchandise as he picked up a set of bangles and let them jangle noisily back onto the counter. Hema arrived half an hour late and spent quite a bit of time asking Ayesha about her knitting.

continued . . . ▶

◄ | *. . . continued*

Alja began to despair of them. "Is there any point in doing this now?" she asked, exasperated. Hema and Ayesha sat up and looked sorry but seemed relieved when Fergal replied "Quite right. Time to go!" and sped off out of the door. Hema's husband arrived to collect her early so Ayesha offered to help Alja put the goods tidily away.

1. Who is the aggressive?

2. Who is the passive aggressive?

3. Who is the *laissez faire*?

4. Later Alja delegated the training to Fergal and it all seemed to go much better. If you were Fergal how would you motivate Ayesha and Hema to attend to the new merchandise appropriately?

Managers

Managers seem to fall into the role of management by virtue of being skilled at something else. Originally hired for a specialist skill they surrender their specialist activity to manage those less skilled than they are in that area. The managerial grid by Rees and Porter (2001) demonstrates this along a timeline against likely activity. It appears that the longer in post the more likely any individual is to be managing. Maintaining flexibility of communication style would facilitate communicating with different types of workers (see Chapter 6, Role of the Manager, pages 160–61 for more information).

A manager usually has seven years' training and expertise in their specialism but perhaps only a few days or a week's training in management. Managerial styles inform manager's communication with some having a high regard for the task and others for those executing the task. In their managerial grid Blake and Mouton (1964) demonstrate how differences become expressed when managers prioritise one over the other. The country club manager is only concerned for the people with an awareness that they are the primary asset. Like footballers' managers they will take care of the individual to secure the talent for the task. The military are more task-based and would feature on the 9.1 section. 1.1 ratings would be for those where the output was not difficult to achieve and those involved were not interested in development. The favoured is the team leader sector where the individual and the task goal is prioritised. On a matrix team, achieving well in the assigned project will help both the individual and the organisation This is because a matrix team must achieve its project goal for the organization but, as the individuals working on that team will soon be assigned to new teams, individual performance will also impact on how much autonomy they have in the next team. Reputations built in matrix teams can be very valuable to both the individual and their own manager who sends them onto the next team, using them as a resource to bargain with in some cases.. Huczynski and Buchanan (2007) assure us that managers try to take an individually tailored approach to problems and may not respond as simplistically as Blake and Mouton's grid may suggest.

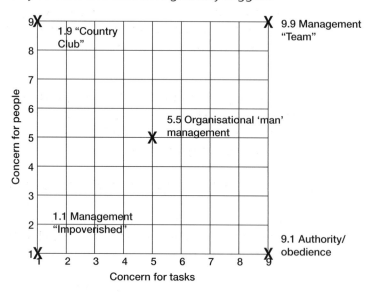

Figure 12.3 Management style – the managerial grid (Blake and Mouton 1964)

 ## Work and communication

A major communication juncture each year is the appraisal process. DeNisi and Pritchard (2006) put communication at the heart of this process and its influence in maintaining engagement (McCartney and Wilmott 2009). It is an opportunity to distill all the elements of this chapter including employee voice, managerial styles of communication as well as the skills learnt in active listening, reading body language, the role of culture and symbols as well as the theoretical concepts of one- and two-way communication and the use of ritual and context in top-down and bottom-up feedback. Allowing it to be a two-way sharing of information and intention is advocated (Murphy and Margulies 2004; Roberts 2002; Losyk 2002). Setting goals together is also key to the transparency of the process (Cascio 1998; Latham and Latham 2000). Fairness and the perception of fairness has been shown to be crucial to the success of the performance appraisal process. Thus communicating performance standards prior to the appraisal helps to establish the ground rules equitably (Grote 2002; Gilliland and Langdon 1998) and engaging in a year-long dialogue with frequent feedback will motivate and highlight achievements (Kluger and DeNisi 1996, 2006). This approach would address some of the concerns raised by a recent survey on employee attitudes and the recession (CIPD 2009) which found that managers were rated poorly by their employees. Yet it appears British managers are not alone in this reluctance to divulge explicit feedback. Indeed Guirdham (2005) notes the variations even between European cultures when communicating. Her study on feedback specifically found that in France performance was seen as linked to the individual's personal qualities making it difficult to separate them out for constructive feedback and development points.

In Germany a need for precision and objectivity was required with feedback relating more to the task than the person. Guirdham (2005) notes that Germans found it difficult both to give and receive feedback but were keen to approach the task with integrity on both sides.

Italians were also found to struggle with giving and receiving feedback and tended to avoid open feedback altogether. While in Spain a manager's criticism was seen as an exercise of power so negative feedback was not given much credence and positive feedback was greeted with confusion as to why it was given in the first place.

Framing: George Lakoff (2004)

Learning to frame a communication so that the recipient can hear it effectively is a key skill for those mediating or using ACAS based training in negotiation. George Lakoff (2004) identified that framing could influence the listener and be persuasive via metaphor, stories, traditions, slogans, artefacts and contrast as well as spin. We have become familiar with these concepts as manipulative rather than benignly influencing devices. Within the appraisal interview helping candidates to reframe failures as learning opportunities or 'been stuck here 11 years' as 'been a loyal employee for over a decade' can help them to re-evaluate their contribution to their team and the organisation as a whole. Active listening sometimes borrows from this as the listener responds with 'so what I hear you saying is. . .' and offers a different interpretation of what the speaker has shared.

ACTIVITY

Try reframing the following communications:

1. a) Why do you always have to be so obstructive here? I'm only trying to get on with my work.
    So what I hear you saying is:
    b) I'm fed up with this level of service, I've been a customer for over 17 years and things are just going from bad to worse.
    So what I hear you saying is:

2. Lana belongs to one of several international operational units. When asked to present their findings they were told to be brief. Lana took this to heart and produced a 10-page report while the French team offered a 42-page report which was praised by the CEO. Lana wants to complain.
   a) How should she frame this?
   b) How would you receive it as her CEO?

12.9 Miscommunication

Miscommunication can happen intentionally, neglectfully or accidentally. Intentional examples are rare and occur when trying to sabotage. This is most common when mergers are being negotiated, when an interested buyer will try to denigrate the value of the company to be acquired (see, for example, Kraft foods recent bids for Cadbury's). Another example is if you were buying second-hand car; you would not enthuse over it even though you might be delighted with it, as the owner may pick up on your excitement and raise the asking price. Neglectful examples occur when the communicator should know better but chooses to behave recklessly. The accidental error could probably not have been prevented and lessons should be learnt from observing previous accidental miscommunications.

ACTIVITY

Decide which of these is intentional, neglectful and accidental:

1. Marijke was off on holiday and was writing an email to her colleague Ayman who was due to step in on selection and contracts. Marijke made a list of contract candidates provisional on their references checking out. She had read a CIPD survey that said 1 in 4 offers were withdrawn owing to incomplete references. Ayman collected the list in the morning and drew up the contracts. He wondered why Marijke always seemed so busy as he couldn't think what else she might have to do and just assumed she had chosen a quiet time to go on leave.
2. a) Baronness Scotland (attorney general) employed a housekeeper whose papers were not in order. The baronness helped to get the legislation through in 2006 so she was well aware of what the relevant law stated. This law often fines new HR graduate trainees £5k personally if they had not checked both of the required lists when recruiting. When she discovered her employee was an illegal worker Baronness Scotland fired her immediately.
   b) Gerald Ratner saw his chain of jewellery stores close in a rapid two-year decline between 1992 and 1994 following his own comments that 'Ratner's has very little to do with quality. . . How can you sell this for such a low

price? . . . I say so because it's total crap" (1991). He also compared his jewellery to a 99p Marks and Spencer prawn sandwich, adding that it probably wouldn't last as long. These lessons in how not to grow your business became known as 'doing a Ratner'.

3. a) Lila had just finished drawing up the shortlist for the board level appointment at the estate agency partnership she worked for. Lila was pleased as she had targets for diversity and this shortlist had one disabled person, two ethnic minorities and three women. Imagine her surprise as her director took his pen and deleted all of the women from the list. 'Find two more suitable candidates,' was all he said as he returned the paper to Lila. Lila stood there astonished. Her silence provoked a justification. 'We can't afford any pregnancies with things as they are: strategic people have to be in place,' he blustered. Unhappy about what had happened Lila picked up the phone to the headhunter again.

b) John Mackey, cofounder and CEO of Whole Foods was investigated in 2007 when it became clear that he had been libelling Wild Oats, a competitor he hoped to acquire, as his Rahodeb pseudonym on the financial bulletin boards of Yahoo.

Summary

This chapter has taken a whistle-stop tour through the areas of communication. From early mechanistic models (Lasswell 1948; Shannon and Weaver 1949) to negotiation strategic negativity (Li and Roloff 2004) and corporate approaches (Cornelissen 2004) of more modern concepts of communication. General tools such as active listening and framing were introduced.

The role of non-verbal communication whether silence, body language or symbolism was discussed and the impact of personal differences and culture outlined. The various vehicles for employee voice and the role of managers in the appraisal system were examined against models such as the managerial escalator (Rees and Porter 2001), Purcell's mapping of managerial styles (2007) and the earlier Blake and Mouton's (1964) managerial grid. The appraisal process as a key developmental communication was looked at and finally miscommunication.

KEY IDEAS

Types of communication

- In the multimedia age we have adapted personally and professionally to a wide range of communication formats.
- Communication can be direct and synchronous or asynchronous, remote and indirect.
- The HR department's role is key to improving internal communication and integrating modern methods to the report, presentation, interview, appraisal, training, disciplinary, meeting and briefing processes.

The purpose of communication

- Communication is used to engage employees and to communicate an organisation's mission and its strategic direction.
- Skilful communicators take into account the target audience, level of previous knowledge, attitude to the information and bias or prejudice of the communicator.
- Codes, short cuts, abbreviations and jargon make communication impenetrable to outsiders and can create elitism within professions.

Early models of communication

- Linear communication: also known as mechanistic or robotic focuses solely on one-way influencing. The listener is passive and the communicator does not define their target audience. The receiver is responsible for decoding the sender's message.
- Psychological approach: culture, attitudes, feelings and perceptions colour our ability to receive a communication as it was originally intended to be interpreted. There could be a variety of perceptions of the same message.
- Autocratic system: information issued in instructions and questions. Feedback is neither invited nor tolerated.
- Social constructionism: communication evolves and is susceptible to being influenced by its environment. Carey (2006) promotes the use of ritual to communicate a cultural understanding.

Recent approaches to communication

- Systematic approach: how messages are processed and how messages evolve when interpreted. Aware of the necessity of feedback and interaction to ensure that the original message is not distorted as it is passed along the communication chain.
- Critical approach: communication is a source of power and can be used to oppress individuals and social groups. Strategic negative communication where the sender takes an artificially negative stance can sometimes have a useful role in negotiations.
- Resource based: Cornelissen (2004), Grunig and Grunig (2007) and Argenti (2007): resource-based approach. Emphasises the importance of key relationships at all levels to deliver successfully.

Non-verbal communication

- Communication is more than the exchange of words.
- Silence is non-verbal communication. Types of silence include acquiescent silence (unvoiced agreement and compliance); defensive silence (self-protective and fear based); and pro-social silence (silence to protect others).
- Body language helps to communicate who we are and what we mean. Sometimes this is an unintentional cue to our inner intentions. Body Language is read by the receiver and enriches and gives context to messages.

continued . . .

. . . continued

- Symbols as a form of communication. Vary between cultures; generations can reinvent what has symbolic value. Corporate and product branding rely on these symbols to differentiate themselves.
- High context cultures: less is explicitly articulated and more is understoood implicitly; relies on clear rules and norms to function. Low context cultures: codify knowledge; explicit in what they want and expect from situations. Low context cultures are easier to adapt to because of their explicit nature whereas high context cultures could take decades to fully understand.

Employee voice
- Unitarist: traditional managerial perspective; hostile to unions. Belief that all share common goals and should conform to work in harmony towards them.
- Sophisticated paternalist: unitarist but focusing on employee well-being, doing away with the need for union representation.
- Standard modern approach: recognises pluralist environment. Line managers recognise unions and work with them to reconcile varied interests.
- Sophisticated moderns: have developed bargaining procedures with unions to aid consultation and conflict resolution.
- Works councils: management-approved worker groups which represent workers' needs; found where unions are discouraged.
- Quality circle: group of similar level interdepartmental managers; meet to discuss problems, to improve processes and practices and to establish a quality approach within their professional dealings with others.

Personality and personal style
- Personality and personal styles impact on our willingness to engage in communication and how we interpret it. We all have our own innate communciation styles.
- Passive: take a laissez faire attitude and avoid confrontation; choose not to engage in the debate and are keen to avoid reaching decisions.

Aggressive: seek out confrontation.

Assertive: articulate their own position and encourage others to express their perspective.

Passive aggressive: will not voice their problems with decisions but their actions will indicate their engagement; lateness, sabotaging tasks and reluctance to join in.

- Communication is influenced by personal experiences and deliberate inputs such as education or training, and influenced by beliefs, myths and stereotypes.
- Managerial styles inform a manager's communication with some having a high regard for the task and others for the people involved.

Work and communication
- Appraisal process is a communication juncture; an opportunity to distill all elements communication (employee voice, managerial styles, skills learnt in active listening, body language, the role of culture and symbols and theoretical concepts).
- Setting goals together is key to transparency. Fairness and the perception of fairness are crucial to the success of the appraisal process.
- A year-long dialogue with frequent feedback will motivate and highlight achievements (Kluger and DeNisi 1996, 2006).

continued . . .

◀

. . . continued

Miscommunication

- Can happen intentionally, neglectfully or accidentally.

- Intentional miscommunication: occurs when trying to sabotage, for example when mergers are being negotiated, an interested buyer may try to denigrate the value of the company to be acquired.

- Neglectful miscommunication: occurs when the communicator should know better but chooses to behave recklessly.

- Accidental errors: probably unavoidable. Observing previous accidental miscommunications will help to learn lessons.

RECOMMENDED READING

For a useful introduction to communication within corporate settings, see Argenti, P.A. (2007) *Corporate Communication*, 4th edn. London: Irwin/McGraw-Hill.

For a useful introduction to HRM, and a guide to more specific issues within the area, look at Bingham, C. (2009) Communication in Porter, C., Bingham, C., Simmonds, D. (2008) *Exploring Human Resource Management*. London: McGraw Hill. Since publication it has become the practitioner's reference book and the academic's bible for HRM used on both undergraduate and postgraduate courses.

Guirdham, M. (2005) *Communicating across Culture at Work*, 2nd edn. London: Macmillan, 218. This text is recommended for those interested in cross-cultural communication both between national cultures and within organisations themselves.

For a useful international reference book for the international HRM practitioner, see Sparrow, P., Brewster, C., Harris, H. (2004) *Globalizing Human Resource Management*. Oxford: Routledge/CIPD.

USEFUL WEBSITES

www.hrmguide.co.uk/relations/future-of-trade-unions.htm
www.cipd.co.uk/subjects/empreltns/psycntrct/psycontr.htm

REFERENCES

Argenti, P.A. (2007) *Corporate Communication*, 4th edn. London: Irwin/McGraw-Hill.

Bandler, R., Grinder, J. (1979) *Frogs into Princes*. Boulder, CO: Real People Press.

Berlo, D. (1960) *The Process of Communication*. San Francisco: Rinehart Press. Cited in Argenti, P.A. (2007) *Corporate Communication*, 4th edn. London: Irwin/McGraw-Hill.

Bingham, C. (2009) Communication in Porter, C., Bingham, C., Simmonds, D. (2008) *Exploring Human Resource Management*. London: McGraw Hill.

Blake, R., Mouton, J. (1964). *The Managerial Grid: The Key to Leadership Excellence*. Houston: Gulf Publishing Co.

Bloisi, W. (2007) *Management and Organisational Behaviour*, 2nd European edn. London: McGraw Hill.

Bryman, A. (2001) *Social Research Methods*. New York: Oxford University Press.

Bureau of Labor Statistics (2009) Union Summary www.bls.gov/cps Released January 2009. Accessed 20 November 2009.

Carey, J. (2006) in Sella, Z. (2007) The Journey of Ritual Communication, *Studies in Communication Sciences* vol. 7, no 1: 117–38.

Cascio, W.F. (1998) *Applied psychology in human resources management*, 5th edn. Upper Saddle River, NJ: Prentice-Hall.

Chowdhury, D. (2009) *Structured Approach to Improve Passive Aggressive Organizational Behavior: An Empirical Research*. Dhiman Deb Chowdhury.

CIPD (2009) *The psychological contract*, January 2009, www.cipd.co.uk/subjects/empreltns/psycntrct/psycontr.htm

Cornelissen, (2004) in Hubner, H. (2007) *The Communicating Company*. Heidelberg: Physica Verlag, 1, 11, 16.

Dasborough, M. T. (2006). Cognitive asymmetry in employee emotional reactions to leadership behaviors. *The Leadership Quarterly*, vol. 17: 163–78.

de Bono, E. (1985; 1999) *Six Thinking Hats*. London: Penguin.

DeNisi, A., Pritchard, R. (2006) Performance Appraisal, Performance Management and Improving Individual Performance: A Motivational Framework, *Management and Organisation Review,* vol. 2, no 2: 253–77.

Galloway, A., Thacker, E. (2007) *The Exploit: A Theory of Networks*. Minneapolis, MN: University of Minnesota Press.

Gilliland, S.W., Langdon, J.C. (1998) Creating performance management systems that promote perceptions of fairness in J.W. Smother (ed.) *Performance appraisal: State of the art in practice*. San Francisco, CA: Jossey-Bass, 209–43.

Grote, R.C. (2002) *The performance appraisal question and answer book: A survival guide for manager*. New York: Management Association.

Grunig, L., Grunig J. (2007) in Toth, E. (2007) *The future of Excellence in PR and Communications Management*. New Jersey: Lawrence Erlbaum Associates, Chapter 2.

Guirdham, M. (2005) *Communicating Across Culture at Work*, 2nd edn. Basingstoke: Palgrave Macmillan, 218.

Hall, E. (1992). *An Anthropology of Everyday Life*. New York: Doubleday/Anchor Books.

Hall, E. (1993) in Shuter, R. (2008) The centrality of culture in Molefi K., Yoshitaka M., Jing Y. (eds), *The global intercultural communication reader*. New York: Routledge, 37–43.

Hofstede, G. (2003) *Culture's Consequences, Comparing Values Behaviours, Institutions and Organisations across Nations*. London: Sage.

Huczynski, A., Buchanan, D., Dunham, R. (2007) *Organisational Behaviour* Harlow: FT Prentice Hall.

Johnson, F., Klare, G. (1961) General Models of Communication Research: A survey of the developments of a decade, *Journal of Communication*, vol.11: 13–26.

Kapucu, N. (2009) Public Administrators and Cross-Sector Governance in Response to Recovery from Disasters, *Administration and Society*, November 2009, vol. 41: 910–14.

Kersley, B., Alpin, C., Forth, J., Bryson, A., Bewley, H., Dix, G., Oxenbridge, S. (2005) *Inside the Workplace: Findings from the 2004 Workplace Employment Relations Survey* (WERS 2004). Abingdon: Routledge.

Kessler, S., Bayliss F. (1998) *Contemporary British Industrial Relations*. Basingstoke: Macmillan.

Kluger, A., DeNisi, A. (2006) Feedback format: does it influence manager's reactions to feedback? *Journal of Occupational and Organizational Psychology*, 1 December 2006, vol. 79, no 4: 517–32.

Lakoff, G. (2004) *Don't Think of an Elephant! Know Your Values and Frame the Debate*. Vermont: Chelsea Green Publishing.

Latham, G., Latham, S.D. (2000) Overlooking theory and research in performance appraisal at one's peril: Much done, more to do in Coper, C. L., Locke, E. A. (eds) *Industrial and Organisational Psychology: Linking theory with practice*. Oxford: Blackwell, 199–249.

LeBaron, M. (2003) Cross-Cultural Communication in Burgess, G., Burgess, H. (2003) *Beyond Intractability*. Boulder: Conflict Research Consortium. University of Colorado. Posted July 2003. www.beyondintractability.org/essay/cross-cultural_communication Accessed 25 September 2009.

Li, S., Roloff, M. (2004) Strategic Negative Emotion in Negotiation. IACM 17th Annual Conference Paper.

Longatan, N. (2009) *Settling in: 10 common myths and one uncommon truth about culture shock*. ExPat Exchange 16 April 2009. www.expatexchange.com/lib.cfm?articleID=3334

Lucas, R., Mathieson, H., Lupton, B. (2007) *Human Resource Management in an International Context*. London: CIPD.

McCartney, C., Wilmott, B. (2009) Employee Outlook: Job seeking in a recession, *Quarterly Survey Report*, Summer 2009, 23 July 2009.

McLean, P. (2008) Employee Voice, MGMT341, *International and Comparative Human Resource Management*, University of Wollongong, delivered 19 August 2008.

Mead, R. (2005) *International Management: cross cultural dimensions*. Chichester: Blackwell.

Mehrabian, A., Wiener, M. (1967) Decoding of inconsistent communications, *Journal of Personality and Psychology*, vol. 6, no 1: 109–14.

Murphy, T., Margulies, J. (2004) Performance Appraisals, ABA Labor and Employment Law Section, Equal Opportunities Committee 2004, Mid Winter Meeting, March 24–27, 2004.

OSullivan, N. (2009) Future of Work in Matthewman, L., Rose, A., Hetherington, A. (2009) *Work Psychology*. Oxford: Oxford University Press.

Pease, A., Pease, B. (2004) *The Definitive Book of Body Language*. London: Orion Books.

Porter, C., Bingham, C., Simmonds, D. (2008) *Exploring Human Resource Management*. London: McGraw-Hill.

Purcell, J. (2007). Mapping Management Styles in Employee Relations, *Journal of Management Studies*, vol. 24, no 5: 533–48.

Rees, W.D., Porter, C. (2001) *Skills of Management*, 5th edn. London: Thomson Learning.

Roberts, G. (2002) Employee Performance Appraisal System Participation: A Technique that Works, *Public Personnel Management*, vol. 31, no 3, Fall 2002: 333–42.

Rogers, C. Farson, R. (1957) *Active Listening*. Chicago, IL: University of Chicago Industrial Relations Center, 25.

Sparrow, P., Brewster, C., Harris, H. (2004) *Globalizing Human Resource Management*. Abingdon: Routledge/CIPD.

Stirling, J., Fitzgerald, I. (2001) European Works Councils: representing workers on the periphery, *Journal of Employee Relations*, vol. 23, no 1: 13–25.

Van Dyne, L., Ang, S., Botero, I.C. (2003) Conceptualizing Employee Silence and Employee Voice as Multidimensional Constructs, *Journal of Management Studies* vol. 40, no 6: 1359–92.

Wurtz, E. (2005) A cross-cultural analysis of websites from high-context and low-context cultures, *Journal of Computer-Mediated Communication*, vol. 11, no 1, article 13.

* Answer to abbreviation activity

Human Resource Management, International Human Resource Management and Strategic Human Resource Management are expected to encompass Learning and Development (including Continuing Professional Development), Reward Management, Management Development, Employee Relations, Performance Management, Employee Voice and an awareness of Organisational Citizenship Behaviour and Corporate Social Responsibility should feature in all ethics policies. Recruitment and Selection requires a knowledge of Genuine Occupational Qualifications and relevant Employee Rights Regulations together with updates in Equal Opportunity legislation and the organisation's Diversity Management potential.

13 Business partnering

'HRM can be regarded as more strategic, more closely aligned with the needs of the business, less rule-bound and less bureaucratic, and having a greater focus on the key role of line managers (than personnel management)'

(Smith in Porter et al. 2006: 7)

CHAPTER OUTLINE

CHAPTER OBJECTIVES

- Understanding what is meant by 'HR business partnering'
- Awareness of the background to the emergence of the concept
- Understanding Dave Ulrich's model of HR roles
- Knowledge of implementing HR business partnering in practice
- Awareness of the issues and potential problems with HR business partnering

13.1 Introduction

Chapter One outlined how, in the early 1980s, human resource management (HRM) developed from personnel management. The personnel function had been subject to various criticisms: the well-known American management writer Peter Drucker (1961), for example, described the job of the personnel manager as being a rather mixed bag of day-to-day activities including administrative duties (like a filing clerk or housekeeper), helping employees with their problems (akin to a social worker) and dealing with trade unions when there was a dispute, or reacting to other problems that arose (firefighter). He paints a picture of a function rather removed from the decision-making centre of the organisation and one that reacted to events rather than being proactive. In a similar vein, Karen Legge (1978) saw personnel management as being caught in a vicious circle, one in which the function was not represented at the 'top table' and therefore not a part of strategic decision-making, including decisions that involved the employees of the organisation. This inevitably led to 'people problems', which the personnel department was expected to deal with, yet the very reactive nature of this led to the 'firefighting' mentioned above and often less than ideal outcomes. This led to the function being somewhat poorly regarded among other managers, which reinforced its lack of representation in senior management decision-making.

The 1980s saw the beginnings of a possibility of change to what has been outlined above with the arrival of human resource management (HRM). Academics at Harvard University developed an approach, the Harvard framework, (Beer et al. 1985) in which it was stressed that HR practices, rather than being separate and piecemeal, should be integrated together. The focus was on gaining employee commitment and using this to drive business performance and meet the strategic objectives of the organisation. A second approach, the matching model (Fombrun et al. 1984), attempted to link the key elements of HR (selection, appraisal, development and rewards) in delivering the business strategy.

In the UK, authors such as David Guest (1987) and John Storey (1992) helped to emphasise the key differences between human resource management and personnel management, with HRM being characterised as being proactive rather than reactive, long term (strategic) rather than short term and based on commitment rather than compliance.

CASE STUDY

As part of a class on HRM the author of this chapter set an exercise in which students were asked to reflect on the key challenges they faced working in HR, as well as what the perceptions were of the HR function from others within their organisations. The students work predominantly in HR or associated roles and are studying part-time for their CIPD qualification as well as a Masters degree.

Some of the key challenges were seen to be as follows:

- The sheer volume of administrative duties and time spent 'firefighting' that their jobs involved.
- The need to measure and evaluate the work of the HR function, and the difficulties involved in doing so.
- The need to convince line managers of the importance of HR.
- The need to keep abreast of on-going legislative changes and to ensure the organisation complied with these.
- Attempting to ensure that line managers applied policies and procedures correctly and consistently.
- The fact that the work involved and impacted on people, whose reaction could be varied and unpredictable.
- Implementing change and communicating the need for such change to employees and other managers.

In terms of perceptions of the HR function from others within the organisation (both employees and other managers), this varied according to the organisation and the specific circumstance. In some organisations, HR was a relatively small function primarily concerned with administration – even then it could be viewed positively if it helped resolve employees queries and issues. In other organisations HR included a more strategic aspect and was viewed as being more important. One respondent replied that employees tended to see the function positively if they had received the answer they wanted from a question, but in a negative light if the answer was less to their liking! Others agreed that HR was often blamed for being the messenger of organisational policies and procedures that were not always popular.

Perceptions of the function by other managers also ranged from the positive, where HR was seen to provide valuable and cost saving advice, in avoiding costly tribunal cases for example or in helping to introduce a better approach to selection, to the more negative where HR was seen as an unnecessary and intrusive constraint on the manager's right to manage. At times the HR department was viewed as being unnecessarily bureaucratic and restrictive, more concerned with policies and procedures than the needs of the business. This was echoed by some other students, who said the HR function in their organisation was viewed as being somewhat removed from 'where the action was' and not directly contributing to business goals.

1. What do the above experiences of the students working in HR tell us about the extent to which things have changed from the 'old days' of personnel management?
2. The students are generally at an early stage of their careers and many are in relatively junior roles. Do you think the answers would have been different if more senior HR managers had been asked the questions?

HR in practice

We have seen above how personnel management has been characterised and thus subject to criticism, and how ideas and models concerning human resource management offered new and different possibilities and the chance for change. The extent to which what academics and management theorists write in text books and journal articles is actually translated into practice is a matter of much debate. It is one thing to say that HR should be more strategic, gain the commitment of employees and thus help to drive business performance in a way that can be demonstrated, and quite another to actually achieve this in reality.

Another complication is the variety of what happens in practice, whether personnel or HR: the way the function operates and what managers in these departments actually do varies enormously between different sectors and organisations. There is also no doubt that, even before HRM came along, some personnel departments were strategic in nature and generated employee commitment. Equally, some departments today, whilst labelled as 'HR' are largely reactive and administrative and would struggle to demonstrate how they help the organisation achieve its business goals, never mind actually driving business performance.

Despite these reservations however, research and survey evidence do point to a general trend of change in the HR function, even if such change is partial. A survey of 1,180 HR professionals by the CIPD entitled 'Where we are, where we're heading' suggested that the function was in the process of moving from 'firefighter' to 'strategic partner'. Thus 72 per cent of respondents believed their influence with senior colleagues had increased, although 35 per cent still saw the function as more operational than strategic and just under half saw the HR function as being more reactive than proactive. The report argues that the survey shows a clear shift in aspiration from a function concerned with reactive HR (firefighting) to one focused on adding business value. However, while two thirds of respondents argued that business strategy was one of the three most important activities in which they personally engaged in, it accounted for a relatively small proportion of their time. (CIPD 2003)

1. In relation to the work of the HR function, what is meant by 'firefighting'? Give examples of what such activities could involve.

Seventy-two per cent of respondents say they have more influence in relation to senior colleagues compared with three years ago
Seven out of ten respondents say their CEO believes HR has a key role to play in achieving business outcomes. A similar proportion state that the executive board frequently discusses HR issues and that HR managers are comfortable discussing business issues
One in three see their current role as that of a strategic partner: more than one in four see themselves as change agent. More than half would like to become strategic partners in the future.
Thirty-five per cent of respondents believe the HR function in their organisation is currently too focused on operational issues, compared with 27 per cent who describe it as heavily strategic. Almost half see the HR function as more reactive than proactive.
Delivery of HR practices by the line is seen as an area requiring substantial improvement.
Most organisations have not significantly increased or reduced their use of external providers in the last three years.

Table 13.1 Key findings of 2003 CIPD survey (CIPD 2003)

1. Summarise the key changes to the HR function shown in the CIPD survey.
2. What are the implications for the HR function of these changes?

(13.3) The role(s) of the HR manager

This brings us to the key focus of this chapter: HR roles in general and the business partner role specifically. You will have gathered from the first two sections above that the personnel/HR function and the personnel/HR managers themselves can and do have different roles. Traditionally these have been seen in terms of an administrative role (for example ensuring that staff get paid the correct salary on time, updating employee records, recording employee leave and sickness records, etc.); a welfare role (helping employees who have problems and issues); and an industrial relations role (negotiating with trade unions for example). A personnel function at a particular site or organisation may have encompassed several of these roles at the same time, and indeed the role of a particular HR manager may also have crossed one or more boundaries.

There have been several attempts to classify these roles, and to update them to reflect the move from personnel to HRM. Storey's (1992) model draws on case-based research to identify four different roles for HR managers: service

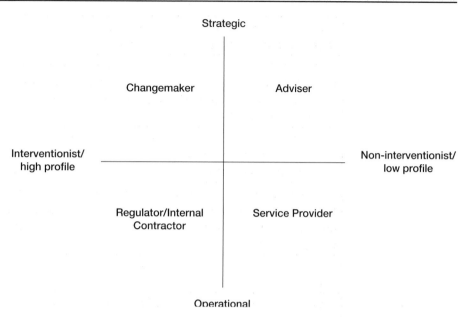

Figure 13.1 Storey's model (adapted from Marchington and Wilkinson 2008: 185), with the permission of the publisher, the Chartered Institute of Personnel and Development, London (www.cipd.co.uk)

providers, regulators/internal contractors, advisers and changemakers. Figure 13.1 illustrates the model, a four-fold categorisation based on two cross-cutting dimensions: the degree to which the function is strategic or operational, and, secondly, the extent to which it is interventionist and high profile versus non-interventionist and low profile.

The service provider role is one in which HR deals with routine operational problems and day-to-day issues raised by line managers (a largely administrative role). The second role, that of regulator/internal contractor, is also operational but is much more prominent and interventionist, either in dealings with trade unions or with other functions within or external to the organisation (for example, if parts of the HR function itself are subcontracted to external providers). Of the two more strategic roles, advisers offer expert advice to line managers, which could be at a strategic level but tends to be behind the scenes and low profile/non-interventionist. And finally, changemaker, which can be seen as the most significant role – such a role aims to link HR to the realities of business performance, to engender employee commitment and to persuade senior managers/directors of the value of HR initiatives.

1. Look at the four roles for the HR function outlined in Figure 13.1. What factors (internal and external to the organisation) might determine which role or roles are found in any particular organisation?

HR business partnering: the Ulrich model

The Ulrich model

John Storey's adapted model outlined above can be seen as both descriptive (that is of how HR roles are and have been) and prescriptive (that is as to how HR can and should change, towards the direction of the change agent quadrant, for example).

In his various writings, David Ulrich argues that there are good reasons for HR's sometimes poor reputation: 'It is often ineffective, incompetent and costly: in a phrase, it is value-sapping' (Ulrich 1998: 124).

He also asks, 'Should we do away with HR?' The answer to his own question would be 'no', but that HR has to change, HR must deliver value: 'HR practices must create value in the eyes of investors, customers, line managers, and employees' (Ulrich and Brockbank 2005). In order to do so he argues, HR needs to adopt new roles (originally four and now updated to five). The original four roles are illustrated below in Figure 13.2.

Figure 13.2 Ulrich's (1997) model (adapted from Ulrich, D. (1997) *Human Resource Champions: The next agenda for adding value and delivering results.* Boston: Harvard Business School Press)

KEY TERMS

Administrative experts Their role is to constantly improve organisational efficiency by re-engineering the HR function and other work processes.
Change agents Their role is to deliver organisational transformation and culture change.
Employee champions Their role is to maximise employee commitment and competence.
Strategic partners Their role is to help to successfully execute business strategy and meet customer needs.

Ulrich's four roles were later amended and updated by Ulrich in conjunction with Brockbank (Ulrich 2005; Ulrich and Brockbank 2005):

- *Administrative experts* were renamed *functional experts*, partly to reflect the fact that the more routine aspects of HR administration can either be outsourced and/or delivered by technology, thus changing the HR role to overseeing such processes, but also to reflect the importance of the expert body of knowledge that HR practitioners have.
- *Employee champions* become *employee advocates*, recognising the key role of employees to organisational success. This role involves both listening to and understanding the needs of the workforce, but also keeping employees in touch with the competitive realities faced by the business. To this role, Ulrich adds another, *human capital developer* which focuses on developing employees for the future, training, career development and coaching.
- *Change agent* becomes part of the *strategic partner* role, partnering line managers to help them reach their goals and helping to come up with winning strategies. It includes involvement in both strategy formulation and execution.

Ulrich links these roles together in a fifth role, that of HR leader. This also means leading the HR function, and collaborating with other functions.

1. What are the main similarities and differences between the Storey and Ulrich models of the HR function?

There is no doubt that Ulrich's ideas have caught the imagination of and had a major impact on the HR profession. This is particularly the case with regard to the business or strategic partner role. Ulrich and Brockbank do point out however that not everyone can operate at a strategic level and that all the roles are important to an organisation. Early on in their careers people working in HR are more likely to fulfil administrative/functional roles, or act as employee advocates. Even then though, it is important that they can see how what they do fits in with the strategic objectives of both the HR function and the organisation as a whole – that is, how their day-to-day job and tasks link to such overall goals. It is also worth pointing out again that there will often be overlap between the roles, so someone who operates mainly in an administrative/functional role may also at times act as an employee advocate, for example.

ACTIVITY

Look through a copy of *People Management*, which is the magazine of the Chartered Institute of Personnel and Development (CIPD) and is available at www. peoplemanagement.co.uk

Look in the appointments section and identify how many job advertisements have 'business partner' in their title, or contain reference to the business partner role. What key words are highlighted in the advert? What sort of sort of activities do these jobs contain?

(13.5) Ulrich's model in practice

Ulrich's ideas have definitely made a strong impression on the HR community in the UK. Many have used his ideas to reorganise and reorientate their function. However, despite the popularity of the model, research by the CIPD (Gifford and CIPD 2007) found that less than 30 per cent of respondents had introduced the model in full, with a further 30 per cent indicating they had introduced it in partial form.

The 'three-legged stool

One way in which the Ulrich model has been adopted (in adapted form) is to restructure the HR function. The CIPD research found that an adaptation of the Ulrich model, known as the 'three-legged stool', has been implemented by some large organisations (CIPD 2008a). This takes the form of structuring the HR function as follows:

- *Shared services* – providing a common service provision of routine HR administration across the organisation. Would commonly include such aspects as payroll, absence-monitoring and advice to common employee queries.
- *Centre of excellence* – a team of HR experts providing specialist and up-to-date advice to managers. The aim is to provide competitive business advantage through innovative HR solutions in areas such as reward, learning, employee engagement and talent management.

- *Strategic business partners* – senior HR professionals working alongside business leaders to influence, formulate and implement strategy. They thus provide input on the 'people dimensions' of business strategy.

Once again, there is likely to be considerable overlap between these three groupings. Any one HR issue may cut across one or more boundaries. HR business partners in particular need to develop good working relationships with their colleagues in shared services and centres of excellence.

1. What is meant by an HR service centre? What sort of activities would such a centre be involved in?

CASE STUDY

XYZ is a large firm involved in food processing, packaging and distribution. It has several different regional centres spread across the UK. Previously each centre had its own small HR team dealing with administration and day-to-day employee queries. Each of these reported to central HR at head office in Manchester. As part of a restructuring, the work of these HR regional centres was transferred to a shared service centre, also in Manchester. This allowed the firm to pool knowledge and resources and share best practice from each centre. It also allowed them to be more consistent in the advice they gave in response to queries from employees and managers. There were also benefits of economies of scale and avoiding duplication of effort and this led to significant cost savings.

A key factor that enabled this change was harnessing information technology: a new HR information system allowed those working in the shared service centre quick and easy access to data and employee records. In addition, for many of the simpler queries and enquiries, employees and managers could find the answer online without having to speak directly to someone in HR.

Overall it was felt that the move to shared services had been a success. Feedback from employees and managers was that generally information was provided with greater consistency, timeliness and accuracy. There were some problems however: some staff missed the face-to-face contact with someone from HR they had enjoyed previously, while there had also been some technical problems with the new system.

This is a fictional case study based partially on material adapted from CIPD fact sheet: HR shared service centres (CIPD 2008b).

1. What led to this organisation implementing an HR shared service centre?
2. What were the key benefits?
3. What were the problems?

Why organisations are implementing business partnering

The move towards some sort of business partner approach can be seen as being part of broader changes in HR. The key drivers of this are as follows (CIPD 2008a):

- *Efficiency and cost savings* – HR departments are increasingly having to measure what they do and show how they contribute to the business in terms of the bottom line (measurable outcomes such as profitability). Shared services in particular can do this, that is, provide improved quality of service while reducing costs.
- *Increasing competitive pressures* – organisations face continuing pressures to be competitive. There is also an increasing recognition that it is the employees of the organisation that are crucial to providing this competitiveness. Organisations need skilled, motivated staff who can demonstrate commitment and thus HR has become central to business competitiveness.
- *Rising expectations of HR* – it is argued that organisations are beginning to expect more of HR, particularly when HR in other organisations is seen to be contributing to strategy and the needs of the business. Business partners are seen as a way of linking HR to the needs of the business.

What then *is* business partnering?

CASE STUDY

Fran Shaw works as an HR manager, business partnering for the University of Hertfordshire. Her answers to questions about how she perceives the business partner role are set out below.

1. What, to you, is meant by the term 'business partner'?

    To me the term means that you are regarded as being part of the management team which makes decisions about the running of a unit, department, school or business. Essential to it is a real understanding of the business in question. What are the key drivers? What are the opportunities and challenges? Who are the main competitors? A real business partner does not provide just the text book HR advice but works with the management team to help them move the business agenda forward.

2. How does your own job relate to this (i.e. to what extent do you consider yourself to be an HR business partner)?

    In the main I think that I have built up the level of trust and understanding to enable me to 'add value'. It is pleasing that managers will generally include HR at the consultative stage rather than seek an opinion at the end of the process or worse still, ask for assistance after the event if it has gone wrong.

continued . . . ▶

◀ . . . *continued*

3. What do you see as the benefits of business partnering (i.e. why are organisations implementing business partnering)?

    The benefit of business partnering for HR is a deeper level of knowledge and understanding of the business. The benefit for the business is people strategy is factored into discussions at the earliest opportunity. The end result should be better decision making.

4. What are the main challenges of the role?

    The main challenges are building up and maintaining effective working relationships with key business contacts. You have to have a high level of trust and respect for business partnering to work. Sometimes the relationship can come under strain because of problems with more transactional HR activities, e.g. mistakes on contracts or on large volume activities, e.g. writing out to all staff after a restructuring. You have to get the basics right first to build up the trust so that you get asked to be involved in more strategic matters.

5. What do you see as the key skills/competencies required for the business partner role?

    Energy, resilience, persuasiveness, patience, empathy, effective communication, commercial appreciation, HR generalist experience, good employment law knowledge.

1. According to Fran, the business partner in the above example, what are some of the key challenges that the role brings?

Ulrich's writings described business partnership as an overriding feature of all four roles that he identified (and later updated to five), from administrative to strategic. In practice, organisations have tended to reserve its use to describe either the more senior posts concerned with strategy (that is, equating to Ulrich's 'strategic business partner'), or for middle-ranking professionals working as advisers or consultants to business units.

KEY TERMS

Business partner Linda Holbeche, Director of Research at Roffey Park Institute, describes a business partner as someone who 'Works alongside senior managers, providing the link between business and organisational strategies, providing support and challenge to the senior team and developing credible initiatives in a setting of cost reduction.' (Holbeche in Kenton and Yarnall 2005: 6)

CASE STUDY

In her article on business partners, Jane Pickard (2004) describes the following examples:

At the Royal Bank of Scotland the term 'business partner' is used to describe the most senior HR role, dealing with strategy. Other HR roles are that of *HR analyst* and *HR consultant* who work directly with business units, *HR technical experts*, in areas such as reward and resourcing, plus an *HR shared service centre* that deals with administration.

At the Prudential, business partners work in business units as consultants, backed up by HR centres of expertise and a shared service centre that deals with administration. It is more a mix of the strategic and the operational than that at the Royal Bank of Scotland. The article describes how one business partner worked with the marketing and innovation function on how to reduce the level of customer complaints. She pulled together the ideas of HR specialists and helped to implement the results.

1. How does the business partner role differ in the two examples given above?

In highlighting the key differences of a business partner compared to that of a more traditional HR role, Kenton and Yarnell argue that the business partner makes an important input to strategic decisions in the business. They would contribute to such aspects as organisational design, strategy development and planning and change initiatives. As such they would spend significantly less of their time on the more routine operational aspects, such as hands-on recruitment and record keeping. They go on to list some of the key functions of the business partner:

- Strategic planning
- Organisational development and design
- Improving productivity and quality in the organisation
- Assisting with mergers and acquisitions
- Looking out for new products and potential new partnerships
- Recruitment and selection (at a strategic rather than operational level)
- Contributing to strategic decisions and giving advice on human resource development, including management development, career planning and performance management
- Pay and reward, including benefits and reward and recognition initiatives
- Overseeing the management of HR information systems
- Overseeing employment relations issues, including trade union negotiations
- Responsibility for legal and regulatory requirements

(Kenton and Yarnall 2005: 7)

CASE STUDY

Charlotte works as an HR business partner at a UK site of one of the world's leading suppliers of fast moving consumer goods (FMCGs). Her answers to questions about how she perceives the business partner role are set out below:

1. What, to you, is meant by the term 'business partner'?

   Somebody who understands the business and the strategic direction and priorities of this business. Taking these into consideration, a business partner can use their insights to lead an agenda that contributes to and progresses the business. A business partner is also there to challenge the business. The business partner can use their knowledge and expertise to suggest different ways of doing things, challenge whether or not the decisions being made are right for the business, but also provide a pragmatic 'business priority focused' agenda. It's about being proactive and leading an agenda, rather than being reactive and 'following orders'. I feel that to be an effective business partner, you have to build credibility and trust with your business managers. Part of the role also involves being networked within the organisation to ensure that you can bring 'best practice' and organisational priorities to the function that you support.

2. How does your own job relate to this (i.e. to what extent do you consider yourself to be an HR business partner)?

   Whilst inevitably my role involves an element of 'administration' and reactive activities such as responding to line manager queries, the focus of my role is contributing to the progression of the HR agenda in line with the function's strategic priorities. I sit on the Leadership Team for the function I support, and am seen as a core member of that team. These meetings and discussions give me an understanding of the bigger picture, i.e. the priorities for the function, which enables me to adapt the people agenda and talent strategy for the function to ensure that it supports and progresses the agenda from a people perspective. I also look for opportunities to be proactive in adding value to the teams in not only what they are working on, but also how they are working from a leadership perspective. Symbolically, I also try and hot-desk with the function, rather than stay in the HR office, in order to build relationships and to have a visibility and presence within the function.

3. What do you see as the benefits of business partnering (i.e. why are organisations implementing business partnering)?

   When business partnering operates effectively, the business partner can bring real value and insights to the functions with which they work. They can implement interventions which make a difference in progressing the function both in terms of their objectives, as well as their ways of working. They can also challenge the function's thinking and ways of working to ensure that things do not remain with the status quo, i.e. just because they have always been done that way.

4. What are the main challenges of the role?

   Establishing yourself as part of the leadership team and a key strategic contributor. Finding your 'hook' in leadership meetings can sometimes be daunting when the focus is project updates and business detail. The challenge is to understand which pieces of this information are relevant for you to be able to build on in driving the people agenda.

continued . . .

◄ *. . . continued*

Also pushing back on 'admin requests'. Making it clear that these should be directed at the shared service centre can seem unhelpful to line managers, but it's necessary to enable you to sfocus on the strategic elements. It can be too easy to get bogged down in operational day-to-day matters, so you have to ensure that you give yourself space to work on the longer-term projects.

5. What do you see as the key skills/competencies required for the business partner role?

Relationship building, questioning skills (asking the right questions to enable a clear understanding of the issues), creativity, adaptability, good planning skills and the ability to see the bigger picture.

1. According to Charlotte, the HR business partner above, what are some of the key benefits that the role can bring to the business functions with which they work?

(13.7) Implementing business partnering

If a move to business partnering is being considered, it is important that there is a clear rationale for any such change. Kenton and Yarnall (2005) argue that a necessary precursor to success is that the HR function is clear as to what it is seeking to achieve and how it can add value to the business, otherwise the danger is that the exercise becomes primarily a name change or rebranding without much substance. As part of any such reflection, is it important to ask what is missing from current or previous approaches? From business partners they spoke to, they highlight the following as key drivers for the change to business partnering:

- Strategic alignment
  - to link and align people management practice to business goals
  - to assist managers in gaining an understanding of the importance of the people they employ to the achievement of business goals

- Service
  - to provide an accessible point of contact for clients (managers, other departments)
  - to improve service levels

- Financial
  - to improve service delivery while containing costs

Business partners may have to market themselves to internal clients to ensure that such clients understand their role and what they can provide.

The CIPD factsheet on HR business partnering (CIPD 2008a) also argues that time and effort needs to be put into preparation. Other people in the organisation, such as senior managers and line managers need to understand the proposed changes and the rationale behind them. In other words, there needs to be receptiveness in the organisation to the proposed change in role of HR. Sufficient time needs to be spent openly discussing partnering and the likely implications for those involved. This is particularly true for line managers who are the ones most likely to be affected by the changes.

The skills needed to perform the business partner role also need to be assessed and matched against existing skills. It is dangerous to simply assume that existing HR managers will have all the necessary skills and abilities for the new role.

It is also a useful exercise to assess the likely possible barriers to achieving a smooth and successful transition to business partnering. This could range from such factors as line managers' reluctance to take on more of the day-to-day people-management responsibilities or lack of skills to do so, through to problems with the current provision of HR transactional services or intranets, which may be slow and/or provide a less than complete service. More fundamental problems could include an absence of a clear and consistent business strategy for HR to attempt to link with.

 1. According to the CIPD, what are some of the key considerations for successful implementation of HR business partnering?

In reviewing the HR business partner model in action, Hunter et al. (2006: 27) summarise the key success factors as follows:

- *Learn the business inside out* – If HR is going to work alongside other managers and report to senior business unit leaders so that what it does is aligned to the business, it has to know the business inside out. This means strategically, operationally and financially. HR will then be in a position to offer relevant people management solutions to issues faced by the business.
- *Build great and diverse relationships* – HR business partners need to network and build relationships with those who are able to support and deliver change and who can provide the necessary information.
- *Be at the leading edge of the business's thinking* – HR needs to be proactive, to anticipate future problems and search out solutions. This means anticipating the organisation's future direction and interpreting the implications for people management of this.
- *Define, track, report and celebrate success* – HR needs to understand the right measures; this is one of the key ways in which strategies are successfully implemented. Measuring and evaluating what HR does and its impact on the business is an important element of the business partner role.

CASE STUDY

Implementing HR Business Partnering at the Department of Work and Pensions (DWP)

The DWP was formed in 2001 out of a combination of the Department for Social Security and parts of the Department for Education and Employment. As well as bringing together welfare policy functions, the DWP delivers welfare services for children, working-age adults and pensioners. It is a very large and complex department with 130,000 staff. The DWP was charged with creating change in welfare delivery, which was linked to a substantial internal change and modernisation programme covering HR, finance, IT and other support services. Part of this change programme involved a fundamental transformation of the HR function.

The HR function, as with the Civil Service as a whole, had many dedicated and talented people working for it. Yet, as a function it was felt to be rather bureaucratic, with a primary focus on the development of policies and procedures; a service provider, yet one which too often was viewed as one which constrained the work of line managers rather than working with them to meet business needs. IT and other systems were slow and ineffective. The DWP had one person working on HR for every 24 employees; a key aim of the review was to change this ratio to 1:50.

A new vision was created and a change of focus driven from the top. This included investment in information systems, targets for service delivery and efficiency improvements, and the start of a programme of external recruitment. The vision was for a smaller, more professional and expert function with excellent information systems supporting centralised shared services, and HR supporting business operations and enabling line managers to deliver results. In this, a new 'HR model' of how HR would operate was designated:

We will not be:	We will be:
administrators	change agents
taking sole ownership of HR issues	business focused
surrogate managers	technical experts
only functionally focused	customer focused
inward-looking	championing values
	fair

This represented a significant cultural shift for both the people working in HR and the DWP line managers.

HR business partners

The introduction of HR business partners was a key element of the new vision and proposed changes. They were tasked with providing linkages between the HR function and business goals and ensuring HR services met business needs. The key to this was viewed as establishing a positive and mutually

continued . . . ▶

. . . continued

reinforcing relationship between HR and line managers. Line managers would take on accountability for an increasing proportion of people management duties, helped and assisted by HR expertise and systems. The expectations for the new HR business partners were as follows:

- Demonstrate an HR focus on business goals, both local and strategic
- Be a change agent, both in terms of the HR function but also across the DWP
- Be a figurehead for an expert and professional HR function that adds value
- Help managers achieve their goals through improved HR service delivery
- Provide coaching for line managers to improve their skills
- Identify and deliver skills training more generally
- Help to ensure that people are put at the heart of the change agenda

A key challenge was seen as ensuring that existing HR roles were not simply rebranded as business partners, that there was real substance to the changes. Clear job descriptions and competency profiles were drawn up and recruitment was both external as well as from within the organisation. This aspect took longer than planned, with some posts remaining unfilled after a year.

Outcomes

Eighteen months on, a sample of business partners and line managers were asked what they thought of the changes business partners had brought. The results showed that they saw the new arrangements as generally successful in delivering the changed relationship between HR and line managers that was wanted. HR was seen as now being more closely aligned to the needs of the business and more expert and accessible. The findings also showed, however, that there was still a long way to go. New information systems hadn't yet been introduced and, as a result, the shared services centres were not yet operating as well as they should have. The findings also showed that more needed to be done to ensure that line managers fully understood what the business partner role was about. There was also a strong desire that business partners should be able to play a more strategic role and spend less time firefighting and on service delivery.

Adapted from *Business partnering – a new direction for HR: a guide.*
(CIPD 2004, with the permission of the publisher, the Chartered Institute of Personnel and Development, London (www.cipd.co.uk))

1. What are some of the key lessons to be learned from the DWP case about the implementation of business partnering?

Requirements of the business partner role

In the preceding sections it has been suggested that the business partner role is different in many fundamental ways from traditional HR. The capabilities required will also be different. In the DWP case study above the organisation had difficulties recruiting new business partners and this situation is mirrored in various research studies. Thus a study carried out for CIPD by Peter Goodge (in Arkin 2007) found that HR people who have what it takes to succeed as business partners are in short supply.

The CIPD factsheet on business partnering argues that the appointment of business partners presents particular challenges and that the skills and behaviours required are different from those found in traditional HR manager roles. Such skill sets include being able to think and act strategically, consultancy skills, business and financial understanding, change management, networking, relationship management, as well as influencing and political awareness skills (CIPD 2008a: 3). Robert Myatt, a consultant, feels there is a considerable gap between where many HR people are now and where they need to be as business partners: 'Business partner implies a two-way, adult-to-adult relationship. Previously, HR did whatever the business needed. Now the function is moving away from taking orders to consultancy. The role of the consultant is to challenge the presenting problem, which may not be the actual problem, and this could be difficult, because they haven't got the power or the confidence' (quoted in Pickard (2004: 2)).

CASE STUDY

Paul Deeprose is a career development professional who runs The Career Gym as a consultancy to focus on the development of HR professionals and their teams, based on his learning from partnering some of the world's best-known companies. He feels that successful business partnering is as much about having the right mind set as a set of skill competencies.

He sets out the requirements of being a business partner as follows:

- *Commercial acumen* - understanding business/competitors/the market, financial aspects and contributing to broader strategy.
- *Consultancy skills* – listening, questioning, challenging and advising. Project management and being solutions-led. Being able to delegate transactional work.
- *Relationships/stakeholder management* – being customer focused. Clarity about who the real stakeholders are and who you are building relationships with.
- *Proactivity, strategic and pre-emptive* – spotting opportunities and acting upon them.
- *External focus* – networking. What are the competition doing? Benchmark your activities.
- *Innovation* – when was the last time you suggested a new way of doing things?
- *Persuasion/influence* – convince me that you can really turn someone's mind around.
- *Delivery/outputs and measurement* – delivery focus, performance improvement. Demonstrate your success. Return on investment.
- *Courageous conviction* – passionately believe in what you are doing. Have the courage of your convictions.
- *Change management* – understand the key drivers for change.
- *Be courageous* – make a difference.

www.thecareergym.co.uk

It is also pointed out that many organisations had accompanied their shift to the business partner model with a significant new training and development programme for the function in order to develop these new skills and competencies.

 ## HR business partnering: issues and possible problems

Dave Ulrich's model of HR roles, and the associated 'three-legged stool' model of the HR function holds out the promise of a transformation of HR and a seat on the top table of strategy formulation and implementation. Yet the application of the model in practice has not always been straightforward. Ulrich describes five (originally four) distinct roles that modern HR professionals need to play: functional expert, employee advocate, human capital developer, strategic partner and HR leader. He sees each of these roles as essential and each as being largely played by different people, all of them business partners. In practice the boundaries between these roles are likely to be blurred, with any one individual's job encompassing more than one role.

In addition, Ulrich warns against taking a hierarchical view of the five roles, although the tendency is to value the strategic ones more highly than the operational. In reality, the term 'business partner' has often been reserved for the relatively senior strategic partner role, or one that combines the strategic with the operational, working with line managers in a particular business unit. One possible danger of this is that the other roles, such as functional expert or employee advocate are devalued, potentially lessening the effectiveness of HR and creating division and resentment amongst its ranks.

We have also seen in this chapter that the skills set required of business partners is different from that of traditional HR and this may cause difficulties when it comes to recruiting for such posts. There are also significant training and development implications involved. Another potential difficulty is the cultural shift needed in both HR and line managers when implementing the change to business partnering, and the length of time this shift may take to be truly embedded.

In relation to the 'three-legged stool' for structuring the HR function – that is into shared services, centres of excellence and strategic business partners – it has been argued that splitting the function into three distinct areas in this way has created boundary problems and sometimes left a hole at the very heart of the operation – 'the Polo problem' (Reilly 2006: 1). Therefore, lines of accountability need to be made clear.

Finally, there is little point in having excellent and dynamic business partners, if shared service centres cannot themselves deliver a first-class service, or if the infrastructure, in terms of fully functioning information systems for example, is not in place.

1. What are some of the potential problems with implementing HR business partnering in practice? What steps can be taken to overcome these?

 ## Summary

The chapter began with an introduction to how the concept of human resource management developed from personnel management and reviewed some of the possible differences between the two. It then considered some of the trends in the aspirations of the HR function, from being largely administrative and reactive to more proactive and concerned with adding business value.

Dave Ulrich's model of HR roles was outlined and the implications for the HR function reviewed. The reasons for organisations implementing business partnering were described and the business partner role in practice was analysed. The following section covered guidelines for implementing business partnering and the requirements of the role and this was followed by a review of some of the issues and possible problems associated with business partnering.

The main points covered in the chapter are summarised below. If you are unsure about any of them, then it is suggested that you revisit the relevant section. If you would like to find out more about any of these topics, further reading is suggested in the next section.

KEY IDEAS

Introduction
- The development of HRM.
- Human resource management (HRM) can be seen to have developed from personnel management.
- Personnel management had been subject to a number of criticisms, including that it was largely administrative and reactive.
- HRM was regarded as more strategic, proactive and aligned to the needs of the business.

continued . . . ▶

. . . continued

HR in practice

- Various surveys suggest both a change in aspiration of the HR function (i.e. how it would like to be) and some evidence of actual change, although the picture is mixed.
- Such changes include moving from reactive firefighting to focusing more on adding business value and adopting a more strategic perspective.

The role(s) of the HR manager

- There have been various attempts to classify personnel and HR roles.
- Storey's model outlines four roles: service provider, regulator/internal contractor, advisor, and changemaker.

HR business partnering: the Ulrich model

- Ulrich originally outlined four roles: Administrative Expert, Employee Champion, Change Agent and Strategic Partner.
- This was later updated to five: Functional Expert, Employee Advocate, Human Capital Developer, Strategic Partner and HR Leader.
- Ulrich's ideas have caught the imagination of the HR community, particularly with regard to the strategic partner role.

Ulrich's model in practice

- CIPD research found evidence that the model has been implemented by organisations, but often only partially.
- One implication has been the restructuring of HR functions. An example would be the 'three-legged stool': shared services, centres of excellence, and strategic business partners.
- The key reasons why organisations are implementing this are seen to be: efficiency and cost savings, increasing competitive pressures, and rising expectations of HR.

What then *is* business partnering?

- Ulrich sees business partner as part of each of his four (or five) roles. In practice, organisations have tended to use the term to describe either the more senior posts concerned with strategy, or for HR middle managers working as advisors or consultants to business units.
- It is argued that key features of an HR business partner in practice are: someone who is part of the management team, understands the business and ensures that people issues are considered when strategies are formulated and implemented. They are proactive and there to challenge the business to consider new ways of doing things.

Implementing business partnering

- When considering the possible move to a business partner model, organisations need to have a clear rationale for doing so: what are they seeking to achieve?
- Key drivers of a move to business partnering can include: to align people management practices to business goals, to provide accessible contact for other managers, and to improve service delivery.
- It is suggested that time and effort needs to be put into planning and preparation for such a change. Line managers in particular need to understand the implications as they are the ones most likely to be affected by the changes.

continued . . .

◀ ... *continued*

Requirements of the business partner role

- The business partner role is different in many ways from a traditional HR role, and therefore has different requirements.
- It is suggested that organisations may have difficulty recruiting people with the right skills set and abilities. There are also implications for learning and development of HR business partners.
- Requirements include: being able to think and act strategically, consultancy skills, business and financial understanding, change management skills, networking and relationship management as well as influencing and political awareness skills.

HR business partnering: issues and possible problems

- There are possible difficulties in application of the model. Organisations may focus on some elements whilst disregarding others and, as a result, such roles as administrative or functional expert may be devalued.
- There may be difficulties in recruiting people with the right skills set to be effective business partners, and substantial training and development may be required.
- Another potential challenge is the cultural shift needed in both HR and line managers; it may be difficult to implement this change.
- Splitting the HR function into three may create boundary problems and sometimes leave a potential gap in responsibilities.
- For HR business partners to be successful there is a need that the other elements of HR are fully functioning and efficient – HR information systems and the operation of shared services, for example.

REFLECTIVE QUESTIONS

1 What are the key ways in which HRM can be seen to differ from personnel management?
2 Name and describe the five roles of Ulrich's updated model of HR.
3 How would you define 'HR business partnering'?
4 What are the key considerations when considering implementing business partnering?
5 List the key requirements of a business partner.

RECOMMENDED READING

The CIPD's factsheet on *HR Business Partnering* (Revised October 2008) provides a useful summary as well as suggestions for further reading.

   Another useful publication on the subject by the CIPD is *Business partnering – a new direction for HR* which explains the concept of HR strategic business partner through a number of case studies. Both of these are available on the CIPD's website (see below) along with a range of articles and commentaries on the topic.

Two useful practical guides to business partnering are Hunter et al's book *HR Business Partners* and that by Kenton and Yarnall *HR – The Business Partner: Shaping a New Direction*.

Caldwell's article on business partner competency models is also worth a look.

Lastly, Ulrich and Brockbank's book *The HR Value Proposition* gives an excellent insight into their ideas.

USEFUL WEBSITES

www.cipd.co.uk The website for the Chartered Institute of Personnel and Development, the professional body that represents HR professionals in the UK. Has factsheets, research reports and more on business partnering. See also the podcast (Number 14) on the changing face of the HR function.

www.peoplemanagement.co.uk Journal of the CIPD, contains articles and news on business partnering plus job advertisements.

www.personneltoday.com Also contains articles and news updates on the subject.

www.shrm.org Website of the body for HR professional in the US.

www.hays.co.uk/hr/hrbusinesspartner/index.aspx Lists HR business partner job vacancies.

REFERENCES

Arkin, A. (2007) 'Street smart', *People Management*, April.

Beer, M., Spector, B., Lawrence, P., Quinn Mills, D., Walton, R. (1985) *Human Resource Management: A general manager's perspective*. Glencoe: Free Press

Caldwell, R. (2008) HR Business Partner competency models: re-contextualising effectiveness, *Human Resource Management Journal*, vol. 18, no. 3.

CIPD (Chartered Institute of Personnel and Development) (2003) *Where we are, where we're heading*. Survey Report. London: CIPD.

CIPD (Chartered Institute of Personnel and Development) (2004) *Business partnering – A new direction for HR: A guide*. London: CIPD.

CIPD (Chartered Institute of Personnel and Development) (2008a) Factsheet: *HR business partnering*. London: CIPD.

CIPD (Chartered Institute of Personnel and Development) (2008b) Factsheet: *HR shared service centres*. London: CIPD.

Drucker, P. (1961) *The Practice of Management*. London: Mercury Books.

Fombrun, C., Tichy, N., Devanna, M. (eds) (1984) *Strategic Human Resource Management*. New York: Wiley.

Gifford, J. and Chartered Institute of Personnel and Development (2007) *The changing HR function: survey report*. London: CIPD.

Guest, D. (1987) Human Resource Management and Industrial Relations, *Journal of Management Studies*, vol. 24, no. 5, 503–21.

Hunter, I., Saunders, J., Boroughs, A., Constance, S. (2006) *HR Business Partners*. Aldershot: Gower.

Kenton, B., Yarnall, J. (2005) *HR – The Business Partner: Shaping a New Direction*. Oxford: Butterworth Heinemann.

Legge, K. (1978) *Power, Innovation and Problem-Solving in Personnel Management*. London: McGraw Hill.

Marchington, M., Wilkinson, A. (2008) *Human Resource Management at Work*. London: CIPD.

Pickard, J. (2004) One step beyond, *People Management*, 30 June.

Porter, K., Smith, P., Fagg, R. (2006) *Leadership and Management for HR Professionals*. Oxford: Butterworth-Heinemann.

Reilly, P. (2006) Falling between two stools, *People Management*, 23 November.

Storey, J. (1992) *Developments in the Management of Human Resources*. Oxford: Blackwell.

Ulrich, D. (1997) *Human Resource Champions: The next agenda for adding value and delivering results*. Boston: Harvard Business School Press.

Ulrich, D. (1998) A new mandate for human resources, *Harvard Business Review*, Jan–Feb, 125–34.

Ulrich, D. (2005) Role call, *People Management*, 16 June.

Ulrich, D. and Brockbank, W. (2005) *The HR Value Proposition*. Boston: Harvard Business School Press.

14 Strategic HRM

'Perhaps one message – more than any other – has been communicated in job advertisements for HR directors over the last few years: whatever you do, help the firm make its HRM consistent with its strategic direction, integrate HR strategy with the wider business strategy'

(Boxall and Purcell 2008: 56)

'The linkage between HRM activities, the needs of the business, and organizational effectiveness is the core of the area called strategic human resource management'

(Schuler and Jackson 2005: 3)

CHAPTER OUTLINE

14.1 Introduction
14.2 What is strategy? An introduction to different approaches
14.3 And strategic HRM?
14.4 Strategic management
14.5 Corporate strategy
14.6 The BCG matrix and implications for human resource management
14.7 Competitive strategy and human resource management
14.8 'Matching' models
14.9 Resource-based approaches
14.10 Strategic HRM: two further issues
14.11 Summary

> **CHAPTER OBJECTIVES**
>
> ● Understand what is meant by strategy, by strategic HRM and by a strategic orientation and be able to distinguish between the various levels of strategy
> ● Appreciate the distinction between classical approaches to strategy and other approaches
> ● Appreciate the links between corporate, business and HR strategies and the contribution of 'matching' models to the development of thinking in strategic HRM
> ● Understand the differences between market and resource-based approaches to strategy and the implications of each for strategic HRM.
> ● Appreciate the role of strategic HRM in contributing to organisational performance and effectiveness

14.1 Introduction

In Chapter 1 we explored the development of human resource management (HRM) as a specific and distinctive approach to the management of people. As the chapters in this book make clear, there has been a move in recent years away from viewing HRM as distinctive (Boxall and Purcell 2008), and indeed the emphasis has shifted to one that acknowledges there are many approaches that can be encompassed within the broad sweep of human resource management. However, one element that has remained is the conviction that it is, or should be, strategic in its approach. What this means and why it matters, is the subject of this chapter, but at the outset we would stress that the term 'strategic' is banded about a great deal in much management literature, although the difficulties of adopting a strategic approach, or indeed of thinking strategically are often played down or ignored.

In this chapter we try and build upon the material we introduced in Chapter 1 to explore more fully what it means to be strategic in the management of people in organisations. We then examine some of the more influential approaches that have been developed to help managers in devising and implementing strategies to manage people effectively, that is in helping organisations to deploy staff in ways that meet organisational, and ideally, staff needs.

14.2 What is strategy: an introduction to different approaches

In discussing the issue of strategy it is useful to start with what Whittington (2002) refers to as the **classical planning** approach, where strategic decisions are constructed on the basis of rational decision-making on the part of senior managers. Within this is the idea of strategic direction, encompassing a vision and sense of purpose about where the organisation (big or small) strives to be at some point in the future. How far ahead in the future and what sort of planning horizon will depend on a variety of factors, including the nature and complexity of the industry, the state of competition and estimates of likely future trends in the market.

In small organisations entering a market for the first time a strategic direction may exist but their planning horizon is likely to be short – possibly six months to a year; there a concern to survive and hopefully secure a niche in a market. In contrast larger organisations that have established themselves in a mature market will often work on significantly longer time horizons. For example, as a result of the huge capital spending involved and the speculative nature of some of their investments, it is not uncommon for the petroleum and motor vehicles industries to develop strategies formally some 10–20 years ahead, and informally 25–50 years ahead. Similarly pharmaceuticals companies like GlaxoSmithKline, and consumer products companies like Unilever and Philips will also tend to work on strategies for the long term. Large capital investments and the potential risk that some research and development activities will not generate a steady income stream into the future mean that they spread risks by having a portfolio of activities which have to be managed and planned for. These longer term strategic decisions tend to focus on the 'big questions' facing them: what businesses do we want to develop, what businesses do we want to be involved in and what kind of a business do we want to be? These and other questions normally associated with business and corporate strategy are detailed below.

KEY TERMS

Human resource strategies Normally thought of as clusters of HR systems.
Human resource system Every HR system is a set of work and employment practices that have evolved to manage a particular hierarchical or occupational group within an organisation (Boxall and Purcell 2008: 24). There may be many of these operating at any one time within an organisation, and therefore a number of different HR strategies.

14.3 And strategic HRM?

Strategy

Following Purcell (1989) it is common to think about strategy operating at a number of levels within organisations. In large multi-divisional companies like Unilever, Proctor and Gamble, Virgin and Nestle this might look something like:

- **First order strategy – corporate strategy** involving decisions about what business(es) should we be in? What should we get out of? Where is the future growth coming from? What markets should we be in – local, national international?
- **Second order strategy – business strategy**; that is strategies for the individual businesses in the organisation involving decisions about how we should compete in the markets we are in? How should we position ourselves? What is our competitive advantage – what is it that means customers come to us to buy goods and services rather than going somewhere else?
- **Third order strategy – functional strategy**, covering Marketing, HRM, IT. In classical strategy these third order decisions largely derive from the first two, particularly the nature of the business strategy being pursued. In terms of HR this would involve, among other things, developing a recruitment strategy to meet the business needs, a reward strategy to aid recruitment and retention of staff, and a strategy for training and development to ensure staff with appropriate skills are available to deliver the overall business strategy.

Purcell's typology is helpful in providing some distinction between the scope and nature of issues dealt with at each level. It is also important in locating HR strategies 'downstream' from corporate and business level decisions, and provides an insight into what strategic human resource management might be concerned with. One perspective on this is provided by Schuler and Jackson (2005) who argue that strategic HRM is concerned with:

- **Vertical integration** – that the organisation needs to fit with its environment and specifically with higher order strategies.
- **Horizontal integration** – that HR systems need to be coherent; that they aim to deliver a consistent set of outcomes.
- **Demonstrating effectiveness** – to show that HRM systems make a difference and contribute to organisational performance.
- **Partnership** – that HR professionals work cooperatively with line managers and non-managerial employees.

In contrast Boxall and Purcell (2008) provide a less prescriptive view, underpinned by a belief in strategic choice, which we explore further below. For them, as a field of study '[s]trategic HRM is concerned with the strategic choices associated with the organisation of work and the use of labour in firms and with explaining why some firms manage them more effectively than others' (2008: 58).

For Boxall and Purcell HR strategies have goals and the means for organising work and people but are subject to a wide range of influences, including – but not exclusively about – corporate and business strategies. Furthermore, by emphasising strategic choice, and the fact that organisations may require different things from different groups of staff, they stress that HR strategies may well vary within organisations as managers develop separate HR systems (sets of work organisation and employment practices) to manage different sets of employees (Boxall and Purcell 2008: 224). It follows that for them, an organisation's HR strategies will tend to comprise clusters of a number of different HR systems.

14.4 Strategic management

Before proceeding further it is worth reflecting on the development of strategy and what it means for managers. The important message of strategic management is that those running organisations are not powerless in the face of hostile environments, particularly impersonal market forces. Rather, through careful analysis, planning and market positioning, senior managers can help shape their organisations' destinies. Furthermore, following Child (1972), they have strategic choices available to them, and if not planned precisely, the future can at least be shaped. It follows that this view of the potency of strategic management to effect change and shape the future invests a great deal in those undertaking this activity, normally seen as the most senior managers in an organisation. They are assumed to have the expertise, the knowledge and the 'helicopter vision' to enable them to understand and evaluate the options available to an organisation in moving forward.

This view of strategy formation has been challenged on a number of fronts (Whittington 2002). Even in terms of its own logic it has problems; whether senior managers really have the necessary insights and information is questionable and even if they do their decision-making may well be constrained by issues of **'bounded rationality'** (Simon 1958). Senior managers often make decisions based on their own experience and what they have done in the past, there is what Johnson and Scholes (2006) have termed an 'organisational recipe', which is strongly shaped by past events and what is deemed 'acceptable'. Organisations may have a tendency or 'path dependency' that makes it more likely for them to operate in particular ways and to respond to particular situations in certain ways. An example of this can be seen in the early work of Miles and Snow (1978) (see Table 14.1). They classified organisations into four types: defenders, prospectors, analysers and reactors, in terms of how they competed in markets. In Table 14.1 we focus on the first two of these as they provide a particularly revealing contrast.

The comparison between 'defender' organisations and 'prospectors' is one between organisations with a narrow range of products that face a relatively stable environment, and those that are more entrepreneurial, relying on new products and services and constantly seeking out market opportunities. The differences lie in how the two types of organisations view their environments

KEY TERMS

Bounded rationality A concept originally developed by Herbert Simon (1958) which emphasises that decision-making is often made on the basis of imperfect or incomplete information. Furthermore, the human mind is only able to process a limited amount of information at any one moment in time and so decisions are rarely, if ever, fully based on rationality.

and their strategic orientation reflects this, with 'prospectors' seeing a more dynamic, fast-changing environment in contrast to the 'defenders', who often protect market share and seek to consolidate market position. As Table 14.1 shows, these also have very different implications for how we might expect core elements of HRM to be managed. Miles and Snow therefore provide us with a link, with a sense of how a strategic direction or orientation may carry with it implications for how people might be managed and the role of HR departments. In doing so, they provide a template for some of the 'matching' models that dominated discussion of HR strategies in the 1980s and 1990s.

How easy it would be for a defender-type organisation to change to become another type is difficult to assess, but we can safely assume that if strategies are developed in relation to their environments, should these environments change in significant ways, organisations are likely to have to go through a difficult period of readjustment if they are to survive. It also reminds us that certain types of organisations can become 'embedded' in particular courses of action and may struggle to meet new demands if customer needs change – IBM in the late 1980s and early 1990s is a case in point here.

Returning to the theme of classical approaches to strategy more generally, a further and longstanding problem with such approaches is that they tend to be far stronger on strategy formation than implementation. It is often the implementation, the 'operationalising' of strategy, which is about getting people not involved in the strategy process to deliver, where many of the difficulties arise and strategies begin to unravel. It is of course this area that is particularly relevant for HR practitioners.

Whittington (2002) also points out that this approach to strategy development is challenged by other 'theories of action', those outside of the classical **paradigm**. The work of Mintzberg (1978) who observed strategy formation in organisations, suggested that it is much more a process involving many layers within organisations than the province of senior managers alone. It follows that instead of being 'top-down' as classical strategy suggests, it tends to be more emergent (as Boxall and Purcell acknowledge in their work), more political and evolves more slowly over time. Whittington suggests further that some

HR Practices	Strategic Configuration	
	Defenders (Internal Employment System)	**Prospectors** (Market Employment System)
Resources	Highly developed internal labour markets Care over recruitment and selection	Buys in labour to undertake tasks
Learning and development	Extensive and long-term focus Well-defined career ladders	Extensive but concern that can always buy-in expertise if required Promoting innovation
Employee relations	Emphasis on partnership, cooperation and involvement Voice mechanisms	Emphasis on performance Little attention paid to mechanisms
Reward management	Clear grading structures Transparent pay systems Mechanisms to encourage retention and L/T orientation such as share ownership	Pay determined by external market comparisons and 'ability to pay' Bonus and incentive payments
HR function	Longstanding and well-established Potentially significant influence	Limited role other than in recruitment and selection and managing external contracts

Table 14.1 Miles and Snow (1987) cited in Marchington and Wilkinson (2007)

contexts may be far more supportive of a longer-term strategic orientation than others. As a consequence some environments, because of their highly competitive nature ('evolutionary') or because of their socio-cultural and institutional frameworks (his '**systemic**' approach to strategy), may hinder the development of such an orientation.

These points are important because they raise questions as to the extent of strategic choice that may be available to senior managers in organisations. Although firms are not fully constrained by their environments, neither are they fully able to create them (Boxall and Purcell 2008: 43), and while there is always some degree of strategic choice in labour management in the firm

(Boxall and Purcell 2008: 57) for some the choices are more constrained than for others. Those organisations facing particularly intense competitive pressures (for example sub-contractors, or those far down the supply chain to a major retailer) may have limited scope to effect a clear strategy, or any strategy may be largely dictated to it by others (Rainnie 1989). In contrast, organisations functioning in a more benign operating environment or where shareholder pressures are counterbalanced by incentives to meet other stakeholder concerns (as in Germany, until recently), may have far more choice available to them in developing strategy. The critical issue for our discussion is that these influences are also likely to have an impact on the choice available to organisations in developing a strategic approach to the management of human resources.

In the following discussion these points should be borne in mind. It may be far easier to develop a longer-term approach to the business and to the management of human resources where pressures to meet short-term targets are less in evidence. In the past, Germany and Japan come to mind and it is no accident that Rhineland and Asian variants of capitalism are frequently contrasted with so-called Anglo-American versions as representing very different business systems and institutional and governance contexts for the operation of business (Hall and Soskice 2001; Whitley 1999). However, in what follows we assume that there is some scope for strategic choice and we begin by focusing on Purcell's first order strategy – corporate strategy in multi-business or divisional organisations.

KEY TERMS

Paradigm The set of ideas, body of knowledge and practices that define a particular discipline or mode of operating at any point in time. Often seen in terms of the dominant thinking and approaches in a particular era.

Processual strategy Derived from the work of Mintzberg and others. His view is that strategy is largely emergent and is shaped by processes within organisations.

Systemic strategy The idea that strategies are shaped by the contexts in which they have developed. In particular the social and cultural contexts; this implies that some contexts are more likely to give rise to particular strategic initiatives than others.

(14.5) Corporate strategy

In the early years of strategy development much of the focus was upon the corporate level and how large diversified conglomerates could effectively manage their portfolios – their collection of assets and businesses. Much of this work took place in the United States where the growth of very large and complex businesses had probably progressed further than elsewhere (Ansoff 1969; Baran and Sweezy 1966). Advice on how such organisations could manage these assets was limited until the work of the Boston Consulting Group in the early 1970s and the development of the so-called BCG Matrix, a development that was quickly followed by a number of increasingly sophisticated matrix models (see the GE matrix, for example). Here we concentrate on the BCG matrix (BCG 1970) because it remains one of the most influential strategic management tools ever constructed. It also remains one of the most controversial, its popularity once described as a major factor in the relative decline in the competitiveness of US corporations throughout the 1970s (Hayes and Abernathy 1980).

Its appeal lay partly in its simplicity and in its rather 'homely', if controversial, terminology, as well as the fact that it fitted well with the dominant 'systemic' orientation at the time. As a portfolio model it encouraged senior managers to view complex organisations as composed of a set of separate and discrete elements with their own income streams. If the elements could be classified in terms of their current and future income-generating potential it would be possible first to treat each of them differently, to operate different strategies for each of them; and secondly to get rid of (divest) those parts that were contributing or likely to contribute little to future income and profitability. It is analogous to an individual who has some wealth (stock of money) and income (flow of money) deciding how to allocate these between competing uses. Some could be invested in a bank, a building society, post office, stocks and shares, or property, with decisions based on the security of an investment, the possible return, the risk involved and so on. Moreover, these decisions could be reviewed on a regular basis.

BCG Matrix

The matrix itself uses two factors or variables: relative market share – that is the share of the market held by the product or service of the organisation relative to that of the largest market share held by any organisation; and market growth. Where a product, service or division is held to have a significant relative market share in a fast-growing market (Intel processors, for example) it would be described as a 'Star'. Where it has a similar market share in a more mature market, or one where growth is more modest, it is normally described as a 'Cash Cow'. Often such products or divisions have been Stars in the past but they have now reached a point in their product life cycle, or the markets in which they operate have slowed down, where the potential for very high income flows no longer exists. Cadbury Dairy Milk or Mars Bars could be examples here, and the matrix suggests that these will continue to generate steady income which can be used to invest in Stars. In the language of the

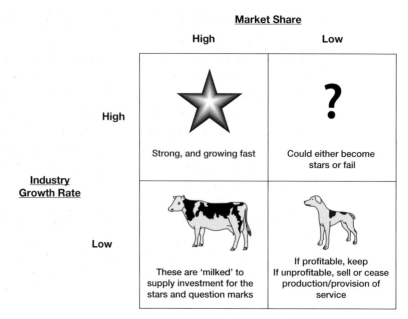

Figure 14.1 BCG Matrix

matrix these should be 'milked' or harvested for the benefit of other parts of the business.

To complete the matrix, those products, services or businesses that have a low relative market share in a slow-growing or declining market should probably be divested they are 'Dogs' that have had their day. The final group, arguably the most complex, are those that lie in reasonably fast-growing markets but where relative market share is low. How senior managers deal with this group will much depend on how long the products or businesses have been in existence, their stage in the product life cycle and their precise position in the quadrant itself. They may have the potential to be Stars but they could also end up becoming Dogs, hence they are termed 'Question Marks'; they are also known as 'Problem Children'.

14.6 The BCG Matrix and implications for human resource management

At this point the reader might ask, 'well, this is very interesting but what does it tell us about HRM in these organisations?' Thomason (1984) has suggested the implications are significant and developed an early version of what we now describe as a 'matching' model. In his view, where a product or business is seen by senior managers to be located within the matrix will to an extent determine how it is treated by management and the nature of policies that

In the **'Dog'** the emphasis of HR would be upon 'downsizing', including cutting costs and managing redundancies.
The **'Cash Cow'** would be concerned with maintaining some order and stability with an established HR presence. HR providing specialist expertise in the administration of pay systems, recruitment and selection and training and development (Redman and Wilkinson 2002).
In the **'Star'** we would expect a focus on flexibility and internal dynamism, with an emphasis on recruitment and selection of highly motivated staff, working towards achieving targets, with retention strategies including internal career ladders, innovative and flexible reward systems and on ongoing training and development.
In the **'Question Mark'**, with a low share of a fast-growing market we might expect to see a concern with internal flexibility and responsiveness to market opportunities. This will be reflected in a tendency towards a flatter organisation structure, a limited number of formal rules, and a limited HR presence. The expectation being that employees will do what they need to do to achieve organisational goals.

Table 14.2 The BCG and HRM (Redman and Wilkinson 2002)

will be followed in individual businesses. In terms of HRM, a business seen as being a Star will construct approaches to *resourcing* the business, *rewarding* and *developing* staff, and managing *employee relations* very different from those in a Cash Cow or a Dog. Table 14.2 provides an illustration of how aspects of HRM might look in each of the four quadrants.

There is little doubt that the influence of the BCG Matrix has been considerable. The structuring of organisations into separate Strategic Business Units (SBUs) operating as profit or cost centres is commonplace and reflects the idea that in managing a complex organisation, separating it out into discrete elements that can be developed or sold off has considerable advantages. Furthermore, the idea that these elements should also adopt functional strategies consistent with their place in the product or business portfolio also appears sensible. A cursory glance at business ownership reveals that many large companies reinforce their multi-divisional structure by ensuring their individual businesses are maintained as separate legal businesses under the control of a parent or holding company. This allows a degree of fragmenting of organisations and their boundaries (Marchington et al. 2005) and makes it easier for them legally to pursue very different approaches to managing people, in particular to rewarding staff.

This latter point can be seen particularly in parts of the public sector. Although the BCG Matrix was developed very much for the private sector (for profit) and this is where it has had most influence, increasingly large sections of the public sector – education, local authorities, the Civil Service (through the creation of Agencies) and the NHS in particular – can be seen to have adopted elements of this approach. As well as reflecting key themes of the BCG Matrix, they also illustrate ways in which developments in strategy have moved on from this, as the emphasis in strategy literature in the 1980s shifted from a concern with conglomerates towards a focus on business strategy and encouraging organisations to look at their **core business**; in essence to concentrate on what they were good at and to divest or contract out (**outsource**) those areas that were non-core.

In the public sector, examples commonly included cleaning and catering services, but on occasions this extended to the contracting out of more specialist services such as legal support, HR departments, and in local authorities frequently reached into core areas of provision such as refuse collection. Often driven by cost considerations these had the effect of reducing headcount (numbers directly employed) and shifted the management of particular groups of staff to a third party, an external contractor. To what extent this constituted a strategy in respect of staff or just a necessity of circumstance is more difficult to unravel. What is clear is that in the public sector, where nationally negotiated common terms and conditions of employment still remain the norm across particular grades of staff, this had the advantage (to the employer) not only of reducing the numbers of those directly employed, but in so doing reducing further the scope of such agreements.

KEY TERMS

Outsourcing Where an organisation subcontracts a service or production process to a third party – an external contractor. This is normally done to reduce costs, to shift risks associated with a service to an outside contractor, or to restructure to focus on core activities.

Summary

Despite its enduring influence the BCG Matrix has considerable weaknesses. One of its attractions (it is a simple 2×2 matrix), is also one of its chief drawbacks, and the fact that it draws an association between market share and market growth means that other key influences on profitability and other measures of business success are ignored. In terms of its underlying assumptions, it draws heavily on product life cycle theory but ignores ways in which this can be extended in often innovative ways. Mars Bars may be Cash Cows for Mars, but Mars ice cream may well be a Star for the organisation.

Two final and more serious deficiencies should also be noted. First, by encouraging a compartmentalised view of organisations it plays down or ignores the sense in which they may be integrated. It is very much an accountant's view of organisations – cash flow forecasting and cost control – which may encourage a kind of financial controller (Goold and Campbell 1987) or financial engineering approach to the running of organisations. In contrast we know that rather than treating their component parts as separate and unrelated, many organisations try and exploit synergies between their various elements. The Virgin group uses Virgin trains and Virgin Atlantic as an important 'window' and outlet for other products of the organisation, such as food and drink, while much of Unilever's vast product range operates from a limited number of base ingredients, particularly vegetable oil, which it uses in everything from margarine to detergents.

Finally, the BCG Matrix is not a model of strategy. It tells us how a product may be performing at a particular point in time and can label it a 'Star' or a 'Cash Cow' but it tells us nothing about *why* or *how* it has become a 'Star' or a 'Cash Cow'. For this we need further analysis but we also require a focus at the level of the individual business, and it is to this that we now turn.

1. Think about the BCG in an organisation known to you – a University, a retail store, a car company. Can you identify a Cash Cow, a Star or a Dog? Is there any evidence that staff who work in these are treated at all differently?

(14.7) Competitive strategy and human resource management

As we noted above, strategic management in the 1980s shifted from a preoccupation with corporate strategy towards strategy at the level of the business unit. Instead of worrying about how the portfolio should be arranged, the focus moved to how businesses could compete, how they could position themselves and develop and sustain **competitive advantage**. Two developments were critical here; the first, the publication of Peters and Waterman's (1982) *In Search of Excellence*, drew heavily on the authors' work with the McKinsey Consulting Group in the US, and focused on US companies that had achieved consistently above-average performance on a number of measures over a 40-year period. They claimed that much of the success of these companies lay in the emphasis they placed on core business and **corporate culture**. These ideas were taken further in subsequent work. In academic writing the ideas that cultures mattered and could be changed (see Deal and Kennedy 1982; Schein 1985; Handy 1986; Hampden-Turner 1994) attracted considerable interest and were given added weight by organisations claiming they had changed cultures (Abbey in the 1990s; BA in the 1980s) or had divested large areas of non-core business. Despite the criticisms levelled at it, this book remains the most popular management text ever written.

KEY TERMS

Competitive advantage Much of strategic management is seen in terms of building sustainable competitive advantage. It is the advantage that an organisation has over its competitors as perceived by its customers. It is therefore the basis for creating value both for the firm and for other stakeholders

Secondly, and arguably more important because of its enduring influence, was the publication of Michael Porter's (1980) book *Competitive Strategy: Techniques for Analyzing Industries and Competitors*. Porter's contribution and the implications of his work for HRM will be discussed in more detail below. Here we note that his 'Five Forces' model (see Figure 14.2) has become one of the most commonly used and cited management tools in the world, and it is not difficult to see why. Through the Five Forces model, Porter provided managers with the tools to undertake not just an *analysis* of an industry, but also the basis to undertake a *diagnosis* of the key issues facing an industry at any point in time, and crucially a set of *prescriptions* as to how they could position their organisations to take advantage of the results of the analysis and diagnosis they had undertaken.

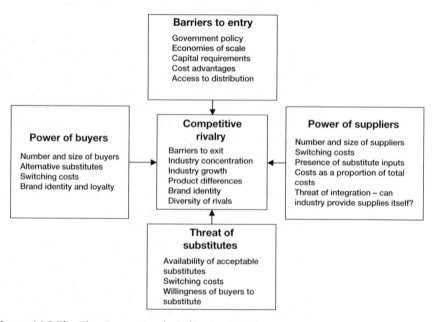

Figure 14.2 The Five Forces Analysis (Porter 1980)

Given this is a book about HRM, it is not our intention to rehearse Porter's Five Forces model in detail, particularly as so many good summaries exist already. Suffice it to say that his model claims to have identified the factors that determine the long-term competitiveness of an industry and uses these to analyse the degree of competition or competitive rivalry existing within an industry. For Porter, these factors are: barriers to entry into an industry; the power of suppliers; the power of buyers; and the threat posed by substitutes. Together these, along with the extent to which the industry is growing, the number and size of firms and their existing strategies will help determine the degree of competitive rivalry. The key point is that this analysis will ensure a better understanding of the dynamics of the industry and in turn provide the basis for a positioning or repositioning of an organisation to take account of 'gaps' or to ensure that an existing position is exploited more effectively.

Before advancing further we should note that Porter is an example of market or market-based strategy. That is, its focus is outside the organisation, on the industry and market. Once you have identified what part or parts of the market to focus upon, you have to consider *how* you are going to do this, what strategy you are going to employ to meet customer needs. For Porter the choice available was clear and deceptively simple. In essence he argued that any organisation has a limited number of **generic strategies** available to it which derive from two sources of competitive advantage; these are:

1 the ability to differentiate themselves from others; or
2 the possession of particular cost advantages.

For Porter an organisation is assumed to follow a strategy based *either* on **differentiation** or **low cost (cost leadership)**, that is to concentrate on building and exploiting competitive advantage in one of these. The next key decision is the focus of the strategy; whether this is to apply to the entire industry, adopting a so-called **broad** (industry-wide) strategy, or a **narrow** (focused), more targeted, niche strategy, for example targeting a particular geographical area or group of customers. A key point for Porter was that organisations are faced with a clear choice and cannot 'mix and match'. In his view once a strategy has been chosen it requires the systematic organising of resources and activities within a business and its supply chain to support the delivery of the chosen strategy. His later work on the value chain (Porter 1985) makes this point clearly. If an organisation's competitive advantage is based on low cost then all the value-adding activities within the organisation's supply chain must be arranged to support this, from procurement (sourcing decisions, purchasing) through to marketing, production, distribution, human resources and customer service. In the case of Ryanair, its low cost strategy is reflected in every part of the company's operations not just in its no pre-assigned seating policy or its plan to charge passengers for using toilets (*Times*

Online 2009). Porter did not take this further, but one implication of his work is that an organisation focusing on low cost would be expected to manage human resources very differently from one focusing on exceptional customer service or product innovation. The business strategy is the driving force for the functional strategies; it follows that as the quote at the start of this chapter put it, the requirement becomes to 'integrate HR strategy with the wider business strategy'.

KEY TERMS

Cost leadership One of Porter's generic strategies, competitive advantage lies in superior cost advantages which an organisation can exploit for example by lowering prices.

Generic strategies Term normally given to the strategic options developed by Michael Porter in terms of broad versus narrow strategy and cost leadership versus differentiation.

(14.8) 'Matching' models

The view that HRM should be contingent on business considerations was first introduced in Chapter 1. As we noted there, a number of writers suggested that the key task for HR practitioners was not only to 'match' HR strategy with the prevailing business strategy (Tichy, Fombrun and Devanna 1982; Schuler and Jackson 1987), but also to ensure a fit among the elements of the HRM strategy (Beer et al. 1984: 13). Thus forging a distinction between **vertical strategy** (and fit) and **horizontal strategy** (and fit) (Bratton and Gold 2007: 51).

In the next section, we explore the detail of matching models further, by focusing on the work of Schuler and Jackson (1987). This study was selected partly because of its significance and continued influence and because it is explicitly concerned with exploring the HR implications of Porter's generic strategies.

In taking Porter's work, Schuler and Jackson (1987) sub-divided the broad **differentiation strategy** into *Quality Enhancement* and *Innovation* and contrasted these with *Cost Leadership*. They then argued that each of these required a distinctive set of what they termed *'employee role behaviours'*. These role behaviours required, in turn, a collection of supportive HR practices about which strategic decisions needed to be made. As we have emphasised above, the essential task for HR is seen as one of fit – between the business and the HR strategies – but it is worth exploring this issue further. The precise nature of what is meant by appropriate employee role behaviours is elaborated upon by Schuler and Jackson (1987) as are the HR implications of these. In the case of an innovation strategy, such as at companies like Nokia, Apple or Microsoft 'this would call for high levels of creative, risk-orientated and cooperative behaviour. The company's HR practices would therefore need to emphasise . . . "selecting highly skilled individuals, giving employees more discretion, using minimal controls, making greater investment in human resources, providing more resources for experimentation, allowing and even rewarding failure and appraising performance for its long run implications"' (Boxall and Purcell 2003: 53–54).

KEY TERMS

Differentiation strategy One of Porter's generic strategies, where competitive advantage lies in seeking to differentiate products or services through such mechanisms as improved quality, customer service, after-sales service, superior distribution channels and product design.

A quality enhancement strategy (Honda is the example given) would require in turn 'relatively repetitive and predictable behaviours, a more long-term or intermediate focus, a modest amount of cooperative interdependent behaviour, a high concern for quality, a modest concern for quantity of output, high concern for process . . . low risk taking activity and commitment to the goals of the organisation' (Schuler and Jackson 1987: 210).

These would then require HRM practices that 'relatively fixed and explicit job descriptions, high levels of employee participation. . . . a mix of individual and group criteria for performance appraisal that is mostly short-term and results-oriented, relatively egalitarian treatment of employees and some guarantees of employment security and extensive and continuous training and development of employees' (Schuler and Jackson 1987: 213).

In contrast, a cost leadership strategy such as at low cost airlines, and budget supermarkets like Netto, Aldi, or Kwiksave would require 'designing jobs which are fairly repetitive, training workers as little as is practical, cutting staff numbers to the minimum and rewarding high output and predictable behaviour' (Boxall and Purcell 2003: 53–4).

These have the clear advantage that the required behaviours and HRM practices can be 'read off' a template and become almost 'best practice' for each of these business strategies, but there are clearly dangers with something as prescriptive as this. The obvious problem is that if the essence of successful strategy lies in it being difficult to imitate, then these strategic options provide little in the way of distinctiveness. Moreover, they also tell us little about why they require a specialist department to develop and administer them. If a template or manual exists, then it simply requires someone, who does not necessarily need to be in HR, to ensure that 'fit' takes place between the business and the HR strategies.

To put this slightly differently:

1 What is distinctive about HR and the HR contribution? If it is simply about 'following the business strategy', the danger is that HR strategy is simply formulaic, 'read off' from a set of prescribed strategic choices.
2 What is the added-value from HR? What is it that HR is providing – the specific skills and knowledge set (see Armstrong 1989) – that helps create added value? Why do we need HR? If there is no claim to specific knowledge, skills or competencies then why can't accountants do this? Something that a number of organisations have already worked out for themselves.
3 HRM could be owned by all managers not just a specific group, something that the early advocates of HRM spotted for themselves.

CASE STUDY

British Airways and Ryanair: A Reprise

In Chapter 1 we contrasted the strategic positioning of McDonald's and Café Rouge, and British Airways and Ryanair. The Schuler and Jackson work allows us to develop those contrasts further in terms of approaches to HRM. Since the mid 1980s British Airways has arguably been following a quality enhancement strategy based on high levels of customer service. Although this has come under threat at various points in time, and may now be focused mainly at higher value-added customers, it has had clear implications for HRM. In Schuler and Jackson's terms, the requirement for consistent role behaviours alongside some loyalty and identification with the organisation has traditionally meant recruiting staff who will 'buy into' this vision and who will stay with the company, something that has necessitated ongoing training and development and building some career ladders for cabin crew. At Ryanair, the cost leadership strategy has meant a focus on passenger volumes and high productivity of staff. In terms of HRM, Ryanair makes considerable use of agency staff, on fixed-term contracts who are, as a result, not direct employees of Ryanair. Cabin crew are recruited as much for their sales skills as for their customer care, and although relatively well-paid when account is taken of commission, they work long hours by comparison with the industry average. Labour costs are then spread over long hours and high passenger volumes.

The other problem is potentially more serious. The approach adopted by Schuler and Jackson is essentially unitarist (see Chapter 1), and assumes away issues of conflict in the management of the employment relationship. Explicitly their argument is that if an organisation can identify 'appropriate role behaviours' then it can develop recruitment, selection, work organisation, rewards and systems of employee involvement that ensure that only those who 'fit' with these are found jobs. Notwithstanding the fact that there may be sound business reasons for organisations to recruit a more diverse workforce, there are dangers, not least in the area of equal opportunities, of such a narrow focus on 'fit', and the concern that organisations may end up 'recruiting to type'. A further concern is that while the models are quite static, environments are dynamic and organisations increasingly require flexibility in their approach to many aspects of business if they are to survive. Focusing narrowly on business strategy may be very short-sighted if the business strategy has to change or be modified in critical respects. Staff recruited on the basis of one set of role behaviours may be poorly suited to engage with another, very different set. The circumstances faced by IBM in the late 1980s and Marks and Spencer in the 1990s illustrate some of the difficulties of business strategies, structures and cultures developed in one set of contexts, proving difficult to sustain in another.

In summary, 'matching' theories of the kind proposed by Schuler and Jackson have considerable intuitive appeal, but they also have inherent weaknesses that make their application problematic. It is notable that in the UK these models have gained less prominence than in the US, due much to the fact that in the UK the HRM framework developed by Beer et al. (1984) has been far more influential. This work suggested a much broader set of contextual influences on HR strategy than just that of business strategy but it still views HR strategy as essentially *reactive*, subservient to 'product market logic' and the corporate strategy (Beer et al. 1984: 51).

A further conceptual problem with matching models relates to the question of whether an organisation really wants to adopt the same HR strategy for all staff. As Atkinson and Meager (1984) pointed out over a quarter of a century ago, senior managers are concerned with various forms of organisational flexibility and it may be that they wish to foster forms of commitment and loyalty from some staff but not all. In McDonald's, those who are viewed as potential store managers on the management track are likely to be viewed, and treated, differently (McDonald's University notwithstanding) from those teenage store workers who combine this with student life or other part-time work. It follows that some organisations may develop a 'core-periphery' employment model along the lines suggested by Atkinson and Meager and practised historically in a number of Japanese companies.

The 'matching model' has also suffered from a lack of empirical support. There has been little hard evidence to support the use of such approaches in practice. Purcell (2004), drawing on the work of Batt and Moynihan's (2002) study of call centres in the USA, suggests that the design of HR systems in such environments is determined less by competitive strategy than by strategic choice, management and leadership orientation and values, findings that are broadly consistent with that found in other studies (e.g Wright et al. 2003).

Before moving on, we must return to a point made earlier in the chapter. A common criticism of much of the traditional strategy literature has been its over-reliance on questions of strategy formation and neglect of implementation issues. To put this another way, the development of strategy in terms of the industry and markets' needs to be matched in a more fundamental way; to the resources and capabilities of the organisation. Considerable market opportunities may exist but without the requisite skills and competencies within the organisation, or accessible to it, the intended strategy is unlikely to be realised. This acknowledgement is important for a number of reasons:

1 It focuses attention back on to the organisation, how it is structured, how work systems are designed and how HR systems contribute to the effectiveness of the organisation.
2 It raises the profile of resources and resource capability. The nature and quality of these resources, how these are combined within an organisation and to what extent they provide it with **core competences** (Hamel and Prahalad 1994) or distinctive capabilities (Kay 1993).
3 In the context of a post-industrial economy where customer service and knowledge are seen as critical, the role of human capital, and the potential for human beings to be viewed as a key *resource* for organisations is significantly increased.

KEY TERMS

Core competence – Derived from the work of Prahalad and Hamel, and linked to resource based views of strategy, a core competency is seen as central to the way a business works and critical to its competitive advantage. They are normally key areas of expertise that are built up over time.
Distinctive capabilities – Linked to the resource-based view of the firm, and often discussed alongside core competencies, they were originally developed by John Kay who describes three sources of such distinctive capability. These are architecture (structure of relational contracts inside and outside organisations); reputation; and innovation, each of which is seen as creating added value for organisations and as an aid to building competitive advantage.

Once we acknowledge the importance of implementation issues in strategy and combine this with a perspective that places more emphasis on the skills and competencies deriving from an organisation's resources, HR ceases to become the 'follower' in strategic management and potentially at least, an 'initiator' of key developments. This has been one of the most important shifts in the strategic management field in recent years and one that has provided HR with considerable potential leverage to increase its role and influence. It is to consideration of this that we now turn.

1. What do you see as the strengths and weaknesses of the 'matching' model offered by Schuler and Jackson?

2. Think about an organisation like British Airways. Identify at least three different groups of staff and think about what BA might be looking for from each of these. How might these be reflected in differences in HR systems within the company.

3. What are some of the implementation issues that traditional strategic management has tended to overlook or play down in importance? Why might HR have an interest in these?

14.9 Resource-based approaches

For many, the development of resource-based approaches to strategy (RBV) marks the single most important advancement in strategic analysis in recent years. It has helped shift the focus of strategy to a concern with issues internal to organisations and to performance rather than planning (Purcell (2004)). As Purcell has argued:

> 'At its heart, RBV seeks to explain the sources of sustained competitive advantage in turbulent conditions where external positioning is uncertain. Looking at internal sources of viability and advantage, emphasis is placed on resources which are critical to organisational success yet are rare, or not commonly available, are not substitutable, and are combined together to form organisational capabilities or processes which are imperfectly imitable, or hard for others to copy' (2004: 14).

He adds that:

> 'The central argument in RBV is that while tangible resources (how technology is used) have often declined in value, intangible and human resources have increased as a source of value . . . the successful firm not only has to have better than average human capital, through recruitment selection and development and then appropriate job design, motivation, communication and involvement systems, but also better processes and capabilities. These combine human and non-human resources together in ways highly appropriate for end-users and markets and in ways other firms find hard to copy' (2004: 14-15).

The implications of the RBV for HRM are complex. For some, it is easy to equate these with so-called 'best practice' notions of HRM, associated with the 'soft' HRM discussed in Chapter 1. Work on 'best practice' high-involvement management and high performance work systems runs with the grain of the value placed on human resources by RBV approaches.

CASE STUDY

RBV: an example

Although it is unwise to make clear-cut distinctions between organisations that follow a market-based strategy and those that have adopted a more resource-based approach because it is often difficult to identify strategy in this way, a number of organisations tend to be consistently cited as examples of the RBV. In the recent past it has been Japanese companies such as Honda, Canon, NEC and Sony that have often been held up as possessing distinctive capabilities or competencies that have helped set them apart from other organisations (Pascale 1991).

The example of Honda is particularly instructive. In the late 1990s the general view was that Honda led the motor industry in a number of areas of technical expertise. More precisely it was felt that Honda's real strengths and core competence lay in the field of engine technology, and that the company used this strength to exploit opportunities in a number of markets: motorcycles, cars, powerboats, lawnmowers. The strength therefore came from within, from internal resources. How these were combined, supported and protected was the source of the distinctive capability, which could then be exploited in a range of different markets. Clearly, the role of human resources in this endeavour was critical, in terms of design, technical competence and expertise, but also by facilitating structures and cultures that encouraged staff to contribute ideas and keep striving for continuous improvement.

Figure 14.3 Honda and the resource-based approach

However, although there may be compatibility between these, the RBV requires a more nuanced approach than 'best practice' prescriptions offer. One framework that allows us to explore the ways in which an organisation's human resources can provide sustainable competitive advantage (Golding 2007) is the VRIO developed by Barney and his colleagues (Barney and Wright 1998). The VRIO framework distinguishes between:

- **Value** – how the HR function can create value, and which human resources are those that contribute to sustainable competitive advantage.
- **Rarity** – what is about the human resources that distinguishes them – what are the rare characteristics of these resources.
- **Inimitability** – as Golding (2007) puts it, 'if an organisation's human resources add value and are rare, they can provide competitive advantage in the short term, but if other companies can imitate these characteristics, then over time, competitive advantage may be lost' (2007: 55). It follows that standard 'best practice' HR solutions require adaptation to particular organisational contents if they are to be of use, and arguably bundled together and embedded in wider organisational networks. It follows that one way in which such resources can be protected and their distinctiveness preserved is through how they are combined through **social architecture** or through **social complexity,** such as a culture which encourages teamworking.
- **Organisation** – this is about the need to ensure that there is appropriate organisation to ensure that a company 'can capitalise on adding value, rarity and inimitability' (Golding 2007: 56). This emphasises 'integrated, coherent HR systems' or bundles of HR practices.

The resource-based view and VRIO focus attention on what Boxall (1996) has termed 'human resource advantage', but they also provide important clues as to how an organisation might retain scarce human resources. How human resources might become 'embedded' in an organisation, what 'resource mobility barriers' (Mueller 1996) might be significant and what factors in the strategic architecture (Kay 1993) might be critical to prevent imitation and 'wastage'. However, as Boxall and Purcell (2008) have noted, rare human resources and human capital are likely to be important to parts of an organisation, not all of it. It follows that the resource-based view may only have relevance to certain groups within an organisation. They make the point that in Hewlett Packard, the 'HP Way', which was a set of guiding principles and core values about the organisation and its valuing of staff, may still apply to its direct employees but only because HP has outsourced much of its routine manufacturing to lower labour-cost areas.

This raises a further issue about ethical aspects of strategic HRM. In any organisation there may be those with high levels of generic and technical skills who do not require firm specific knowledge to practice. As a result they may have more boundaryless identities, requiring what Boxall and Purcell (2008) term more market-based as opposed to commitment-based HR. This may give rise to a core–periphery model along the lines developed by Atkinson and Meager reflected in diverse HR systems within and beyond the firm to the supply chain. At the time, the Atkinson and Meager model was criticised for its explicit promotion of employment segmentation and that the consequent two- or three-tier workforce consigned some to a life of part-time, temporary or subcontracting work. It is certainly the case that many organisations combine 'good' and 'bad' jobs but increasingly, in our globalising world, 'bad' jobs may well be 'outsourced' or get relocated elsewhere, to other parts of the organisation's supply chain. This may permit a resource-based approach to operate for a select group of key, core staff. From these the organisation may be willing to provide some guarantees of employment security, training and development opportunities, career progression and other benefits in return for commitment, loyalty, engagement and long service. Those deemed to be non-core are more likely to be exposed to the risks, uncertainties and insecurities of the external labour market and may be those who are already disadvantaged in employment terms.

Summary

As Boxall and Purcell (2008) have argued, senior managers have some choice in their HR systems; that is in the nature of their work systems and their employment practices. In organisations with mixed groups of staff, with different skill sets and expectations it is likely that they will develop a number of systems for different groups, with HR strategy consisting of clusters of these different HR systems. This takes us some way from the models that seek to match HR with business strategy by extending the idea of matching to encompass a broader range of factors.

We have already discussed the broader 'matching' involved in the so-called 'Harvard' framework, devised by Beer et al. (1984) to encompass other environmental factors. Boxall and Purcell build on this but, in emphasising strategic choice, diverge from the 'matching' literature. Furthermore, the RBV and the VRIO framework suggest the need to craft HR initiatives which are distinctive, or at least are difficult for others to copy. It follows that the RBV may only be appropriate for some within an organisation and care needs to be taken over how different HR systems can coexist in the light of equal opportunities and broader ethical considerations. This becomes an even bigger issue where work has been outsourced or relocated overseas. The concern to be seen as a 'good' or 'ethical' employer, concerned with wider social responsibilities may be less far-fetched than in the past. Even where 'bad' jobs can be outsourced or relocated, ignoring labour standards and basic issues of labour treatment might come back to haunt an organisation as it has threatened to do with

Primark, (*BBC Panorama* 2008), Gap (*Observer* 2007), Walmart (*Associated Press* 2005) and Nike (*Independent* 2001).

1. The CIPD (Chartered Institute of Personnel and Development) has particularly welcomed the developments in resource-based strategy in recent years. In what ways does this offer a more upbeat message for HRM and how does it suggest HR departments should respond to the opportunities it provides?
2. Compare and contrast the Schuler and Jackson 'matching' model of strategy with the implications of the resource-based view for HR. What are the strengths and weaknesses of each and which do you feel is most appropriate for modern service organisations and why?
3. Given the experience of some 'household name' employers how can a balance be found between ethical HR practices and effective business performance?

(14.10) Strategic HRM: two further issues

Before we draw this chapter to a close there are two further areas we should draw attention to. The first is the role of strategic HRM in relation to mergers and processes. The second, closely associated with the RBV, is the link (if any) between HRM and organisational effectiveness and performance.

Taking the first of these, mergers and takeovers are an increasingly important issue for modern organisations and there is an acknowledgement of their impact, even where they do not take place, in influencing the management of human resources. For example, the threatened takeover of Pilkingtons Glass by the conglomerate BTR in the late 1980s had a considerable impact on the company, and although Pilkingtons managed to resist the takeover, it ushered in major changes in operations and HR management (Caulkin 1987; Lorenz 1996); a focus on efficiency replaced a more paternalistic family orientation. Indeed, where mergers and takeovers have taken place, HR-related issues are frequently a major source of a number of problems, particularly in those acquisitions that fail (Hunt et al. 1987) and this suggests a need to give greater prominence to HR issues when mergers and takeovers are being considered.

The second issue has been the subject of considerable academic and practitioner interest in recent years, and much of the research relies upon quantitative studies based upon large-scale survey data or on case study research. In Chapter 1 (Section 1.8) we drew attention to some of this work, particularly that of the Bath University group who have explored issues surrounding the 'black box' problem of how HR practices link to performance (Purcell et al. 2003). Figure 14.4 replicates a model developed by Boxall and Purcell (2008) to explain the links between HR systems and organisational performance.

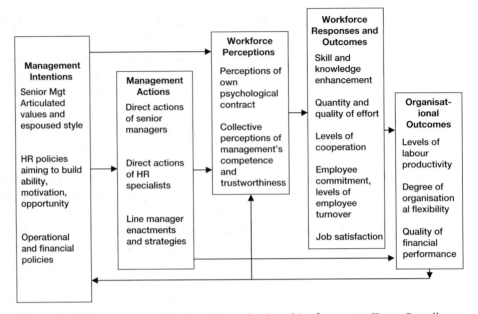

Figure 14.4 HR Systems and Links to Organisational Performance (Peter Boxall and John Purcell, *Strategy and Human Resource Management*, published 2002, Palgrave Macmillan, reproduced with permission of Palgrave Macmillan)

In Figure 14.4 above, moving from left to right, the extreme left-hand box contains the **intended elements** of HRM, for individuals and for collective relations. The next box focuses on the **actions** of various management groups and together these feed into a box representing workforce perceptions. These perceptions are influenced both by the intended and espoused actions of management, and emphasise that where gaps open up between these, they may undermine perceived fairness of treatment and levels of trust towards management. These perceptions in turn influence how the workforce responds to management, which may include such acts as quitting, and these, along with management actions, feed into a range of organisational outcomes including measures of performance.

Boxall and Purcell see the value of the model in helping organisations identify weak links in their HRM-performance chain (2008: 223) and certainly it has considerable value as a diagnostic tool, particularly in large and complex organisations where inconsistencies between the various elements in the model are likely to be at their greatest. However, the model has value in other ways. In allowing a distinction to be made between what managers say they are trying to do (intended values, style and strategy) and what they actually do in practice (espoused values, style and strategy) the model permits insights into why some strategies fail, and helps focus on specific problems of implementation. Furthermore, in a world of strategies, structures and systems the model is a timely reminder of the importance of human agency in influencing the success and effectiveness of any initiatives. In many respects this is the key value of this approach. In unlocking and exploring the 'black box', Purcell and his colleagues have been less interested in the 'what' of strategic initiatives than 'how' such initiatives are enacted within organisations, in essence their implementation. It also reminds us that 'management is about getting things done through people' (Salaman 1995), and that it is the *processes* by which things happen in organisations that need to be thought about and reflected upon and which the Bath studies have thrown back into sharp focus.

In recent years strategic management has taken the issues of strategic implementation far more seriously and the 'new management accounting' literature associated with Kaplan and Norton (1996), has made great strides in helping organisations and line managers to translate business strategies into outcomes at the operational levels. However, the studies by Purcell and his colleagues for the CIPD remind us of the importance of the local contexts in which strategies are enacted as well as the social and behavioural factors that shape the success or otherwise of strategies 'on the ground'.

 ## 14.11 Summary

In this chapter we have attempted to provide an overview of the development of Strategic HRM and have tried to link this with chronological developments in the field of strategic management. The emergence of interest in corporate strategy, and the influential work of the Boston Consulting Group, carried with them clear implications for HR policies and practices. With the shift in focus to competitive advantage and business strategy in the 1980s there was a parallel interest in business-driven HRM which in turn led to a flurry of interest in 'matching' business strategy and HR strategy. Common to all these approaches has been the recognition of HRM as a 'downstream' activity, that along with other functional strategies, HRM is a second or third order strategy; its task is to fit with the prevailing environment, specifically the particular business strategy in operation at the time.

This rather downbeat assessment of strategic HRM has been challenged in recent years, at least in academic circles. The emergence of HRM, the rise of the resource-based view of strategy, the shift to a service economy with an emphasis on people and knowledge as key sources of competitive advantage, and a growing recognition of the importance of implementation issues in the success of strategies have all contributed to a reappraisal of the role and contribution of HR in organisational effectiveness. These developments have been further aided by an increasing focus on performance within organisations and by work that has sought to establish clear links between aspects of HR and measures of organisation performance.

However, despite these very positive developments, as we noted in Chapter 1, HRM still struggles to establish itself and the extent to which strategic HRM is as widespread or as effective in organisations is hard to assess. All of which brings us back to the discussion of Whittington's (2002) work at the beginning of the chapter and the alternative 'theories of action' that can inform discussion of strategy. In order to move forward, we perhaps need to take more notice of his 'systemic' and '**processual**' approaches to strategy. As Boxall and Purcell – who incorporate significant elements of emergent (processual) strategy into their discussion of HR strategy – note, organisations are political spaces and strategies, like other developments within organisations, are likely to develop through networks, negotiations and compromises. It reminds us, in case we need it, that as well as strategies informed by a range of contextual factors, we need informed human beings, human agency to ensure that managers have sufficient political and social skills to really 'walk the talk'.

KEY IDEAS

What is strategy?
- The concept of strategy and classical approaches to strategic management.
- The concept of strategic direction.
- The ideas of levels of strategy – corporate, business (competitive) and functional – introduced with HR seen as downstream strategy in conventional accounts of strategy.

Strategic HRM and strategic management
- Contrasts between classical and other approaches to strategy using ideas developed by Whittington (2002).
- Classical approaches, based on models of rational decision-making where senior managers analyse environments and make long-term planning decisions about what an organisation should be trying to achieve and how it plans to achieve this.
- An outline of the problems associated with classical approaches presented and 'flagged up' as issues to be borne in mind when considering examples of these in the remainder of the chapter.
- The idea that strategy involves certain choices and that although strategy may be constrained in important respects, a degree of choice exists.
- An introduction to what is meant by strategic human resource management; contrasting the approaches of Boxall and Purcell; that it is concerned with strategic choices about the organisation of work; and the use of labour in organisations with that of Schuler and Jackson; that it is concerned with vertical and horizontal integration, partnership and demonstrating effectiveness.

Corporate strategy/the BCG matrix and human resource management
- For much of 1960s and 1970s strategic management concerned itself with corporate strategy in large multi-divisional companies or conglomerates.
- In corporate strategy the strategic task is about managing a portfolio of businesses.
- Some of the most influential approaches designed to help with this task were portfolio matrix models, the best known of which was the Boston Consulting Group Matrix.
- The BCG Matrix carried with it important implications for HR strategy and policies, and along with the work of Miles and Snow began a concern with linking HR with business strategies.

continued . . .

◀ *. . . continued*

Competitive strategy and human resource management/matching models

- In the 1980s strategic management shifted to a concern with core business and sustainable competitive advantage.
- Prominent in these developments was the work of Michael Porter and his 'Five Forces' model examining competitive rivalry within an industry.
- Porter's work suggested that any organisation has a limited number of strategic options available to it based on exploiting competitive advantage in low cost or differentiation.
- A number of writers suggested that these choices had implications for lower order, functional strategies. Schuler and Jackson in particular offered a framework that indicated what the HR implications would be of an organisation following an innovation, quality enhancement or cost leadership strategy.

Resource-based approaches

- Developed since the 1990s, resource-based approaches have significantly changed the way we think about strategy, focusing attention on core competencies and distinctive capabilities; factors inside an organisation or within its broad network of alliances.
- In a world where customer service and knowledge are assumed to have increased in importance as factors in competitive advantage, people as a resource are highlighted of particular importance. One significant contribution of resource-based approaches is their elevation of people and the human resource function as potentially critical to organisational success.
- The implications of the RBV for specific HR policies are less clear. For some this provides an opportunity for 'best practice' HR in the form of high performance work practices to be 'rolled out' throughout organisations, for others there is a need to adapt such policies to the specific circumstances faced by individual organisations.
- The chapter has also underlined the Boxall and Purcell argument that HR strategy is about clusters of HR systems, so that large organisations are likely to operate different HR systems for different groups of staff. Whether an RBV is appropriate for all staff in an organisation is doubtful, and a key question then becomes who should be covered by such an approach and who should be excluded.

Strategic HRM: two further issues

- The implications of acquisitions for strategic HRM and revisited the question of how HRM contributed to organisational performance.
- It is clear that people issues are an important but often neglected factor in mergers and acquisitions, and the HR issues involved in bringing staff together from different organisational structures, systems and cultures given insufficient weight or attention.
- In discussing the links between HRM and performance, the focus was less upon the exact nature of policies and interventions and more on the importance of 'softer' skills in making strategies work on the ground.
- The model developed by Boxall and Purcell was employed to show how gaps between espoused/intended actions can contrast with what actually takes place in practice and how strategies can often fall short of their intended outcomes because of implementation issues.
- The final contribution of the model emphasises the role of human agency in achieving strategic outcomes, and reminds us that management is a social and political process, that relies on networking, influencing, negotiating and persuading to make things happen. This helps us to understand *how* strategies get translated into *action*, and why they may be more successful in some contexts than in others.

RECOMMENDED READING

As you are no doubt now aware, Strategic HRM is a difficult area and one that repays a good deal of reading around the subject. In general, you are unlikely to explore it in too much detail until you are well into your undergraduate studies but the following will be of help if you wish to try and understand aspects of what has been covered in this chapter in more detail

Boxall, P., Purcell, J. (2008), *Strategy and Human Resource Management***, Basingstoke: Palgrave MacMillan**

A book designed for postgraduate students but the first two chapters are worth persevering with. A great deal of knowledge about Strategic HRM can be gained from a close reading of these.

Golding, N. (2007) 'Strategic Human Resource Management' in Beardwell, J., Claydon, T. (eds), *Human Resource Management: A Contemporary Approach* **(5th ed.), Harlow: FT/Prentice Hall**

A book designed for postgraduate and final-year undergraduate students but it does provide a detailed treatment of Strategic HRM that builds upon coverage in the present chapter. It is particularly useful in its coverage of the resource-based view, HRM and performance and on the balanced scorecard.

For what still remains a classic example of the 'matching' approach you are encouraged to read

Schuler, R., Jackson, S (1987), 'Linking competitive strategies and human resource management practices', *Academy of Management Executive* **vol. 1, no. 3, 207–19.**

For a similarly influential treatment of the resource based view look at **Prahalad, C, Hamel, G. (1990), 'The Core Competence of the Corporation',** *Harvard Business Review***, May–June 79–91.**

For those seeking an accessible way into the 'new management accounting' work associated with Kaplan and Norton, the second half of the final chapter of Boxall and Purcell is useful.

REFERENCES

Ansoff, H. (1965), *Corporate Strategy*, London: Penguin

Atkinson, J., Meager, N. (1984), 'Manpower strategies for flexible organisations', *Personnel Management*, 28–31 August

Baran, P., Sweezy, P. (1966), *Monopoly Capital: An Essay on the American Economic and Social Order*, New York: Monthly Review Press

Barney, J, Wright, P. (1998), 'On becoming a strategic partner: the role of human resources in gaining competitive advantage', *Human Resource Management*, Spring, vol. 37, no. 1

Bartel, Batt, R., Moynihan, L. (2002), 'The viability of alternative call centre production models', *Human Resource Management Journal*, vol. 12, no. 4, 14–34

Bartlett, C., Ghoshal, S. (1998), *Managing Across Borders: The Transnational Solution* (2nd ed.), Boston: Harvard Business School Press

Beer, M., Spector, B, Lawrence, P., Mills, Q., Walton, R. (1985), *Managing Human Assets*, New York: Free Press

BCG (1970), *The Growth-share Matrix* (**www.bcg.com**)

Boxall, P., Purcell, J. (2008/2003), *Strategy and Human Resource Management* (2nd ed./1st ed.) Basingstoke: Palgrave MacMillan

Bratton, J., Gold, J. (2007), *Human Resource Management: Theory and Practice* (4th ed.), London: Palgrave MacMillan

Caulkin, S. (1987), 'Pilkington after BTR', *Management Today*, June

Child, J. (1997), 'Strategic choice in the analysis of action, structure, organizations and environment: retrospect and prospect', *Organization Studies* vol. 18, no. 1 43–76

Child, J. (1972), 'Organizational structure, environment and performance: the role of strategic choice', *Sociology* vol. 6, no. 3 1–22

Deal, T., Kennedy, R. (1982), *Corporate Cultures: Rites and Rituals of Corporate Life*, Perseus books

Fombrun, C., Tichy, N., Devanna, M. (1985), *Strategic Human Resource Management*, New York: Wiley

Golding, N. (2007) 'Strategic Human Resource Management' in Beardwell, J., Claydon, T. (eds), *Human Resource Management: A Contemporary Approach* (5th ed.), Harlow: FT/Prentice Hall

Goold, M, Campbell, A, (2002), *Designing Effective Organizations: How to Create Structured Networks*, San Francisco: Jossey-Bass

Goold, M., Campbell, D. (1987), *Strategies and Styles: The Role of the Centre in Managing Diversified Corporations*, Oxford: Blackwell

Goold, M., Campbell, D., Alexander, M. (1994), *Corporate Level Strategy: Creating Value in the Multi-Business Company*, New York: Wiley

Hall, P., Soskice, D. (2001), *Varieties of Capitalism: The Institutional Foundations of Comparative Advantage*, Oxford: OUP

Hamel, G., Prahalad, C. (1994), *Competing for the Future*, Boston: Harvard Business School Press

Hampden-Turner, C. (1994), *Corporate Culture: From Vicious to Virtuous Circles*, London: Piatkus

Handy, C. (1986), *Understanding Organisations*, London: Penguin

Hayes, R., Abernathy, W. (1980), 'Managing our way to economic decline', *Harvard Business* Review, July–August, 67–77

Hunt, J., Lees, S., Grumber, J., Vivian, P. (1987), *Acquisitions: The Human Factor*, London: London Business School and Egon Zehnder International

Johnson, G., Scholes, K. (2006), *Exploring Corporate Strategy: Texts and Cases* (7th ed.), London: FT/Prentice Hall

Kay, J. (1993), *The Foundations of corporate Success: How Business Strategies Add Value*, Oxford: OUP

Lorenz, A. (1996), 'Pilkington picks up the pieces', *Management Today*, March

Marchington, M., Wilkinson, A. (2005), *Human Resource Management at Work: People Management and Development* (3rd ed.), London: CIPD

Marchington, M., Grimshaw, D., Rubery, J., Willmott, H., (2005), *Fragmenting Work: Blurring Organizational Boundaries and Disordering Hierarchies*, Oxford: OUP

Miles, G., Snow, C. (1978), *Organizational Structure, Strategy and Process*, San Francisco: Stanford University Press

Mintzberg, H. (1994), *The Rise and Fall of Strategic Planning*, New York: Free Press

Mueller, F. (1996), 'Human resources as strategic assets: an evolutionary resource-based theory', *Journal of Management Studies*, vol. 33, no.6, 757–785

Paauwe, J. (2004), *HRM and Performance: Achieving Long Term Viability*, Oxford: OUP

Penrose, E. (1959), *The Theory of the Growth of the Firm*, New York: Wiley

Peters, T., Waterman, R. (1982), *In Search of Excellence: Lessons from America's Best Run Companies*, New York: Harper and Row

Porter, M. (1985), *Competitive Strategy: Creating and Sustaining Superior Performance*, New York: Free Press

Porter, M. (1980), *Competitive Strategy: Techniques for Analyzing Industries and Competitors*, New York: Free Press

Purcell, J. (2004), 'Business strategies and human resource management: uneasy bedfellows or strategic partners'? Working paper, University of Bath, School of Management.

Purcell, J. (1989), 'The impact of corporate strategy on human resource management', in Storey, J. (ed.) *New Perspectives on Human Resource Management*, London: Routledge

Purcell, J., Kinnie, N., Hutchinson, S., Swart, J., Rayton, B. (2003), *Understanding the People-Performance Link: Unlocking the Black Box*, London: CIPD

Rainnie, A. (1989), *Industrial Relations in Small Firms: Small Isn't Beautiful*, London: Thomson

Redman, T., Wilkinson, A. (2002), *Contemporary Human Resource Management: Text and Cases*, Harlow: Pearson

Salaman, G. (1995), *Managing*, Milton Keynes: Open University Press

Schein, E. (1985), *Organizational Culture and Leadership*, New York: Jossey-Bass

Schuler, R., Jackson, S, (1987), 'Linking competitive strategies and human resource management practices', *Academy of Management Executive*, vol. 1, no. 3, 207–19

Simon, H. (1947), *Administrative Behaviour: A Study of Decision-Making Processes in Administrative Organizations*, New York: The Free Press

Simon, H., March, J. (1958), *Organizations*, New York: Wiley

Thomason, G. (1984), *A Textbook of Industrial Relations Management*, London: Institute of Personnel Management

Whitley, R. (1999), *Divergent Capitalisms: The Social Structuring and Change of Business Systems*, Oxford: OUP.

Whittington, R. (2002), *What is Strategy and Does it Matter?* Oxford: Blackwell

Wright, P., Gardner, T., Moynihan, L. (2003), 'The impact of HR practices on the performance of business units', *Human Resource Management Journal*, vol. 13, no. 3

INDEX